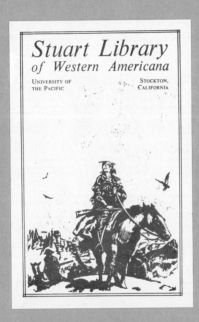

A Journal
of Travels into the
ARKANSAS TERRITORY
During the Year 1819

THE EDITOR

SAVOIE LOTTINVILLE, a graduate of the University of Oxford, was Director of the University of Oklahoma Press for thirty years and founder and editor of the series of which this book is a volume. He was for several years Regents Professor of History in the University of Oklahoma. Among the several books he has written or edited are *The Rhetoric of History* (1976) and *Travels in North America, 1822–1824,* by Paul Wilhelm, Duke of Württemberg (1973), both published by the University of Oklahoma Press.

The American Exploration and Travel Series

Thomas Nuttall in 1824

A Journal
of Travels into the
ARKANSAS TERRITORY
During the Year 1819

By Thomas Nuttall, F. L. S.

Honorary Member of the American Philosophical Society
and of the Academy of Natural Sciences, &c.

EDITED BY SAVOIE LOTTINVILLE

University of Oklahoma Press: *Norman*

By Savoie Lottinville

Life of George Bent: Written from His Letters by George E. Hyde (editor, Norman, 1968)

Soldier in the West: Letters of Theodore Talbot During His Services in California, Mexico, and Oregon (editor, with Robert V. Hine, Norman, 1972)

Paul Wilhelm Duke of Württemberg, *Travels in North America, 1822–1824*. Translated by W. Robert Nitske (editor, Norman, 1974)

The Rhetoric of History (Norman, 1976)

Thomas Nuttall, *A Journal of Travels into the Arkansas Territory During the Year 1819* (editor, Norman, 1979)

Library of Congress Cataloging in Publication Data

Nuttall, Thomas, 1786–1859.
  A journal of travels into the Arkansas Territory during the year 1819.

  (The American exploration and travel series; v. 66)
  First published in 1821 by T. H. Palmer in Philadelphia under title: A journal of travels into the Arkansa Territory, during the year 1819.
  Bibliography: p. 339
  Includes index.
  1. Southwest, Old—Description and travel.
2. Arkansas River—Description and travel. 3. Arkansas —Description and travel. 4. Oklahoma—Description and travel. 5. Ohio River—Description and travel.
6. Mississippi River—Description and travel.
7. Indians of North America—Southwest, Old.
8. Nuttall, Thomas, 1786–1859. I. Lottinville, Savoie, 1906– II. Title. III. Series: American exploration and travel series; v. 66.
F396.N98 1979   917.6′04′3   79-4742

Contents

Illustrations

MAPS

Editor's Introduction

THOMAS NUTTALL, the former printer's apprentice from Liverpool, England, was publishing his second book in 1821, a many-sided recounting of his adventures in the Near Southwest two years before. Its dedicatory page suggests how far the young man, a native of Long Preston in the West Riding of Yorkshire, had come since his arrival in Philadelphia at age twenty-two on April 23, 1808. The persons honored were the Abbé José Francisco Corréa da Serra (1750–1823), the Portuguese minister to the United States from 1816 to 1820, a notable botanist; Zaccheus Collins (1764–1831), the Philadelphia businessman and philanthropist; John Vaughan (1756–1841), a distinguished figure in the scientific and intellectual life of the city and the Republic; and William Maclure (1763–1840), the well-known geologist and philanthropist. They were Nuttall's associates in the American Philosophical Society and the Academy of Natural Sciences of Philadelphia. Maclure was president of the academy from 1817 until his death. Collins was vice-president of the academy. Vaughan was treasurer and librarian of the American Philosophical Society. Corréa had been honored by membership in the Royal Society, London.

They were indeed more. Each had contributed fifty dollars to a fund to finance Nuttall's ambitious thrust into the area embracing the territory of Arkansas (which then embraced most of present Oklahoma) and on, by way of one or more rivers, to the Rocky Mountains.[1] He would leave Philadelphia on October 2, 1818, with this small resource, a few personal belongings, and his indispensable "pocket microscope" for examining botanical and paleontological specimens. He had a firearm, but on his last association with the gun, on his voyage up the Missouri River with the John Jacob Astor land brigade in 1811, he had found it chiefly useful for digging plants and roots, for which the French Canadian boatmen thought him *fou*. He was now, as he had been earlier, incapable of fear of the still savage and largely unexplored frontier of the American West.

[1]GRAUSTEIN, 131.

Gifted men do not give their friendship—much less their financial support—to the untried. Philadelphia, at Nuttall's first arrival in 1808, a short twenty-five years after the close of the American Revolution, was entitled to a certain amount of discretion in welcoming newcomers. It was the center of intellectual life in the Republic, aside from having been its capital from 1790 to 1800. The president of the United States was also president of the American Philosophical Society, a post he had held for four years before he went to Washington in 1801 and would continue to hold for five years after his second term ended in 1809. Thomas Jefferson was, if not the society's most distinguished Indian linguist, then certainly its most consistent collector of vocabularies.

The Academy of Natural Sciences, shortly to be founded (1812), would come to include in its membership most of the figures interested in scientific developments. In the Medical College of the University of Pennsylvania, Benjamin Smith Barton (1744–1815), John Redman Coxe (1773–1864), and Caspar Wistar (1761–1818) were raising up botanists as well as future medical practitioners, for plants, rather than a still largely unexplored chemistry, provided most of the materia medica of the times. And it was botany that drew young Nuttall to such men as these, and they, with surprisingly little delay, to him.

He had been impelled to cross the Atlantic in the stormy spring of 1808 so that he might find plants as yet undescribed or little known in the continental reaches of North America. Aborigines (as he called the Indians) knew these reaches, but white men did not, certainly not in the ways Nuttall wished to know them. He had nearly starved in London, after leaving his Uncle Jonas Nuttall's Liverpool printing and publishing establishment in 1807. That he might starve in Philadelphia or on some distant prairie seems not to have disturbed him. He set about finding an American manual of botany almost from the moment he left ship. There was one, by Dr. Benjamin Smith Barton, of the Medical College, he seems to have been told. Unable to find a copy for sale, he sought out the author in person.

It was a characteristic approach to his further education that young Nuttall was adopting, as his biographer, Jeannette E. Graustein, has spiritedly developed for us.[2] He had learned what botany he knew in

[2] *Ibid.*, 7–13.

association with a better-educated young friend, on botanizing excursions while he was on vacation at Long Preston from his printing apprenticeship in Liverpool. He was indebted in this respect to John Windsor, of Settle, nearby in Yorkshire, and would remember him in a botanical nomenclature to be.

At school-leaving, aged fourteen, Nuttall still lacked command of languages essential to the pursuit of botany as a science—Latin, Greek, and French (he was getting started in the fast-developing years of Alexander von Humboldt and his French colleague Aimé Bonpland). He had therefore spent his spare time from printing duties gaining mastery over them. How well he then and later pursued self-teaching would appear in his first book, published nine years after he had touched shore at Philadelphia.

Whether Nuttall met Dr. Barton at his home, as Professor Graustein thinks likely, or at his new series of botany lectures, which began April 26, 1808, three days after Nuttall's arrival, is less important than the outcome, which in many ways would determine Nuttall's future career in North America. The fact is that Barton soon saw in the young Yorkshireman a possible successor to the German botanist Frederick Pursh (1774–1820), who had collected for and assisted Barton in ordering his herbarium during the seasons of 1806 and 1807. Pursh, in his turn, would also influence the English newcomer indirectly and directly. The larger circumstantial influence, however, was the Lewis and Clark Expedition, whose principals had sent a rich trove of natural-science specimens from Fort Mandan on the Upper Missouri in 1805 and had brought back to Washington in the summer and autumn of 1806 a still larger one. The first shipment had been entrusted for study to Barton, on Thomas Jefferson's instructions, but the busy Barton had done nothing with them.

It is unclear whether Barton intended to use Pursh for describing the plants sent from Fort Mandan. But Pursh would have a second chance. It came when Meriwether Lewis, the senior officer of the Lewis and Clark Expedition, retrieved the plants from Barton and entrusted their study and description, as well as the cultivation of the Lewis and Clark seed collection, to Bernard M'Mahon (1775–1816), the seed merchant and author of *The American Gardener's Calendar* (Philadelphia, 1806), whose store in Philadelphia was well known to all interested botanists in the city.[3] M'Mahon retained Pursh for the task of describing and drawing the plants in the Lewis and Clark herbarium, the date being some time after Pursh had returned late in 1807 from his last collecting trip for Barton. The botanical findings were intended to form a separate and additional volume, to follow the publication of the Lewis and Clark journals of the Voyage of Discovery to the Pacific.

At Meriwether Lewis's death at Grinder's Tavern on the Natchez Trace in Tennessee, October 11, 1809, the task of securing the Pursh descriptions and drawings, as well as compensating Pursh, fell to William Clark. Pursh had meantime left Philadelphia for New York, and later would go on to London, carrying his drawings, many duplicate specimens, and cuttings from those that were unique.[4] When his *Flora Americae Septentrionalis* appeared in two volumes (London, 1814), it contained descriptions of 124 plants collected by Lewis and Clark.[5]

Under these circumstances William Clark approached Benjamin Smith Barton to take up once again the responsibility at which he had earlier failed. The latter's acceptance is indicated in Clark's letter of May 22, 1810, to him, written well after the discussions.[6] Barton, still more in need of an assistant, turned to Thomas Nuttall, but with a plan which, though explicit enough, was even more leisurely in its pace than his first undertaking on the Lewis and Clark specimens. However leisurely, it would ultimately put Nuttall on the route of the Voyage of Discovery of 1804–1806, to gather western flora and to authenticate what the discoverers had found before. It is safe to say that the young Englishman would henceforth be committed to the Far West, even when, later, he was for so long shackled to Augustan Cambridge, Massachusetts. Barton's "second chance" directed him there, and the young Republic, still alive to the achievements of Jefferson's captains, even after a delay in publication now more than four years long, wished for the story of what was found to the far extremity of the Louisiana Purchase.

In a contract which Barton drew, Nuttall agreed to devote himself to collecting "animals, vegetables, minerals, Indian curiosities, etc."—a

[3]CUTRIGHT, 358.
[4]*Ibid.*, 361; PURSH, I, x.
[5]CUTRIGHT, 363.
[6]Clark to Barton, May 22, 1810, in CUTRIGHT, 362.

less lucid list than Thomas Jefferson had given Lewis and Clark, but one which both men well understood. His pay would be eight dollars a month, payable on his return. He left Philadelphia on April 12, 1810, for the sixty-mile ride to Lancaster over the only macadamized road in North America at the time, thence to Pittsburgh. His further itinerary, difficult to relate geographically to the understood objectives of the journey, would take him, Barton planned, along the southern shore of Lake Erie to Detroit, on to Chicago on Lake Michigan, then to Green Bay, across country to Lake Superior, thence by the Lake of the Woods route to Lake Winnipeg. Thereafter he was to move southeast to the Missouri River, then to the Mississippi, down the Mississippi to the mouth of Illinois River, thence eastward to Fort Vincennes on the Wabash, and back to Philadelphia by way of Kentucky and Virginia.[7]

Nuttall started the Pittsburgh-to-Cleveland leg of the trip manfully on foot, at times greatly weakened by malaria, which he had contracted on a collecting venture for Barton into the swamps along Delaware Bay the year before. The disease would attack him repeatedly on the present expedition and others in the years to come.[8] At the mouth of Huron River he went by boat along the western extremity of Lake Erie, through Lake Saint Clair, then by birchbark canoe, on which he was offered a ride by Aaron Greeley (1773–1820), the surveyor of Michigan Territory, along the west side of Lake Huron to Mackinac Island, the site of Michilimackinac, the fur-trade center, in the Straits of Mackinac. He arrived August 12.[9]

Here fortune favored his western destination far better than Barton's plan. He met—just when is unclear from his 1810 diary—Wilson Price Hunt (1783–1842) and other leaders of the land brigade of the Astorians, representing John Jacob Astor's Pacific Fur Company, destined for the mouth of the Columbia (the sea brigade would round South America and rendezvous with the land party for the founding of Astoria in 1811). They departed Michilimackinac about September 3 by canoes, taking Nuttall with them, and arrived at La Baye, near the mouth of Fox River at the lower extremity of Green Bay, Wisconsin, September 9.[10]

[7]NUTTALL [4], 77–80.
[8]*Ibid.*, 41.
[9]*Ibid.*, 68.
[10]*Ibid.*, 68; IRVING [3], 131.

Nuttall's 1810 diary breaks off, except for unrelated fragments and notes, at the party's arrival September 10 at the Portage on Fox River, above its confluence with the Wisconsin. It would be the only surviving diary or journal, except his full-statured *Journal of a Tour into the Arkansas Territory* of 1818–20. The later course of the Astorians was down the Wisconsin to its mouth on the Mississippi at the long-established fur-trade center Prairie du Chien, Wisconsin, thence down the Mississippi to Saint Louis, arriving late in September, 1810. Here Nuttall would spend the winter, while Hunt took his brigade up the Missouri to the mouth of the Nodoway River, upstream from present Saint Joseph, Missouri.

The winter's stay was notable for the opportunity it gave Dr. Barton's explorer to botanize in the area around Saint Louis and to get to know another Englishman interested in botany, John Bradbury (1768–1823), a member of the Linnean Society of London who had come to the United States to collect living plants for the Liverpool Botanic Garden. He got to know also Henry Marie Brackenridge (1786–1871), of Pittsburgh, a friend of Bradbury's trained in law but temporarily casting about for a connection. Bradbury, like Nuttall, was invited to go up the Missouri and overland to the mouth of the Columbia with Hunt, Ramsay Crooks (1787–1859), Donald McKenzie (1783–1851), Robert McClellan (1770–1815), and Joseph Miller, the Pennsylvania trapper and fur trader. The Astoria partners were a very blue book then and later of the American fur trade (though the Scots named were then based on Canada). The brigade would ultimately exceed sixty persons.[11]

Henry Marie Brackenridge got his invitation from a different, competing enterprise, that of Manuel Lisa (1772–1820), the senior partner with Andrew Henry and Reuben Lewis, Meriwether Lewis's only brother, in the Missouri Fur Company.[12] Lisa and Brackenridge would meet the Astorians June 2, 1811, twelve hundred miles up the Missouri from Saint Louis. Among the members of Lisa's party were Toussaint Charbonneau, Lisa's French-Canadian interpreter (as he had been for the Lewis and Clark Expedition), and Charbonneau's Shoshoni wife, Sacagawea, the mother of Jean Baptiste, nicknamed Pomp (short for Pompey) by Lewis and Clark soon after his birth, February 11, 1805, at their

[11]IRVING [3], 138; PORTER, 103–12.
[12]BRACKENRIDGE [2], 30–31.

winter quarters at Fort Mandan, seven miles below the mouth of the Knife. Here, once more, the West, like the East, was associating its best representatives with the botanical explorer out from Philadelphia. [13]

Nuttall had been taking advantage of every boat stop or encampment for collecting seeds, plants, roots, and bulbs. With Bradbury and Brackenridge along he gathered additional energy for his task, though he worked mostly alone. He was often heedless of distance and sometimes confused about his location or directions—tendencies he would later repeat, as he would also a seeming indifference to Indian hostility.

The summer's and fall's collecting were crowned for Nuttall at the Mandan Post of the Missouri Fur Company, after the Astorians had left the Missouri to proceed by land from the Arikara village between the mouth of Grand River and the mouth of the Cannonball. The Mandan Post was located farther north, near the mouth of the Knife. [14] Here he met Reuben Lewis, and at the end of the summer Andrew Henry, also a Lisa partner and one of the most intrepid fur men working in the distant areas of the West. Nuttall appears to have advanced in this interval from the Mandan Post as high up the Missouri as the mouth of the Yellowstone. But the most reliable portrait of the young scientist as western explorer comes from the accounts written by his companions, Bradbury and Brackenridge, and from Washington Irving in *Astoria*, published twenty-five years later. The long descent of the Missouri, which would put him down once more at Saint Louis, probably took from some time in September until past mid-October. He was accompanied downriver by Lisa, Lewis, and Henry, surrounded by their furs.

The year 1812 was now swiftly approaching, and with it a state of war between the United States and Nuttall's homeland, Great Britain. When Nuttall descended the Mississippi by boat to New Orleans, he found a ship at the Gulf port ready to sail for Liverpool. He took passage, thus delaying for the time being, he apparently thought, the fulfillment of the grand project formed for him by Benjamin Smith Barton, to subject the Lewis

[13]BRADBURY, in THWAITES [1], note 105. The meeting of the two parties was at Cedar Island, the site of Régis Loisel's trading fort. Jean Baptiste may not have been returning to the Mandan villages with his parents; he was being educated by Gen. William Clark and his wife in Saint Louis.

[14]Not to be confused, however, with the Fort Mandan of the Lewis and Clark Expedition, which was downstream and on the east side of the Missouri.

and Clark natural-science collections to scientific reexamination and to expand them as fully as possible.

In England during the war years Nuttall innocently slipped into some scientific misjudgments and achieved an honor which must have meant much to him. He permitted Fraser's Nursery, Chelsea, to publish in 1813 *A Catalogue of New and Interesting Plants, Collected in Upper Louisiana, and Principally on the River Missourie, North America,* developed from Nuttall's seeds, roots, and bulbs collected on the route of the Astorians. The names were mostly without scientific description. Frederick Pursh, who had meantime arrived in England, was preparing his *Flora Americae Septentrionalis* (1814), and into it he introduced many of Nuttall's species with descriptions of his own. Others subsequently went into synonymy, but a few retain the Nuttall name.[15] The ultimate fate of the Lewis and Clark Herbarium has been told by Paul Russell Cutright, who gave it order after its rediscovery at the American Philosophical Society and its transferrence to the Academy of Natural Sciences of Philadelphia.[16]

The honor Nuttall achieved was his election to the Linnean Society, London, in 1813.[17] It came just over five years after his first departure for the United States. He was now only twenty-seven years of age, but he had still "miles to go and promises to keep." They were of his own making, and he would soon see to them.

From the time of his return at war's end in 1815, Nuttall had to have some means of sustaining himself in Philadelphia. Through seedsmen like Bernard M'Mahon and, in London, John Fraser and James Dickson he had learned about the steady even if modest rewards to be had from selling seeds of new or little-known species. This source of income rather than the craft of printing he used to complement whatever largesse his Uncle Jonas in Liverpool may have forwarded to him. He had long been away from printing in the Philadelphia establishment of D. Heartt, who had taken him on soon after his arrival from England in 1808. The lapse was five years, from 1810, when he started for the Great Lakes, to his return from England.[18]

[15]Edward L. Greene, "Reprint of Fraser's Catalogue," *Pittonia,* II (1890), 114–19.
[16]CUTRIGHT, 364–75.
[17]GRAUSTEIN, 90.
[18]*Ibid.,* 98.

He had meantime developed an ambitious project for the writing of an American flora. Toward that end, but also for earning current income, he made two trips, the first, in the latter half of 1815, as far south as Savannah, Georgia, and the second, principally on foot, through northwestern Pennsylvania, down the Ohio drainage to Kentucky, on into Tennessee, the southern Appalachians, and through North and South Carolina to Charleston, in 1816 and into January, 1817. The botanical collections Nuttall achieved in both expeditions were substantial and tell us, in his publication to-be, where he had found many specific plants.

When the author's first book appeared in July, 1818, the measure of his greatness as a taxonomist became known on both sides of the Atlantic. *Genera of North American Plants with a Catalogue of the Species through 1817*, in two volumes, was printed for Nuttall by his old employer, D. Heartt, at his own expense. Since Nuttall was at no time in his American career ahead of the hounds financially, there is room for the conjecture that he may have set some of the type and fed sheets through the press.

The botanical classification of genera in Nuttall's work is Linnaean, but the descriptions often develop the relationships advanced taxonomically by the post-Linnaean school of Jussieu and De Candolle, with a considerable degree of indebtedness to John Ray still earlier, in the eighteenth century. The compromise was, in all likelihood, a concession to a system to which Americans had become accustomed. Nuttall, although increasingly able to manage Latin descriptions, chose English for this work, but with clear exposition of derivations.

Nuttall's election to the Academy of Natural Sciences of Philadelphia was not a consequence of his first book-length publication. It came in January, 1817, before he had started the writing and eighteen months before its completion. Similarly, his election to the American Philosophical Society in October, 1817, was ahead of the fact. But joined to his 1813 election to the Linnean Society of London, these recognitions were bright ornaments to the growing scientific reputation of the thirty-one-year-old. They also conferred upon him the privilege of using the book and manuscript collections held by the academy and the Philosophical Society. That they were of immense value to him appears in both *Genera* and his second book, which would emerge from his lonely journey, about to begin.

A slow-dying tradition has it that Thomas Nuttall wished to go out to the Near Southwest of present Arkansas and Oklahoma, and thence to the Rocky Mountains, in some measure to beat the Stephen Harriman Long Expedition of 1819–20 to those distant exploring and scientific goals. As a matter of fact, he had projected himself into the Near Southwest on at least three occasions before the Long Expedition was conceived in Washington.[19] And when he organized himself for his solitary undertaking, he was a year and a half ahead of the deflection of the Yellowstone Expedition from its destination up the Missouri to a new route and an entirely different objective across the Great Plains to the mountains and back by way of Fort Smith, under Long's command.

There is substantial basis for believing that John Bradbury's original plan, developed for himself in the autumn of 1810, to go from Saint Louis to "Ozark [Arkansas Post], a town on the mouth of the Arkansas," in May, 1811, planted in Nuttall the germ of the idea of a southwestern journey.[20] The Arkansas drainage was understood by at least two scientific explorers to be a rich area botanically. One of them—Thomas Nuttall—would have the exploring opportunity in 1819.

Actually Nuttall set out from Philadelphia for Lancaster on October 2, 1818. With his patrons' money in his pocket he went by stage, as he had done in 1810, for the first leg of his journey. At Lancaster, however, he chose to travel on foot—a better way for a botanist forever searching. Our need at this point is minimal, however, for a narrative analysis of an exploring journey which would ultimately take Nuttall from Philadelphia to Pittsburgh, down the Ohio to its mouth, thence down the Mississippi to the mouth of the Arkansas, up that river to the Three Forks (the confluence of the Grand and Verdigris rivers with the Arkansas in present eastern Oklahoma), and on to a point at approximately the location of present Guthrie, Logan County, Oklahoma. Counting his observations on the lower Mississippi to New Orleans in 1820, the author's journey

[19]Nuttall to Aylmer Bourke Lambert, January 26, 1816, quoted in GRAUSTEIN, 102; W. P. C. Barton to Brigadier General Daniel Parker, June 30, 1817, *ibid.*, 129; Nuttall to Daniel Drake related to George Wilkins Short, January 10, 1817, *ibid.*, 112 and note 55.

[20]John Bradbury to William Roscoe, November 28, 1810, in H. W. Rickett, "John Bradbury's Explorations in Missouri Territory," Letter 13, American Philosophical Society *Proceedings*, XCIV, No. 1 (1950), 70.

extended for more than half a continent. The journal which follows, with its explanatory annotations, affords us all, or almost all, that we may need. The account, as it unfolds along the route, is pivotal not only to an understanding of the natural science stores in the Near Southwest fifteen years after the Louisiana Purchase but also to an understanding of the past and contemporary history of an explosive region, hemmed on the south and west first by Spain, then by Mexico, fluid with Indian migration and conflict, and disturbed by the beginnings of white settlement.

This much must be said, however: Nuttall was making his journey without benefit of an accompanying expedition or a complement of exploring friends, except when he went south from Fort Smith with Major William Bradford and a corporal's guard, to Red River. He was almost always a welcome guest on boats proceeding upstream on the Arkansas, however, and his stays with settlers are gratefully noted. On the final leg of his progress toward the distant Rockies, up Little Deep Fork River toward the Cimarron in present Oklahoma, he was with a Mr. Lee, a trapper who is without further identification. That Nuttall's intention to go all the way to the Rocky Mountains was rash is demonstrated by his fate and Lee's. He almost died from malaria, and they were both turned back by odds which he, at least, had underestimated all along.

Nuttall's acuteness as an observer, his ability to gather from acquaintances on his route the stuff of which future history would be made, and his nearly insatiable interest in Indian antiquities and contemporary life make of his account a rich, abundantly detailed assemblage. Comparatively, it offers many more rewards than the often limited number which emerge from the impressionistic, generalized accounts of his contemporaries writing from their experiences in the trans-Mississippi West.

Nuttall in his Preface promised himself and us a second volume to accompany the Arkansas *Journal*. It would embrace aboriginal antiquities, he wrote, essays on the languages of the western Indians, and an "oral and graphical" view of languages in general. The volume, if it was ever written even in part, never appeared. The reasons are analyzed in the Editorial Note to Nuttall's Appendix. In a word, he would not have the time, and his linguistic and anthropological background for the task, unlike his command of natural sciences, was too little advanced.

What here may be described as Barton's Law is that, if procrastination in the pursuit of scientific ends can defeat them, it surely will. Nuttall's large botanical harvest in the Near Southwest, shown in his *Journal* and in the accompanying editorial annotations, was not published scientifically over his name until 1837, fourteen years after the Long Expedition *Report* appeared.[21] The Long Expedition, in its return phase in 1819–20, covered much of the territory Nuttall had originally set out to exploit botanically, and it yielded descriptions of many species which he otherwise might have claimed.[22] But there were causes of Nuttall's procrastination, as a synopsis of his career after 1820 will show.

The 1819 *Journal* appeared in Philadelphia in 1821. This time Nuttall had a publisher, T. H. Palmer. The date was early enough to afford Edwin James, the compiler of the Long Expedition *Report*, an opportunity to consult and acknowledge many points of interest from Nuttall's general experience.

The copy of the journal that has been available to me is that of the Frank Phillips Collection in the Western History Collections of the University of Oklahoma. It has a spine length of 22.5 cm., a paper page of 21.7 cm. × 13.5 cm., a type page of 21 picas × 38 picas (including running head and folio). There are five plates of southwestern scenes and a folding map of the Arkansas River drainage. The binding is ¼ leather on tan-brown-blue marbled paper over boards, the die stamping gold, including plain rules on front and back leather corners. The endsheets are blue. The book sold at two dollars. It was reliably reprinted (from type

---

[21]NUTTALL [3], 139–203. The paper was completed in 1834, but its publication, as indicated, did not occur until 1837. The Long Expedition narrative report came soon after the publication of Nuttall's *Arkansas Journal*, which appeared in November, 1821. It was Edwin James's compilation, *Account of an Expedition from Pittsburgh to the Rocky Mountains, Performed in the Years 1819 and '20 . . . Under the Command of Major Stephen H. Long*, 2 vols. and Atlas (Philadelphia, H. C. Carey and I. Lea, 1823).

[22]Edwin James, "Catalogue of Plants Collected during a Journey to and from the Rocky Mountains during the Summer of 1820," American Philosophical Society *Transactions*, II (1825), 172–90.

John Torrey, "Descriptions of some new or rare Plants from the Rocky Mountains, collected in July, 1820, by Dr. Edwin James," *Annals of the Lyceum of Natural History of New York*, I (1824), 30–36; "Descriptions of some new Grasses collected by Dr. E. James, in the Expedition of Major Long to the Rocky Mountains, in 1819–1820," *ibid.*, 148–56; "Some Account of a Collection of Plants made during a journey from the Rocky Mountains in the summer of 1820, by Edwin P. James," *Annals of the Lyceum of Natural History of New York*, II (1828), 161–254.

newly set) in THWAITES [1], Volume XIII, but without the extensive historical and scientific annotations it demands today.

To attempt an extended recounting of Nuttall's career after he had returned to Philadelphia in April, 1820, would be to intrude upon Graustein's brilliant biography, *Thomas Nuttall, Naturalist: Explorations in America, 1808–1841* (Cambridge, Harvard University Press, 1967), which encompasses a good deal more than its title suggests—the young life before the Philadelphia years began and the mature life and death (September 10, 1859) in England, as well as the American experience. Nuttall's interests were complex, but in good hands, that is, Graustein's, they become unified and imbued with purpose. The personal drives, almost always realized, and at least two large frustrations are clearly evident. But for our purposes at least a small capsule of the post-southwestern career is needed.

From his return to Philadelphia after his explorations in the Southwest, Nuttall was busy with the writing of his *Journal* and thereafter with a number of projects, perhaps none more interesting than his paper on the geological structure of the Mississippi Valley (ANS *Journal*, II, 14–52). In it the correlations between certain North American formations and those of England anticipate the findings of geologists much later in the nineteenth century. Nuttall also immersed himself in mineralogy, acquired new friends, John Torrey (1796–1873) among them, and accepted a number of lectures in the eastern area. His correspondence was becoming large with his reputation, but its flow was one-sided, largely to him rather than from him.

With the death of William Dandridge Peck (1763–1822), the professor of natural science at Harvard and curator of the Cambridge Botanic Garden, the board of visitors of the professorship began the search for a successor in the autumn of 1822. Their collective eye fell on Thomas Nuttall, and by mid-March, 1823, he had become a lecturer in natural science and curator of the Botanic Garden. He was an anomaly in that setting, for he had no degrees. With interludes in England in the first half of 1824 and during the same season of 1828, in the South on botanical missions in the winter and early spring of 1829–30, and late in 1831 and the spring of 1832, for collecting in, respectively, New Hampshire and the Middle West and the southern states, he graced Harvard and the

Botanic Garden. In the autumn of 1832 he was off again, this time to the Azores, and from there to England, reporting back to the Harvard Corporation finally on July 7, 1833, shortly after his return after an absence of more than eight months.[23] He had not proved to be a stationary figure on a becalmed academic sea. By the beginning of March, 1834, he had written a letter of resignation to Josiah Quincy, the president of Harvard.[24]

Nuttall's frustrations during the Harvard years were his inability to work there with trifling library resources, in contrast to their relative abundance in Philadelphia, and his own restless attraction to the wilderness of the Far West. His accomplishments, on the other hand, were not minor. Like countless teachers before and after him, Nuttall was impelled to write his own textbook, *An Introduction to Physiological and Systematic Botany*, which he published in the spring of 1827 with Hilliard and Brown, Cambridge. By 1832 he was publishing *A Manual of the Ornithology of the United States and Canada: The Land Birds* (Cambridge, Hilliard and Brown), followed in 1834 by its second volume, *The Water Birds* (Boston, Hilliard, Gray). The two bird volumes represented Nuttall's prose at its best. They would continue to appear even to 1903. Coming at the end of his Harvard career, they not only justified a later estimate of his worth as "easily the first man of science in Augustan Harvard"[25] but demonstrated once more the great range of his versatility.

The great spine of the Rocky Mountains had been on Nuttall's mind since at least 1811, when near the mouth of the Yellowstone he was still short of his goal. And California had been equally strong in his plans since at least 1816. When he received from Nathaniel Jarvis Wyeth (1802–56), of Cambridge, now on his first trading expedition into the Far Northwest, a letter of July 4, 1833, telling of a plant shipment he was making and inviting Nuttall to join him a year hence on another expedition, the die was cast. By January 15, 1834, the two men were giving form to their plans, and three weeks later Wyeth learned from Nuttall that John Kirk Townsend (1809–51), a Philadelphia ornithologist and friend of Nuttall's, had been invited to go along.[26] Meantime, Nuttall had been

[23]GRAUSTEIN, 266.
[24]*Ibid.*, 291–92.
[25]MORISON, 217.
[26]Wyeth to Nuttall, July 4, 1833; Wyeth to Nuttall, January 15, 1834; Wyeth to

analyzing and describing Wyeth's herbarium from the Far West: it included 112 species of flowering plants, 51 of them new to science, he believed.[27]

Nuttall and Townsend left Philadelphia for Pittsburgh on March 13, 1834, and went by boat thereafter to Saint Louis. From the staging point at Independence, Missouri, the large cavalcade led by Wyeth and Milton Sublette, of the Rocky Mountain Fur Company, struck out by Wyeth's land route of 1833. Its mission was the delivery of his goods contracted to the fur company, which was headed by William Sublette and Robert Campbell, at what proved to be the Green River Rendezvous of 1834, more accurately the Rendezvous on Ham's Fork of the Green, in present Lincoln County, Wyoming.

It was the season of Sir William Drummond Stewart, whom they would meet in the Northwest; of Captain B. L. E. Bonneville, a romantic figure signalized later by Washington Irving (1837); of Dr. John McLoughlin, Chief Factor for the Hudson's Bay Company at Fort Vancouver, who was their host near the end of the journey to the mouth of the Columbia; and of many others. But it was also a season of collecting, for Nuttall in botany and for Townsend among the birds. Wyeth wrote from the Green River that "Mr. Nuttall has made an immense collection of new plants."[28] How immense would appear in the fullness of time. On the Willamette there were, however, disbelievers. They consisted of a number of Nuttall's French-speaking boatmen of 1811, now settled in the far country, puzzled as ever by the scientist's search for roots and bulbs and plants.[29]

A young Harvard man, Richard Henry Dana (1815–82), was quite as puzzled when he encountered Nuttall on a San Diego beach, "with his trousers rolled up to his knees, picking up stones and shells."[30] Nuttall would later be a passenger on the *Alert*, whose complement included the deckhand Dana, on his return around the Horn to New York, arriving in September, 1836. Many readers of Dana's uncertain classic, *Two Years*

Nuttall, February 4, 1834, in WYETH, 67–68, 103–104, 106–107. TOWNSEND is our principal source for events of the long expedition to the Pacific.

[27]NUTTALL [7], 5–60.

[28]WYETH, 137.

[29]LEE AND FROST, 132.

[30]DANA, Chap. 30 of varying pagination in many editions.

before the Mast (1840), have concluded that the former Harvard faculty member was distant on board to the undergraduate on leave. Far from it: on Dana's evidence, they had many a short chat at night when he was at the wheel of the ship.

The moral of the episode on the San Diego beach, however, is that, from the time of his arrival at the mouth of the Columbia in the autumn of 1834, Nuttall had been assiduously collecting Mollusca as well as plants and minerals. The description of his harvest here and southward to California was entrusted to J. W. Randall.[31]

Nuttall made two trips to Hawaii, one for the period from January 5, 1835, to April 16, the other in the winter of 1835–36. And following his two excursions he had his opportunity to see California and collect there.

Nuttall's papers after his return east were, as before, many in number and of great significance scientifically. He was sometimes in Philadelphia, sometimes in Cambridge, and for a long period in 1838 and 1839 he was traveling in the South.[32] Shortly thereafter he began work on a revision of François André Michaux's *Histoire des arbres forestiers de l'Amérique septentrionale* (2 vols., Paris, 1810–13), for which he completed a three-volume supplement, arranged for handsome plates, and saw through to completion most of the sheets. *North American Sylva* was to take seven years in the publishing, however, the last volume appearing in 1849[33] long after Nuttall had to return to England (1842) to take up manor life at Nutgrove, his Uncle Jonas Nuttall's estate, descended to him for his remaining lifetime through his Aunt Frances. The terms of the inheritance made it mandatory for Nuttall to remain in England for at least nine months out of any calendar year.[34] Thus Nuttall was remanded to his native country. He could not resist his old haunts, however, and on November 5, 1847, he was back in Boston, then in Cambridge and Philadelphia, finally departing for England in mid-March, 1848. It would be his last visit.[35]

[31]RANDALL, 106–47.

[32]GRAUSTEIN, 343.

[33]Vol. I, Part I, 1–56, Part II, 57–136 (Philadelphia, Judah Dobson, 1842 and 1843, respectively); Vol. II (Philadelphia, T. Ward, 1846); Vol. III (Philadelphia, Smith and Wistar, 1849).

[34]GRAUSTEIN, 334.

[35]*Ibid.*, 372–76.

Editorial Procedures

THE TEXT: Thomas Nuttall's original *Journal* published in 1821 is the source from which the present edition has been prepared. It contains obvious English spellings, occasional misspellings, abbreviations, and variant punctuation, all of which I have retained in the text but have shown correctly in the editor's notes when meaning or historical identification would otherwise fail. Thus also I have retained a few inconsistencies in spelling, the most striking being Nuttall's alternate uses of "Chicasaw" and "Chickasaw." The only significant changes appearing in the present edition are the addition of a terminal *s* to his use of Arkansa in the title of the work and the elimination of subtitle data: "With Occasional Observations on the Manners of the Aborigines. Illustrated by a Map and Other Engravings." The accompanying reproduction of the original title page, however, will make clear Nuttall's own choice. I have chosen a redrawing rather than a duplication of the author's long foldout map drawn for him by H. S. Tanner, showing the lower Arkansas River drainage, partly because more modern data will serve present-day readers better, partly because tipping in a map of this character would be an expensive hand operation in an already expensive undertaking.

TYPOGRAPHY: This new edition conforms typographically, within obvious limits, to Nuttall's original. I have added in capital and small capitals his name at the end of each note which he himself wrote. All other notes are mine. In the latter, genera and species, or the one or the other, not italicized, even when the author may have used italics, are so handled because they did not achieve acceptance on any of a number of grounds, of which Nuttall's failure to publish a name scientifically was one. All scientific designations in Nuttall's account and notes have been made current in my annotations, from the manuals and scientific papers available today. Where I have found it necessary to add material to a Nuttall note, I have enclosed it in brackets.

SOURCES: In the notes I indicate sources in small capitals, using in most cases the surname of the author or editor (NASATIR, II, 212, for example), relegating full bibliographical detail to the appended listing in Sources Cited by the Author or Cited or Consulted by the Editor; or, similarly, using the name, often abbreviated, of an agency or collection (TERR. PAPERS, XIX, 303, for example). When I cite from two or more works by the same author, I bracket the number of the author's work corresponding to the bracketed number of its full bibliographical listing in the appended Sources Cited. At some points full author and title treatment is given, especially when such data are needed for a thorough understanding of contemporary or comparative detail.

THE BIBLIOGRAPHY (Sources Cited), a greatly expanded one, is partly of Nuttall's doing, inasmuch as his not infrequent references must now be more thoroughly related to others then available or to more recent works, critically assessed. At no point will this need be more apparent than in the editorial tracing of the De Soto sources, which otherwise might be thought to have little relationship to the author's explorations in the Southwest.

Acknowledgments

THE CORDIAL SPIRIT of helpfulness accorded me by many of my colleagues in the University of Oklahoma has made my pursuit of Thomas Nuttall in the Southwest a far less difficult task than it might otherwise have been. Three of them read all of the typescript and made valuable suggestions, respectively, in botany, geography, and western history. They are:

George J. Goodman, Regents Professor of Botany Emeritus and Curator Emeritus of the Bebb Herbarium, who is a wise and much-needed scientific counselor. To him I owe many taxonomic retracings and the kind of precision one would expect of one of North America's most distinguished botanists.

John W. Morris, Professor of Geography Emeritus, who is thoroughly in command of Nuttall's territory, east and west.

Arrell M. Gibson, George Lynn Cross Research Professor of History, whose southwestern research and writing are distinguished.

A number of interesting geological problems in Nuttall's account had the attention of Professor Leon Reiter, formerly of the School of Geology and Geophysics, and George G. Huffman, Professor of Geology and Geophysics. Professor Thomas J. Love, a native of Arkansas and a member of the Engineering Faculty in the University of Oklahoma, provided needed data on the lower Arkansas drainage, as Dr. Tom Dillard, President of the Pulaski County Historical Society (Arkansas) did for Arkansas settlements which long ago disappeared.

Richard G. Taft and Judson S. Woodruff, attorneys of Oklahoma City, helped me avoid some of the easier assumptions about Cherokee-Choctaw Indian treaty lands. And to another attorney, Anton J. Pregaldin, of Clayton, Missouri, I am indebted for precise genealogical data on the Joseph Bogy family.

The bibliographical pursuit of Nuttall in two hemispheres was greatly facilitated by gifted specialists John S. Ezell, David Ross Boyd Professor of History and Curator of Western History Collections in the University of Oklahoma, and Wayne Morris, his former assistant; and Dorothy Hill Gersack, formerly of the National Archives and Records Service, Washington, D.C.

Graphic representation of Nuttall's travels in the period 1818–20 for this edition of his work was undertaken by Frank O. Williams, a highly skilled cartographer as well as scholarly editor, to whom I am greatly indebted, particularly for his tracing of the Nuttall thrust towards the Rocky Mountains from Three Forks in present Oklahoma. The tracing of this route also had the careful attention of D. Horton Grisso, whose training in Oklahoma geology proved immensely helpful in the solution of a difficult problem.

Cluff E. Hopla, George Lynn Cross Research Professor of Zoology in the University of Oklahoma, and John Francis McDermott, the distinguished historian of the Mississippi Valley, of Saint Louis, were generously responsive to inquiries. To Carolyn B. Powell, Map Librarian of the School of Geology in the University of Oklahoma, and to Irene Endicott, Proofreader at the University of Oklahoma Press and my indispensable typist, my warm thanks for their clearly evident contributions to this volume. And for editorial care at the publication stage, my gratitude to Doris Radford Morris, Managing Editor of the University of Oklahoma Press; and for still another indispensable index, equally my gratitude to Mrs. H. C. Peterson.

SAVOIE LOTTINVILLE

Norman, Oklahoma
May 28, 1979

A JOURNAL OF TRAVELS
INTO THE ARKANSAS TERRITORY
DURING THE YEAR 1819

A

JOURNAL

OF

TRAVELS

INTO THE

ARKANSA TERRITORY,

DURING THE YEAR

1819.

WITH OCCASIONAL OBSERVATIONS ON THE MANNERS OF THE

ABORIGINES.

ILLUSTRATED BY A MAP AND OTHER ENGRAVINGS.

———◆———

BY THOMAS NUTTALL, F. L. S.

HONORARY MEMBER OF THE AMERICAN PHILOSOPHICAL SOCIETY, AND OF
THE ACADEMY OF NATURAL SCIENCES, &c.

———◆———

PHILADELPHIA:

PRINTED AND PUBLISHED BY THOS. H. PALMER.

1821.

Permit me to lay before you the humble narrative of a journey, chiefly undertaken for the investigation of the natural history of a region hitherto unexplored. Excuse the imperfect performance of the gratifying task which you liberally had imposed, but which was rendered almost abortive by the visitations of affliction.

If, in so tiresome a volume of desultory remarks, you should meet with some momentary gratification, some transient amusement, or ray of information, the author will receive the satisfaction of not having laboured entirely in vain.

AUTHOR'S PREFACE

To THOSE who vaguely peruse the narratives of travellers for pastime or transitory amusement, the present volume is by no means addressed. It is no part of the author's ambition to study the gratification of so fastidious a taste as that, which but too generally governs the readers of the present day; a taste, which has no criterion but passing fashion, which spurns at every thing that possesses not the charm of novelty, and the luxury of embellishment. We live no longer in an age that tolerates the plain "unvarnished tale." Our language must now be crowded with the spoils of those which are foreign to its native idiom; it must be perplexed by variety, and rendered ambiguous and redundant by capricious ornament. Hermes, no longer the plain messenger of the gods, exercises all his deceit, and mingles luxury in the purest of intellectual streams.

Had I solely consulted my own gratification, the present volume would probably never have been offered to the public. But, as it may contain some physical remarks connected with the history of the country, and with that of the unfortunate aborigines, who are so rapidly dwindling into oblivion, and whose fate may, in succeeding generations, excite a curiosity and compassion denied them by the present, I have considered myself partly excused in offering a small edition to the scientific part of the community, just sufficient to defray the expenses of the printer, who kindly undertook the publication at his own risk. I may safely say, that hitherto, so far from writing for emolument, I have sacrificed both time and fortune to it. For nearly *ten* years I have travelled throughout America, principally with a view of becoming acquainted with some favourite branches of its natural history. I have had no other end in view than personal gratification, and in this I have not been deceived, for innocent amusement can never leave room for regret. To converse, as it were, with nature, to admire the wisdom and beauty of creation, has ever been, and I hope will ever be, to me a favourite pursuit. To communicate to others a portion of the same amusement and gratification has been the only object of my botanical publications; the most remote idea of personal emolument arising from them, from every circumstance connected with them could not have been admitted into calculation. I had a right, however, reasonably to expect from Americans a degree of candour, at least equal to that which my labours had met in Europe. But I have found what, indeed, I might have reason to expect from human nature, often, instead of gratitude, detraction and envy. With such, I stoop not to altercate; my endeavours, however imperfect, have been directed to the public good; and I regret not the period I have spent in roaming over the delightful fields of Flora, in studying all her mysteries and enigmas, if I have, in any instance, been useful to her cause, or opened to the idle wanderer one fruitful field for useful reflexion.

Not wishing to enlarge the present publication, or retard it by the addition of a voluminous appendix, I reserve for a subsequent volume, which will shortly be issued, A *general view and description* of the *aboriginal antiquities* of the *western states,* and some *essays on the languages of the western Indians,* and their connection with those of other parts of the world, involving, in some measure, *a general view of language, both oral and graphical.*

The surveys and collections towards a history of the aboriginal antiquities, have remained unpublished in my possession for several years, and would have been longer withheld, in hopes of rendering them more complete, had not an unexpected anticipation obliged the author to hasten to do justice to himself, and claim, at least, that which was due to his personal industry.

The aboriginal languages of America, hitherto so neglected and unjustly consigned to oblivion as the useless relics of barbarism, are, nevertheless, perhaps destined to create a new era in the history of primitive language. In their mazes is unfolded a history of morals, of remote connections, of vicissitudes and emigrations, which had escaped the circumstantial pen of history; and yet, however strange it may appear, are more durably impressed than if engraven upon tablets of brass, and possessed of an intrinsic veracity nothing short of inspiration.

The literary character of the aboriginal languages of America, have, of late years, begun to claim the attention of the learned both in Europe and America. The reports and correspondence of the Historical committee appointed by the American Philosophical Society, stand meritoriously preeminent in this research; and it must be highly gratifying to the public to know, that the same members continue still to labour in the field with unabated vigour. These various efforts united, I may venture to predict, will be crowned with successful discoveries which could not have been anticipated and which will ultimately contribute towards the development of that portion of human history, which, above all others, appeared to be so impenetrably buried in oblivion.

Philadelphia, November, 1821.

CONTENTS

———————

APPENDIX

A JOURNEY
INTO THE INTERIOR OF
THE ARKANSAS TERRITORY

CHAPTER I.

ON THE MORNING of the second of October, 1818, I took my depar-ture from Philadelphia in the mail stage, which arrived safely in Lancas-ter, sixty-three miles distant, a little after sun-set. Though always pleas-ingly amused by the incidents of travelling, and the delightful aspect of rude or rural nature, I could not at this time divert from my mind the most serious reflections on the magnitude and danger of the journey which now lay before me, and which was, indeed, of very uncertain issue.

Scarcely any part of the United States presents a more beautiful succes-sion of hill and dale, than that which succeeds between Philadelphia and Lancaster; the valley, however, of Chester county, including Down-ingston, exceeds every other, except the site of Lancaster, in fertility and rural picture. It is about twenty-five miles in length by one in breadth, and pursues from hence a north-east direction. The rock throughout this valley is calcareous, and the soil is consequently of a superior quality. This lime-stone, which has been assiduously examined by the mineralogists and naturalists of Philadelphia, though not very dissimilar to that of the western states, except in the high inclination of the strata and the predominance of spar, has never yet been found to contain any kind of organic remains, and scarcely any metals more than traces of iron, man-ganese, titanium, and lead.

3D.] From Lancaster, I continued my route on foot, as affording greater leisure, and better opportunity for making observation. The rain, however, to-day prevented me from proceeding more than seventeen miles on the road to Harrisburgh.[1] About twelve miles east of Middleton,[2] I had again occasion to observe certain ledges of the prevailing calcareous rock, dipping at an angle scarcely under that of 45°, traversed by sparry veins, occasionally intermingled with epidote, in which are also imbedded bright brown-red rhombic masses of felspar and amorphous quartz, a circumstance which had formerly fallen under my notice in a pedestrian tour on this road; I was now, however, enabled to trace this appearance into a connection with the transition formation which almost immediatley succeeds, presenting masses of agglomerated rock, chiefly calcareous, of which the fragments are both angular and arrounded. Beyond this, on the first succeeding hill, occur layers of the old or transition sand-stone, not always red, though some of that colour appeared in the vicinity, interlayed with brown-red slate-clay. Afterwards, and in connection with this information, appears the green-stone of the Germans, and the bottoms of the valleys only are calcareous. Twelve miles west of Lancaster, we enter the fine fertile tract, once known to the natives of the Susquehannah by the name of *Pe-Quay,* or the Pleasant Fields.[3]

4TH.] To Middleton, grunstein and argillaceous trap, with sand-stone conglomerate, and Spanish-brown slate-clay alternate and succeed each other, affording an indifferent soil, and forming lofty hills, with precipitous declivities and narrow valleys. The sylvan hills of the Susquehanna are, however, calcareous and underlayed with common bluish grey and chlorite slate, which as at Lancaster abounds with scattered or imbedded

---

[1]Harrisburg, in swampy land originally called *Peshtank* or *Peixtan* by the Delaware Indians, corrupted to Paxtang by whites, was the site of John Harris's trading post before 1725, later the location also of his ferry across the Susquehanna. The actual town was laid out by John Harris, Jr., sometime after his father's death in 1748. The seat of Dauphin County, it also became the state capital in 1812. Lancaster, named the county seat of Lancaster County in 1729, and temporary state capital from 1797 to 1812, was then and later a center for German immigrants, mostly from the Palatinate. P.C.P., III, 355–56, 380–81, 384–86.

[2]Middletown, still older than Harrisburg, was declining in 1818, when this middle town between Lancaster and Carlisle lost commercial ground to Baltimore. CUMING, in THWAITES [1], IV, 36.

[3]Pequea, originally a Shawnee village on Pequea Creek in Lancaster County, from 1694 to 1730. *Pequea* = dust or ashes.

cubic pyrites.[4] The long bridge of a mile and a quarter, connecting with a small island, crosses a wide and shallow part of the river, whose bed is of slate (or argillite).

5TH.] About half past seven, I left Harrisburgh, and in the course of the day proceeded through Carlisle to within five miles of Shippensburg,[5] a distance of about 31 miles, over a deeply undulated country, evincing, by the ease and comfort of its scattered population no inconsiderable degree of fertility in the soil, which is calcareous. The first considerable chain of hills, proceeding from north-east to south-west, clad with unbroken forests, appeared on our left during most part of the day, and indicated an approach to the mountains.

6TH.] This evening I arrived at Cammels'-town,[6] situated at the foot of the North Mountain. The intermediate and surrounding country is deeply undulated with hills of a softish sandstone and slate clay. The more conspicuous hills of shale, accompanied by organic remains, commence at Chambersburg,[7] and, as in Virginia, are characterised by the appearance of Pine (*Pinus inops*),[8] and scrub oak (*Quercus ilicifolia*); here also occurs the fragment sumach (*Rhus aromaticum*).[9]

The road, on which several bands of labourers were employed, was now nearly completed to Pittsburgh, affording that convenience and facility to the inland commerce of the state which had been so long neglected. The states of New-York and Virginia, equally interested in the advance-

---

[4]The Chlorite slate of the Wissahickton, near Germantown, considered as primitive, contains similar pyrites with octahedral crystals of iron ore. —NUTTALL.

[5]Carlisle, county seat of Cumberland, dates from the establishment by the Frenchman James le Tort of a trading post at what became Le Tort Springs about 1720. Lewis Evans's map of 1749 does not show it, but his of 1755 does. It was the site of Carlisle Fort, chosen by Gov. Robert Hunter Morris in 1755, terminated in 1758. P.C.R., VI, 517, 732–33; for the Le Torts see *ibid.*, I, 340, 396, 435; II, 562; III, 187; IV, 237.

Shippensburg, named for Edward Shippen, who owned the land on which it was laid out in 1749, was the site of Fort Morris, named for the then provincial governor, who authorized its construction in 1755. It was not regularly garrisoned after 1759. HUNTER, 450–63.

[6]Cammels'-town [Campbell's Town], extinct, derived its name from one or more Scotch-Irish settlers there before the last third of the eighteenth century.

[7]Chambersburg, named for Edward Chambers, was the site of a stockade dating from 1756. The present city occupies the same site, in Franklin County. P.A., 2d Ser., II, 695.

[8]*Pinus inops* Ait. (1789) gives way to *Pinus virginiana* Mill. (1768).

[9]*Rhus aromatica* Ait., rare in Pennsylvania.

ment of their internal trade, now begin to show themselves as the serious rivals of Pennsylvania, which till lately, with the exception of New-Orleans, enjoyed the most considerable portion of the commerce of the west.

7TH.] To-day I proceeded about 21 miles, over a very poor and mountainous country. From the little village, or cluster of cabins, called Loudon,[10] we commence the ascent over the North Mountain, by an easy and well-levelled turnpike. From its summit appeared a wide and sterile forest extending across the glen, and, only at small and distant intervals, obscurely broken by scattered farms. The soil is here argillaceous, a slate-clay passing into argillaceous trap and siliceous sandstone, occasionally changing into an almost homogeneous quartz, predominates. At Loudon, there is a small iron-furnace, and ore in inconsiderable quantities found in the neighbourhood. Passing this range, sometimes called the Cove or North Mountain, we descend to M'Connels'-town,[11] which now presents itself in bird's-eye view before us, here the soil is calcareous, but still, to all appearance, destitute of organic remains. Deep and narrow valleys, steep hills every where presenting shale devoid of impressions, though often so far bituminous as to blaze, abound, but no coal is to be met with nearer than the valley of the Juniata, where organic impressions also commence. Within the great valley of the North Mountain, are several other lower and interrupted ranges. The chain also called the North Mountain, proceeding much to the east in its southern course, presents in that direction acuminated peaks, and appears interrupted as towards Staunton in Virginia. From this summit we are distinctly enabled to mark the direction of the South Mountain, so low where we crossed it as to afford an almost imperceptible ascent.

[10]Loudon, a mile west of Fort Loudon, was described by James Flint, in *Letters from America* (1822), in THWAITES [1], IX, 69–70, as "a few houses only, two of them taverns." The date, September, 1820, two years after Nuttall's visit. The fort was erected in 1756. HUNTER, 463–73.

[11]M'Connels'-town, present McConnellsburg, Franklin County, originally at the "Sugar Cabins" near Fort Lyttleton, the latter constructed in 1756, like Loudon and other forts, following Braddock's Defeat in 1755. For the stay of Christian Friedrich Post with the Cherokees and other Indians in early November, 1758, as Gen. John Forbes marched to the conquest of Fort Duquesne from the French, see Post, *The Journal of Christian Frederick Post, on a Message from the Governor of Pennsylvania* . . . [1758], in THWAITES [1], I, 239–40; also P.C.R., VIII, 132, 142, 145, 147.

What still remained of the old road,[12] appeared here as bad as can well be imagined; a mere Indian trace, without any choice of level, over rocky ledges and gullies, threatening at every instant the destruction of the carriages which ventured over it.

8TH.] After travelling about 28 miles, I arrived, in the evening, at the very pleasant and romantically situated town of Bedford,[13] hemmed in by a cove of mountains to the south and west, near whose declivity issue the chalybeate springs, occasionally the resort of the sick and convalescent. Very little of the road over which I came to-day was yet turnpike, and as bad as may naturally be supposed over a succession of mountain ridges, which, though scattered, and interrupted by the passage of waters, scarcely fall short of the North Mountain in point of elevation. These ridges, of which in the above distance there are three or four, are all often confounded in the name of Cove Mountain.

I crossed the Juniata by a wooden toll-bridge, which, like all other private accommodations in the United States, does not exempt the pedestrian traveller. The valley of the river is narrow and romantic, embosomed by cliffs, rudely decorated with clumps of sombre evergreens, particularly the tall Weymouth pine and spruce, with the splendid Rhododendron and the *Magnolia acuminata*.[14] As we approach towards Bedford the valleys widen, are more fertile, and present calcareous strata still inclined at a lofty angle, and generally destitute of organic remains. Every elevation, and most of them short and steep, presents a predominance of argillaceous earth, either red or greenish and slatey, as it may happen to contain an admixture of iron or chlorite; there are, however, no iron furnaces nor ore

[12]The "old road": Nuttall, walking from Shippensburg southwest to Chambersburg, west to McConnellsburg, thence northwest to Rays Hill, was on what had originally been an Indian trace, subsequently a well-traveled route chosen by Indian traders. At Rays Hill he struck the "new road," part of the route built by Pennsylvanians (Benjamin Franklin among them) to supply Braddock's advance in 1755 from Maryland on Fort Duquesne. The new road began at Shippensburg and continued on by way of Raystown (now Bedford). It coincides with present Pennsylvania Turnpike westward. HUNTER, 31–32.

[13]First Rae's Town, later Rays Town, and by Nuttall's time Bedford, four miles east of the point where news of Braddock's defeat in 1755 called a halt to the "new road" being built to supply his forces up from Fort Cumberland. Construction was resumed on Gen. John Forbes's plans to move westward across Pennsylvania in 1758 for the second attack on Fort Duquesne. HULBERT, 32–33. Fort Raystown (1758) was renamed in 1759 for the Duke of Bedford.

[14]Popularly, the cucumber tree, deciduous.

in this quarter nearer than the vicinity of Huntingdon.[15] Seams of coal have been discovered on the banks of the Juniata, but unworthy of notice or difficult to drain. Fifteen miles from Bedford, coal begins to appear. Indeed, about a mile from the town I observed in the siliceous sandstone made use of for repairing the road, and which was obtained in the vicinity, casts of *orthoceratites?* or something resembling them, collected into fascicles or clusters, and aggregated over the surface of the rocks in which they are found; the transverse septa or channels are all proximate, and their circumference is about two inches.[16] Excepting a second impression, something similar, but much smaller (and which rather resembles some alcyonite),[17] no other reliquiae appeared in this stone, which is also the first occurrence of the kind on my journey to the westward.

The mountain scenery, at first so grand and impressive, becomes at length monotonous; most of the cimes, terraces, and piles of rocks lose their effect beneath the umbrageous forest which envelopes them, and which indeed casts a gloomy mantling over the whole face of nature.

To judge of the inland commerce carried on betwixt Philadelphia and Pittsburgh, a stranger has but to view this road at the present season. All day I have been brushing past waggons heavily loaded with merchandise, each drawn by five or six horses; the whole road in fact appears like the cavalcade of a continued fair.

9TH.] To-day I proceeded about 20 miles from Bedford on the way to Pittsburgh, and in the evening lodged at a tavern situated on the top of the Alleghany ridge. About nine miles from Bedford I first observed the occurrence of fossil shells, consisting of terebratulites, and amongst them the *Anomia trigonalis* of Martyn,[18] with some other species. They occur in the sandstone employed for mending the road, with which also alternates much liver-brown argillaceous shale. From hence the dip of the strata gradually diminishes, and the hills are no longer so short and steep; slate-clay with appearances of coal are also visible, but as yet there are no *zoophytic*, or, as some consider them, *phytolithic* or vegetable impressions. The ascent to the summit of the Alleghany from the east is much

---

[15]Thirty-nine miles northeast of Bedford.

[16]A fossil nautiloid cephalopod of the genus *Orthoceras*.

[17]A soft coral of the genus *Alcyonium*.

[18]One of the thin-shelled bivalve mollusks, here geologically of the Mesozoic era.

more gentle than that of the North Mountain, or the other mountains scattered through this valley. The Alleghany, here from 10 to 20 miles broad, is apparently the boundary of the transition, and the long slopes and salient coves of its western declivity are within the range of the secondary formation. Much of the *Quercus Primos monticola* (or mountain chesnut oak)[19] presents itself on the mountain, together with the *Magnolia acuminata* and *Sorbus americana* or service-berry.[20]

10TH.] To-day I walked nine miles to Stoystown,[21] if a handful of houses like this deserves such an appellation. The declivity of the surface is much more gentle and inconsiderable than that which I had passed. Indications of coal were also apparent along the margin of the road. The valleys are now broader, and the soil of a better quality. The inhabitants, however, chiefly Irish, are indigent, and considerably deficient in prudence and cleanliness. I spent most part of the day in collecting seeds of the *Magnolia acuminata*.

11TH.] To-day I proceeded 18 miles to the little hamlet of Ligonier[22] lately begun, and passed through Loughlins-town,[23] equally inconsiderable, except for dram shops, improperly called taverns, with which this road abounds. The turnpike is completed nearly throughout this distance, and also to Greensburgh. Towards evening I crossed the Laurel Mountain, and found abundantly on its western declivity the *Circaea alpina*. In the valley on the eastern ascent I likewise saw the *Betula glauca*,[24] and a profusion of the common *Rhododendron*, which gives the

[19]Apparently a manuscript name only, possibly a combination of *Q. prinus* Linn., which now prevails, and *Q. montana* Willd. Nuttall's own *Quercus michauxii* Nutt., swamp chestnut oak, prevails also.

[20]*Sorbus americana* Marsh. is American mountain ash. "Service-berry" may have been a slip for "service tree," one of the several common names for this plant.

[21]At Stoystown, Nuttall had descended from Allegheny Ridge. Here Lt. Col. Henry Bouquet, Gen. John Forbes's second-in-command against Fort Duquesne, had built a small fort in 1758. Nuttall's route from Bedford makes us know he was following Forbes's "new road," now Highway 30 to Pittsburgh. Cf. FLINT [1], 78.

[22]Ligonier, site at former Loyalhanna, Westmoreland County, of a fort named for John, Field Marshal Earl Ligonier, of the British army; built by General Forbes's army in 1758, it often served as Colonel Bouquet's headquarters to the end of that year. Bouquet to Forbes, July 21, 1758, and Bouquet to Sir John St. Clair, BOUQUET, II, 248–56, 433–34, *et passim*.

[23]Loughlintown, S.E. of Ligonier, is still a farming village. Nuttall had passed over Laurel Hill Summit four miles S.E. of Loughlintown.

[24]*Circaea alpina* is one of the species of enchanter's nightshade (Onagraceae). *Betula*

name of Laurel to this mountain. Indications of coal, and a continued declension in the dip of the strata are still obvious. The sandstone, which is almost the only rock I have seen throughout the course of the day, is remarkable for tbe absence of organic reliquiae. In some places it appears like grauwacke blended with angular fragments of a soft slate. Near the western base of the Laurel ridge the usual zoophytes make their appearance, chiefly *Culmaria striata* (*Striaticulmis* of Martyn), also casts of enormous channelled *Culmariae* like those of Bradford, in Yorkshire (England).[25] Vegetation at this advanced season still appeared very luxuriant on the western descent of the Laurel, and the valleys bore the appearance of fertility.

12TH.] This evening I arrived at Greenburgh,[26] 18 miles west of Liganier. The last considerable mountain range to the west on this route is Chesnut Ridge, which I crossed to-day. Here I met with the *Imperatoria lucida* of Sprengel, also abundance of the *Cimicifuga americana* and

---

glauca, doubtless often remarked by natural scientists reading this journal, is otherwise unaccounted for in botanical literature, until *Betula glauca* Wender (1846).

[25]Although we are as yet unacquainted with the internal and essential physical structure of these organic remains, which have hitherto been considered as plants, I have thought it necessary to assume the above generic name as preferable to the improbable, and at any rate merely ordinal name of *Phytolithus*. The CULMARIAE, as I have termed them, are striated or grooved and somewhat compressed, cylindric, articulated bodies, gradually attenuating from joint to joint, mostly undivided or simple, but occasionally bifid, and at length terminating in a point. On one of the sides they commonly possess a deep and central channel, and in some species at the joints present alternate small protruberances and cavities. Their soboliferous propagation appeared to originate from these joints, in the form of wart-like or areolate protruberances, and, unlike plants, they never seem to have produced anything similar to leaves, flowers, or seeds.

The tessellated zoophytes, by others also considered as vegetable remains which I have termed STROBILARIAE are subcylindric and often somewhat conic, but inarticulated; some of the species protruded, as occasion required, from the centre of these tessellae, bodies resembling hollow spines, or (as would appear from a specimen in my possession from Bradford, in Yorkshire) suckers or hollow cylinders, with circular contractile and striated mouths. The whole of these processes, when exserted mistaken for leaves, could be withdrawn within the body of the animal, and indeed most of the casts present this quiescent or contracted state. These bodies likewise exhibit in some specimens a complicated internal structure. —NUTTALL. [The author's comparison of invertebrates here and in England anticipates subsequent correlations between the United States Devonian period and the English Carboniferous.]

[26]Greensburg, named for Gen. Nathaniel Greene of the American Revolution, founded 1785, is the burial site of Gen. Arthur St. Clair, prominent in the French and Indian War and the American Revolution but routed by the Miami Indians under Little Turtle in Ohio in 1791.

Asplenium angustifolium. [27] The dip of the strata becomes now more and more inconsiderable, but organic remains, except those peculiar to the coal formation, are scarcley to be met with, and there is a predominance of slaty and argillaceous sandstone.

13TH.] The turnpike was now completed through the last 40 miles up to Pittsburgh, and scarcely any undertaking promises more advantage to the state in general. It will tend to check the competition of the inland navigation of the state of New York, as well as that of the state of Virginia, through which the United States have established a national road as far as the town of Wheeling on the Ohio.

14TH.] West of Greensburg, and indeed east of it, from the base of the Chesnut Ridge, the surface of the country is deeply undulated, and laborious to travel. The land upon the height is sterile and thinly populated; still every five or six miles we meet with some poor-looking hamlet, which commonly, out of 12 to 20 log cabins composing it, contains six or seven licensed dram shops, besides three or four stores for the retailing of merchandise. How much is a scattered and independent population like that of the honest and industrious Germans inhabiting the eastern parts of Pennsylvania to be preferred to these towns whose inhabitants are brought together by no prospect of general industry or economy. To say that coal is common throughout this country, and that it is generally employed for fuel, is repeating a fact familiar to every one who has ever visited the western country.

15TH.] To-day I arrived again in Pittsburgh, and endeavor as I may to drive away my former prejudices against this very important commercial and manufacturing city, I find it impossible. Nothing appears to me to predominate but filth and smoke and bustle. The rivers and surrounding country are engaging and romantic—its situation—the Thermopylae of the west, into which so many thousands are flocking from every christian country in the world—its rapid progress, and the enterprising character of its inhabitants, are circumstances which excite our admiration. In national industry, the true source of wealth and independence, Pittsburgh is

[27] *Imperatoria lucida* Spreng., one of the Umbelliferae (parsley family), is now in the genus *Angelica* (sometimes *Coelopleurum*), which is coastal. Nuttall may have been viewing one of two or three other very similar species of *Angelica* occurring in the area. *Cimicifuga americana* Michx., mountain bugbane. *Asplenium angustifolium* Michx. is *A. pycnocarpon* (Spreng.) Tidestr., glade fern.

now scarcely inferior to any of the older and larger towns in the Union. The shores of the Monongahela were lined with nearly 100 boats of all descriptions, steam-boats, barges, keels, and arks or flats, all impatiently and anxiously waiting the rise of the Ohio, which was now too low to descend above the town of Wheeling. A bridge at this time nearly completed across this stream, and one of the piers of another across the Alleghany was also laid.[28]

The day after my arrival I went through the flint-glass works of Mr. Bakewell, and was surprised to see the beauty of this manufacture, in the interior of the United States, in which the expensive decorations of cutting and engraving (amidst every discouragement incident to a want of taste and wealth) were carried to such perfection. The productions of this manufacture find their way to New Orleans, and even to some of the islands of the West Indies.

The president Monroe, as a liberal encourager of domestic manufactures, had on his visit to those works given orders for a service of glass, which might indeed be exhibited as a superb specimen of this elegant art.

Mr. Bakewell was now beginning to employ the beautiful white and friable sandstone which had been observed near to a branch of the Merrimec by Mr. Bradbury and myself, as well as others, in the winter of 1809. It promises every important requisite for the production of the purest flint-glass, and exists in inexhaustible quantities.[29]

16TH.–18TH.] Still at Pittsburgh, waiting for an opportunity to descend the river, which was now almost impracticable in consequence of the lowness of the water.

---

[28]This was Nuttall's third visit to Pittsburgh. His first trip west across Pennsylvania had been made entirely by stage, leaving Philadelphia on April 12, 1810, and arriving April 19. (His subsequent encounter with the leaders of John Jacob Astor's Pacific Fur Company brigade, outfitting at Michilimackinac for a second voyage of the Lewis and Clark route to the Pacific and the establishment of Astoria, gave him an opportunity to ascend the Missouri from Saint Louis, departing March 13, 1811.) His second visit, in June, 1816, had been prompted by his attempt to find a replacement specimen for *Collinsia verna* Nutt., originally found in mid-May, 1810, but subsequently lost. The search was unsuccessful, and he went on by a circular route to Cincinnati, Lexington, northern Tennessee, Cumberland Gap, Asheville, Morganton, and Charleston. Cf. NUTTALL [4], *Nuttall's Travels into the Old Northwest: An Unpublished 1810 Diary*, ed. by Jeannette E. Graustein, *Chronica Botanica*, Vol. XIV, Nos. 1, 2 (1950–51), 21–27; GRAUSTEIN, 42–77, 105–13.

[29]Benjamin Bakewell, the uncle of Lucy Bakewell Audubon and a friend of Joseph Priestly's, had come from England to the United States in 1793, setting up an importing business in New York, where John James Audubon worked from 1806 to mid-1807.

19TH.] This morning I took a walk to Grant's Hill, from whence there is a delightful view of Pittsburgh, and on the hill itself some very pleasing rural retirements of the wealthy citizens.

My attention, as usual, was directed to the surrounding minerals and stratification, which are no unimportant matters in the economy of this settlement. The coal basin, or rather bed, which has been so long wrought on this hill, about six feet thick, is almost exactly horizontal, and consequently worked by a simple parallel drift without making any inconvenient quantity of water. The coal bassets out towards the edge of the hill, and so near the summit as to present scarcely any other overlay than a thin shale, more or less friable, and no sandstone. The dip, such as it is, is to the north of east, but scarcely manifest. It is bituminous or inflammable, and of a very good quality. Beneath this single bed of coal, occurs a fine grained, micaceous sandstone, rendered greenish from an admixture of chlorite earth; still lower in the series appears a compact calcareous rock, in which I did not perceive any reliquiae. At the southern extremity of the hill, where it approaches the Monongahela, the laminated micaceous sandstone, however, exhibits great clusters of *culmariae* (*striaticulmis* of Martyn), almost ancipitally compressed, and with the striatures very fine. Here the calcareous rock beneath the micaceous sandstone exhibits masses of terebratulites, some of which are very minute, but in great quantities. Near to the precipitous termination of Grant's Hill, and in several other contiguous places, the sandstone appears to have been disintegrated with violence, and the angular fragments again to have been cemented by a stalactitial deposition of calcareous spar, of a fibrous texture, almost similar to arragonite. Seams of fibrous gypsum, possessing a silky lustre, have also been discovered in this vicinity.

In the course of this ramble I found abundance of the *Monarda hirsuta*, which as well as *M. ciliata*, do not much resemble the legitimate species of the genus.[30]

On the failure of Bakewell's business he moved to Pittsburgh and set up his glass factory, the early stages of which Nuttall had seen in late April, 1810 (Nuttall misdates the 1810 visit by one year). FORD, 41–72.

John Bradbury, fellow of the Linnean Society, London, was Nuttall's travel companion on the Missouri River trip and its recorder in *Travels in the Interior of North America, in the Years 1809, 1810, and 1811 . . .* (London, 1819).

[30]These species of the Labiatae (mint family) are now placed in the genus *Blephilia* rather than *Monarda*, which they closely resemble, as *Blephilia hirsuta* (Pursh) Benth., wood mint, and *B. ciliata* (L.) Benth.

CHAPTER II.

———

21ST.] To-day I left Pittsburgh in a skiff, which I purchased for six dollars, in order to proceed down the Ohio. I was fortunate enough to meet with a young man who had been accustomed to the management of a boat, and who, for the consideration of a passage and provision, undertook to be my pilot and assistant. We set out after 11 o'clock, and made 19 miles. Here we were overtaken by a thunderstorm, accompanied by very heavy rain, which continued during most part of the ensuing night. We had no choice, and therefore took up our abode for the night in the first cabin which we came to, built of logs, containing a large family of both sexes, all housed in one room, and that not proof against the pouring rain. Provided, however, with provision and beds of our own we succeeded in rendering ourselves comfortable, and were pleased with the hospitable disposition of our landlord, who would scarcely permit any of his family to receive from us the moderate compensation which we offered.

22D.] At day-break we again betook ourselves to the voyage; but after proceeding about nine miles, the strong south-west wind forced us to a delay of several hours.

In this distance from Pittsburgh the Ohio meanders through a contracted alluvial flat, thickly settled, and backed with hills, which are often peaked and lofty, fringed, at this season, by a forest of the diversified, but dying hues of autumn. The water was extremely low, and we passed through several rapids, in which bare rocks presented themselves in such quantity, as to deny the passage of any thing but boats drawing 9 or 10 inches of water.

After proceeding about two miles below Beavertown[1] we landed in the dark, and went to the tavern to which accident had directed us, but finding it crowded with people met together for merriment, we retired to a neighbouring hovel, in order to obtain rest and shelter from the weather, which was disagreeably cold. Our prospect of repose was soon, however, banished, as our cabin, being larger than the tavern, was selected for a dancing room, and here we were obliged to sit waking spectators of this riot till after one o'clock in the morning. The whiskey bottle was brought out to keep up the excitement, and, without the inconvenience and delay of using glasses, was passed pretty briskly from mouth to mouth, exempting neither age nor sex. Some of the young *ladies* also indulged in smoking as well as drinking of drams. Symptoms of riot and drunkenness at length stopped the dancing, and we now anticipated the prospect of a little rest, but in this we were disappointed by the remaining of one of the company vanquished by liquor, who, after committing the most degrading nuisance, at intervals disturbed us with horrid gestures and imprecations for the remainder of the morning. On relating in the neighbourhood our adventure at this house, we were informed that this tavern was notorious for the assemblage of licentious persons.

23D.] After an hour or two of interrupted repose we again embarked, and found that there had been a slight fall of snow. The wind was still adverse, and so strong as perfectly to counteract the current; with some labour we got down to Georgetown,[2] and warmed ourselves by a comfortable fire of coal. The tavern was very poorly accommodated, a mere cabin without furniture, of which its owner was from habit scarcely sensible.

[1]Beavertown, now Beaver, at the mouth of the Beaver River on the Ohio, was the site of a Delaware Indian "old town," associated with two headmen, King Beaver and Shingas. It was referred to by Conrad Weiser ("The Journal of Conrad Weiser..." [1748], P.C.R., V, 349) as Beaver Creek. It became the county seat of Beaver in 1800. Cf. P.C.R., VI, 675–76; VIII, 305–13.

[2]Fortescue Cuming described Georgetown as enclosed by hills above the river as in an amphitheater, but then (1807) declining, with only twenty-five occupied houses. CUMING, 84.

About two o'clock in the afternoon we again landed at a poor log-cabin to warm ourselves, and were very kindly welcomed by the matron of the house, who, without the benefit of education, seemed possessed of uncommon talents. I had read, in the first settlement of Kentucky, of remarkable instances of female intrepidity, brought forward by the exigencies of a residence on a dangerous frontier, and our hostess appeared to be equally an Amazon, modest, cool, and intrepid. I listened to her adventures with much interest. She and her husband, with a small family, had some years ago followed the tide of western emigration to the banks of the little Miami, near Cincinnati. Here, after a tedious and expensive journey, they had settled on a piece of alluvial land, and might probably have prospered, but for the dreadful effects of continued sickness (ague and bilious fever), which urged them to sacrifice every other interest for that of their emaciated offspring, and to ascend the Ohio in search of a situation which might afford them health. She pointed to some remains of decent furniture which the cabin scarcely sheltered, saying, with an affectionate look at her poor children, "we once had a decent property, but now we have nothing left; emigration has ruined us!" With six children around her, and accompanied by another family, ascending the Ohio in a flat-boat, they were struck by a hurricane. She herself and one of her children had taken their regular turn at the oar, the master of the boat, who had also his family around him, became so far alarmed and confused as to quit his post in the midst of the danger which threatened instantly to overwhelm them, tremendous waves broke into the boat, which the affrighted steersman knew not how to avoid. This woman seized the helm which was abandoned, and by her skill and courage saved the boat and the families from imminent destruction.

24TH.] The wind still south-west, but abating a little. We proceeded at 11, and about 18 miles from Steubenville, landed and took up our lodging on an island, with no other shelter than the canopy of heaven; but we slept comfortably, with our feet to a warm fire, according to Indian custom.

25TH.] This evening we arrived at Steubenville,[3] which appears to be a

---

[3]Steubenville, named for Baron Friedrich Wilhelm Augustus von Steuben, the German soldier who helped train American troops during the Revolution, had become the county seat of Jefferson County, Ohio, in 1797, two decades before Nuttall's visit.

place of industry and manufacture. Two miles below the town we lodged in the cabin of a poor tenant farmer.

The banks of the river are exceedingly romantic, presenting lofty hills and perpendicular cliffs of not less than 300 feet elevation, every where covered or fringed with belts of trees in their autumnal foliage, of every bright and varying hue, more beautiful even than the richest verdure of summer. The uplands being calcareous are found to be exceedingly fertile, and we consequently perceive houses and fences on the summits of the loftiest hills which embosom the river. From 50 to 70 dollars per acre was demanded for these lands, which are better for wheat than the alluvial soils. Flour was here four dollars per barrel, and beef six cents per pound.

26TH.] This evening we arrived at Wheeling,[4] consisting of a tolerably compact street of brick houses, with the usual accompaniment of stores, taverns, and mechanics. It is also the principal depot for the supply and commerce of the interior of this part of Virginia. A number of boats had been fitted out here this season, which could not navigate from Pittsburgh in consequence of the lowness of the water. At this place the great national road into the interior, from the city of Washington, comes in conjunction with that of Zanesville, Chillicothe, Columbus, and Cincinnati. At the northern extremity of the town there is a very productive bed of coal, and equally horizontal with that of Pittsburgh; its thickness is about six feet, and as it occurs *beneath* the limestone it must of course be considered as a *second* bed. Every where along the banks of the river, particularly at this low stage we perceive adventitious boulders and pebbles of sienite, which cannot have originated nearer than the mountains of Canada, situated beyond the lakes. Proceeding about four and a half miles from Wheeling, we took up our night's residence at a cabin near to the outlet of M'Mahon's creek.[5]

[4]Wheeling, in what became the West Virginia Panhandle, took its name from a creek already identified as "Wealin or Scalp Creek," noted in his journal by Christopher Gist, exploring for the Ohio Company of Virginia in 1751. The site and surrounding lands were claimed in 1769 by Ebenezer Zane, of Virginia, who settled his family and his brothers Silas's and Jonathan's families there in 1770. It was the location of Fort Fincastle (1774) during Lord Dunmore's War, rechristened Fort Henry during the American Revolution, and the starting point for Zane's Trace from Wheeling to Limestone, Ky., from 1797. MULKEARN, 38; PALMER, II, 109, 131, 394; III, 359; VI, 55, 243; VIII, 238.

[5]Flowing into the Ohio one mile below Bellaire, Ohio. Nuttall's "adventitious" geological debris is, by implication, from the eastern extremity of the Canadian Shield.

27TH.] To-day I again observed a bed of coal in the bank of the Ohio, worked *beneath* the limestone, situated nearly opposite to Little Grave creek. This superincumbent limestone does not appear to abound with organic remains, and is nearly horizontal, with a slight dip, perhaps 10°, to the south-east. Ten or 12 miles further, the same coal bed still bassets out from beneath the calcareous rock, and so near to the present low level of the river as not to admit of being worked at any other stage of the water. The shale (or bituminous slate clay) above and below the coal is extremely superficial, being only a few inches in thickness, and interspersed with small masses of bitumen and reliquiae which imitate charred wood, but are destitute of the characterizing cross grain.

At the mouth of Little Grave creek we landed, to view the famous mound, said to be 75 feet high. The ascent is extremely steep: it is indeed a pyramid, and of an elegant conic figure; at the summit there is a circular depression indicative of some excavation, and it is surrounded by a shallow ditch, across which, there are left two gateways. It appears to be elevated at about an angle of 60°, and the earth, as in many other similar monuments, has evidently been beaten down to resist the washing of rains. It is remarkably perfect and compleat, and would probably continue a monument as long as the walled pyramids of Egypt. Amongst other trees growing upon it, there was a white oak of not less than two centuries' duration. In the immediate vicinity, there is likewise a small ditched circle with two entrances, and a smaller ditched mound.[6]

At this place, I took in a young man going down to Big Sandy creek, who assisted in working his passage with us. At dark we landed on the Ohio shore, and lodged with a poor but hospitable resident.

28TH.] Tired of the boat, I got out and walked 10 or 12 miles, on the Virginia side of the river. Many of the settlers here appear to be Yankees, from Vermont and Connecticut, and in prosperous circumstances. A mile and a half above Sistersville, and 35 from Marietta, in Virginia,

---

[6]Moundsville of today, seat of Marshall County, W.Va., product of the consolidation of Elizabethtown, named for the wife of James Tomlinson about 1798, and Mound City, adjoining, founded 1831, in 1865. Grave Creek Mound occupies the center of the present city. It is of the prehistoric Adena Culture, dating from A.D. 500–900, and is 79 feet high, more than 900 feet in circumference, and 50 feet in diameter at the top, the largest such mound in the United States. MARTIN, 262–67.

there is a small aboriginal station, consisting of five or six low mounds, and a circle containing an area of about an acre.

29TH.] Twenty-six miles above Marietta, on the Virginia side, on the estate of Mr. Cohen, there was on the platform of the third, or most ancient alluvial bottom, a large, but low mound, grown over with brambles; and, at the distance of about a quarter of a mile below, a small square embankment containing near an acre, with only one or two openings or entrances.

Most part of the afternoon, I continued walking along the Ohio bank, and observed, as I have done for near 30 miles above, the alluvial lands to be more extensive, occupying often both banks of the river, and a sensible diminution in the elevation of the hills. The bottoms here abound with elm, and there are also extensive and undrainable tracts covered with beech.

30TH.] At day break, we again betook ourselves to our laborious journey, which, in consequence of the adverse wind, was nearly as toilsome as a voyage up, in place of down the stream; in addition to which, we had also to encounter the severe and benumbing effects of frost. We passed Marietta,[7] remarkable for its aboriginal remains, and in the evening, encamped on the beach of the river, but did not rest very comfortably, in consequence of the cold.

31.] Passed Belpre settlement, an extensive portion of fertile alluvial land, and thickly settled.[8] All the prevailing rock here, for some distance, is a massive sandstone, either brownish, greenish, or grayish, fine grained and micaceous, and occasionally exposing something like impressions of alcyonites, but appearing in no place indicative of coal. This evening we

[7]Marietta, seat of Washington County, was founded 1788 by Gen. Rufus Putnam and the Rev. Manasseh Cutler, of Massachusetts, a significant early American botanist, and other New Englanders constituting the Ohio Company of Associates, in April, 1788, at the confluence of the Muskingum with the Ohio. The Marietta mounds, of which the conical member was most prominent, were of the prehistoric Hopewell culture (A.D. 900–1300) and had been mapped and described by Capt. Jonathan Heart, 1787, and General Putnam, 1788 (original at Marietta College). Cutler, moreover, had applied tree-ring dating to the site and accounted for some prehistoric human remains. CUTLER, II, 14–17.

[8]Belpre, like Marietta, had been settled by veterans of the Revolutionary War, but a year later, in 1789.

lodged at a house, four miles above the mouth of Shade river,[9] where the bottoms are extensive and fertile. In a rocky situation, I found abundance of the *Seymeria macrophylla*, near six feet in height; also a new species of *Aster*, in full bloom, at this advanced season.[10]

November 1ST.] We proceeded about 19 miles without any material hindrance, when the south-west wind, which had so constantly opposed our descent, blew up a thunder-storm with rain, which detained us for the remainder of the day. Below Marietta, the alluvial lands become still more extensive, and appear to be held at a price considerably above their real value by speculators, who thus prevent the population from ac-cumulating. We scarcely, indeed, see any thing in this quarter but the miserable log cabins of tenants so poor and ill provided, even with the common necessaries of life, that, had we not taken the precaution of providing ourselves with provision, we must often have had either to fast, or sit down to nothing better than mush and milk; which, though an agreeable, is not a sufficiently nourishing diet for a traveller.

In descending the river, we uniformly find rapid water along the is-lands and bars; a circumstance appearing to indicate the former union of such islands with the land. Nearly all the sugar here made use of by the inhabitants, is obtained from the maple (*Acer saccharinum*), which, by more careful management, might be refined equal to muscovado.[11]

2D.] We were again detained a considerable part of the day by the contrary wind, and, during the delay, fell in with a descending family, which had passed us the preceding day. In a short time after meeting, two hounds belonging to our companion, which had been let loose in the woods, chased a buck to the river: my companion and the old migratory hunter instantly launched the skiff in the pursuit, and succeeded in shoot-ing the unfortunate deer in the water; a method commonly resorted to in this country, where the chase is more a matter of necessity than amuse-ment.

[9]Shade River empties into the Ohio at Long Bottom, Ohio.

[10]*Seymeria macrophylla* Nutt., mullein-foxglove, which Nuttall had collected with Dr. Daniel Drake, the Cincinnati physician, on the banks of the Little Miami during his first trip on the Ohio River drainage in 1816; and the *Aster* would become *A. amethys-tinus* Nutt. NUTTALL [2], II, 49; GRAUSTEIN, 106, 133.

[11]*Acer saccharinum* L., now reserved to the silver or soft maple, was in Nuttall's time applied to *Acer saccharum* Marsh., the hard or sugar maple. *Muscovado* in Spanish = unrefined cane sugar.

3D.] This morning I walked up the right bank of the river, to view an aboriginal station, said to be situated on the present estate of Mr. Warf, on Park's bottom; but, on proceeding about two miles through an en-swamped beech forest, I relinquished the undertaking, finding it to be more than three miles above Mill creek, which I had crossed the preceding day. I understood that this work was a circular embankment, including an area of three or four acres; and in the vicinity of which, were several inconsiderable mounds.[12] Beech woods, flanked by elevated cliffs, still continued for four miles on the Virginia side, to Le Tart's rapids, where the boat was to wait my arrival. On the way I found abundance of the *Dracocephalum cordifolium* with long slolons like ground ivy, also *Hesperis pinnatifida*, but I was more particularly gratified in finding the *Tilia heterophylla*. Nothing is here more abundant than the *Stylophorum* (*Chelidonium*. MICH.).[13] This evening, we were 16 miles above Galiopolis;[14]

4TH.] About 11 miles from which, I observed a bed of coal, now worked on the bank of the river, some distance above the base of a high cliff, and overlaid by a massive micaceous sandstone, constituting the main body of the hill, and, as usual, horizontally stratified. Beneath the coal appeared a laminated limestone. Not many miles from hence, nitre is also obtained in caves.

The wind still continued against us, and with considerable labour we got five miles below Galiopolis, at which and Point Pleasant there are several mounds and aboriginal remains.

5TH.] This evening we had proceeded about 26 miles below

[12]Nuttall's right bank is the Ohio side of the river, in the area in Meigs County defined by Syracuse, Ohio, and the point at which Mill Creek, in Jackson County, W.Va. flows into the Ohio. It is nearly impossible to pinpoint the prehistoric "works" to which he refers, inasmuch as there are ten such sites, mostly of the Adena culture, in the area. The Kanawha River drainage at and upstream from Point Pleasant, W.Va., nearby is rich in such remains. SHETRONE, 166.

[13]*Dracocephalum cordifolium* is probably an error for Nuttall's *D. cordatum,* which he had recently described and which = *Meehania cordata* (Nutt.) Britt. *Hesperis pinnatifida,* of the Cruciferae (mustard family) was transferred to the genus *Iodanthus* as *I. pinnatifidus* (Michx.) Steud. *Tilia heterophylla* Vent. is the white basswood. *Stylophorum* (*Chelidonium* Michx.) is *S. diphyllum* (Michx.) Nutt., wood poppy.

[14]Sixteen years before Nuttall's present visit to Gallipolis, F. A. Michaux, following in his French father's footsteps of August 23, 1793, had found sixty notched cabins, the rude settlement bought by Parisians during the revolution from the Scioto Company of Ohio in 1790. Most even then had been abandoned. MICHAUX, F. A., 98–102.

Galiopolis. Yesterday and to-day, I remarked, parallel with the present level of the river, and often surmounted by a lofty and friable bank of earth, beds of leaves compressed and blackened, giving out ferruginous matter to the water which oozed through them. On examination, they proved to be the same kind of foliage as that of the trees which compose the present alluvial forest; as platanus, beech, oak, poplar, &c.

About Steubenville I observed the first occurrence of misletoe (the *Viscum verticillatum* of the West Indies), which now appears very prevalent and conspicuous. The fruit of the popaw (*Porcelia triloba*) here comes to perfection, and is rich and finely flavoured, while above, and in a few localities where it exists in Pennsylvania, it is scarcely eatable.[15]

I was again informed of the existence of aboriginal mounds and entrenchments on the fertile alluvial lands called Messer's Bottom, which are of several miles extent, commencing almost immediately below Galiopolis on the Virginia side, but after several unsuccessful inquiries, the ignorance and supineness of the settlers, though numerous, prevented me from discovering them.[16]

6TH.] We proceeded about nine miles, and were as usual prevented from continuing further by the reiterated violence of the pertinacious south-west wind, accompanied by a haze, which made every object appear as if enveloped in smoke.

7TH.] This evening, we passed the mouth of Big Sandy creek, the boundary of Kentucky. Near to this line commences the first appearance of the cane (*Arundinaria macrosperma*), which seems to indicate some difference in the climate and soil.[17] The settlements are here remote, the people poor, and along the river not so characteristically hospitable as in the interior of Kentucky. Landing rather late, we took up our lodging where there happened to be a corn-husking, and were kept awake with idle merriment and riot till past midnight. Some of the party, or rather of the two national parties, got up and harangued to a judge, like so many lawyers, on some political argument, and other topics, in a boisterous and

[15]The American mistletoe here observed is now *Phoradendron serotinum* (Raf.) M. C. Johnston. *Porcelia triloba* = *Asimina triloba* L., pawpaw.

[16]The discovery might have required weeks, for the archaeological remains in the Kanawha Valley of West Virginia extend for one hundred miles.

[17]*Arundinaria macrosperma* Michx. = *A. gigantea* (Walt.) Muhl., giant cane.

illiberal style, but without coming to blows. Is this a relic of Indian customs?[18]

The corn-fields, at this season of the year, are so overrun with cuckold-burs (*Xanthium strumarium*),[19] and the seeds of different species of Bidens or Spanish-needles, as to prove extremely troublesome to woollen clothes, and to the domestic cattle, which are loaded with them in tormenting abundance. In consequence of these weeds, the fleece of the sheep is scarcely worth the trouble of shearing. The best remedy for checking the growth of these noxious plants, would be to plow them in about the time of flowering, which would exterminate them, and improve the crop of corn.

The people here, living upon exigencies, and given to rambling about instead of attending to their farms, are very poor and uncomfortable in every respect; but few of them possess the land on which they live. Having spent every thing in unsuccessful migration, and voluntarily exiling themselves from their connections in society, they begin to discover, when too late, that industry would have afforded that comfort and independence which they in vain seek in the solitudes of an unhealthy wilderness. We found it almost impossible to purchase any kind of provision, even butter or bacon, nothing appearing to be cultivated scarcely but corn and a little wheat.

I was again informed of the existence of aboriginal remains in the vicinity of the place where we arrived this evening.

8TH.] We were delayed nearly the whole of the day by the usual adverse wind.

9TH.] To-day, however, we were fortunate enough, at last, to obtain the breeze in our favour, and proceeded about 28 miles, encamping three miles below the town of Portsmouth.[20]

[18]Kentucky, the fifteenth state, dating from 1792, had been partly settled by frontiersmen from Virginia, Maryland, Pennsylvania, and the Carolinas, representing English, Scots, Irish, German, and French stocks. Many of its pioneers, still with travel in their blood, had begun moving still farther west by 1804, to Illinois, Missouri, and Arkansas. Its settlers on the Ohio River border were scarcely more primitive than those on the Missouri River west of Saint Louis in this period, as other travelers noted.

[19]*Xanthium strumarium* L., cocklebur, once thought adventive from Europe, now seems likely, with the other members of the genus, to be native to America.

[20]Portsmouth, Ohio, on the east bank of the Scioto River at its confluence with the

10TH.] The wind still continuing in our favour, accompanied by a considerable current, we proceeded about 32 miles, and encamped 12 miles below Salt creek, and 17 above Maysville. In this course the river appears very meandering, and from Portsmouth, the hills, which are considerable, come up diagonally to the margin of the river and present serrated or conic summits.[21] At the lowest stage of the water we perceive horizontal ledges of calcareous rock filled with terebratulites, &c. The salt at Adamsville appears to be made from water issuing out of the alluvial argillaceous soil near to the outlet of Salt Creek, but in many parts of the Western country coring for salt water is frequently continued some hundreds of feet, (sometimes as much as 400 feet) below the surface, through calcareous and sand-stone rocks, and occasionally through beds of coal.

11TH.] We proceeded seven miles below the thriving town of Maysville, formerly called Limestone[22] from the rock in its neighbourhood, and experienced heavy rains during the whole day, which in our open skiff proved very unpleasant, and, to augment our uncomfortable situation, we encamped at a late hour on a very disagreeable muddy shore, where it was not possible to kindle a fire.

The farmers along the river for many miles down appear to be in thriving circumstances. Their houses are very decent in external appearance, but so badly finished and furnished that many of the rooms are unoccupied, or merely serve the purposes of a barn, and the family are commonly found living in the kitchen. Most of these ostentatious shells of frame houses are the work of the New-England settlers, who are very

---

Ohio, may be one of the oldest townsites in the United States, since it was the center of prehistoric Hopewell Indian culture (A.D. 900–1400), the aboriginal works extending east and west along both the Ohio and the Kentucky banks of the Ohio. Christopher Gist described the lower Shawnee town occupying the same site in late January, 1751, during his explorations for the Ohio Company, as consisting of one hundred houses and a ninety-foot council house on the Ohio bank and forty houses on the Kentucky side. As a white settlement Portsmouth dated from fifteen years before Nuttall's visit, i.e., 1803. SHETRONE, 260–61; Christopher Gist, "Journals," in Lois Mulkearn, ed., *George Mercer Papers*, 16–18, 497–98.

[21]En route to Maysville, Nuttall had passed the mouth of Brush Creek, in Adams County, Ohio, above which lies Great Serpent Mound, which has been classified in the Adena culture from the excavation of a burial mound four hundred feet from it.

[22]Maysville had already become the principal supply port for Kentucky as early as 1793, the year after statehood, when the French botanist André Michaux described it in his journal (in THWAITES [1], III, 35). Although it had only a few settlers in 1773, it was of sufficient stature in 1787 to be incorporated as a town.

industrious, and not without more or less of their usual economy and sagacity.

12TH.] We were again retarded by the south-west wind. The shore on which we landed was thickly strewed with fragments of calcareous rock filled with terebratulites, alcyonites, flustras, encrinal vertebrae, &c. &c. Some specimens which I here collected of the encrinal vertebrae were coated with a cellular epidermis, in appearance resembling a millepore; they are also remarkably dichotomous. In one of the calcareous fragments which I broke occurred the *Trilobites paradoxus.*

The wind abating, we passed down to Augusta,[23] and with our emigrant companions encamped on the opposite shore. Here the insolence of my companion rendered our separation absolutely necessary. It is to be regretted, that so many of those wandering New-Englanders (who, like the Jews in Europe, are to be met with in every part of the union), should prove so disgraceful to their country. My impression now was, that this young man was a refugee from justice or deserved infamy, and in all probability I narrowly escaped being robbed.

13TH.] To-day I arrived at Cincinnati,[24] and was again gratified by the company of my friend Doctor I. Drake,[25] one of the most scientific men west of the Alleghany mountains.

[23]Augusta, once but not now the seat of Bracken County, Ky.

[24]Cincinnati, as yet less than thirty years old, had already acquired its share of historical myths, most of which Jacob Burnet, who settled there as early as 1796, tried to lay to rest. John Cleves Symmes, of New Jersey, had contracted with the Continental Congress in 1788 for one million acres between the Miami and Little Miami rivers, subsequently known as the Miami Purchase. A fraction plus a full section opposite the mouth of Licking River, in Kentucky on the Ohio, was acquired from him by Matthias Denman, who paid in Continental currency the equivalent of 15d. an acre, or 13 cents of a later hard U.S. currency. The town was laid out in the autumn of 1789 by Denman and his partners, Robert Patterson and Israel Ludlow, with the principal part of early settlement coming in the spring of 1790. BURNET, 31–49.

[25]Dr. Daniel (not I.) Drake (1785–1852), whom Nuttall had met in 1816 on his first descent of the Ohio and to whom he had confided his proposal to voyage down the Ohio en route to California, was a graduate of the Medical College of the University of Pennsylvania, where Benjamin Smith Barton (1766–1815) taught materia medica, and botany and natural history as well, and encouraged many medical students avocationally into botany. His advocacy of a medical college in Ohio was successful: *An Inaugural Discourse on Medical Education Delivered at the Opening of the Medical College of Ohio in Cincinnati, 11 November, 1820* (Cincinnati, 1820). Cf. Daniel Drake, *Physician to the West: Selected Writings of Daniel Drake on Science and Society,* ed. by Henry D. Shapiro and Zane L. Miller; GRAUSTEIN, 112 & n.

The town appeared to have improved much, both in appearance and population, since my last visit; it is, indeed, by far the most agreeable and flourishing of all the western towns. Here I had the good fortune, through Dr. D., to be introduced to Mr. H. Glenn, lately sutler to the garrison of Arkansa; from whom I had the pleasure to learn something more explicit concerning the probable progress of my intended journey.[26]

A medical college was, I understood, about to be established in Cincinnati. Dr. D., who delivered a very appropriate introductory oration, will, probably, be the principal of the institution. But such undertakings are yet rather premature, and the student would derive many exclusive advantages by acquiring a medical education in the universities already established.

17TH.] About 12 o'clock I left Cincinnati in my skiff, and was accidentally joined by two strangers going to Lawrenceburgh, 25 miles distant, where we arrived this evening.[27] This is a neat and thriving town, situated near the estuary of the Great Miami, and on the line of the state of Indiana.

18TH.] I departed at day-break, but, after descending five miles, discovered my gun had been forgotten at the tavern where I lodged. The day was dismal and cloudy, with showers of snow and gales of wind, undis-

[26]Hugh Glenn (1788–1833), a Virginian who had settled at Cincinnati before the War of 1812, in which he had captained a company, was a government contractor with Jacob Fowler from 1814 to 1817. In the latter year he contracted to supply a number of United States forts, among them Belle Point, later Fort Smith. He had been visited by members of Maj. Stephen Harriman Long's Yellowstone Expedition (in which Nuttall's Philadelphia friends had hoped for his appointment as botanist) in Cincinnati in May preceding Nuttall's present visit. The latter would carry letters of introduction from Glenn to the authorities at Belle Point. Glenn is best remembered for his successful attempt in 1821 with Fowler and Nathaniel Pryor to open the Santa Fe trade. For his vicissitudes with his government contracts see Harry R. Stevens, "Samuel Watts Davies and the Industrial Revolution in Cincinnati," *Ohio Historical Quarterly*, Vol. 70, No. 2 (April, 1961), 95–127; AM. ST. PAPERS, MILITARY AFFAIRS, II, 73. His New Mexican ventures appear in Jacob Fowler, *The Journal of Jacob Fowler*, ed. by Elliott Coues; and in Thomas James, *Three Years Among the Mexicans and Indians*, ed. by W. B. Douglas, 108–109, 109n.

[27]Lawrenceburg, county seat of Dearborn County, Ind., had its beginnings only sixteen years before Nuttall's visit. It was noted by Nuttall's contemporary travelers James Flint, *Letters from America . . .* [1818–20], in THWAITES [1], IX, 158; and George W. Ogden, *Letters from the West . . .*, in THWAITES [1], XIX, 68. Maximilian zu Wied Neuwied (1832–34) saw it too (*Reise in das innere Nord-Amerika . . .*, in THWAITES [1], XXIV, 142).

sembled winter. In the evening I arrived at a little town called the Rising Sun,[28] from its tavern, 13 miles below Lawrenceburgh.

19TH.] A fine morning and but little wind.—I now continued alone to navigate the Ohio, which is here exceedingly crooked. The alluvial lands are extensive, with the hills low, and the rock, as usual, calcareous and filled with organic impressions. I descended about 30 miles, and lodged with a very polite and hospitable Frenchman, three miles above the Swiss towns of Vevay and Ghent.[29] He informed me that he had emigrated the last summer from Grenoble, and had purchased land here at the rate of 10 dollars per acre, including the house and improvements which he occupied. He complained how much he had been deceived in his expectations, and that if he was home again, and possessed of his present experience, he would never have emigrated. He did not give a very favourable account of the settlement of Vevay, and he and others, particularly a Swiss whom I called upon, informed me that the wine here attempted to be made was of an inferior quality. It sold at 25 cents the bottle, but soon became too sour to drink, and that instead of obtaining the northern vines for cultivation, as those around Paris, they had all along attended to the southern varieties. So the vineyards of Vevay, if not better supported, will probably soon be transformed into corn-fields. The wine which they have produced is chiefly claret, sometimes bordering on the quality of Burgundy, for the preservation of which their heated cabins, destitute of cellars, are not at all adapted; we do not, however, perceive any obstacle to the distillation of brandy, which could be disposed of with great facility and profit. The quantity of wine said to be yielded to the acre, is about 500 gallons, which, if saleable, ought to produce a considerable emolument, and materially benefit the country, by diminishing the foreign demand. Several gentlemen of science, wealth, and patriotism in Kentucky and Mississippi Territory, are now also beginning to devote their attention to this important and neglected subject, and are commenc-

[28]Rising Sun, seat of Ohio County, dating from a decade later than Lawrenceburg and, like it, noted by Ogden and Maximilian.

[29]Vevay was laid out five years before, in 1813, following the colonization of twenty-five hundred acres by eleven Swiss families led by John James Du Four, largely for the purpose of developing a wine culture, according to John Bradbury, Nuttall's companion in 1811 on the upper Missouri. BRADBURY, in THWAITES [1], V, 316. Ghent, across the Ohio in Carroll County, Ky., was a product of the same thrust.

ing by the cultivation of improved varieties of the native species of vine, which promise, above those of Europe, every requisite of fertility, hardihood, and improved flavour.

20TH.] To-day I passed the rising town of Madison,[30] and the outlet of Kentucky river.—The sun was setting when I arrived and just served to disclose the beauty of the surrounding scenery. On one side of the river rose a lofty fascade of calcareous rocks, fretted like net-work; on the opposite extended the low alluvial lands of Kentucky, thickly lined with an almost unbroken rank of tall poplars, (*Populus angulisans*), resembling a magnificent vista planted by the hand of man.[31]

21ST.] Late in the evening I arrived at Bethlehem, a miserable little hamlet in speculation, containing about half a dozen houses.

22D.] To-day I came within 11 miles of Louisville, and lodged with a hospitable and industrious Irishman, who had emigrated from Belfast about 17 years ago.

23D.] At length I arrived at the large and flourishing town of Louisville, but recently a wilderness.[32] Labour and provision rated here much above the value which they commonly bore in the state and the surrounding country. The markets were very negligently supplied, and at prices little inferior to those of New Orleans. In fact, the vortex of speculation, this commercial gambling, absorbed the solid interests of the western states, and destroyed all mercantile confidence. The whole country was overrun with banks, which neither deserved confidence nor credit. Not a note in Kentucky commanded specie, the capital was altogether fictitious, and ought to have been secured by every species of property possessed by the stockholders. A more ruinous and fraudulent system of exchange was never devised in any Christian country; it is truly a novelty to see a whole

[30]Madison, which dates from the first decade of the nineteenth century, is the seat of Jefferson County, Ind.

[31]*Populus* angulisans is perhaps a *lapsus calami* for *P.* angulata = *P. deltoides*, eastern cottonwood.

[32]Louisville, a few months later, in 1820, claimed 4,012 inhabitants, though at the time of the visit of Paul Wilhelm, the Duke of Württemberg, in 1823 there appear to have been only 250 houses. WÜRTTEMBERG, 159–65. The site had been visited by Gen. George Rogers Clark and his troops in 1778, when they rested at Corn Island. Shippingport, immediately below the Falls of the Ohio, now part of Louisville, afforded a dock and warehouses for the large tonnage undergoing transshipment upstream from the falls, and equally downstream.

community, at least the wealthy part of it, conspiring in a common system of public fraud.

The love of luxury, without the means of obtaining it, has proved the bane of these still rude settlements of agriculturists, naturally poor in money by reason of their remoteness from the emporium of commerce, and their neglect of manufactures. When one heard a farmer demand a price for his produce in Kentucky, equal nearly to that of Philadelphia, we might be certain that he expected payment in depreciated paper.

A stranger who descends the Ohio at this season of emigration, cannot but be struck with the jarring vortex of heterogeneous population amidst which he is embarked, all searching for some better country, which ever lies to the west, as Eden did to the east. Amongst the crowd are also those, who, destitute of the means or inclination of obtaining an honest livelihood, are forced into desperate means for subsistence.

In my descent from Pittsburgh to Louisville, I found the wind, excepting about two days, constantly blowing up the river. The north-west or south-west winds, in fact, continue almost three quarters of the year. The deep valley which the river has excavated forms a vortex, into which the rarified air of the land rushes for equilibrium. The south-west wind is uniformly, at this season of the year, attended with a dense and bluish atmosphere, charged with vapours, which appear like smoke, and sometimes accumulate so as to obscure the land.

I was detained at Louisville until the 7th of December, trying various means of descending the river. The lowness of the water prevented the descent of the steam-boats, and the price of passage to Natchez was now no less than 50 dollars. Wearied by delay, I at length concluded to purchase a flat-boat, and freighted it nearly at my own cost, which, for an inexperienced traveller, was certainly an act of imprudence, as the destruction of the boat, which frequently happens, would probably have plunged me into penury and distress.

The wealth and population of Louisville are evidently on the increase, and a canal is now proposed, to obviate the difficulty of navigating by the Falls.

I perceive no material variation in the soil or river scenery. The surface is deeply undulated, fertile, and much sunk into circular depressions or water-swallows. The rock is all calcareous, but destitute of coal, or indeed any kind of overlaying of stratum in this neighbourhood.

The Falls, at this stage of the water, roar in terrific grandeur; the descending surges resemble the foaming billows of the sea, and do not now admit the passage of vessels drawing more than 12 inches of water, though at other seasons there is a sufficiency for the largest boats on either side of the island which divides the falls. The calcareous ledge over which the water thus pours is nearly as horizontal as a floor, and filled with the reliquiae of terebratulites, caryophillites, corallines, encrinites, &c. It also contains an unusual portion of pyrites, illinitions of blende ore of zinc, and a bluish green pulverulent substance, which is perhaps an ore of copper, or an oxide of nickel. Wood in a state of petrifaction has been discovered near the island which divides the cataract, and that in considerable quantity. The steam-boats, which ascend as far as Shippingsport, below the Falls, are of no less tahn 3 to 500 tons burthen, and are handsomely fitted up for the accommodation of passengers. Sometimes they descend to New Orleans in eight or ten days, affording a facility of communication heretofore unprecedented.

CHAPTER III.

ON THE 7TH, towards evening, I left Shippingsport in the flat-boat which I had purchased, accompanied by an elderly gentleman and his son [Mr. Godfrey and Edwin], who intended to proceed to New Orleans. The river had now taken a sudden and favourable rise of eight or ten feet perpendicular. We floated all night, keeping an alternate watch, and before the expiration of 24 hours, on the 8th, the current alone had carried us without labour near 80 miles! We accompanied another vessel of the same kind, and, for mutual convenience, our boats, according to custom, were lashed together side by side, thus also facilitating our progress by obtaining a greater scope of the current.

9TH.] We continued at the same rate, floating along without any labour, except that of occasionally rowing out from the shore, or avoiding submerged trunks of trees, called snags or sawyers, as they are either stationary or moveable with the action of the current; by the French they are called *chicos*. In the night we passed the town of *Troy*, an insignificant handful of log-cabins, dignified by this venerable name; here we stopped a few minutes to unload some salt, which, in consequence of the scarcity, incident to the low stage of water, sold at four dollars per bushel. Nearly all the salt which supplies this country descends the Kanhaway.

On the 10th we arrived at Owensville,[1] more commonly called Yellow

[1]Now Owensboro, seat of Daviess County, Ky., so renamed after the Battle of Tippecanoe, November 7, 1811, in which Abraham Owen, colonel and aide-de-camp to

Banks, from the ochraceous appearance of the argillaceous friable bank of the river. This is another insignificant cluster of log-cabins, and the seat of a county. Flour sold here at 10 dollars per barrel. In consequence of the want of mills, they depend altogether on the upper country for their supplies of this important article. Mills are much wanted, and, in order even to obtain cornmeal, every one has to invent something of the kind for himself. At this place the store-keepers were busily collecting pork for the market of New Orleans, at the rate of five dollars per hundred, in exchange for dry-goods and groceries. No other produce appeared in this place. No orchards are yet planted, and apples were worth one dollar and a half the bushel.

We floated as usual till towards midnight, but the north-west wind arising, at length put a stop to our progress. Having proceeded about 18 miles below Owensville, we endeavoured to land on the Kentucky side, but, in the attempt, ran an imminent risk of grounding on an extensive bar; with considerable labour we rowed our unmanageable flat to the opposite shore, where we found deep water, and a good harbour from the wind.

11TH.] About day-break we were accosted by a back-woods neighbour, anxious for a dram of whiskey, which we had foreseen and provided for. We were detained all day by the wind, and the hunters went out in quest of turkeys. The improvidence of these hunting farmers, is truly remarkable: annually mortgaging their produce for the meanest luxuries of civilized life; still destitute of flour, of the produce of the orchard, of country spirits, and, indeed, of coffee and sugar for a great part of the year; at the same time, that they might become independent, with even moderate industry.

Potatoes are very indifferent in this country, but pulse and all kinds of grain excellent and productive.

Here, at Mountplace[2] as it is called, there are two or three Indian mounds, upon one of which our visitor had built his house, and in digging had discovered abundance of human bones, as well as several stone pipes, and fragments of earthen ware.

Indiana Territorial Governor and Commander William Henry Harrison, lost his life to the Shawnee and allied Indians under the Prophet. Harrison to the Secretary of War, November 18, 1811, in ESAREY, I, 618–34.

[2]Once but not now near Newburgh, Warrick County, Ind.

12TH.] About 9 o'clock, we pushed out and proceeded. Towards evening, 15 miles from Hendersonville, in Indiana,[3] we passed a small town called Evansville, apparently a county seat, by the appearance of a court house.[4] We continued to float throughout the night, which was very fine and moonlight, but cold, the thermometer being down at 20°. We passed Henderson in the night, and, about 5 o'clock in the morning of the 13th, came in sight of the large and beautiful broad island, called the Diamond, with the river, on either side of it, apparently a mile in breadth. At two intervals of 10 miles each, we had passed two other islands, and about one o'clock, found ourselves carried by good fortune, and at an easy rate, opposite to the Wabash and its island, which mark the commencement of the territory of Illinois.

From Owensville, cane begins to be tall and abundant. The prospect of an approaching storm caused us to come to shore at an early hour, where we remained for the night, having our boat tied to a stout branch or stem of the *Borya acuminata*,[5] which grows here in abundance, and is nearly as thorny as a sloe bush, sending up many straight stems from the same root.

14TH.] We rode over to Shawneetown,[6] a handful of log cabins, with

---

[3]Rather, Kentucky. Henderson sheltered John James and Lucy Audubon, who had come there as early as 1810 and built a cabin among the 250 others lining the unsurfaced streets. This was the locus of Audubon's early commercial disaster, a large gristmill promoted by Thomas Bakewell and joined by Thomas Pears and David Prentice, the millwright, beginning in the spring of 1816. To the Audubon cabin in the summer of 1818 came Constantine Samuel Rafinesque-Schmaltz, gross in attire and ambition, and after him George Keats, brother of the English poet John, and Georgina, George's young wife. Nuttall, however, would not meet Audubon until the summer of 1832, in Boston. FORD, 74–102; Audubon to Dr. Richard Harlan, August 14, 1832, in GRAUSTEIN, 242.

[4]Evansville was scarcely six years old in 1818, in which year it became county seat of Vanderburgh County, Ind. It was named for Gen. Robert Morgan Evans, militia commander in the War of 1812.

[5]Now *Forestiera acuminata*. —NUTTALL. [*F. acuminata* (Michx.) Poir., swamp privet.]

[6]Shawneetown, below the mouth of the Wabash in Gallatin County, Ill., then and now occupies a more ancient Shawnee Indian site. Father Marquette, who identified the Wabash in 1673 (THWAITES [2], LIX, 143–47), saw the Chaouanons, or Shawnees, who at that time, he wrote, had twenty-three villages in one district and fifteen in another and were docile, beset by the Iroquois "like flocks of sheep." This tribe, of the central Algonquian linguistic group, outlived the description, moving later, as they apparently had done earlier, from Tennessee and South Carolina to Pennsylvania and Ohio, after the Treaty of Greenville (1795) to Missouri, later to Kansas, and after 1831 to the Canadian River in present Oklahoma. Marquette's description of the flora of the Wabash confluence with the Ohio closely resembles Nuttall's.

some of them shingled, commanding an agreeable view of the river, but not situated beyond the reach of occasional inundation. I learned, on inquiry, that Mr. Birkbeck's settlement was not so unhealthy as had been reported, and that it was continually receiving accessions of foreigners.[7] After floating some distance, we came up with three other flat boats, and lashing to them proceeded all night. The river is here very wide and magnificent, and checquered with many islands. The banks at Battery Rock, Rock in the Cave,[8] and other places, are bold and rocky, with bordering cliffs. The occidental wilderness appears here to retain its primeval solitude; its gloomy forests are yet unbroken by the hand of man, they are only penetrated by the wandering hunter, and the roaming savage.

15TH and 16 TH.] Got down below fort Massac,[9] and remained ashore most part of the night, being detained by the wind. On the night and morning of the 15th, the thermometer fell to 10°. In a cypress swamp, near to the shore, grew the *Gleditsia monosperma* and the *Cephalanthus*, with pubescent leaves and branchlets, which grows in Georgia and Louisiana, also the *Asclepias parviflora*.[10]

17TH.] Between 2 and 3 o'clock in the afternoon, we arrived at the

---

[7]Morris Birkbeck, a native of Wanborough, England, and George Flower, both owners of English landed estates, pioneered on what became known as the English Prairie, between the Wabash and Little Wabash rivers, Edwards County, Ill., beginning 1817. Birkbeck's town, Wanborough, contained twenty-five cabins and a number of commercial establishments in 1820. Flower's settlement, Albion, was two miles east of Birkbeck's. William Cobbett, in self-imposed exile from England raising rutabagas on Long Island, was critical of this English colonization venture, as was his friend Thomas Hulme. John Woods, *Two Years Residence in the Settlement on the English Prairie, in the Illinois Country* . . . (London, 1822), 158–63. Cf. Richard Flower, *Letters from Lexington and the Illinois* (London, 1819); Birkbeck, *Notes on a Journey in America* (London, 1817), and *Letters from Illinois* . . . (London, 1818); William Cobbett, *A Year's Residence in the United States of America* (New York, 1818; London, 1828).

[8]Cave-in-Rock, Hardin County, Ill., handsomely described by Fortescue Cuming in 1810 (in THWAITES [1], IV, 272–73).

[9]Fort Massac, on the north bank of the Ohio ten miles below present Paducah, Ky., had been a French post before it was reactivated beginning May 24, 1794, during Maj. Gen. Anthony Wayne's campaign against the Ohio Indians. It had been abandoned since 1814. Henry Knox, Secretary of War, to General Anthony Wayne, March 31, 1794, AM. ST. PAPERS, FOREIGN AFFAIRS, I, 458–59.

[10]*Gleditsia* monosperma = *G. aquatica* Marsh., water locust; *Cephalanthus occidentalis* var. *pubescens* Raf., hairy buttonbush; *Asclepias parviflora* = *A. perennis* Walt., swamp milkweed.

mouth of the Ohio, and were considerably mortified on perceiving the Mississippi to be full of floating ice. Governed by the conduct of the boats which we had for three days accompanied, we came to on the Kentucky shore, and remained in company with several other boats, this and the whole of the following day.

The summit of the bank, at the foot of which we had landed, was surmounted by an almost impenetrable and sempervirent cane brake; we measured several canes upwards of 30 feet in height.[11] These wilds afford but little gratification to the botanist, their extreme darkness excluding the existence of nearly [every] herbaceous plant. Among the trees, we still continue to observe the coffee-bean (*Gymnocladus canadensis*), now loaded with legumes, the seeds of which, when parched, are agreeable to eat, but produce a substitute for coffee greatly inferior to the *Cichorium*.[12]

The whole country here, on both sides of the Mississippi and the Ohio, remains uninhabited in consequence of inundation, and abounds with various kinds of game, but particularly deer and bear, turkeys, geese, and swans, with hosts of other aquatic fowls; though, with the exception of the white pelican, they are such as commonly exist in many other parts of the Union.

While amusing ourselves on the 17th, we were visited by a couple of the Delaware Indians,[13] and shortly after by a hunting party of Shawnees, who reside some miles west of St. Louis. I invited one of them into our cabin, and prevailed upon him to take supper, with which he appeared to be well satisfied and grateful. On the following day, a number of the Shawnees came with our evening guest, and desired to purchase gunpowder. They behaved with civility, and almost refused to taste of spirits,

[11]*Arundinaria gigantea* (Walt.) Muhl., giant cane.

[12]*Gymnocladus* canadensis = *G. dioica* (L.) Koch. *Cichorium* is chicory.

[13]The Delaware Indians belong linguistically to the Central Algonquians and according to their own tradition had a common origin with the Shawnee, Nanticoke, Mahican, and, with more remote connection, the Sauk and Fox tribes, the Shawnee claiming a close relationship with the latter. They called themselves *Lenape* or *Leni-lenape;* the French, *Loups,* wolves; the English, Delawares, from their residence on Delaware River in eastern Pennsylvania and New Jersey in William Penn's time. Pressure from the Iroquois forced them to the Susquehanna in 1742; a decade later they were in eastern Ohio; many were in Indiana by 1770, others by 1789 were in Missouri and Arkansas, and in 1820 some seven hundred were in Texas. Their reservation life began in 1835 in Kansas, but in 1867 they were removed to Indian Territory, present Oklahoma. HODGE, I, 385–87.

but their reluctance was at length overcome by some of our neighbours, and the night was passed at their camp with yells and riot. Although the Delawares and Shawnees are proximately allied to each other, yet we perceive the existence of that jealousy among them, which has ever been so fatal to the interest of the aborigines, from the conquest of Cortes to the present moment. The Delawares cautioned me against the Shawnees, among whom they were continually hunting, and stigmatized them as rogues; I found them, however, all equally honest in their dealings, as far as I had any intercourse with them; still the history of the Shawnees, on many occasions, has long proved the truth of the character which is given of them by the Delawares. Scarcely any of the Indian tribes have migrated so often and so far, as the restless and intriguing Shawnees; who, since their first discovery on the banks of the Savannah, in Georgia, have, in the space of a century, successively migrated through the western states to the further bank of the Mississippi. Ever flying from the hateful circle of civilized society, which, probably in their own defence, they have repeatedly scourged, so as, indeed, to endanger their safety; averse to agriculture and systematic labour, they still depend upon the precarious bounty of the chase for their rude subsistence. Retreating into the forests of the western interior, according to their own acknowledgment destitute of lands, they are reduced to the misery of craving the favour of hunting ground from the Cherokees and Osages,[14] excepting the uninhabitable wilds of the Mississippi, which, as in former times, still continue the common range of every tribe of native hunters.

These Indians possess the same symbolical or pantomimic language, as

[14]The Osages, forming with the Omahas, Poncas, Kansa, and Quapaws the Dhegiha division of the Siouan family, had long occupied the central Missouri region from the confluence of Osage River with the Missouri southward. But by 1802 dissident groups from both the Grand and Little Osages, encouraged by the Chouteau fur-trading interests, had moved southwestward to the Three Forks area in present Oklahoma formed by the confluences of the Grand and Verdigris rivers with the Arkansas. The Osage hunting range in Nuttall's time extended south to Red River and far to the west into the High Plains.

The Cherokees, a detached tribe of the Iroquoyan family, were traditionally friendly to the Shawnees, notably when the latter were occupying the middle Savannah River in South Carolina and, in a separate band, the Cumberland Basin of Tennessee, before the northeastward movement of both bands in the eighteenth century, first to Pennsylvania, later to Ohio. Historically the Cherokees were claimants to the vast mountain region of the southern Alleghenies, in southwestern Virginia, western North Carolina and South

that which is employed by most of the nations with which I have become acquainted. It appears to be a compact invented by necessity, which gives that facility to communication denied to oral speech.

Carolina, northern Georgia, eastern Tennessee, and northeastern Alabama.

The presence of the westward migrating Cherokees from Tennessee in central and western Arkansas in the spring of 1819, clearly in confrontation with the Osages, will be of major importance to Nuttall's subsequent account.

CHAPTER IV.

Embark amidst the ice of the Mississippi—Run aground on Wolf's island in attempting to land—relieved from this situation—but find ourselves again involved in it, and are imposed upon by the extortion of a neighbouring voyager—Pass the Iron banks—Cypress—Solitude of the country—New Madrid—Oscillations of the earth still frequent—Point Pleasant—Vestiges of the great earthquake—The Little Prairie settlement almost destroyed by it—The Canadian reach—A dangerous and difficult pass of the river— The first Chicasaw Bluffs—Additional danger and uncertainty of the navigation—Stratification of the Bluff—A dangerous accident—The second Chicasaw Bluffs—Observations on their stratification.

19TH.] This morning, after breakfast, our more than usually timid neighbours and ourselves ventured into the floating ice of the Mississippi, which we soon found to be less formidable than we had imagined, though still not without some danger of drifting imperceptibly or unavoidably upon some sunken tree, of which there are no small abundance throughout the bed of the Mississippi. Carried upon these by the rapid current, our boats might be staved or entirely overturned, accidents which not infrequently happen to those who give way to negligence or incaution.

About half an hour before sun-set, our company came to alongside a breaking sand-bar, where lay also two other boats; governed by their example we attempted to land, but floated by the current to a distance below, and here, unfortunately, attempting to make a landing, and trusting too confidently to the lightness of our boat, we were instantly carried upon a shallow and miry bar. I was sensible of the dilemma into which we had fallen, and lost no time to plunge into the water, though at the point of freezing, attempting, but in vain, to float off the boat by a lever. The effort was beyond my strength, and after remaining in the water nearly an hour, I had reluctantly to submit to our situation. At length, two boatmen offered their assistance, for the consideration of five dollars, with which I complied, and in a few moments we again floated. They took us in the dark about 100 yards further down, and there made a landing. I still felt suspicious of our situation, notwithstanding their assurances of safety: and at day-light, we found ourselves (in consequence of the rapid falling of the river) as far as ever grounded upon the bar; to obviate which, all our strength and ingenuity availed nothing. The boatmen also, who had assisted us the preceding night, and put us off our guard by false assurances, now passed us with indifference, and denied us the assistance which they had promised. We immediately commenced unloading, and had proceeded pretty far in our labour, when we were visited by the owner of a neighbouring boat, who, pretending to commiserate our situation, offered to assist us gratuitously; and hearing how we had been cheated out of five dollars, expressed his dislike at any boatman having acted with such want of fellow-feeling. We had scarcely time to breakfast, before our yankees arrived with two skiffs; and one of them now assured us that we should never be able to get off until the rise of the river; though, as appeared in the sequel, merely with the friendly view of putting a good price upon his services. The other, instead of the gratuitous assistance which he had offered, made a tender of his services at three dollars. At length, like genuine Arabs, they demanded the value of eight dollars, with which I was reluctantly obliged to comply. After about ten minutes further unloading, a lever placed under the bow, set us readily afloat in one minute; so much had these kind gentlemen deceived us, as to our real situation. They now also refused to fulfil the bargain of assisting us to reload, until brought to some sense of duty by remonstrance.—I shall not indeed soon forget Wolf's island, and its harbour of sharpers.

20TH.] The day was far advanced when we got off, and after floating 10 miles we moored for the night, taking care to have deep water.

The land appears low and uninhabited on every side, except at the Iron-banks (called Mine au Fer by the French)[1] we passed yesterday, and which are cliffs of friable and argillaceous earth, the upper bed being ferruginous, beneath which occurs a very conspicuously-coloured band of pink clay about 12 inches thick, and below are white beds of the same material, improperly considered chalk.

[1]Iron Banks (Mine au Fer) on the Kentucky side of the Mississippi, some twenty miles below the mouth of the Ohio.

The cyprus (*Cupressus disticha*)[2] which continues some distance along the Ohio above its estuary, is here much more common, and always indicates the presence of annual inundation and consequent swamps and lagoons, but we do not yet meet with the long moss (*Tillandsia usneoides*),[3] a plant so characteristic of the prevalence of unhealthy humidity in the atmosphere.

21ST.] We commenced our voyage at the dawn of day, and continued to float along without interruption. The river here appears truly magnificent, though generally bordered by the most gloomy solitudes, in which there are now no visible traces of the abode of man. It is indeed a sublime contrast to the busy hum of a city, and not altogether destitute of interest. In the course of the day we passed a number of capacious islands, but all as they ever were from their creation, and most of them even without names, the property of any one who will assume the possession; but they are in general, I suspect, annually submerged by inundation.

This evening we were 10 miles above New Madrid, and moored opposite to one of the islands which had been convulsed by the earthquake of 1811.

22D.] We commenced our voyage early, and arrived before noon at New Madrid.[4] We found both sides of the river unusually lined with sunken logs, some stationary and others in motion, and we narrowly avoided several of considerable magnitude.

New Madrid is an insignificant French hamlet, containing little more than about 20 log houses and stores miserably supplied, the goods of which are retailed at exorbitant prices: for example, 18 cents per pound for

[2] Now *Taxodium distichum* (L.) Richard, bald cypress.

[3] Spanish moss.

[4] Nuttall had visited New Madrid and examined some of its prehistoric remains in 1811, on his return from his trip to the upper Missouri, shared with John Bradbury, the English botanist, and Henry Marie Brackenridge, of Pittsburgh (NUTTALL [4], 72). He had missed the great earthquake of December 16 in that year, but Bradbury, who was short of money and had taken charge of a boat laden with lead consigned to New Orleans, witnessed it all, including the destruction of New Madrid.

The town, formerly a trading post called l'Anse a la Graisse, later the site of Spanish Fort Céleste (1791), was the capital site chosen by Col. George Morgan in 1787 for his imperium within Spanish Louisiana. It was in part settled in 1789, but Morgan's vast domain of some 15 million acres stretching down the Mississippi to the mouth of the Saint Francis at present Helena, Ark., was rescinded by Esteban Miró, Spanish governor of Louisiana, in the summer of the same year, not without the advice of Gen. James Wilkinson. Cf. HOUCK [1], I, 275–315.

lead, which costs seven cents at Herculaneum;[5] salt five dollars per bushel; sugar 31 1-4 cents per pound; whiskey one dollar 25 cents per gallon; apples 25 cents per dozen; corn 50 cents per bushel; fresh butter 37 1-2 cents per pound; eggs the same per dozen; pork six dollars per hundred; beef five dollars. Still the neighbouring land appears to be of a good quality, but people have been discouraged from settling in consequence of the earthquakes, which, besides the memorable one of 1811, are very frequently experienced, two or three oscillations being sometimes felt in a day. The United States, in order to compensate those who suffered in their property by the catastrophe, granted to the settlers an equivalent of land in other parts of the Territory.

The site of the town, as we learn from La Vega, the historian of Soto, bears unequivocal marks of an aboriginal station; still presenting the remains of some low mounds, which, as usual, abound with fragments of earthen ware.[6]

23D.] We proceeded about six miles, and came to at another small French hamlet called Point Pleasant.[7] Here I saw the Catalpa (*Catalpa*

[5]Herculaneum, Jefferson County, Mo., down the Mississippi from Saint Louis, had been an important center for the smelting of lead and at this time had two shot towers, among other facilities.

[6]See the Appendix, and the account of De Soto's incursion. —NUTTALL.

In the immediate vicinity of the town I met with *Barbera glandulosa, Erigeron (Caenotus) divaricatum, Verbena stricta, V. Aubletia, Croton capitatum,* and *Helenium quadridentatum.* On the banks of the river *Oxydenia attenuata* and the *Capraria multifida* of Michaux. —NUTTALL.

[Nuttall's retracing of the Hernando de Soto Expedition route, only mentioned above but given in detail in his Appendix, is more fully annotated at the latter point. Here it may be noted that the nearly conclusive evidence in our time discourages the notion that the expedition actually reached the site of New Madrid in 1541. But the evidences Nuttall mentions of prehistoric cultural remains have been sustained by modern archaeological excavations reported by Carl H. Chapman in "A Preliminary Survey of Missouri Archaeology, Part II: Middle Mississippi and Hopewellian Cultures," *Missouri Archaeologist,* X (April, 1947), 64ff. For the De Soto Expedition see U.S. De Soto Expedition Commission, John R. Swanton, Chairman, *Final Report of the United States De Soto Expedition Commission,* 76 Cong., 1 sess., *House Document No. 71* (10328), (1939).

[Nuttall's species noted above: Barbera glandulosa = *Barbarea vulgaris* R. Br., yellow rocket. *Erigeron divaricatus* Michx., fleabane (the Nuttall division *Caenotus* stands). *Verbena stricta* Vent., hoary vervin, is native in Missouri. *Verbena* Aubletia = *V. canadensis* (L.) Britt. *Croton* capitatum = *C. capitatus* Michx., hogwart. *Helenium quadridentatum* Hook. is a sneezeweed (three other species of *Helenium* and one variety were named by Nuttall). *Oxydenia attenuata* Nutt. gives way to *Leptochloa attenuata* (Nutt.) Steud. Capraria multifida Michx. = *Leucospora multifida* (Michx.) Nutt., an erect, hairy annual herb of the Scrophulariaceae (Figwort family).]

cordifolia) in the forests, apparently indigenous, for the first time in my life, though still contiguous to habitations.

This place and several islands below were greatly convulsed by the earthquake, and have in consequence been abandoned. I was shown a considerable chasm still far from being filled up, from whence the water of the river, as they say, rushed in an elevated column. The land is here of a superior quality, but flat, and no high grounds have made their appearance since we passed the Iron-Banks, no rock is any where to be seen; the banks of the river are deep and friable; islands and sand-bars, at this stage of the river connected with the land, are almost innumerable. In the midst of so much plenty provided by nature, the Canadian squatters[8] are here, as elsewhere, in miserable circumstances. They raise no wheat, and scarcely enough of maize for their support. Superfine flour sold here at 11 dollars per barrel.

The dresses of the men consist of blanket capeaus, buckskin pantaloons, and mockasins.

25TH.] Christmas-day. We left Point Pleasant, and floated along without encountering any material obstacle, except glancing against an enormous moving log (or sawyer), which for the moment threw us into terror. Indeed the submerged trees become more and more numerous.

In the evening we arrived at the remains of the settlement called the Little Prairie, where there is now only a single house, all the rest, together with their foundations, having been swept away by the river, soon after the convulsion of the earthquake, in consequence (as the inhabitants say, and as they also affirm in New Madrid) of the land having sunk 10 feet or more below its former level.[9]

26TH.] After continuing about 10 miles below the Little Prairie, we were detained for the remainder of the day by commencement of a storm,

[7]Point Pleasant, New Madrid County, Mo., ten miles downstream from New Madrid itself. (His *Catalpa* cordifolia = *C. speciosa* Warder.) The evidences of earthquake destruction here and at points subsequently mentioned by Nuttall may be related to the modern determination that earth shock of this magnitude could be felt over an area of 750,000 square miles.

[8]Such as cultivate unappropriated land without any species of title. —NUTTALL.

[9]For a historical account of this country, once thickly inhabited by the natives, see the abridged relation of its discovery, and pretended conquest, by Ferdinand de Soto, in the Appendix. —NUTTALL.

[As Note 6 *supra* suggests, the accounts of the De Soto Expedition written by a

which towards evening increased to violence, and continued so throughout the night. I felt under some apprehension that we should break our cable, and so be cast away upon some of the many snags and sawyers which obstruct the river.

27TH.] Towards noon, the north-west wind moderating, we continued as usual, and proceeded about 12 miles through a portion of the river filled with islands and trunks of trees. No habitations whatever appeared since we left the Little Prairie.

28TH.] Proceeded a few miles, to the head of the 25th island, as marked in the Pittsburgh Navigator,[10] and remained about four hours, waiting the abatement of the wind, which did not permit us to proceed in safety. Our company did not appear inclined to advance towards the Canadian reach until the following morning; but not wishing to spend any time unnecessarily, we continued about five miles further.

29TH.] Proceeding at day-break, we looked with apprehension for the dangers described by the Navigator, but passed along with so little difficulty as almost to doubt our actual situation. A few miles below, however, we observed the river contracted within a narrow space by a spreading sand-bar (or island), and planted almost across with large and dangerous trunks, some with the tops, and others with the roots uppermost, in a perpendicular posture. The water broke upon them with a noise which I had heard distinctly for two miles, like the cascade of a mill-race, in consequence of the velocity of the current; with all our caution to avoid them, the boat grazed on one, which was almost entirely submerged, and we received a terrific jar. All day we had experienced uninterrupted rain, but it was now pouring down in torrents. About two o'clock in the afternoon, as soon as the fog had cleared away, we perceived ourselves again

---

Gentleman of Elvas, Garcilaso de la Vega, Juan Bautista Muñoz (from an anonymous "official" report), and Rodrigo Ranjel shed no direct light on the aboriginal inhabitants of New Madrid County, since the expedition never reached that area. But it did encounter many villages of the Casqui on and east of White River, and of the Pacaha in the lowlands near the present mouth of Saint Francis River. The archaeological findings for New Madrid County indicate substantial populations at or just before the Spanish incursion. U.S. DE SOTO EXPEDITION COMMISSION, 249–53. Cf. "Middle Mississippi Culture in New Madrid County," CHAPMAN, 61–63.]

[10]Popularly so called, *The Navigator* was published under varying titles in twelve editions to 1824 by Zadok Cramer and his associates in Pittsburgh. It dealt with navigation of the Monongahela, Allegheny, Ohio, and Mississippi rivers. Nuttall is here referring to the tenth (1818) or an earlier edition.

moving towards the field of danger. I counted, in the space of a minute, about 100 huge trees fixed in all postures, nearly across the whole river, so as scarcely to leave room for a passage. We proceeded towards a bank of willows on the Louisiana side, thinking to land for the night, in consequence of the unremitting and drenching rain, but found it impracticable, by reason of the rapid current. At length we descended to water which had the appearance of an eddy, and here I was strongly urged to land, in which attempt the boat would, in all probability, have been sunk amidst a host of snags and half-concealed trunks which lined the shore. With all our exertions in rowing off, we but narrowly escaped from being drawn into the impassable channel of a sand island which spread out into the river, presenting a portion of water resembling a sunken forest. The only course which we had left appeared no less a labyrinth of danger, so horribly filled with black and gigantic trunks of trees, along which the current foamed with terrific velocity—Scylla on one hand, and more than one Charybdis on the other. Fortunately, however, our voyage was not destined to end here, and, after an hour's drenching amidst torrents of rain, we at length obtained a landing place about 10 miles above the first Chicasaw Bluffs.[11] On the point of one of these bars at Flour island, we observed the wreck of two large flat boats which we supposed might have been lost during the earthquake. Northing still appeared on every hand but houseless solitude, and gloomy silence, the inundation precluding the possibility of settlement.

30TH.] We proceeded as soon as the dense fog this morning would permit, but could not ascertain our situation any longer by the vague

---

[11]The Chickasaw Bluffs, often but mistakenly limited to the Fourth Bluffs at present Memphis, Tenn., begin with the First Bluffs at present Fort Pillow State Park, Lauderdale County, Tenn., some fifty miles upstream from Memphis. The high headlands continue interruptedly, with the Second Bluffs in Tipton County, downstream from the first; the Third Bluffs in Shelby County, E. of Meeman-Shelby Forest State Park, extending some six miles to a point N.W. of Memphis and embracing somewhere within this distance the site of René Robert Cavelier, Sieur de La Salle's Fort Prudhomme of 1682; and, finally, the Fourth Chickasaw Bluffs at the river extremity of Memphis, overlooking Wolf River Lagoon and Mud Island. The Fourth was the site of Fort Pickering, subsequently mentioned by Nuttall. Cf. U.S. Geological Survey topographic maps; CUMING, 262–69; William H. Goetzmann, exploration routes, in *National Atlas of the United States*, U.S. Department of the Interior, Geological Survey (Washington, D.C., 1970), Plates 134, 135; MARGRY, I, 545–70, 593–616, II, 164–80, 196–205, 216–12; COX, I, 18, 131 ff.

trifling of the Navigator, and after proceeding some distance at the beck of the current, came in sight of Flour island. Here the Navigator says, "the channel is on the right side, but some prefer the left," but the very sight of the right-hand channel was to me sufficient, and finding the main body of the river carrying us to the left, I felt satisfied to go farther round rather than venture through such a horrid pass, which indeed resembled a submerged forest, and through which no flat boat, I should suppose, could ever proceed with safety, however deep might be the water. That we had got a passable channel to the left, I was fully satisfied on perceiving the intersection of the first Chicasaw Bluffs or hills, all the high lands of the Mississippi being uniformly washed at their base by a deep and rapid current. Here we landed for a few moments, to survey those hills, the only ones we had seen since leaving the Iron banks. The ascent was steep, and the elevation between 2 and 300 feet above the level of the river. These banks appeared to consist of a stratified, ferruginous, and bluish sandy clay, probably a disintegrated sandstone, which it perfectly resembled to the eye, though altogether friable to the touch. In some places, lower down the river, we observed masses of ferruginous conglomerate blackened by the atmosphere, the pebbles chiefly hornstone, and some of them quartz. The *debris* of which this conglomerate consists is entirely adventitious, or unconnected with the existing rocks, which form the basis of this ancient deposit.

At this place, we saw the first cabin since our departure from the Little Prairie. On approaching the 34th island from the mouth of the Ohio, which presents itself rounding, and nearly in the middle of the river, we had at first determined to take the left-hand side, set down by the Navigator as the channel, but finding ourselves to float very slowly, we rowed a little, and then submitted to the current. It was soon observable, that we drifted towards the right-hand channel, though much the narrowest, and my companion advised that we should keep the left, especially as it was the nearest, and as the wind accompanied by rain blew strongly up the river. However, on finding still that the current drew to the right, even against the wind, and having arrived at the commencement of the bar of the island, I determined, at all events, to keep to the right. At length, after considerable labour, we landed at a neighbouring cabin, and were informed that the left channel had not in places more than 12 inches of water, being nearly dry, and almost destitute of current. Here, again, we made a fortunate escape. We also learnt, that not more than two days ago, a flat boat was sunk by the snags, which filled the right-hand channel of Flour island.

At this place, we met with two or three families of hunters, with whom were living some individuals of the Shawnees and Delawares.[12] They had lately caught an unusual abundance of beaver in the neighbourhood, and were anxious to barter it for whiskey, though scarcely possessed either of bread or vegetables. Amongst their furs, I also saw a few skins of the musk-rat, (*Arctomys monax*, L.) which are never met with further to the south.[13]

31ST.] We continued our voyage as usual at daylight, and floating with a brisk current down the right side of the 34th island, had nearly cleared ourselves of a host of snags and sawyers, when at last, puzzled on which side of one of these terrific objects to steer, we unfortunately struck it with considerable force, and the young man who accompanied us (the son of Mr. G.), an amiable youth of 16, was precipitated headlong into the river, together with the steering oar, which was suddenly jerked off by the snag; our boat was at the same instant careened over so far, as at first to appear overturning, but I instantly had the satisfaction to see that she was free, had received no injury, and that Edwin on this emergency could swim, and, though much alarmed, had come within our reach, and got safely on board. As to our steering oar it remained across the snag, and was now become a sawyer; working horizontally upon the back of the black and fearful trunk which had so justly thrown us into consternation.

The wind springing up against us, we came to under the second Chicasaw Bluff, and had time to examine and contemplate these romantic cliffs, now doubly interesting after such a monotonous and cheerless prospect of solitary brakes and enswamped forests. This fasçade, or perpendicular section, precisely of the same materials and consistence as that of the Iron banks above, continues, I think, uninterruptedly for near two

---

[12]For the presence of the Shawnees and Delawares in this area see Chapter III, note 13 *arte*.

[13]Arctomys monax L. = *Ondatra zibethicus zibethicus* (L.), now difficult to trace distributionally because of its introduction, along with others of its genus, in many areas to which it was not native (by introduction it has even become Eurasian).

miles, and is about 150 feet high. The uppermost bed (all of them as nearly horizontal as may be), 12 to 20 feet thick, commencing immediately below the present vegetable loam, consists of a yellowish, homogeneous, now friable, sandy, and argillaceous earth, which is succeeded by a thinner and more ferruginous bed; below occurs a layer or band of *pink*-red clay, now and then variegated with white specks, and, though constant in its appearance and relative position, no where exceeding 18 inches in thickness; below again occur ferruginous earths and clays more or less sandy, then a bed of a brownish-black colour, and about 18 inches in thickness, which, on examination, I found to be lignite, or wood-coal, containing less bitumen than usual, and so distinctly derived from the vegetable kingdom, exhibiting even the cross grain of the wood, as to remove all doubts of its origin. To the taste it was sensibly acid, and smelt in burning like turf. Beneath this coal, and in connection with it, occurs a friable bed of dark-coloured argillaceous and sandy earth, in which I could very distinctly perceive blackened impressions of leaves of an oak, like the red oak and the willow oak, with *Equisetum hiemale* or Shave-rush,[14] and other vegetable remains, not much unlike the black beds of leaves which occur along the banks of the Ohio, but much more intermingled with earth. In this bed also occur masses or nodules of a hard and very fine-grained light gray sandstone, bordering almost upon hornstone, likewise charged with vegetable remains, resembling charred wood, together with leaves of oaks and of other forest trees. Nearly on a level with the present low stage of the river, there was a second bed of this coal, more interrupted than the first in its continuity, though constant in its locality, no less in some places (like basins) than 8, 12 or 15 feet in thickness. Below, clays again succeeded, and terminated the visible stratification.

In two or three places, I observed that the mud, which was very deep, had been boiling up into circular masses like fumeroles, and have no doubt, but that the decomposition of this vast bed of lignite or wood-coal, situated near the level of the river, and filled with pyrites, has been the active agent in producing the earthquakes, which have of late years agitated this country. The deposition of vast rafts of timber, thus accidentally

---

[14]*Equisetum hyemale* L., scouring rush.

brought together by the floods of the river, are continually, even before our eyes, as I may say, accumulating stores of matter, which, in after ages, will, no doubt, exert a baneful influence over the devoted soil, beneath which they are silently interred! How much has the vegetable kingdom to do with the destiny of man! The time, though slowly, is perhaps surely approaching, which will witness something like volcanic eruptions on the banks of the Mississippi. The inhabitants frequently, and almost daily, experience slight oscillations of the earth: I have even witnessed them myself while descending the river.[15]

[15]Nuttall's assumption that earlier earthquakes in this area had stemmed from decomposition of lignite seams at or not far below ground level was faulty. Moreover, he was too good a scientist to equate "earthquake" with "volcanic." Hence his forecast of volcanic activity is also faulty. Hadley and Devine conclude that earthquakes in the Mississippi embayment trough (which includes parts of western Tennessee, western Kentucky, southern Illinois, southeastern Missouri, and eastern Arkansas) "are believed to have been caused by movements on members of the northeast-trending New Madrid and Wabash River fault systems." Jarvis B. Hadley and James F. Devine, "Seismotectonic Map of the Eastern United States," accompanying *Map Folio 620*, Department of the Interior, United States Geological Survey (1974).

The Fourth Chickasaw Bluffs at Memphis experienced earthquake intensities of IX–X on the Modified Mercolli Scale of 1931 in the years between 1638 and 1864. By contrast the New Madrid quake attained XI–XII in 1811. Cf. *National Atlas of the United States*, Plate 67; Richard G. Stearns and Charles W. Wilson, Jr., "Geology and Seismic Hazard in, and East of, the New Madrid Earthquake Zone," in Geological Society of America, *Abstracts with Programs*, Vol. 5, No. 5 (February, 1973), 437.

CHAPTER V.

JANUARY 1ST, 1819.] We proceeded slowly, in consequence of adverse wind; and at length, came in sight of the third Chicasaw Bluff, quite similar in appearance and conformation with that of the second above described. The 35th island of the Navigator intervened betwist us and the cliff, there being no water to the left of it; the channel at this stage of the river, was completely choked up by a bed of sand.

We came to for the night on a sand-bar, opposite the centre of the island, resembling an Arabian desert, and scattered in every direction with lignite or bovey coal, washed probably from the basis of the Bluffs. The shore of the island was horribly strewed with the wreck of the alluvial forest, brought down by the overwhelming current of the river at its highest stage, and thrown confusedly together in vast piles.

In the course of the day, we stopped awhile at a Shawnee camp, and bartered for some venison and wild honey, which they had in plenty. The honey, according to the Indian mode, was contained in the skin of a deer taken off by the aperture of the neck, thus answering, though very rudely, the purpose of a bottle.

On the 2d, we passed the "Devil's Race-ground," as it has been very formidably termed, but observed no obstructions in the river equal to that at Plumb point, where we saw the wrecked boats. We observe, however, every day, wrecks of flat boats, drifted along the shores. We continued to the lower end of the "Devil's Elbow," and again found the difficulty greatly exaggerated. The whole surrounding country still continues a desolate wilderness, abandoned to inundation, presenting impenetrable cane brakes and gloomy forests: none of the trees, however, attain that enormous magnitude, which they so frequently present along the borders of the Ohio. This appearance may perhaps be attributed, in part, to the perpetual revolutions of the soil, occasioned by the overwhelming force and inundations of the river.

A dog lost in the forest, and perishing with hunger, came up to the bank of the river, yelling most piteously; but would not enter our skiff, which was sent for it, and continued to follow us for some distance, but the danger of the shore, and the rapidity of the current, rendered our endeavours to assist the miserable animal perfectly useless, and, after some time, he fell back, stopped and yelled, till he reluctantly disappeared.

3D.] We proceeded only a few miles in consequence of the wind, and came to at the point of a sand-bar, seven miles above the fourth Bluff. Here we observed a flat-boat lying aground, and dry upon the bar, for want of precaution in landing during the falling state of the river.

4TH.] This morning we descended to the fourth Chicasaw Bluffs, and, after endeavouring in vain to proceed, were obliged to desist for the wind, and come to under fort Pickering.[1] The strata are here again similar to those of the second Bluffs, even the seam of pink clay occurs, and near the level of the river we likewise perceive the lignite in a bed of about six feet thickness; but not probably continuous. Along the shore we saw masses which looked precisely like burnt logs, but all this coal, at length, blazes in the fire, and gives out, as usual, a smoke partaking of the odour of coal and turf.

We found a store here for the supply of the Indians and the settlers of

[1]Fort Pickering, completed at Chickasaw Bluffs on October 22, 1797, at present Memphis, was named first Fort Adams, later Fort Pike, and finally for Timothy Pickering, U.S. secretary of war. Its site was near that of Fort Assumption, created by the French, later replaced by the Spanish Fort San Fernando de las Barrancas, erected in the spring of 1795. Spain's withdrawal followed the Treaty of San Lorenzo (known as Pinckney's Treaty) in 1797. The fort's complement was thin after 1804. The adjoining government factory traded heavily with the Chickasaw Indians, among others, for hides, furs, tallow, and beeswax until, at the request of the Chickasaws, it was closed in 1819. AM. ST. PAPERS, MILITARY AFFAIRS, I, 176–77; AM. ST. PAPERS, INDIAN AFFAIRS, I, 772, II, 56; PRUCHA, 55, 58, 65, 73.

the neighbourhood, besides that of the United States.[2] The advance upon articles sold to the natives is very exorbitant: for example, a coarse Indian duffell blanket four dollars, whiskey, well watered, which is sold almost without restraint, in spite of the law, two dollars per gallon, and every thing else in the same proportion. Yet the Indians get no more than 25 cents for a ham of venison, a goose, or a large turkey.

On visiting a neighbouring encampment of the Chicasaws, we found many of them in a state of intoxication. They are generally well dressed, extravagantly ornamented, and, from the fairness of many of their complexions, and agreeable features, appear to have profited by their intercourse with the whites. Several of them possessed some knowledge of English, and a considerable number are making advances towards civilization. General Jackson purchased from them a tract of land, said to be of more than 300 miles extent, and bounded by Wolf river, a small stream which enters the Mississippi at the commencement of the Bluffs.[3] On the river lands I here first noticed the occurrence of *Brunichia, Quercus lyrata,* and *Carya aquatica (Juglans,* MICH.).[4]

[2]The store here referred to (not to be confused with Banjamin Foy's across the Mississippi in Arkansas) was apparently privately owned, possibly by the Colbert family (Levi, George, and William), Chickasaw mixed-bloods, who, in the period from 1793 onward, had dominated Chickasaw tribal affairs, closing the Chickasaw domain in Tennessee, Mississippi, and Alabama to white traders in 1816 through United States intervention. Whisky, by federal statute, could not be sold at government factories. CUMING, 291–92; James Wilkinson to the Secretary of War (Henry Dearborn), October 25, 1801, AM. ST. PAPERS, INDIAN AFFAIRS, I, 651–52; KAPPLER, II, 135–36; Andrew Jackson to Isaac Shelby, August 11, 1818, in JACKSON, A., II, 387; GIBSON [1], 99ff., 134–35.

[3]The Chickasaws, of the Muskhogean linguistic family (Choctaws, Chickasaws, Creeks, Seminoles, fourteen small tribes of the Chickasaw-Choctaw division of the Muskhogean family, and others), were historically a warlike group, culturally advanced. The great extent of their territorial domain (*supra*) caused them to be cultivated by French, Spanish, and, in the last decade of the eighteenth and first two decades of the nineteenth centuries, American officials. Settlement pressures in Alabama, Mississippi, and Tennessee after 1800 produced the treaties of 1805 and 1816, progressively constricting the Chickasaw land holdings, until, less than three months before Nuttall's arrival at Fort Pickering, Gen. Andrew Jackson and Isaac Shelby, treaty commissioners for the United States, negotiated on October 19, 1818, the treaty confining the tribe to northern Mississippi and an adjoining 495,936 acres in N.W. Alabama. Although the Chickasaws would be the last of the so-called Five Civilized Tribes to agree to remove across the Mississippi to Indian Territory (present Oklahoma), they finally had to yield in 1837. KAPPLER, II, 79–80, 135–37, 174–77; AM. ST. PAPERS, INDIAN AFFAIRS, II, 499.

[4]Brunichia = *Brunnichia ovata* (Walt.) Shinners, ladies'-eardrops; *Quercus lyrata*

On the 5TH we passed President island, of considerable magnitude, contiguous to which there is a rapid current. The left channel was now choked up with sand at its entrance. Here we again observed a settlement of two or three families. In the evening we came to alongside a sand-bar or willow island, at least so in high water, though now connected with the land by a dry sand-bar, like many other of the transient islands noticed in the Navigator. We, at length, began to observe a rise in the bed of the river.

6TH.] To-day we saw a few widely-scattered log-cabins along the bank, and came within 14 miles of the mouth of St. Francis.

7TH.] We proceeded by the left channel of St. Francis island, and found it very shallow and difficult, abounding with snags and bars, upon one of which lay a flat-boat aground, which had been detained here 12 days. We endeavoured to make a landing at the uppermost house of the settlement, near the mouth of the St. Francis, but found the water much too rapid; we succeeded, however, in eddy water half a mile below, but found a considerable difficulty in ascending the broken bank.

I made some enquiries respecting the Arkansa, 95 miles from hence. The Osages bear a very bad character with these hunting farmers, of whom we saw but two individuals, and one inhabited house, excepting that we had first endeavoured to make. This settlement appears to be nearly abandoned, and very undeservedly. I walked out two or three miles into the woods, and found the land considerably elevated above the reach of inundation, and of a good quality. Nearly opposite island 60, a few miles below, we were informed of the existence of hills within a quarter of a mile of the river.

How many ages may yet elapse before these luxuriant wilds of the Mississippi can enumerate a population equal to the Tartarian deserts! At present all is irksome silence and gloomy solitude, such as to inspire the mind with horror.[5]

I was greatly disappointed to meet with such a similarity in the vegetation, to that of the middle and northern states. The higher lands produce

---

Walt., overcup oak; *Carya aquatica* (Michx. f.) Nutt., water hickory. (The genus of hickories is Nuttall's.)

[5]Any inclination to associate Nuttall with popular tendencies in this the Romantic period must be dispelled by this and many subsequent observations by the author. His natural scientific zeal is often difficult to reconcile with his gloomy view of the landscape.

black ash, elm (*Ulmus americana*), hickory, walnut, maple, hackberry (*Celtis integrifolia,* no other species),[6] honey-locust, coffee-bean, &c. On the river lands, as usual, grows platanus or button-wood, upon the seeds of which flocks of screaming parrots were greedily feeding,[7] also enormous cotton-wood trees (*Populus angulisans*), commonly called yellow poplar,[8] some of them more than six feet in diameter, and occasionally festooned with the largest vines which I had ever beheld. Here grew also the holly (*Ilex opaca*), *Aplectrum hiemale,* (*Ophrys hyemale,* LIN.), *Botrychium obliquum,* and *Fumaria aurea.* Nearly all the trees throughout this country possessing a smooth bark, are loaded with misletoe (*Viscum verticillatum*).

8TH.] About a mile below the place where we spent the last night, is the settlement called the Big Prairie, consisting of three or four log-cabins, and two families, but in a state of abandonment since the shock of the earthquake, which the inhabitants assert to have produced a depression of the ordinary level, that exposed the settlement to inundation; and, in fact, by a sudden encroachment of the river, which carried off the land for more than a quarter of a mile in breadth, all the habitations, except the two now surviving, were swept into the river. About a mile and a half below commences the 60th island of the Navigator; the right channel was now choked up with sand at its outlet. A little distance below we landed at a store to purchase some necessaries. Considerable tracts of good and elevated land, once numerously peopled by the natives, appear in this quarter, over which the conspicuous devastations of a hurricane now added horror to solitude.

[6]What Nuttall saw was what he in part named, *Celtis occidentalis* L. var. *integrifolia* Nutt. To the author also belongs *C. tenuifolia* Nutt., thin-leaved.

[7]Their most favourite food in the autumn is the seeds of the cuckold bur (*Xanthium strumarium*). —NUTTALL. [The author's parrots were Carolina parakeets (*Conuropsis carolinensis ludovicianus* [Gmelin] in this range), now extinct, which were observed in large numbers by other travelers in the Mississippi Southwest before settlement encroached.]

[8]This and the species that follow were, not *Populus* angulisans, which is either an unpublished name or a slip for *P. angulata* = *P. deltoides* Marsh., the eastern cotton-wood, one common name for which is Nuttall's "yellow poplar"; *Ilex opaca* Ait., American holly; *Aplectrum hyemale* (Muhl.) Torr., one of the Orchidaceae, in which Nuttall is well represented; Ophrys hyemale L., on the other hand, is unidentifiable; *Botrychium dissectum* Spreng. var *obliquum* (Muhl.) Clute, moonwort, one of the adders'-tongue family; Fumaria aurea = *Corydalis aurea* Willd., golden corydalis of the poppy family; Viscum verticillatum = *Phoradendron serotinum* (Raf.) M. C. Johnston.

The scrub-grass or rushes, as they are called here (*Equisetum hiemale*), from about 50 to 60 miles above, to this place, appear along the banks in vast fields, and, together with the cane, which is ever-green, are considered the most important, and, indeed, the only winter fodder for all kinds of cattle. The cane is unquestionably saccharine and nutritious, but the scrub-grass produces an unfavourable action on the stomach, and scours the cattle so as to debilitate and destroy them if its use be long continued.

We proceeded, without any accident worthy of remark, about six miles, below the "Little Round island," noticed in the Navigator, which from its uncommon aspect affords a pretty good local object for the boat-men. While passing the island we were accosted by some, to us, suspicious characters, mimicking distress to draw us to land, but in vain. We had been well assured of the existence of gangs of pirates occasionally occupying these solitudes.

9TH.] We continued, as usual, soon after day-break, and were about to stop by reason of the wind, when it unexpectedly abated, so far as to prevent us, and we proceeded to the *Three Islands,* as they ought to be called for the sake of distinction, and which are not intelligible as the 62d and 63d of the Navigator. These islands lie nearly parallel, and present themselves at the commencement of a left hand bend in the river. Two of them which first appear are small willow islands, with adjoining sand-bars. The channel of the first was now dry; that of the second smooth, but apparently shallow. The principal insulated forest is crescent-formed like Flour island, or deeply and circularly indented on the right-hand side. We had proceeded past the two willow islands nearly to the principal one, when we perceived, unexpectedly, that the greater part of the river was pouring along with headlong velocity between the main and second willow island. To the left, the channel round the third island appeared broad and shallow, indeed nearly deserted by the river. We now entered the torrent almost too late for precaution, which, towards the main island, the side to which we had been inadvertently drawn, was planted full of black and fearful logs. It was only with the utmost exertion that we saved ourselves (by rowing out towards the bar) from the fate of some unfortunate boat-men, which presented itself to us with more than usual horror. This was a large flat-boat, which hung upon the trunk of an implanted tree, by which it had been perforated and instantly sunk.

We passed islands 64 and 65, and came to the shore in the bend opposite the middle of 66, which appeared to be about three miles in length. From New Madrid to this place the river appears singularly meandering, sweeping along in vast elliptic curves, some of them from six to eight miles round, and constantly presenting themselves in opposite directions. The principal current pressing against the centre of the bend, at the rate of about five miles per hour, gradually diminishes in force as it approaches the extremity of the curve. Having attained the point of promontory, the current proceeds with accumulating velocity to the opposite bank, leaving, consequently, to the eddy water, an extensive deposition in the form of a vast bed of sand, nearly destitute of vegetation, but flanked commonly by an island or peninsula of willows. These beds of sand, for the most part of the year under water, are what the boatmen term bars. The river, as it sweeps along the curve, according to its force and magnitude, produces excavations in the banks; which, consisting of friable materials, are perpetually washing away and leaving broken and perpendicular ledges, often lined with fallen trees, so as to be very dangerous to the approach of boats, which would be dashed to pieces by the velocity of the current. These slips in the banks are almost perpetual, and by the undermining of eddies often remarkable in their extent. To-day we witnessed two horrid sinkings of the bank, by each of which not less than an acre of land had fallen in a day or two ago, with all the trees and cane upon them, down to the present level of the river, a depth of 30 or 40 feet perpendicular. These masses now formed projecting points, upon which the floating drift was arrested, and over which the current broke along with more than ordinary velocity. Just after passing one of these foaming drifts, we narrowly escaped being drawn into a corresponding eddy and vortex that rushed up the stream, with a fearful violence, and from which we should not have been easily extricated. I now sufficiently saw the reason why the flat-boats were always kept out from the shore, and towards the bars which occupy the opposite side of the river.

The encroachments in the centre of the curves of the meanders, proceeding to a certain extent, at length break through and form islands, in time the islands also disappear, and so the river continually augmenting its uncontroulable dominion over the friable soil, alternately fills up one channel, and more deeply excavates or forms another, in proportion to the caprice of the current.

In regard to landing, eddy or silent water is constantly to be found beyond the point of the bends or curves of the river. The bars are also generally safe, when sufficiently high, and the water deep. In such situations, the counter current, though inconsiderable, affords also a singular facility to vessels which are ascending.

A rude cabin, which we passed to-day, was the only habitation we had seen for 30 miles.

This evening we were visited by three young men, a boy, and a squaw of the Osarks, a band of the Quapaws or Arkansa Indians. Their aspect was agreeable, their features aquiline, and their complexion comparatively fair; my first impression was that they somewhat resembled the Osages. Their errand was whiskey, and I regretted that it was not possible to satisfy them without it. They drank healths in their own language, and one of them could mumble out a little bad English. They informed me, partly by signs, that their company was about five or six families or fires, as they intimated, out on a hunting excursion. I was sorry to find that they were beggars, and that one of them proved himself to be a thief.[9]

10TH.] This morning we left the 66th island, opposite the middle of which we came to last evening, but found our situation hazardous from the sliding in of the bank around, and which might easily have involved us in difficulty. By the time we had proceeded about a mile and a half along the bend or right hand channel of 67 and 68, which lie opposite to each other, a fog sprung up, so very dense as to render our situation amidst almost unseen obstacles extremely dangerous. We had no alternative but rowing over to the bar of the island on our left, in which attempt we at length succeeded, not, however, without a risk of grounding. Here we lay until towards evening, when we proceeded to the termination of the 68th island, and made an indifferent landing. On exposing the thermometer to

---

[9]Osark = Ozark, from the French *Aux Arcs*, for Henri de Tonty's post of 1686 amidst the Ozark, i.e., Quapaw, Indians. (Arkansas Post remains, as a small village, on the Arkansas River upstream from its confluence with the Mississippi in Arkansas County.) The name *Quapaw* for these Indians precedes *Ozark* chronologically and linguistically, for *Pacaha* had been conferred upon them by De Soto's expedition, 1539–42, possibly from the Indians' own *Ugakhpa*, or "Downstream People," to distinguish them from other (upstream) members of the Dhegiha division of the Siouan linguistic group, including the Omahas, Poncas, Osages, and Kansa. Although the designation Ozark was giving way to Quapaw after 1800, Nuttall here and Henry Ker in 1816 (*Travels Through the Western Interior of the United States . . .*) were influential in the preservation of the former for some years. Cf. HODGE, II, 180, 333–36.

the air, it rose and remained at 62°. In the water it fell to 42°; the difference being 20°, which readily accounted for the dense fog that exclusively enveloped the river. This coldness of the water was no doubt occasioned by the thawing of ice in the upper part of the river, or some of its more considerable tributary streams, in consequence of which, the vapours of the moist and warm air were perpetually precipitated over it. The air, of unequal temperature, now and then felt extremely warm.

On the 11th we were again detained by the fog and heavy rain, but turned out about 10 o'clock. After proceeding opposite the commencement of the 69th island we stopped in consequence of the fog. Here, on ascending the bank, I found the woods almost impenetrably laced with green briars (*Smilax*), supple-jacks (*Œnoplia volubilis*), and the *Brunichia*, and for the first time recognised the short-podded honey-locust (*Gleditscia brachycarpa*), a distinct species, intermediate with the common kind (*G. triacanthos*), and the one-seeded locust (*G. monosperma*), differing from *G. triacanthos* in the persisting fasciculated legumes, as well as in their shortness and want of pulp.[10]

We proceeded a few miles further amidst torrents of rain, and were again obliged to land in consequence of the fog. Here we met with two hunters, who informed us of the existence of a considerable settlement on the banks of White River.[11]

The wind springing up in the evening from the northwest, the thermometer fell to 52°, and the water to 40°, from which time the dense fog that had exclusively enveloped the river began to disperse, and in the night we had a storm.

12TH.] Coming along the bend of the 71st island, we struck upon an enormous planter, or immoveable log, but again escaped without accident. About noon we landed at Mr. M'Lane's, a house of entertainment.[12] Here I was advised to proceed with my small cargo and flat-boat

[10]Of the foregoing only the following require further identification: Oenoplia volubilis is *Berchemia scandens* (Hill) K. Koch; Nuttall's "short-podded honey-locust, a distinct species," is a hybrid, ×*Gleditsia texana* Sarg., from *G. aquatica*, water locust, and *G. triacanthos*, the common honey locust; *G.* monosperma is *G. aquatica*.

[11]Saint Charles and Crockett's Bluff in N.E. Arkansas County of the present may have qualified as the sites the hunters had in mind, though, as Henry Rowe Schoolcraft, traveling at this time on the Saint Francis and White rivers, found, there were many primitive small settlements. SCHOOLCRAFT [1], 86–87 *et passim*.

[12]Neil McLane, who kept a tavern at the mouth of the White, would in 1819 become

to the port of Osark, on the Arkansa, by the bayou, which communicates between the White and Arkansa rivers, in both of which it was now conjectured there was back-water from the Mississippi. Concluding upon this measure, I hired a man at five dollars to assist me, and parted here with Mr. G—— and son, who soon, to my satisfaction, got a further passage on board a flat-boat. The idea of so soon arriving on the ground which I more immediately intended to explore, did not fail to inspire me with hope and satisfaction.

a member of the territorial legislature of Arkansas, now separated from Missouri Territory, to which it had been attached as a separate district since 1812. Arkansas Post, *infra*, was its first territorial capital.

CHAPTER VI.

Proceed up White river for the Arkansa—Suspicious conduct of one of the boatmen—Pass through the connecting bayou, and proceed up the Arkansa; its navigation; soil and surrounding scenery—A small French settlement— Extraordinary mildness of the season—Mounds—Changes in the alluvial lands produced by the agency of the river—Land speculators—Vegetation of the alluvial lands—The town or Post of Arkansas—Enormous land claims—Difficulty of navigating against the current—The Great Prairie —First settlement on the Arkansa; its present state—Agricultural advantages arising from the mildness of the climate—Storax—Aboriginal remains —The Quapaws or Arkansas—Their traditions and character.

13TH.] To-day I was detained at Mr. M'Lane's, waiting the drunken whim of the Yankee, whom necessity had obliged me to hire. In the course of a few hours he had shifted from two bargains. At first, I was to give him five dollars for his assistance, and in case that should prove inadequate, I had agreed to hire an additional hand on the Arkansa. Now he wished to have the boat for bringing her completely to the Port, and next he wanted 10 dollars!

I endeavoured to amuse myself in the neighbourhood, by a ramble through the adjoining cane-brake. Here I found abundance of the *Celtis integrifolia* (entire-leaved nettle tree) and the common and one-seeded honey-locust; also *Forrestiera acuminata* of Poiret (*Borya acuminata*, WILD.). The day was as mild and warm as the month of May, and the *Senecio laciniata*, so common along the banks of the Mississippi, already showed signs of flowering.[1]

14TH.] To-day we proceeded up White river with considerable difficulty, and hard labour, the Mississippi not being sufficiently high to

---

[1]*Celtis* integrifolia = *C. laevigata* Willd., sugar hackberry. *Forestiera acuminata* (Michx.) Poir. is swamp privet. *Senecio* laciniata, an unpublished name, could be *S. aureus* L. or *S. obovatus* Muhl., both of which occur in Arkansas.

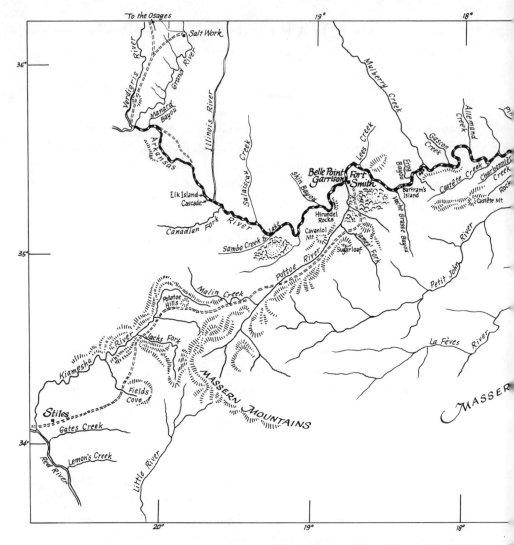

The Arkansas River, from H. S. Tanner

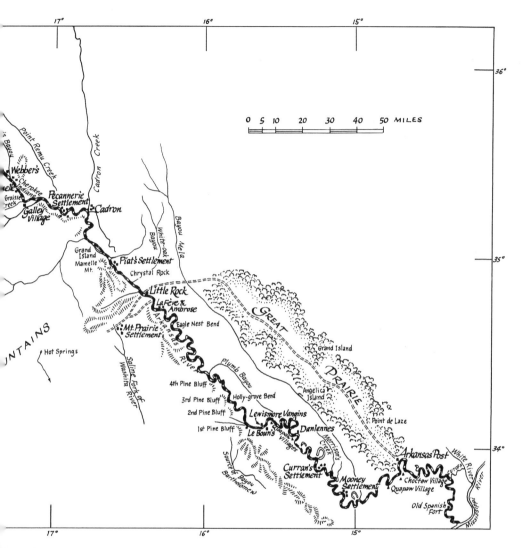

map in Nuttall's first edition, 1821

produce any eddy. The course which we made, in the two miles that we ascended, was west by north. I now found the boatman whom I had hired, one of the most worthless and drunken scoundrels imaginable; he could not be prevailed upon to do any thing but steer, while myself and the other man I had hired, were obliged to keep constantly to the oar, or the cordelle (tow-rope). In the evening we left the boat without any guard, intending to repair to it in the morning from Mr. M'Lane's, where we returned again this evening, being only three miles distant across the forest. Here I discovered that the Yankee intended to proceed to the boat in our absence and rob me, pretending some business to the mouth of the Arkansa, for which he must depart by moon-light. Unknown to him, however, and accompanied by a young man whom I had hired in his place, we repaired to the boat, waiting under arms the approach of the thief, but unable to obtain a boat, he had relinquished the attempt, and saved himself from chastisement.

In the neighbouring woods I was shewn a scandent leguminous shrub, so extremely tenacious as to afford a good substitute for ropes, and commonly employed as a boat's cable. A knot can be tied of it with ease. On examination I found it to be the plant which I have called *Wisteria speciosa (Glycine frutescens*. WILLD.) the Carolina kidney-bean tree.[2]

15TH.] We continued with hard labour ascending White river to the bayou, in a direction of west to north-west, the bayou or cut-off continuing to the south-west. In this distance, there are no settlements, the land being overflowed by the back water of the Mississippi. We passed nearly through the bayou, in which there are four points of land and a half; the current carrying us almost three miles an hour towards the Arkansa, which it entered nearly at right angles, with a rapid current, and a channel filled with snags. The length of the bayou appears to be about eight or nine miles.

16TH.] Leaving the bayou, we entered the Arkansa, which was very low, but still red and muddy from the freshets of the Canadian. Most of the larger streams which enter into it from the south, are charged with red and turbid water, while those of the north are clear. Every where I ob-

---

[2]The name of *Thrysanthus*, given by Mr9 Elliott, has been already employed for another genus. —NUTTALL. [*Wisteria* speciosa (Glycine *frutescens* Willd.) = *Wisteria frutescens* (L.) Poir. The genus, honoring Caspar Wistar, is Nuttall's.]

served the chocolate or reddish brown clay of the salt formation, deposited by the southern freshets. The Arkansa had here a very gentle current, and was scarcely more than 200 yards wide, with its meanders on a small scale, similar to those of the Mississippi. In consequence of the unrestrained dominion of the inundation, no settlements yet appeared in this quarter. We proceeded chiefly by means of the cordelle, but at a very tedious and tiresome rate, for, after the utmost exertion, with our unwieldy boat, we were this evening only six and a half miles above the outlet of the bayou.[3]

17TH.] We found the labour of towing our boat exceedingly tiresome, in consequence of the sudden falling of the river, produced by a corresponding ebb of the Mississippi. With painful exertions, and after wading more than three hours in the river, we passed only two bars in the course of the day.

18TH.] To-day we towed along two bars, much more considerable than any preceding bends, but had the disappointment to spend the night only a single mile below Madame Gordon's, the place of our destination with the boat, and only 16 miles above the bayou, by which we entered the Arkansa. This house is the first which is met with in ascending the river. Nearly opposite to the foot of the last bar but one which we passed, a vast pile of drift wood marks the outlet of a bayou, which is open in high water, and communicates with the Mississippi.

The three last bends of the river, like the four first, tending by half circles to the north-west, are each about two and three miles in circuit. As in the Mississippi, the current sets with the greatest force against the centre of the curves; the banks of which are nearly perpendicular, and subject to a perpetual state of dislocation. In such situations we frequently see brakes of cane; while, on the opposite side, a naked beach of sand, thinly strewed with succulent and maritime plants, considerably wider than the river, appears to imitate the aridity of a desert, though contrasted at a little distance by skirting groves of willows and poplars.

[3]The Arkansas River, 1,450 miles in length, rises in Lake County, Colo., above modern Leadville, flows s. then E., emerging from the mountains at Pueblo, thence E. across Colorado and Kansas to Great Bend, thereafter S.E. to Wichita, across N.E. Oklahoma and central Arkansas to the Mississippi in E. Desha County. Its largest tributaries are the Canadian, Cimarron, and Grand (or Neosho) rivers, which empty into it in Oklahoma.

No other kind of soil appears than a friable loam, and the beds of red clay, which so strongly tinge the water at particular periods of inundation. The sand of the river appears to be in perpetual motion, drifting along at the beck of the current; its instability is indeed often dangerous to the cattle that happen to venture into the river, either to drink or traverse the stream.

The land, although neglected, appears in several places, below Madame Gordon's, high enough to be susceptible of cultivation, and secure from inundation, at least for some distance from the immediate bank of the river.

No change, that I can remark, yet exists in the vegetation, and the scenery is almost destitute of every thing which is agreeable to human nature; nothing yet appears but one vast trackless wilderness of trees, a dead solemnity, where the human voice is never heard to echo, where not even ruins of the humblest kind recall its history to mind, or prove the past dominion of man. All is rude nature as it sprang into existence, still preserving its primeval type, its unreclaimed exuberance.

19TH.] This morning we had extremely hard labour, to tow the only mile which remained of our tiresome voyage. I was obliged to plunge into the water up to the waist, and there work for some time, to disengage the boat from a hidden log upon which it was held; the men I had employed, being this morning scarcely willing to wet their feet, although I had to pay them exorbitant wages.

A mile and a half from Madame Gordon's there was a settlement, consisting of four or five French families, situated upon an elevated tract of fertile land, which is occasionally insulated by the overflowings of the White and Arkansa rivers.

20TH.] To-day, and indeed for more than a week past, the weather, except being cloudy, has felt to me like May; towards mid-day the thermometer rose to 67°. The birds had commenced their melodies; and on the high and open bank of the river near to Madame Gordon's, I had already the gratification of finding flowers of the same natural family as many of the early plants of Europe; the Cruciferae; but to me they were doubly interesting, as the first fruits of a harvest never before reaped by any botanist.

In the afternoon, I walked about a mile from the river to the house of

Monsieur Tenass, an honest and industrious farmer. The crop of cotton, and of corn, here the last summer was, I understand, very indifferent, for want of rain. The first sold here, at five to six dollars per hundred weight, in the seed; and flour at 10 dollars per barrel.

The climate is said to be too warm for apples, but quite suitable for peaches. The land on which this gentleman and his neighbours resided, in tolerable independence, is very considerably elevated and open, bearing a resemblance to the lands about the Chicasaw Bluffs, and at first view, I thought I discovered a considerable hill, but it was, in fact, an enormous mound, not less than 40 feet high, situated towards the centre of a circle of other lesser mounds, and elevated platforms of earth. The usual vestiges of earthenware, and weapons of hornstone flint, are here also met with, scattered over the surrounding soil.[4]

In any other direction from this settlement, the lands are totally overflowed in freshets as far as the Mississippi. On this side of the Arkansa, the floods cover the whole intermediate space to White river, a distance of 30 miles. Within this tract, cultivation can never take place without recourse to the same industry, which has redeemed Holland from the ocean. The singular caprice of the river, as it accidentally seeks its way to the sea, meandering through its alluvial valley, is truly remarkable. The variation of its channel is almost incredible, and the action which it exercises over the destiny of the soil, can scarcely be conceived. After pursuing a given course for many ages, and slowly encroaching, it has, at length, in many instances cut through an isthmus, and thus abandoned perhaps a

[4]This mound site, evidently consisting of a central temple mound surrounded by grave mounds, like Menard Mound four miles up the Arkansas from its confluence with its bayou connection with the White, is representative of the Middle Mississippian culture (A.D. 1300–1700). Prehistoric remains, as yet unworked archaeologically in Nuttall's time, were abundant from the mouth of the Arkansas to a point near that stream course at Spiro, in eastern Oklahoma, perhaps the richest find of all. The Arkansas drainage sites, perhaps of Muskhogean origin (of which Creek, Choctaw, and Chickasaw Indians are modern representatives), could have resulted from the northward spread of Marksville culture of Louisiana (A.D. 900–1300), later by Deasonville and Coles Creek cultures (A.D. 1300–1500), not unmixed however with Caddoan culture s. of the Arkansas River, along the Red. Cf. Clarence Bloomfield Moore, *Certain Mounds of Arkansas and Mississippi: Part 1, Mounds and Cemeteries of the Lower Arkansas River* (Philadelphia, P.C. Stockhausen, Printer, 1908); Cyrus Thomas, *Report on the Mound Explorations of the Bureau of American Ethnology*, Bureau of American Ethnology, *12th Annual Report*, 1890–91 (Washington, D.C., 1894); M. R. Harrington, *Certain Caddo Sites in Arkansas* (New York, Museum of the American Indian, Heye Foundation, 1920).

course of six or eight miles, in which the water stagnating, at length becomes totally insulated, and thus presents a lagoon or lake. One of these insulated channels, termed a lake, commences about two miles from hence, and approaches within four miles of the Arkansas or the Post of Osark, affording a much nearer communication than the present course of the river.

Towards evening, two keel boats came in sight, one of which was deeply loaded with whiskey and flour; the other, a small boat fitted out by a general Calamees and his brother, two elderly men out on a land speculation, who intended to ascend the river as far as the Cadron, which is 300 miles from hence by water, or to the Fort, which is 350 miles further. I perceived that they noted down every particular which came to their knowledge, but appeared to be illiterate men, and of course, I found them incapable of appreciating the value of science. On application, they merely condescended to offer me a passage, provided I would find my own provision, and work as a boatman. Such was the encouragement, which I at length wrung from these generous speculators; not, I dare say, exploring the Missouri territory with the same philanthropic views as the generous Birkbeck.[5]

21ST.] About 12 o'clock, the thermometer was again at 67°. In the course of the forenoon, I took a solitary ramble down the bank of the river, and found along its shelving border, where the sun obtained free access, abundance of the *Mimosa glandulosa* of Michaux; also *Polypremum procumbens, Diodia virginica, Verbena nodiflora,* LIN. *Eclipta erecta,* MICH. *Poa stricta, Panicum capillaceum, Poa reptans* as usual in vast profusion, and *Capraria multifida.* The trees and shrubs are chiefly the Pecan, *(Carya olivoeformis) C. aquatica;* the black walnut, *(Juglans nigra),* but very rare; *Fraxinus quadrangulata, Liquidamber* and *Platanus,* but rarely large or full grown; also *Celtis integrifolia;* the swamp oak *(Quercus aquatica),* nearly sempervirent, the red oak *(Q. rubra),* the scarlet oak *(Q. coccinea),* Spanish oak *(Q. falcata); Populus angulisans,* the cotton wood, of greater magnitude than any other tree in this country, with the wood yellowish, like that of the Tulip tree, answering the pur-

[5]Lewis or Louis Calame, who had been successively a private and a sergeant, 1809–12, in the U.S. Army, and an ensign, third lieutenant, and second lieutenant in the War of 1812, was probably the "general" here referred to. HEITMAN and POWELL both unravel the riddle. For Birkbeck, see Chapter III, note 7.

pose of fence rails, and being tolerably durable. The smaller white poplar *(P. monilifera)*, never so large as the preceding, commonly growing in groves like the willows, and presenting a bark which is white and even. Different kinds of honey locust, as the common species *Gleditscia triacanthos*, the one-seeded *G. monosperma*, and the short podded *G. brachyloba*. There is no sugar-maple, as I understand, nearer than the upper parts of the St. Francis and White river.[6]

The alluvial soil is here sandy and light; by no means luxuriant, except on the very margin of the river. We no where see such enormous trees as those which so frequently occur along the banks of the Ohio; this, however, may in part be occasioned by the instability of the soil, from whence they are occasionally swept at no very distant intervals. The tulip tree *(Lyriodendron tulipifera)*, which attains the acme of its perfection and magnitude in Kentucky, is not met with on the banks of the Arkansa.

In consequence of the many saline streams which fall into this river, its waters are frequently found to be almost impotable.

22D.] The path, which I this morning pursued to the Post, now town of Arkansas,[7] passed through remarkably contrasted situations and soil. After leaving the small circumscribed and elevated portion of settled lands already noticed, and over which were scattered a number of aboriginal

[6]The foregoing species are Mimosa glandulosa Michx. = *Desmanthus illinoensis* (Michx.) MacM., prickle weed; *Polypremum procumbens* L., a small annual/perennial of the Loganiaceae; *Diodia virginiana* L., buttonweed; Verbena *nodiflora* (L.) = *Lippia nodiflora* (L.) Michx., fog fruit; *Eclipta erecta* Michx. = *E. alba* (L.) Hassk., one of the composites; *Poa* stricta = *Windsoria stricta* Nutt. = *Tridens strictus* Nash; *Panicum* capillaceum = *P. capillare* L., old witchgrass; *Poa reptans* Michx. = *Eragrostis reptans* (Michx.) Nees, now placed by some in a monotypic genus *Neeragrostis reptans* (Michx.) Nicora., creeping love grass; *Capraria multifida* = *Leucospora multifida* (Michx.) Nutt., of the Scrophulariaceae; *Carya* olivoeformis = C. *illinoiensis* (Wang.) K. Koch; *Carya aquatica* (Michx. f.) Nutt., bitter pecan; *Fraxinus quadrangulata* Michx., four-angled, or blue, ash; *Liquidambar styraciflua* L., sweet gum; *Platanus occidentalis* L., sycamore; *Celtis* integrifolia = C. *laevigata* Willd., sugar hackberry; *Quercus aquatica* = *Q. nigra* L. (not *Q. nuttallii* E. J. Palmer); skipping to *Populus angulisans*, we have either *P. heterophylla* L., swamp cottonwood, or *P. deltoides* Bartr. (Marsh. in T. and G.), the so-called eastern cottonwood; *P.* monilifera Ait. = *P. deltoides* Bartr.; the locusts, previously identified, need only *Gleditsia* brachyloba, which may be *G. texana* Sarg. Nuttall's tentative information on the maples *Acer saccharum* Marsh. and *A. nigrum* Michx. f., neither with a natural range in Arkansas but present on the Saint Francis and White rivers in Missouri, was correct; *Acer saccharinum* L., however, is found in the upper three-fourths of the state.

[7]Arkansas Post dated from 1686, when Henri de Tonty, La Salle's lieutenant, built a small fort a few miles above the mouth of the Arkansas River, Poste aux Arkansas, now

mounds, I entered upon an oak swamp, which, by the marks on the trees, appeared to be usually inundated, in the course of the summer, four to six feet by the back water of the river. The species are principally *Quercus lyrata, Q. macrocarpa* (the over-cup Oak);[8] *Q. phellos* (the willow oak); *Q. falcata* (the Spanish oak); and *Q. palustris* (the swamp oak); with some red and scarlet, as well as black and post oak on the knolls, or more elevated parts. In this swamp, I also observed the *Nyssa aquatica, N. pubescens* (Ogechee lime, the fruit being prepared as a conserve), as well as *N. biflora,*[9] and *Gleditscia monosperma.* After crossing this horrid morass, a delightful tract of high ground again occurs, over which the floods had never yet prevailed; here the fields of the French settlers were already of a vivid green, and the birds were singing from every bush, more particularly the red bird (*Loxia cardinalis*),[10] and the blue sparrow (*Motacilla sialis*).[11] The ground appeared perfectly whitened with the *Alyssum bidentatum.*[12] The *Viola bicolor,*[13] the *Myosurus minimus*[14] of Europe, (probably introduced by the French settlers) and the *Houstonia serpyllifolia* of Michaux, (*H. patens* of Mr. Elliott)[15] with bright blue flowers, were also

---

twice removed to a point 55 miles upstream. The French continued to garrison it and the Jesuits to minister to its soldiers and French settlers nearby in the eighteenth century, as reflected in *Jesuit Relations and Allied Documents* (ed. by Reuben Gold Thwaites), to 1763. The post was almost if not quite pivotal in the Mississippi River frontier between New Orleans (founded 1718) and Fort de Chartres in the Illinois Country. Under the Spanish regime, 1764–1800, it remained so, as reflected in Spanish colonial documents (*Papeles de Cuba*), under its new names, Fort Carlos III and Fort Estevan. It was garrisoned by the United States in 1804 as Fort Madison, with the Louisiana Purchase, and between 1805 and 1810 had a government factory for the Indian trade. Fortescue Cuming noted in 1808 "a good settlement of French, Americans, and Spaniards" (*Sketches of a Tour to the Western Country,* 272). At the time of Nuttall's visit it was about to become the territorial capital of Arkansas (March 2, 1819). David W. Parker, *Calendar of Papers in Washington Archives Relating to the Territories of the United States.* . . .

[8]*Quercus macrocarpa* Michx., mossy-cup oak, or bur oak.

[9]*Nyssa aquatica* L., water tupelo; *N. pubescens* is unpublished, but Ogeechee lime is *N. ogeche* Marsh., and it and *N. biflora* Bartr. are without an Arkansas range. What Nuttall saw was *N. sylvatica* Marsh., black tupelo, or sour gum, and the var. *dilatata* Fern.

[10]Now *Richmondina cardinalis* (Linnaeus).

[11]Motacilla *sialis* = *Sialia sialis sialis* (Linnaeus), bluebird.

[12]An unpublished name, *Alyssum bidentatum* = *Draba brachycarpa* Nutt., a small annual herb of the Cruciferae, mustard family.

[13]*Viola* bicolor = *V. emarginata* (Nutt.) Le Conte, blue violet.

[14]*Myosurus minimus* L., mousetail.

[15]*Houstonia serpyllifolia* Michx., thyme-leaved bluet, which does not have an Arkan-

already in bloom. After emerging out of the swamp, in which I found it necessary to wade about ankle deep, a prairie came into view, with scattering houses spreading over a narrow and elevated tract for about three miles parallel to the bend of the river.

On arriving, I waited on Monsieur Bougie, one of the earliest settlers and principal inhabitants of the place, to whom I was introduced by letter. I soon found in him a gentleman, though disguised at this time in the garb of a Canadian boatman. He treated me with great politeness and respect, and, from the first interview, appeared to take a generous and active interest in my favour. Monsieur B. was by birth a Canadian, and, though 70 years of age, possessed almost the vigour and agility of youth. This settlement owes much to his enterprise and industry.[16]

The town, or rather settlement of the Post of Arkansas, was somewhat dispersed over a prairie, nearly as elevated as that of the Chicasaw Bluffs, and containing in all between 30 and 40 houses. The merchants, then transacting nearly all the business of the Arkansa and White river, were Messrs. Braham and Drope, Mr. Lewis, and Monsieur Notrebe, who kept well-assorted stores of merchandize, supplied chiefly from New Orleans, with the exception of some heavy articles of domestic manufacture obtained from Pittsburgh. Mr. Drope, to whom I was also introduced by letter, received me with politeness, and I could not but now for awhile consider myself as once more introduced into the circle of civilization.[17]

---

sas range, here makes Nuttall's second choice, *H. patens.* Ell., small bluet, more probable.

[16]Joseph Bogy *père* was baptized at Beauport (Quebec), Canada, April 13, 1752. He could have been 70 at Nuttall's first meeting with him, and may well have been if his baptism had been deferred. Like other historical figures he was "never young nor old," for at 20 (if Nuttall's estimate of his age is correct), he was carrying messages from Spanish officials at Arkansas Post to those at Saint Louis, in 1769. But his Spanish Louisiana homeland seems to have been Kaskaskia, Ill., where he was married to Marie Louise Duguay Du Plassy on August 18, 1778, and where Joseph *fils* was born to them April 24, 1782. In all, there would be six Joseph Bogys and one Louis Vital Bogy, born to Joseph *fils* and Marie Beauvais Bogy, who would become U.S. senator from Missouri.

Bogy was already well established as a trader at Arkansas Post by 1786. Later he became secretary to Juan Ventura Morales, the Spanish intendant for Upper Louisiana. He was one of the "expert" appraisers, from long residence in the Arkansas Post area, when Captain Francisco Casa y Luengo inventoried the post proper preparatory to turning it over to Lieut. Joseph B. Many for the United States, March 23, 1804. From 1808 he was a partner with Hewes Scull trading up the Arkansas River. Anton J. Pregaldin to Savoie Lottinville, March 24, 1976; HOUCK [1], II, 216–17; BILLON [2], 50; SCHARF, I, 1491–92; Scull and Bogy Letterbook, microfilm, Bizzell Memorial Library.

The improvement and settlement of this place proceeded slowly, owing, in some measure, as I am informed, to the uncertain titles of the neighbouring lands. Several enormous Spanish grants remained still undecided; that of Messrs. Winters, of Natchez, called for no less than one million of acres, but the congress of the United States, inclined to put in force a kind of agrarian law against such monopolizers, had laid them, as I was told, under the stipulation of settling upon this immense tract a certain number of families.[18]

The cotton produced in this neighbourhood, of a quality no way inferior to that of Red river, obtained this year from six to six and a half dollars per cwt. in the seed, and there were now two gins established for its preparation, though, like every thing else, in this infant settlement of the

[17]"Braham" could have been Jacob Barkman, who had been trading at Arkansas Post and New Orleans since 1812. He became postmaster of Clark, Clark County, in 1819. Farrar Newberry, "Jacob Barkman," *Arkansas Historical Quarterly*, Vol. XIX, No. 4 (Winter, 1960), 314ff.

Eli J. Lewis, postmaster at Arkansas Post from July 5, 1817, to June 2, 1830, was clerk of Arkansas County and magistrate as well, 1819–27. He died as postmaster of Helena in 1833. TERR. PAPERS, XIX, 155.

Frederick Notrebe, late of the Napoleonic armies and more recently a merchant of New Orleans, was described in Nuttall's time as "opulent" for his brick house and store at Arkansas Post. He would win in November, 1819, at the end of Nuttall's Arkansas River sojourn, election to the Territorial Legislative Council, and in 1820 appointment as a common pleas judge. TERR. PAPERS, XIX, 24, 118, 385, 400.

William Drope, businessman at Arkansas Post, would be active in November, 1819, in petitioning Congress for a mail route serving the territorial capital. He was unfortunate in purchasing the buildings of the U.S. Trading Factory to the Cherokees at Spadre Bayou at its closing in 1823, losing them in a recapture by the Indian Office because the sale was unauthorised. TERR. PAPERS, XIX, 35, 528; XX, 388–90, 501–502.

[18]The Winters grant on the Arkansas of one million arpents (1 arpent = 0.75 acre), more or less, made in 1797 by Baron Francisco Luis Hector de Carondelet, Spanish governor of Louisiana, to Elisha Winters and his sons William and Gabriel, was being pressed for confirmation within a year of the transfer of Louisiana to the United States. But in 1807, Congress limited grants antedating the Louisiana Purchase to two thousand acres. The Commissioners of Land Claims continued to investigate the claim to 1834, and it was finally disallowed in 1848. *House Journal*, 23 Cong., 1 sess., 372; TERR. PAPERS, XIV, 463–64; XIX, 114–15, 233, 401. Other Spanish grants were to Don Carlos Villemont, 14,000 arpents in 1795 at Point Chicot; to Baron de Bastrop, twelve leagues square on the Ouachita; to the Marquis de Grande Maison, 100,000 acres adjoining the Bastrop grant, subsequently transferred to Daniel Clark. TERR. PAPERS, XV, 179–80; IX, 408, 414, 468–69, 512. Cf. acts: March 2, 1805 (2 STAT. 324–29); April 21, 1806 (2 STAT. 391–96); March 3, 1807 (2 STAT. 440–42), together with relevant lower court and Supreme Court decisions.

poor and improvident, but little attention beyond that of absolute necessity, was as yet paid to any branch of agriculture. Nature has here done so much, and man so little, that we are yet totally unable to appreciate the value and resources of the soil. Amongst other kinds of grain, rice has been tried on a small scale and found to answer every expectation. The price of this grain, brought from New Orleans, was no less than 25 to 37½ cents per lb. by retail. Under the influence of a climate mild as the south of Europe, and a soil equal to that of Kentucky, wealth will ere long flow, no doubt, to the banks of the Arkansa.

I again made application to the land speculators, trying to prevail upon them on any terms, to take up my baggage, as far as the Cadron, which would have enabled me immediately to proceed on my journey, across the great prairie, but they remained inexorable.[19]

23D.] To-day, I returned to Madame Gordon's, which, though only six miles distant by land, is not less than 15 by water. I was now obliged more deeply to wade through the enswamped forests, which surround the habitable prairie lands, in consequence of the late rain. In these ponds, I am told, the Proteus or Syren is occasionally met with. There are also alligators, though by no means numerous.

24TH.] This morning I again proceeded up the river with my flat boat, by the assistance of two French boatmen, full of talk, and, at first, but indifferently inclined to work; we succeeded, however, by night, to get to the third of the five sand-bars or bends, which intervene between this place and the village of Arkansas. The following day in the evening, after a good deal of hard labour and wading, on my part, and that of the negro in my employ, we arrived at Monsieur Bougie's, and the next day I parted

---

[19]Missouri and Arkansas territories in 1819 were feverish with speculation in public lands being offered at auction to citizens and as bounties offered by lottery to soldiers in the War of 1812 holding entitlements by warrant. The traffic in warrants, bought up by speculators, was considerable. Two million acres of military bounty lands were made available by the Act of 1811 for the Louisiana Territory, to which Arkansas was then attached. The Arkansas share lay between the Saint Francis and Arkansas rivers. Not even the ongoing depression, induced by the Bank of the United States's constriction of credit in the summer of 1818, halted the land excitement. Wrote Timothy Flint (*Recollections of the Last Ten Years*, 145–46), "Land-claims, settlement-rights, preemption rights, Spanish grants, confirmed claims, unconfirmed claims, and New Madrid claims . . . made up the burden of the song in all social meetings." Cf. Malcolm J. Rohrbough, *The Land Office Business: The Settlement and Administration of American Public Lands, 1789–1837*, 71–142.

with a sort of regret from the boat, which, with all its difficulties, had afforded me, through the most inclement season of the year, no inconsiderable degree of comfort and convenience.

On the 26th, I proceeded with my baggage and property to the village in Monsieur Bougie's perogue, accompanied by one boatman. Near to the town, we grounded on the inner side of a recent, and still augmenting bar, and, after falling a little back, we crossed over, but here the current would not permit us to advance with the oars. The shore was high, and the water too deep for poles, so that we had again to attempt the side we had left; here, in drifting with velocity again on the bar, our fickle boat or canoe was so near overturning, notwithstanding our exertions, that, for a moment I considered every thing as lost; getting out, however, into the water, we with some difficulty set the perogue afloat, and for safety dragged her along, up to our waists in water. The sand was here so moveable, as to bury our feet at every step. We at length succeeded, and came to shore, under a bank 100 feet high, without any kind of practicable landing for merchandise, that of last year being now choked up with moving sand.

In the meanest garb of a working boatman, and unattended by a single slave, I was no doubt considered, as I had probably been by the land speculators, one of the canaille, and I neither claimed nor expected attention; my thoughts centered upon other objects, and all pride of appearance I willingly sacrificed to promote with frugality and industry the objects of my mission.

An insignificant village, containing three stores, destitute even of a hatter, a shoe-maker, and a taylor, and containing about 20 houses, after an existence of near a century, scarcely deserved geographical notice, and will never probably flatter the industry of the French emigrants, whose habits, at least those of the Canadians, are generally opposed to improvement and regular industry. During my stay, I took up my residence with Dr. M'Kay, and found in him an intelligent and agreeable companion; but such is the nationality of these ignorant people, that French quackery has hitherto been preferred to the advice of a regular physician. Blanket capeaus, mocassins, and overalls of the same materials, are here, as in Canada, the prevailing dress, and men and women commonly wear a handkerchief on the head in place of hats and bonnets.

28TH.] This morning I accompanied the doctor to shoot wild geese, as they passed to a neighbouring lake, about two miles in the rear of the town. Here a vast prairie opens to view, like a shorn desert, but well covered with grass and herbaceous plants. Over this vast plain, which proceeds a little to the west of north, computed to be not less than 30 leagues in length, by 10 to 15 in breadth, passes the road to the Cadron, and the settlements of Red river.

Among other plants already in flower in these natural meadows, we saw abundance of a new and fragrant species of *Allium* with greenish-white flowers, and destitute of the characteristic odour of the genus in common with *A. fragrans*, to which it is allied.[20] The *Houstonia serpyllifolia* and *Claytonia caroliniana*[21] were also in full bloom at this early season.

February 3D.] This afternoon I walked to Mr. Mosely's, six miles distant by land, and 15 by water. The prairie, in consequence of the late rains, appeared almost one continued sheet of water. I observed springing up, the *Eryngium aquaticum*, occasionally employed as a medicine by the inhabitants, acting as a diuretic, and in larger doses proving almost emetic.[22] Crossing the prairie, which is bordered with settlements, we entered the alluvial forest, containing oak, hickory, box elder (*Acer negundo*), elm, &c. nearer the river cotton-wood appears as usual. I saw here a prickly-ash (*Zanthoxylion Clava Herculis*),[23] the size of an ordinary ash, but the same species as that of the southern states, and the bark proving equally efficacious for allaying the tooth-ache.

The first attempt at settlement on the banks of the Arkansa, was begun a few miles below the bayou which communicates with White river. An extraordinary inundation occasioned the removal of the garrison to the borders of the lagoon near Madame Gordon's, and, again disturbed by an overflow, they at length chose the present site of Arkansas. The first band of hunters who attempted to reside here, were, it is said, obliged to remove, in consequence of the swarms of rats, with which they found the

[20]*Allium* = *Nothoscordum bivalve* (L.) Britt., false garlic.
[21]*Claytonia caroliniana* Michx., out of range; perhaps better *C. virginica* L., spring beauty, or its wide-leaved phase, *C. virginica* forma *robusta* (Somes) Palm. and Steyerm.
[22]*Eryngium aquaticum* L., eryngo, of the Atlantic Coast. What he saw was *E. yuccifolium* Michx., rattlesnake master, button snakeroot.
[23]*Zanthoxylum Clava-Herculis* L., southern prickly ash.

country infested. These animals, which are native, differ specifically from the European species, are much larger, and commit the most serious depredations.[24]

The poverty of the land in the immediate vicinity of this place, will probably operate as a perpetual barrier to its extension. The encroachments of the river upon the precipitous and friable bank in front of the town, and the enlargement of the ravines by which it is intersected, renders the site altogether precarious, and prevents the practicability of any thing like a convenient landing for merchandise. During the period of high water, however, the adjoining bayou, or channel of communication with a neighbouring lake, affords this convenience.

The love of amusements, here, as in most of the French colonies, is carried to extravagance, particularly gambling, and dancing parties or balls. But the sum of general industry is, as yet, totally insufficient for the support of any thing like a town.

The houses, commonly surrounded with open galleries, destitute of glass windows, and perforated with numerous doors, are well enough suited for a summer shelter, but totally destitute of comfort in the winter. Without mechanics, domestic conveniences and articles of dress were badly supplied at the most expensive rate. Provision produced in the country, such as beef and pork, did not exceed six cents per pound; but potatoes, onions, apples, flour, spirits, wine, and almost every other necessary article of diet, were imported at an enormous price, into a country which ought to possess every article of the kind for exportation to New Orleans. Such is the evil which may always be anticipated by forcing a town, like a garrison, into being, previous to the existence of necessary supplies. With a little industry, surely every person in possession of slaves might have, at least, a kitchen garden! but these Canadian descendants, so long nurtured amidst savages, have become strangers to civilized comforts and regular industry. They must, however, in time give way to the introduction of more enterprising inhabitants.

The enormous claim of Messrs. Winters, containing about a million

[24]North America has its share of Cricetid rodents, but the rats here described probably were European introductions, Old World Murids—*Rattus norvegicus*, of which there are several subspecies, here seemingly *R. norvegicus norvegicus* (Berkenhout), or one of the subspecies of the black rat, *R. ratus ratus* (Linnaeus), with a normal southern range favoring the latter, smaller species. HALL AND KELSON, 768–69.

of acres of this territory, and which will yet probably for some time remain undetermined, proves a considerable bar to the progress of the settlement. Besides a great portion of the neighbouring prairie, it embraces much of the finest land on the northern border of the river, and continues for near one hundred miles along its bank.

The great prairie of which we have already spoken, said to be 90 miles in length, contains an invaluable body of land, and, where sufficiently drained, which is pretty generally the case, except during the rains of winter, would produce most species of grain in abundance. As a pasture it is truly inexhaustible, though in the hottest months of summer occasionally deprived of water.[25]

The cattle throughout this country are generally left to provide for themselves, and suffered to range at large, excepting such as are in domestic use. That they may not become entirely irreclaimable, they are now and then enticed to come up to the fold by a handful of salt, or a few ears of corn. No hay is provided for fodder, nor does it indeed appear necessary, except to assist in fattening for the stall, but this piece of economy, like almost every thing else which might promise comfort, is neglected, and the cattle are killed just as they are hunted up from the prairie or the cane-brake. It is from the prevalence of the cane, and the shave-rush (*Equisetum hiemale*), that the cattle are kept in tolerable condition, and often even fat, through the severest part of the winter. Indeed, at this early, but perhaps uncommonly advanced season of the year (not yet the middle of February), there was already a few inches of green herbage, and only one night during this month have I seen any ice. The thermometer, towards noon, rises to $70°$, and the peach and plum-trees, almost equally naturalized, have nearly finished blooming. The fig, however, unprotected by the shelter of a wall, though sufficiently vigorous, appears every year to die down nearly to the ground. Grapes succeed so as to promise wine, but without the advantage of cellars it soon becomes subjected to the acetous fermentation.

The sweet gum tree (*Liquidambar styraciflua*), which produces no resin

[25]Timothy Flint visited Arkansas Post and the Grand Prairie a few weeks later, in May, 1819. His impressions of the latter resemble Nuttall's, upon whom he may have drawn for his own book, not published until 1826. Part of the Grand Prairie would be devoted to rice farming, with modern Stuttgart representing the industry. FLINT, 191–92.

in the northern states, where it is equally indigenous, here, as in Mexico and the Levant, exudes the odoriferous Storax of the shops.

As to the breed of domestic animals, no selection of those commonly raised has yet been attended to, nor any foreign ones introduced from parallel climates, so as to afford us any idea of the resources and conveniences which might here be brought into existence. The horned cattle increase and fatten without any labour or attention, more than the trouble of occasionally ascertaining their existence in the wilderness through which they are at liberty to roam without limit. It is in consequence of this unrestrained liberty, and the advantage of a perpetual supply of food, that the horse has become already naturalized in the southern parts of this territory, and the adjoining province of Spain. By this means, however, the domestic breed has been, in some respects considerably deteriorated; the horses of this country are rather small, though very hardy, and capable of subsisting entirely upon cane or grass, even when subjected to the hardest labour. They were commonly sold from 30 to 50 and 100 dollars a piece, though paid for in the depreciated currency of the country, bearing a discount of from 10 to 20 per cent.

The singular temperature and general mildness of this climate, which may be presumed from a cursory inspection of its flora and agriculture, and then again the occurrence of considerable frosts in the winter, are circumstances which justly excite astonishment when we survey the same parallels of latitude in the transatlantic regions. Here, in the latitude of the Cape of Good Hope, in that of Sidon, and even south of Candia and Cyprus, with its groves of myrtle, near to the latitude of Madeira, and in that of the empire of Morocco, we find the fig annually levelled to the ground by frosts. Not even the low palmetto (*Sabal minor*) indigenous, consequently no prospect of naturalizing the date, so common in the same parallels of Africa; no olive, nor any well-grounded prospect of its success; wines, for which Madeira has so long been celebrated (at least any of superior quality), appear also proscribed from this part of America. No evergreens of any description, except the holly, appear throughout the dreary forests. The north-western winds, sweeping over the arctic deserts of eternal winter, have extended the temperature of northern Europe over all the regions of the United States, nearly to the very limits of the tropic. The climate of Arkansas, scarcely elevated more than 5 or 600 feet above the level of the sea, is not more ardent and less temperate than that of the south of France.

For several miles in and round the town, the accumulation of low mounds or Indian graves, scattered with those fragments of pots, which were either interred or left on the graves with offers of food, by the affectionate friends of the deceased, mark the ancient residence of the natives. In one of the tumuli, on the bank towards the bayou, intersected by the falling away of the earth, a pot of this kind, still employed by the Chicasaws and other natives for boiling their victuals, had fallen out of the grave, and did not appear to be of very ancient interment. Whether these monuments had been the slow accumulation of natural and casual mortality, or the sad remains of some overwhelming destruction, was now impossible to determine. From the ashes of fires, and fragments of charcoal, besides the accompaniment of many indestructible weapons, utensils, and pots broken into fragments by force, I suspect that these mounds are merely incidental, arising from the demolition of the circular dwelling in which the deceased had been interred, a custom which was formerly practised by the Natchez,[26] Cherokees, and other of the natives. Indeed, the sacrifices and offerings which the Indians formerly made to the manes of the deceased father, were sometimes almost ruinous to his family, though no longer blackened by the immolation of human victims. Father Charlevoix relates, that stopping, as he descended the Mississippi, at a village of Ouyapes (or Wyapes), the same with the Quapaws (or, as they call themselves, O-guah-pas), then living near the confluence of White river with the Mississippi, he found them in great distress from the ravages of the small-pox. Their burying-place appeared "like a forest of poles and posts newly set up, and on which there hung all

[26]The Natchez, of the Muskhogean linguistic group, which consisted of the Creeks, Choctaws, Chickasaws, Seminoles, and a number of other tribes, speaking related though distinct dialects, were in the main a sedentary people living historically on Saint Catherine's Creek, east and south of present Natchez, Mississippi. The Taensas lived nearby but the linguistic relationships with the Natchez are now unknown. Their neighbors, the Chitimachas, were not related linguistically.

Fort Rosalie, built in their midst on the E. bank of the Mississippi at modern Natchez in 1716 by the French, became both an irritant to them and a pretext by the French for their removal. The Natchez massacred the French garrison and its commander, Sieur de Chopart; nearly seven hundred Frenchmen lost their lives. Between 1729 and 1731 the French nearly annihilated the Natchez. LE PAGE [1], III, 231–62.

manner of things: there is every thing which the savages use." The men and women both continued lamenting throughout the night, and repeating without ceasing, "*Nihahani*, as the Illinois do, and in the same tone." A mother weeping over the grave of her son, poured upon it a great quantity of Sagamitty (or hominy). Another kindled a fire near one of the tombs, probably for the purpose of sacrificing food, as I have seen practised by the Pawnee-Rikasrees of the Missouri.[27]

The aborigines of this territory, now commonly called Arkansas or Quapaws and Osarks, do not at this time number more than about 200 warriors. They were first discovered about the year 1685, by Chevalier de Tonti.[28] From what source Father Charlevoix ascertains that they were very numerous in the time of Ferdinand de Soto, I am unable to learn. In the abridged relation of this expedition by Purchas, I cannot possibly discover any thing relating to them.[29] The people of Quigaute must have occupied a country not far from the Arkansa, and are said by La Vega to

[27]Charlevoix's Historical Journal, p. 307, London Edition. —NUTTALL. [Pierre F. X. de Charlevoix, S.J., earlier a teacher at College Louis-le-Grand, Paris, whom Voltaire the student had found "a bit on the talkative side," published *Histoire et description générale de la Nouvelle France* . . ., 3 vols. (Paris, Nyon fils, 1744), and with it (Vol. 3) his direct observations in *Le Journal historique d'un voyage fait par l'ordre du roi dans l'Amérique Septentrionale* for the period 1720–22, describing the Arkansas (Quapaw) Indians, much as Bénard de La Harpe was doing at the same time (Pierre Margry, *Découvertes et établissments des Français dans l'ouest et dans le sud de l'Amérique Septentrionale, 1614–1754*, 6 vols., VI, 365). Nuttall's "Pawnee-Rickasrees of the Missouri" are the Arikaras, whom he had encountered on the Upper Missouri with the Astoria party of 1811. They, the Pawnees of the Platte and Loup rivers of Nebraska, the Wichitas of Kansas, the Kichai of Trinity River, Texas, the Caddos of Red River, and the Kadohadachos of E. Texas were all linguistically related as Caddoans.]

[28]For the Quapaws encountered by the De Soto expedition, see footnotes 6 and 9 in Chapter IV of the present work. The Capaha of Garcilasco de la Vega's account and the Pacaha of the Gentleman of Elvas' were the Quapaws. One hundred and forty-one years later, on March 13 and 14, 1682, Henri de Tonty witnessed his superior's, René Robert Cavelier, Sieur de La Salle's, ceremony on the Arkansas River, raising a cross in the center of the principal Quapaw town of that time. MARGRY, II, 181. Four years later, in 1686, Tonty, searching for the lost La Salle, was again at the mouth of the Arkansas, establishing Post aux Arkansas above it.

[29]Samuel Purchas (1575–1626), the English cleric and friend and successor to Hakluyt in the compilation and publication of voyages and explorations, was a native of Essex, from which, on his own admission, he had not ventured farther than two hundred miles. Contrary to Nuttall's statement, Purchas did include De Soto evidence concerning the Pacaha, or Quapaws, and the Casqui, or Kaskaskias (later of the Illinois Confederacy), enemies of the former, noting repeatedly the large numbers of the Quapaws in 1541. Purchas, *Hakluytus Posthumus, or Purchas his pilgrimes* (reprinted from the original of 1625 by MacLehose & Sons, Glasgow, 1906, 20 vols.), Vol. 18, pp. 25–33. For

have been numerous and powerful, but that they were the same people as the Arkansas or O-guah-pas, seems by no means probable. From their own tradition it does not appear that they were visited by the whites previous to the arrival of La Salle; they, that many years had elapsed before they had any interview with the whites, whom they had only heard of from their neighbours.

In a council held with the Quapaws some years ago, concerning the boundaries of the lands which they claimed, a very old chieftain related to the agent, that at a very remote period his nation had descended the Mississippi, and after having proceeded in one body to the entrance of a large and muddy river (the Missouri), they had there divided, one party continuing down the Mississippi, and the other up the miry river. The descending band were checked in their progress by the Kaskaskias, whose opposition they at length subdued. In their further descent they were harassed by the Chicasaws and Choctaws, and waged war with them for some considerable time, but, at length, overcoming all opposition, they obtained the banks of the Arkansa, where they have remained ever since. Some of them, reverting apparently to the period of creation, say, that they originally emerged out of the water, but made many long and circuitous journeys upon that element, previous to their arrival on the banks of this river.

As their language scarcely differs from that of the Osages, Kanzas, Mahas, and Poncas of the Missouri, it is presumable that these sprung from the band which ascended the Missouri. They say, they remained separated from a knowledge of each other for many years, until mutually discovered on a hunting party, taking each other at first for enemies, till assured to the contrary by both uttering the same language.

They bear an unexceptionally mild character, both amongst the French and Americans, having always abstained, as they say, from offering any injury to the whites. Indeed, to do them justice, and to prove this opinion concerning them is no modern prejudice, I cannot do less than quote the testimony of Du Pratz, made about a century ago. Speaking of the Arkansa territory, he adds, "I am so prepossessed in favour of this country, that I persuade myself the beauty of the climate has a great influence on

an informed critical estimate of Purchas, see E. G. R. Taylor, "Samuel Purchase," *Geographical Journal*, LXXV, 536–39 (1930).

the character of the inhabitants, who are at the same time very gentle, and very brave. They have ever had an inviolable friendship for the French, uninfluenced thereto, either by fear or views of interest; and live with them as brethren, rather than as neighbours."[30] They say, that in consequence of their mildness and love of peace, they have been overlooked by the Americans; that they are ready enough to conciliate by presents those who are in danger of becoming their enemies, but neglect those who are their unchangeable friends.

The complexion of the Quapaws, like that of the Choctaws and Creeks, is dark, and destitute of any thing like the cupreous tinge. The symmetry of their features, mostly aquiline, often amounts to beauty, but they are not to be compared in this respect to the Osages, at least those of them which now remain. Charlevoix says, "The Arkansas (as he calls them) are reckoned to be the tallest and best shaped of all the savages of this continent, and they are called, by way of distinction, *the fine men.*"[31] I question, however, whether this epithet is not similar to that of the Illinois, and the Llenilenape, or "original and genuine men," as it is translated, of the Delawares. The name of Akansa or Arkansa, if ever generally assumed by the natives of this territory, is now, I am persuaded, scarcely ever employed; they generally call themselves O-guah-pa or Osark, from which last epithet, in all probability, has been derived the name of the river and its people; indeed, I have heard old French residents in this country, term it Riviere des Arks or d'Osark.

They employ artificial means to eradicate that pubescence from their bodies, which is, indeed, naturally scanty. The angle of the eye is usually elongated, but never turned up exteriorly, as it is said, in common with the Tartars, by Humboldt, to be the case with the Mexicans.

[30]Best known for his *Histoire de la Louisiane* (Paris, 1758), Simor Le Page du Pratz was also witness to much of the history he wrote, as one of the some eight hundred men who came out to the French colony in John Law's West India Company, beginning in 1718, staying on for the next eighteen years.

[31]Beaux Hommes for the Quapaws in Charlevoix became "Handsome Men" in Thomas Jefferys, *The Natural and Civil History of the French Dominions in North and South America*, Parts I and II (London, 1761), I, 144. Beaux Hommes was applied by the French also to the Siksikas or Blackfeet, of the Algonquian linguistic group. The half-dozen Algonquian tribes in the Illinois Confederacy were not similarly designated by the French or the English. But the Delawares, most important of the Algonquian stock, called themselves Lenape ("real men") or Leni-Lenape ("native, genuine men"). Nuttall's Llenilenape is unique in the synonymy. HODGE, I, 385–86.

Although they may be said to be taciturn, compared with Frenchmen, their passions are not difficult to excite.

As hunters, they are industrious, but pay little attention to agriculture; and pleased by intercourse with the whites, they are not unwilling to engage as boatmen and hunters.

About a century ago, father Charlevoix describes the Arkansas as occupying four villages; that which he visited was situated on the bank of the Mississippi, in a little meadow, which was (in 1819) M'Lane's landing, the only contiguous spot free from inundation. The people called Akansas by this author, were then made up of the confederated remnants of ruined tribes. The villages which he visited, called themselves Ouyapes, evidently the O-guah-pa. On the Arkansa, six miles from the landing, there was a second village, consisting of the Torimas and Topingas. Six miles higher were the Sothouis, and a little further was the village of the Kappas; these are again the same people as the Quapaws or O-guah-pas.[32]

In the time of Du Pratz, the Arkansas had all retired up the river of this name, and were living about twelve miles from the entrance of White river. They were still said to be pretty considerable in numbers, and had been joined by the Kappas, the Michigamias,[33] and a part of the Illinois. He likewise remarks, that they were no less distinguished as warriors than hunters, and that they had succeeded in intimidating the restless and warlike Chicasaws.[34] Indeed, the valour and the friendship of the Arkansas is still gratefully remembered by the Canadians and their descendants, and it is much to be regretted that they are making such evident approaches towards total destruction. The brave manner in which they opposed the Chicasaws, has long ensured them the quiet possession of their present country. Among the most perfidious Indians, is the story which has been

[32]Torimas, better Tourimas = Quapaws and the name of their specific village, which apparently had not shifted since the early eighteenth century. Topingas = Tongigua, residents of the small Quapaw village Tongigua, placed by Joutel on the E. bank of the Mississippi River in 1687, at or above modern Rosedale, Miss. MARGRY, III, 457. Sothouis = Uzutiuhi, again a Quapaw band. JEFFERYS, I, 134. Kappas (Quapaws) here probably trace to Le Page du Pratz's Kapas. Nuttall's original notes, *infra*, "Charlevoix, Hist. p. 306. Lond. Ed."

[33]The Michigameas, first visited by Father Marquette in 1673, possibly at Big Lake, between the Mississippi and Saint Francis rivers, west of present Blytheville, Mississippi County, Ark., were the most southerly tribe of the Illinois Confederacy.

[34]Du Pratz, Hist. Louisiana, p. 318. —NUTTALL.

related to me by major Lewismore Vaugin,[35] one of the most respectable residents in this territory. The Chicasaws, instead of standing their ground, were retreating before the Quapaws, whom they had descried at a distance, in consequence of the want of ammunition. The latter understanding the occasion, were determined to obviate the excuse, whether real or pretended, and desired the Chicasaws to land on an adjoining sand-beach of the Mississippi, giving them the unexpected promise of supplying them with powder for the contest. The chief of the Quapaws then ordered all his men to empty their powder-horns into a blanket, after which, he divided the whole with a spoon, and gave the half to the Chicasaws. They then proceeded to the combat, which terminated in the killing of 10 Chicasaws, and the loss of five prisoners, with the death of a single Quapaw.

I am informed, that it is a custom of the Quapaws, after firing the first volley, to throw aside their guns, and make a charge with their tomahawks.

The treacherous Osages, to whom they are naturally allied by the ties of consanguinity, at one period claimed the assistance of the Quapaws, with the secret intention of betraying them to destruction. Arriving near the scene of action, and discovering, as was said, the encampment of the supposed enemy, the Osages parted from their friends, under pretence of ambuscading the enemy. Their conduct, however guarded, had not, it seems, been sufficient to remove the suspicions of the wary leader of the Quapaws, who now concerted measures of security. The Quapaws made their fires as usual, but secretly left them, in order to watch the motions of the Osages, who, as it had been suspected, crept up to their encampment in the dead of night, and fired a volley near the fires, not doubting but they had destroyed those who had seemingly confided in their friendship. But at this instant, the Quapaws, sufficiently prepared, arose from their concealment, and exercised a just chastisement on the traitors.

The social regulations, as well as the superstitions and ideas of the

[35]Although the Vaugines appear in Arkansas history from the Spanish period (1764–1800), the "Major Lewismore Vaugin" of Nuttall's account remains a puzzle. But François Vaugine of Arkansas Post was appointed major of militia for the District of Arkansas by Gen. James Wilkinson, governor and commander-in-chief of Louisiana Territory, July 14, 1806. He had been justice of the peace and in 1814 would become county judge. TERR. PAPERS, XIII, 540, 544–49; XIV, 795; XXI, 76, 82.

supernatural entertained by the Quapaws, are no way materially distinct from those which are practised by their eastern and northern neighbours. The most simple testimonies of attachment, without the aid of solemn vows, are thought sufficient to complete a conjugal felicity, which, where all are equal, in wealth and property, can only be instigated through the desire of personal gratification or mutual attachment, and can but seldom be attended with that coldness and disgust, which is but too common, where this sacred tie is knit by avarice. Neither is this contract controlled by any unnatural and overruling policy. The obligation to decorum and the essential ties of society are not abandoned by the Indian, in consequence of his being freed from that perpetual restraint, which appears to have been requisite in civilized society. The father can recall his daughter from the habitation of one who has rendered himself odious to his child. The husband can abandon the wife who has made herself obnoxious to his house and family. They are only united by the bonds of mutual esteem and reciprocal friendship; they will, of course, endeavour to deserve it of each other, as affording a gratification to themselves, no less than to their parents and relatives.

As the marriage is never ostentatious, or strictly ceremonious, so its disavowal, when not induced by any thing flagrant, is not a matter to alarm the repose of society. The male children go with the father, the females attend upon the mother. Children, however begotten, are dear to a society ever on the brink of extermination.

That any ceremonies, more than the celebration of a frugal and sober feast, are constantly practised by any of the natives of this country, is much more than can be satisfactorily proved. Among the Quapaws, I have been informed, that the husband, on the consummation of his marriage, presents his wife with the leg of a deer, and she, in return, offers him an ear of maize, both of which are so many symbols of that provision against the calls of necessity, which they are mutually accustomed to provide.[36]

The young and unmarried women of the Quapaws, according to a custom equally prevalent among many other tribes of Indians, wear their

---

[36]A ceremony similar to this, was also, according to Adair, practised among the Creeks. —NUTTALL. [James Adair, *The History of the American Indians* (London, 1775).]

hair braided up into two parts, brought round to either ear in a cylindric form, and decorated with beads, wampum, or silver. After marriage these locks are all unfolded, the decorations laid aside for her daughters, and her hair, brought together behind in a single lock, becomes no longer an assiduous object of ornament. According to the History of the Costume of all Nations, this manner of braiding the hair appears to have been equally prevalent among the women of Siberia, Tartary, Turkey, and China. As an expression of the greatest grief and misfortune, anciently practised by many other nations of the world, I have, amongst the aborigines of the Missouri, not unfrequently seen both men and women shave away their hair. It is not, however, I believe, practised by the Indians of the Mississippi, nor among the Quapaws or Osages.

The ideas of supernatural agency, entertained by the Arkansas, are very similar to those which prevail among the natives of the Missouri. Every family, for example, chooses its *penates*, or guardian spirit, from among those various objects of creation which are remarkable for thier sagacity, their utility, or power. Some will perhaps choose a snake, a buffaloe, an owl, or a raven; and many of them venerate the eagle to that degree, that if one of those birds should happen to be killed during any expedition, the whole party immediately return home. The large feathers of the war-eagle, which they consider talismanic, are sometimes distributed throughout the nation, as sacred presents, which are expected to act as sovereign charms to those who wear them.

The cure of diseases, though sometimes attempted with rational applications, is not unfrequently sought, among the Quapaws, and many other natives of the continent, in charms and jugglery.

As to the future state, in which they are firm believers, their ideas are merely deduced from what they see around them. Their heaven for hunters is at least as rational as that of some of our own fanatics.

For some considerable time after the interment of a warrior and hunter, his grave is frequented with provision, which, if still remaining, after a reasonable lapse of time, is considered as a sure presage that the deceased has arrived at a bountiful hunting ground, and needs no further supply from the earth.

The Quapaws, though no greater proficients in music than the rest of the Indians, have, however, songs appropriated to love, to death, and to battle, but which are merely so many simultaneous effusions of the heart, accompanied by rude and characteristic airs and dances.

It is hardly necessary to detail the dress of the Arkansas, which scarcely, to my view, in any respect, differs from that of the Delawares, Shawnees, or Chipeways. Its component parts are, as usual, mocasins for the feet; leggings which cover the leg and thigh; a breech-cloth; an overall or hunting shirt, seamed up, and slipped over the head; all of which articles are made of leather, softly dressed by means of fat and oily substances, and often rendered more durable by the smoke with which they are purposely inbued. The ears and nose are adorned with pendents and the men, as among many other Indian tribes, and after the manner of the Chinese, carefully cut away the hair of the head, except a lock on the crown, which is plaited and ornamented with rings, wampum, and feathers. Many of them, in imitation of the Canadian French, wear handkerchiefs around their heads, but in the manner of a turban. Some have also acquired the habit of wearing printed calicoe shirts next to the skin.

The younger Indians, as I am informed, notwithstanding the neglect of renewing their dress, are so partial to cleanliness of the skin, that they practice bathing both winter and summer.[37]

[37]Cf. J. Owen Dorsey, "Omaha Sociology," U.S. Bureau of American Ethnology, *Third Annual Report,* 1881–82, 205–370.

CHAPTER VII.

————

Departure from Arkansas—Indian villages—Mooney's settlement—Curran's settlement—Interview with the Quapaw chief—The Pine Bluffs—Soil, climate, and productions—The Little Rock—Roads—Mountains—Vegetation—The Mamelle—Cadron settlement—Tumuli—Soil and climate —Pecannerie settlement—Mountains—Cherokees—The Magazine mountain—Dardanelle settlement—Manners and customs of the Cherokees— Their war with the Osages.

From Arkansas to the Cadron, a distance of about 300 miles by water, I now understood there existed a considerable line of settlements along the north border of the river, and that the greatest uninhabited interval did not exceed 30 miles. Though the spring was premature, and the weather still subject to uncomfortable vicissitudes, the want of society and of employment induced me to embrace the earliest opportunity of continuing my journey into the interior of the territory, where I hoped to find additional employment and gratification in my researches connected with natural history. For this purpose I again embarked on the river in a large skiff, which was proceeding to the Baird's-town settlement;[1] but as most of our company were fond of whiskey, the only beverage in the country, except water or milk, it was difficult to get them parted from their companions and conversation; however, after many efforts to make a start, we at last got off, though merely to make one or two miles, so as to be disengaged, at any rate, for the morning. Our encampment was a sand-bar or beach, skirted by willows, and though in itself a situation by no means interesting, yet far from disagreeable to him who can enjoy the simple fare of the hunter, and the calm and unsullied pleasures of nature.

On the following day (February the 27th) we proceeded about 21

[1]Beards Town appears on early Arkansas maps west of Little Meto Creek and opposite a village no longer on maps, Heckatoo. It was upstream thirty-five miles from Arkansas Post.

miles, or seven points up the river, and in some places against a current of considerable velocity, which had been augmented by a southern freshet, communicating a muddiness and chocolate-brown colour to the stream. In the evening, to avoid the attacks of musquitoes, we again chose a sand-beach for our place of encampment.

In the course of the day we passed the outlet of the bayou, or rather river, Meta,[2] which diagonally traverses the Great Prairie, also two Indian villages on the south bank, which continues to be the Quapaw line as far as the Little Rock. The first was the periodical residence of a handful of Choctaws, the other was occupied by the Quapaws. On this side of the river there appeared to be considerable bodies of very fertile land elevated above inundation.

The peach-trees, now in bloom, were considerably disseminated beyond the immediate precincts of the Indian villages, and seemed to be almost naturalized, but, in common even with the wild fruits of the country, they are occasionally robbed of fruit by the occurrence of unseasonable frosts.

On the 28th, after ascending about 13 miles, we arrived at the settlement begun by colonel Mooney,[3] consisting of three or four families. I was here very hospitably entertained by Mr. Davison. Near this house, and about 200 yards from the river, there was a fine lake of clear water, of considerable extent, communicating with the river by a bayou, which enters a few miles below. Its bed appeared to be firm and sandy. The neighbouring land was of a superior quality, either for corn or cotton, but all conditionally held on the uncertain claim of Messrs. Winters. Notwithstanding the extent of inundated lands, the climate was considered

---

[2]Bayou Meto, flowing s.e., enters the Arkansas below the town of Bayou Meto. The bayou, first large tributary to the Arkansas, forms the boundary between Arkansas and Jefferson counties.

[3]Daniel Mooney, prominent at Arkansas Post, which was now within days of becoming the territorial capital of Arkansas, had come to the area soon after the Louisiana Purchase. He was appointed sheriff, census taker, and successively captain, major, and lieutenant colonel of militia, respectively by Louisiana Territorial Governors Meriwether Lewis and Benjamin Howard and by Missouri Territorial Governor William Clark between 1808 and 1817. (Arkansas was part of Louisiana Territory to 1812, and of Missouri Territory thereafter to 1819, when it achieved its own territorial status.) TERR. PAPERS, XIV, 430, 472, 528, 545, 795; XV, 277; BATES, II, 25–28, 143–44, 200, 237, 281, 289.

unusually healthy, and the soil, with but little labour, capable of insuring a comfortable independence to the cultivator.

March 1st.] This morning a slight white frost was visible, though, yesterday and the day before, thermometer rose, at noon, to 70°, and the Red-bud (*Cercis canadensis*) was commonly in flower. We proceeded about 10 miles, and encamped opposite to an island; the water now falling as rapidly as it had risen. Leaving the boat, and walking through the woods, I was surprised to find myself inadvertently at the Quapaw village we had passed yesterday, situated upon a small prairie, constituting the isthmus of a tongue of land, which, six or seven miles round, was here scarcely half a mile across. Endeavouring now to obtain a nearer route to the river, than that of returning by the path, I found myself in a horrid cane-brake, interlaced with brambles, through which I had to make my way as it were by inches. The delay I thus experienced created alarm among my companions, who fired three guns to direct me to the spot where they waited, and where I soon arrived, pretty well tired of my excursion.

2d.] A slight frost appeared again this morning. We proceeded slowly, passing in the course of the day three points of land, one of which was about six miles, the others three each, and in the evening encamped a mile below Morrison's bayou.[4] Nearly opposite to this stream there was another village of the Quapaws, containing about 15 cabins, and called, by the French, ville de Grand Barbe, from their late chief, who, contrary to the Indian custom, wore a long beard.[5] It stands on the edge of the forest, surrounded by good land, and elevated above the overflows.

3d.] To-day we arrived at Curran's settlement,[6] consisting of six families, who had chosen for their residence a body of very superior land. From 1000 to 1500 pounds of cotton have been produced upon the acre,

[4]Possibly named for Moses Morrison, one of the early residents of Arkansas Post.

[5]This and the preceding Quapaw village and others that follow are identifiable largely, sometimes only from Nuttall's account. Much the same can be said of the wide-spaced clusters of white cabins, which have now entirely disappeared. Timothy Flint, who visited many of them and preached at Arkansas Post in 1819, compared their inhabitants adversely with Missouri settlers, who, in his view, were less "rough and untamed." *Recollections of the Last Ten Years . . .*, 194.

[6]Named for one or both members of the Currin family, Lemuel, named coroner, and James, township judge, for Arkansas County by Missouri Territorial Governor William Clark, October 1, 1814. TERR. PAPERS, XIII, 795.

and of a staple no way inferior to that of Red river. As to maize, it is as luxuriant as possible. But what most recommended this settlement, in my estimation, was the unequivocal appearance of health and plenty. We landed for the night nearly opposite what is called the Old River, four miles above Curran's, an elliptic curve of the river, 11 miles in circuit, cut off at the isthmus in the course of a single night, as was witnessed by a French trader encamped on the spot, who fled in terror from the scene of devastation. On the borders of this bend, now become a lake, and which explains the origin of similar bodies of water along this river, there were three families now settled.[7]

4TH.] The middle of the day, and early part of the afternoon, felt warm and sultry as summer. About noon I arrived at the cabin of Mr. Joseph Kirkendale, four miles above the cut-off in the river, where I tasted nearly the first milk and butter which I had seen since my arrival on the banks of the Arkansa. This farm, like those below on Old River, was situated upon a small and insulated prairie or open and elevated meadow, about 15 miles from the Great Prairie. The drought which was experienced last summer throughout this territory, proved, in many places, nearly fatal to the crops of corn and cotton, so that the inhabitants were now under the necessity of importing maize for provision, at the rate of one dollar and a quarter per bushel.

At Mr. Kirkendale's, I had an interview with the principal chief of the Quapaws, who landed here on his way down the river. His name, to me unintelligible, was Ha-kat-ton (or the *dry man*).[8] He was not the hereditary chief, but received his appointment as such, in consequence of the infancy of the children of the Grand Barbe. His appearance and deportment were agreeable and prepossessing, his features aquiline and symmet-

[7]At present Lake Dick in Jefferson County. Actually, the lake is an oxbow as a cutoff from the Arkansas.

[8]Ha-kat-ton, The Dry Man, appears often as a signatory and a chief of the Quapaws in treaties with the United States: as Krakaton in the Treaty of August 24, 1818, at Saint Louis, ceding the major part of the Quapaw lands in Arkansas to the United States; as Hackehton in the Treaty of August 15, 1824, at Harrington's, Ark., ceding the remainder of the Quapaw lands in Arkansas; as Kackatton in the Treaty of May 13, 1833, at an unnamed site, relinquishing the Quapaw lands occupied in the Caddo country s. of Red River and relocating the tribe between the Senecas and the Shawnees in Kansas; as Heckatoa in the Treaty of Camp Holmes, Indian Territory, August 24, 1835, pledging friendship and peace with the Plains Comanches and Wichitas. KAPPLER, II, 160–61, 211, 435, 962.

rical. Being told that I had journeyed a great distance, almost from the borders of the great lake of salt water, to see the country of the Arkansa, and observing the attention paid to me by my hospitable friend, he, in his turn, showed me every possible civility, returned to his canoe, put on his uniform coat, and brought with him a roll of writing, which he unfolded with great care, and gave it me to read. This instrument was a treaty of the late cession and purchase of lands from the Quapaws, made the last autumn, and accompanied by a survey of the specified country. The lines of this claim, now conceded for the trifling sum of 4000 dollars in hand, and an annuity of a thousand dollars worth of goods, pass up White river, until a south line intersects the Canadian river of Arkansa, then continuing along the course of this river to its sources, afterwards down Red river to the great Raft, and thence in a north-east direction to point Chicot, on the Mississippi, and so in a north-west line to the place of commencement, near White river. Their reservation (situated exclusively on the south bank of the Arkansa) commences at the post or town of Arkansas, and continues up that river to the Little Rock, thence in a southern direction to the Washita, which continues to be the boundary, to a line intersecting the place of commencement.[9] To this deed were added the names of no less than 13 chiefs. This tract contains probably more than 60,000 square miles. Such are the negociating conquests of the American republic, made almost without the expense of either blood or treasure!

Hakatton informed us, that he had lately returned from the garrison, where, in concert with a fellow chief and the commander, they had succeeded in rescuing from bondage some unfortunate prisoners and females of the Caddoes, of whom about 15 or 20 had been killed by the Osages.

[9]The Quapaw copy of the treaty, which Nuttall had before him, described the cession as "beginning at the mouth of the Arkansas river; thence extending up the Arkansas, to the Canadian fork, and up the Canadian fork to its source; thence south, to Big Red river, and down the middle of that river, to the Big Raft; thence, a direct line, so as to strike the Mississippi river, thirty leagues in a straight line, below the mouth of the Arkansas; together with all their claims to land east of the Mississippi and north of the Arkansas river, excepting a point opposite the Post of Arkansas running a due southwest course to the Washita [Ouachita] river; thence up the latter to Saline fork, and up Saline fork to a point from whence a due north course would strike the Arkansas river at the Little Rock; and thence down the right bank of the Arkansas to the place of beginning." The latter description became the Quapaw reservation to 1824. But here and in Nuttall's description, the "Washita" must be understood as the Ouachita of Arkansas, not the Washita of present Oklahoma. KAPPLER, II, 160–61.

The former reside on the banks of Red river, into whose territory the Osages occasionally carry their depredations. This chief warned me from trusting myself alone amongst the Osages, who, if they spared my life, would, in all probability, as they had often done to the hunters, strip me naked, and leave me to perish for want. But in his nation, he took a pride in assuring me, if I was found destitute, I should be relieved to the best of their ability, and conducted, if lost, to the shelter of their habitations, where the stranger was always welcome. His late journey to the seat of government, appeared to have inspired him with exalted ideas of the wealth and power of civilized society.[10]

To my inquiries, respecting the reputed origin of the O-guah-pas, he answered candidly, that he was ignorant of the subject; and that the same question had been put to him at St. Louis, by governor Clarke.

[10]Ha-kat-ton's warnings about the Osages, his Siouan cousins, reflect the then current tensions on the Indian frontier S.W. of Saint Louis. Three thousand Osages under Clermont and Ka-Zhi-Ci-Grah, or Makes-Tracks-Far-Away, had been induced by Pierre Chouteau, of Saint Louis, to move from Osage River when the Chouteaus lost their Osage monopoly to Manuel Lisa in 1802, in favor of a site on the Verdigris River above the Three Forks (the Arkansas, Verdigris, and Grand, or Neosho). Here they soon found themselves in conflict with the Caddos on and south of Red River, westward migrating Choctaws and Cherokees, and Kansa and other Plains tribes north of them. The Grand and Little Osages remaining on Osage River signed a treaty in 1808 with Gen. William Clark ceding most of their Missouri and Arkansas lands and accepting resettlement in an area consisting of all of present Oklahoma lying north of the Arkansas and Canadian rivers. This done, the Osages on the Verdigris, called Cheniers (of the Oaks) by the French and Arkansas Osages by Americans (from the stream, not the future territory and state), soon knew of the coming of a Cherokee advance party from east of the Mississippi and the appearance of Choctaws from the S.E., followed in 1817 by a large tide of Cherokees into what is now Arkansas, part of the old Osage hunting domain. The year 1817 also saw the establishment of Hugh Glenn's trading post at Three Forks, a friendly competitor with the Chouteau enterprise. By 1820 it was estimated that some scores of Anglo-American and French-speaking fur gatherers were working out of the Three Forks.

The always vague western limits of the Louisiana Purchase were finally defined less than two weeks before Nuttall's meeting with Ha-kat-ton, in the Adams-Onís Treaty of February 22, 1819. The long-pending removal of Indians from east of the Mississippi to Arkansas Territory and the Osage lands west of the present Arkansas-Oklahoma border was about to begin.

Zebulon Montgomery Pike, "Dissertation on Louisiana," in *The Journals of Zebulon Montgomery Pike, with Letters and Related Documents*, ed. by Donald Jackson, 2 vols., II, 19–42, contains an excellent contemporary view of the Osages. See also Thomas Jefferson to Albert Gallatin, July 12, 1804, and Jefferson to Robert Smith, July 13, 1804, in *Letters of the Lewis and Clark Expedition, with Related Documents, 1783–1854*, ed. by Donald Jackson, 199–200 n.; TERR. PAPERS, XV, 378; John Joseph Mathews, *The Osages*, 341 ff.

This morning I observed the wife of the chief, preparing for her family a breakfast from the nuts of the Cyamus (or Nelumbium).[11] They are first steeped in water, and parched in sand, to extricate the kernals, which are afterwards mixed with fat, and made into a palatable soup. The tubers of the root, somewhat resembling batatas or sweet potatoes, when well boiled, are but little inferior to a farinaceous potatoe, and are penetrated internally and longitudinally, with from five to eight cavities or cells.

5TH.] We were again visited by the Quapaw chief, who appeared to be very sensible and intelligent, though much too fond of whiskey. I took an opportunity to inquire of him, whether the Quapaws considered smoking as in any way connected with their religion, to which he answered, that they merely regarded it as a private gratification or luxury; but that the Osages smoked to God, or to the sun, and accompanied it by a short apostrophe: as, "Great Spirit, deign to smoke with me, as a friend! fire and earth, smoke with me, and assist me to destroy mine enemies, the Caddoes, Pawnees, Mahas, &c.! my dogs and horses, smoke also with me!"

Among the most remarkable superstitious ceremonies practised by the Quapaws, is that which I now found corroborated by Hakatton. Before commencing the corn-planting, a lean dog is selected by the squaws, as a sacrifice to the Indian Ceres, and is, with terrific yells and distorted features, devoured alive. This barbarous ceremony, which we derided, he assured us gravely, was conducive to the success of the ensuing crop. After the harvest of the maize, and subsequent to the Green-corn Dance, they have also a succession of dances and feasts, which they support like our Christmas mummers, by going round and soliciting contributions.

The Quapaws are indeed slaves to superstition, and many of them live in continual fear of the operations of supernatural agencies.[12]

---

[11]Not Calamus (*Acorus Calamus* L.), the *maka[n]-ninida* of the Omahas, according to J. Owen Dorsey, "Omaha Sociology," in Bureau of American Ethnology, *Third Annual Report* (1885), 308; but possibly *Nelumbo lutea* (Willd.) Pers., water chinquapin, pond nut.

[12]For the Dhegiha Siouans, specifically the Omahas and comparatively the others of the group, including the Quapaws, see DORSEY [1], 211 ff. Nuttall was touching upon what became, under anthropological investigation, a complex structure of customs and religion.

On the 7th, we proceeded to Mr. Morrison's, [13] a few miles distant, but did not accomplish it until the succeeding morning, in consequence of the prevalence of a violent storm from the south-west.

On the 8th, I remained at Mr. Morrison's farm, agreeably situated on a small prairie, contiguous to the river, surrounded with an extensive body of good land, continuing a considerable distance from the bank. These small prairies often appear to have been the sites of ancient Indian stations.

A number of Quapaw canoes passed down the river, and several drunken Indians, accompanied by Paspatoo, their chief, now 75 years of age, were straggling about in quest of whiskey, which if not *prohibited*, would, in all probability, be less plentifully supplied.

The adjoining forest was already adorned with flowers, like the month of May in the middle states. The woods, which had been overrun by fire in autumn, were strewed in almost exclusive profusion with the *Ranunculus marilandicus*, [14] in full bloom, affording with other herbage, already an abundant pasture for the cattle. Towards evening, Mr. Drope, with his large and commodious trading boat of 25 tons burthen, passed this place on his way to the garrison, with whom I was to embark on the following morning.

9TH.] I walked about four miles to Mr. Dardennes', [15] where there were two families residing on the bank of the river, which is agreeably elevated, and here I had the satisfaction of joining Mr. Drope. Lands of the same fertile quality as that on the border of the river, extend here from it for eight miles without interruption, and free from inundation. The claim of Winters' still continues up to an island nearly opposite Mr.

[13]"Mr. Morrison" may be Moses Morrison, mentioned in note 4 *ante*, but William Morrison (1763–1837), a Pennsylvanian who came out to Kaskaskia after 1790 to form the trading partnership with his uncle Guy Bryan known as Bryan and Morrison, was joined later by his brothers Robert, James, Jesse, Samuel, and Guy. His operations in the fur and mercantile trades extended from Prairie du Chien, Wis., to New Orleans, and from the Rocky Mountains to Pittsburgh. One of the Morrisons may have had the farm here visited. BILLON [2], 219–21; LeRoy R. Hafen, "New Light on LaLande, First American in Colorado," *Colorado Magazine*, 24 (1947), 194–97.

[14]*Ranunculus marilandicus* Poir., = *R. hispidus* Michx. var *marilandicus* (Poir.) Benson, crowfoot or buttercup; *R. micranthus* Nutt. is the tiny-flowered species.

[15]Toussaint Dardenne was married at Fort de Chartres, the French post near Kaskaskia, Ill., in 1747. His son Jean Baptiste had a Spanish grant on the north bank of the Arkansas. HOUCK [2], II, 97–98.

Lewismore's,[16] but the survey of all this land, now ordered by Congress, seems to imply the annihilation of this claim, which for the benefit of the settlement ought promptly to be decided.

Four miles above Dardennes', commences the first gravel-bar, accompanied by very rapid water.

10TH.] We now passed Mr. Mason's,[17] 18 miles above Dardennes', where likewise exists an extensive body of rich and dry land, along the borders of Plum bayou. We encamped at the upper point of the sand-beach, about three miles above Mason's, on the margin of a small and elevated prairie, which, from the abundance of Chicasaw plum bushes forming a grove, I fancied might have been an ancient aboriginal station. The day was exceedingly wet, accompanied with thunder, which had continued with but little intermission since the preceding night.

11TH.] Passed Mr. Embree's,[18] and arrived at Mr. Lewismore's. Six miles above, we also saw two Indian villages, opposite each of those settlements. The land is here generally elevated above the inundation, and of a superior quality; the upper stratum a dark-coloured loam, rich in vegetable matter.

The Indians, unfortunately, are here, as usual, both poor and indolent, and alive to wants which they have not the power of gratifying. The younger ones are extremely foppish in their dress; covered with feathers, blazing calicoes, scarlet blankets, and silver pendents. Their houses, sufficiently convenient with their habits, are oblong square, and without any other furniture than baskets and benches, spread with skins for the purpose of rest and repose. The fire, as usual, is in the middle of the hut, which is constructed of strips of bark and cane, with doors also of the latter split and plaited together.

[16]"Lewismore" here evidently refers to Major Lewismore Vaugine, the son of François Vaugine, who held a Louisiana-Missouri territorial militia appointment, as his father did, about whom we shall hear more from Nuttall shortly.

[17]Mason's identity is conjectural. Thomas and Edward Mason were Kaskaskia traders, contemporaries of another trader, Pierre Mason, of Sainte Genevieve and Saint Charles, Mo., during the Spanish regime. HOUCK [2], II, 65, 76. Plum Bayou mentioned immediately following parallels the Arkansas on the N.E. in Jefferson and Lonoke counties and enters the Arkansas N.E. of Pine Bluff.

[18]Moses Embree, of Arkansas County, was a petitioner at this time for the appointment of territorial judges as the territory of Arkansas came into being. His holding was on the north side (left bank) of the Arkansas, opposite the land reserved in the Quapaw treaty of 1824 to James Scull. TERR. PAPERS, XIX, 20; XX, 107; KAPPLER, II, 210–11.

The forest was already decorated with the red-bud, and a variety of humble flowers. A species of *Vitis*, called the June grape, from its ripening at that early period, was also nearly in blossom. It does not appear to exist in any of the eastern states; in leaf it somewhat resembles the *vigne des batures* (or *Vitis riparia* of Michaux), while the fruit, in the composition of its bunches, and inferior size, resembles the winter grape.[19]

We spent the evening with major Lewismore Vaugin, the son of a gentleman of noble descent, whose father formerly held a considerable post under the Spanish government.

Fifteen miles above this place, Monsieur Vaugin informed me of the remains of an aboriginal station of considerable extent, resembling a triangular fort, which the Quapaws on their first arrival in this country say, was inhabited by a people who were white, and partly civilized, but whom, at length, they conquered by stratagem. The hunters possess an opinion, by no means singular, that this embankment is of antediluvian origin.[20]

12TH.] This morning we met captain Prior and Mr. Richards, descending with cargoes of furs and peltries, collected among the Osages. The former was one of those who had accompanied Lewis and Clarke across the continent.[21] Six miles above Mr. Vaugin's, at Monsieur

[19] The infertile plant cultivated in the vicinity of the city of London, has received the name of *Vitis odoratissima*, by gardeners, an epithet which does not express any peculiar character. —NUTTALL. [What Nuttall saw in Arkansas suggests *V. riparia* var. *praecox* Engelm., June grape.]

[20] The site, described by archaeologists as the Knapp Group, sixteen miles downstream from Little Rock at the western edge of Lonoke County, consists of an embankment five to six feet high and a mile in length, enclosing an area of eighty-five acres on three sides, with Mound Lake on the fourth side. Within are fifteen mounds of varying size. SHETRONE, 358–69. For the character of prehistoric material cultures on the Arkansas River see William H. Holmes, "Illustrated Catalogue of a Portion of the Collections Made by the Bureau of Ethnology During the Field Season of 1881," Smithsonian Institution, Bureau of American Ethnology *Third Annual Report (1885)*, 468–89.

[21] Nathaniel Pryor (1775–1831), one of the "nine young men from Kentucky" enlisted for the Lewis and Clark Expedition in August, 1803, at the Falls of the Ohio (present Louisville), became a sergeant at Wood River, above Saint Louis, in 1804, as the expedition prepared to embark upon its two-year Voyage of Discovery to the Pacific. After service as an ensign in an abortive attempt at returning Shahaka, the Mandan, to the Upper Missouri in 1807, he became a trader at present Galena, Ill., but was wiped out by the Winnebagos. He served with distinction in the War of 1812, attaining a captaincy, then resumed the Indian trade from Arkansas Post with Samuel Richards and later with Hugh Glenn. His interest, however, had begun to center up the Arkansas River, at Three Forks, even before he received a license to trade with the Osages des Chênes at the end of

Michael Le Boun's,[22] commences the first appearance of a hill, in ascending the Arkansa. It is called the Bluff, and appears to be a low ridge covered with pine, similar to the Chicasaw cliffs, and affording in the broken bank of the river the same parti-coloured clays. Mr. Drope remained at the Bluff, trading the remainder of the day with the two or three metif families settled here, who are very little removed in their habits from the savages, with whose language and manners they are quite familiar. In the evening, a ball or dance was struck up betwixt them and the *engagées*. The pine land is here, as every where else, poor and unfit for cultivation. Over this elevated ground were scattered a considerable number of low mounds.

13TH.] To-day I walked along the beach with Mr. D., and found the lands generally dry and elevated, covered with cotton-wood (*Populus angulisans*), sycamore (*Platanus occidentale*), maple (*Acer dasycarpa*), elm (*Ulmus americana*), and ash (*Fraxinus sambucifolia* and *F. platicarpa*).[23] We observed several situations which appeared to have been formerly occupied by the Indians. A canoe of the Quapaws coming in sight, we prevailed on them to land, and, during the interval of our boat's arriving, I amused myself with learning some of their names for the forest trees. While thus engaged, I observed, that many of their sounds were dental and guttural, and that they could not pronounce the *th*. In the evening we came to a little above the second Pine Bluff.

14TH.] We proceeded to Mons. Bartholome's,[24] where Mr. D. stayed

---

November, 1819, eight months after Nuttall met him. He married among the Osages, opened a trading post a mile and a half above the mouth of the Verdigris, joined Hugh Glenn and Jacob Fowler, 1821–22, in an expedition to Santa Fe and the San Juans, became a subagent for the tribe, and died in 1831. D. JACKSON [2], 118, 312–13, 381 n., 642–43n., 645–46; Walter B. Douglas, "Documents, Captain Nathaniel Pryor," *American Historical Review*, Vol. XXIV, No. 2 (January, 1919), 263–65; FOWLER, 4–5.

[22]Michel Bonne, as he signed himself, was from the Quapaw Nation, suggesting a *métif*, or mixed-blood, status, with a holding on the south (right) bank of the Arkansas, at or close to present Pine Bluff, which locality is described *infra* by Nuttall. TERR. PAPERS, XIX, 756.

[23]*Populus* angulisans is here *P. deltoides* var *missouriensis* (Henry) Rehd; *Platanus occidentalis* L., sycamore; *Acer* dasycarpa (*Acer dasycarpum* Ehrh.) = *A. saccharinum* L., soft, or silver, maple; *Fraxinus sambucifolia* Lam. = *F. nigra* Marsh., black ash; *F. platycarpa* = *F. caroliniana* Mill., water ash.

[24]Louis Barthélemy, one of eleven signatories of Indian descent (Quapaw) to a petition of May 4, 1826, to Congress to quiet title to their lands on the south (right) bank of

about two hours. Mons. B. and the two or three families who are his neighbours are entirely hunters, or in fact Indians in habits, and pay no attention to the cultivation of the soil. These, with two or three families at the first Pine Bluffs, are the remains of the French hunters, whose stations have found a place in the maps of the Arkansa, and they are in all probability the descendants of those ten Frenchmen whom de Tonti left with the Arkansas, on his way up the Mississippi in the year 1685. From this place we meet with no more settlements until our arrival at the Little Rock, 12 miles below which, and about 70 from hence, by the meandering course of the river, we again meet with a house. We proceeded about eight miles from Bartholome's, and about sun-set came in sight of another pine bluff of about 100 feet elevation, and a mile in length. On the right hand bank the land appeared fertile and elevated. Near our encampment there was a small lake communicating with the river by a bayou. The horizontal beds of clay in this cliff or precipice are precisely similar to those of the Chicasaw Bluffs.

15TH.] The land appeared still, for the most part, on either bank, elevated above inundation. Some cypress clumps,[25] however, were observable on the Quapaw side. On the opposite we saw a cluster of Hollies (*Ilex opaca*), which were the first we had seen any way conspicuous along the bank of the river. The forests every where abound with wild turkeys, which at this season are beginning to be too poor for food. We came about 16 miles above the last pine bluff, and were there detained the remainder of the evening by the commencement of a strong south-west wind, which in the night veered round to the north-west. The land on the Indian side, contiguous to the river, abounded with thickets of Chicasaw plum-trees, which appear to have overgrown the sites of Indian huts and fields, but, except in a few elevated places, the first alluvial platform or terrace is subject to inundation. The second bank, where the large cane commences, is, however, free from water. The right side of the river appeared universally high, and rich cane land with occasional thickets and openings.

---

the Arkansas granted by the United States treaty with the Quapaws in 1824, was evidently the "Mons. Bartholome" Nuttall referred to. All others, except James Scull, were of French-Quapaw families of long standing, just possibly descendants of the men of Tonty's garrison at Poste aux Arcs of 1686. TERR. PAPERS, XX, 238–40.

[25]Cupressus disticha. —NUTTALL. [*Taxodium distichum* (L.) Richard, bald cypress.]

Throughout this country there certainly exists extensive bodies of fertile land, and favoured by a comparatively healthy climate. The cultivation of cotton, rice, maize, wheat, tobacco, indigo, hemp, and wine, together with the finest fruits of moderate climates, without the aid of artificial soils or manures, all sufficiently contiguous to a market, are important inducements to industry and enterprize. The peach of Persia is already naturalized through the forests of Arkansa, and the spontaneous mulberry points out the convenience of raising silk. Pasturage at all seasons of the year is so abundant, that some of our domestic animals might become naturalized, as in Paraguay and Mexico; indeed several wild horses were seen and taken in these forests during the preceding year.

The territory watered by the Arkansa is scarcely less fertile than Kentucky, and it owes its luxuriance to the same source of alluvial deposition. Many places will admit of a condensed population. The climate is no less healthy, and at the same time favourable to productions more valuable and saleable. The privations of an infant settlement are already beginning to disappear, grist and saw-mills, now commenced, only wait for support; and the want of good roads is scarcely felt in a level country meandered by rivers. Those who have large and growing families can always find lucrative employment in a country which produces cotton. The wages of labourers were from 12 to 15 dollars per month and boarding, which could not then be considered as extravagant, while cotton produced from five to six dollars per hundred weight in the seed, and each acre from 1000 to 1500 pounds.

16TH.] At sunrise the thermometer was down to 28°, and the wind at north-west. This sudden transition, after such a long continuance of mild weather, felt extremely disagreeable, and forboded the destruction of all the fruit in the territory. This morning we passed the fifth Pine Bluff, and the last previous to our arrival at the Little Rock; the fasçade was about the same height and of the same materials as the preceding. Among the pebbles of a gravel beach which I examined were scattered a few fragments of cornelian, similar to those of the Missouri, and abundance of chert or hornstone containing organic impressions of entrocites, caryophillites, &c.[26] here and there were also intermingled a few granitic fragments,

[26]Paleozoic invertebrates.

which, if not more remotely adventitious, had probably descended from the mountains.—We proceeded to-day about 17 miles.

17TH.] This morning we had the disagreeable prospect of ice, and the wind was still from the north-west, but abating. To-day we progressed about 20 miles. The sixth point we passed, since our encampment of the preceding night, was called the Eagle's Nest, which is here seen situated on the opposite side of the bend before us, of six miles in circuit, and only about 100 yards across at the isthmus.

The almost uninterrupted alternation of sand-bars in the wide alluvial plain of the Arkansa afford, as on the Mississippi, great facilities to navigation, either in propelling the boat by poles, or towing with the cordelles. As the bars or beaches advance, so they continually change the common level of the river, and driving the current into the bend with augmenting velocity, the curve becomes at length intersected, and the sand barring up the entrances of the former bed of the river, thus produces the lakes which we find interspersed over the alluvial lands.

In the present state of the water, which is remarkably low, considering the rains which have fallen, it is difficult to proceed with a large merchant boat more than 18 or 20 miles a-day.

18TH.] We now passed an island or cut-off two miles long, and forming a point four or five miles round. Near its commencement we were again gratified with the sight of a human habitation.

Although the lands along the bank of the river here, appear elevated above the inundation, yet, betwixt the lower settlement and Mr. Twiner's,[27] where we now arrived, the surveyor found considerable tracts subject to the overflow, and in one place a whole township so situated. On the opposite side, or Indian reservation, the hills approach within six or eight miles of the river, and, like most of the southern pine lands, promise but little to the agriculturist, but the intermediate alluvion is as fertile as usual. The Great Prairie, as I am told, on our right, lies at the distance of about 18 or 20 miles; the intermediate space, unbroken by hills, must necessarily afford an uninterrupted body of land little removed from the fertile character of alluvial.

[27]Robert Twiner was an early settler in Phillips County, between the White and Mississippi rivers, but George Twyner, who lived much closer to Nuttall's present location, seems more likely. TERR. PAPERS, XIX, 401, 598.

Towards evening we arrived at Monsieur La Feve's, where two families reside, at the distance of about eight miles above Mr. Twiner's; these are also descendants from the ancient French settlers.[28]

19TH.] This morning we met with a boat from the garrison, commanded by lieutenant Blair, on his way to Arkansas.[29] We also passed Trudot's island,[30] and Mr. D. stopped awhile at the elder La Feve's, for the purposes of trade. Monsieur F. by his dress and manners did not appear to have had much acquaintance with the civilized world. In the evening, we arrived at the house of Mr. Jones, where we were very decently entertained.[31]

20TH.] Two miles further lived Mr. Daniels, in whose neighbourhood a second family also resided.[32] The land in this vicinity appeared to be of a very superior quality, and well suited for cotton. Some of it, obtained by the grant of the Spaniards, and since confirmed by the United States, is held as high as ten dollars the acre. From this place proceeds the road to St. Louis, on the right, and Mount Prairie settlement, and Natchitoches on Red river, on the left. From all I can learn, it appears pretty evident that these extensive and convenient routes have been opened from time immemorial by the Indians; they were their war and hunting-paths, and such as in many instances had been tracked out instinctively by the bison in their periodical migrations. It is in these routes, conducted by the Indians, that we are to trace the adventurers De Soto and La Salle, and by which we may possibly identify the truth of their relations. From the appearances of aboriginal remains around Mount Prairie we may safely infer the former existence of the natives on that site, and it appears also

---

[28]Jean Le Feve was living on the Arkansas in 1819 and, from his dress and manner, is a better candidate than Pierre Lefèvre *père,* who was an expert chosen by Casa y Luengo, captain and commandant of the Louisiana regiment for France, as Arkansas Post was inventoried and turned over to the United States March 23, 1804. Place names, however, are persistent, e.g., Fourche la Fave River flowing east through Perry County, N.W. of Little Rock. HOUCK [1], I, 128–29; II, 341–43; TERR. PAPERS, XIX, 24.

[29]Lt. William Preston Smith Blair, of Kentucky, from the garrison at Fort Smith, Nuttall's destination.

[30]Trudot's Island, a corruption of Trudeau's Island, named for Zenon Trudeau, lieutenant governor of (Spanish) Upper Louisiana, succeeding Manuel Pérez, July 21, 1792–August 2, 1799. NASATIR, I, 151 ff.

[31]The large Jones tribe here narrows to Hugh Jones, visible along the Arkansas as territorial status impended early in 1819. TERR. PAPERS, XIX, 16–17.

[32]Wright Daniel would become a mail carrier between Little Rock and Arkansas Post in 1824. TERR. PAPERS, XIX, 652.

probable, that this must have been the fertile country of the Cayas or Tanicas described by La Vega, a people who are at this time on the verge of extermination.[33]

The distance from Mr. Daniels', on the banks of the Arkansa, to Red river, is believed to be about 250 miles. The Great Prairie, bearing from hence to the north-east, is said to be 40 miles distant, and there is likewise a continuation of open plains or small prairies, from hence to the Cadron settlement. White river lies about 100 miles distant to the north.

In the course of the day we passed the sixth Pine Bluff, behind which appeared the first prominent hill that occurs to view on the banks of the Arkansa. The fasçade or cliffs, in which it terminates on the bank of the river, is called the Little Rock, as it is the first stone which occurs in place.[34] The river, no longer so tediously meandering, here presents a stretch of six miles in extent, proceeding to the west of north-west. In the evening we arrived at Mr. Hogan's,[35] or the settlement of the Little Rock opposite to which appear the cliffs, formed of a dark greenish coloured, fine-grained, slaty, sandstone, mixed with minute scales of mica, forming what geologists commonly term the *grauwacke slate*, and declining beneath the surface at a dip or angle of not less than 45° from the horizon. The hills appear to be elevated from 150 to 200 feet above the level of the river, and are thinly covered with trees.

[33]Garcilaso de la Vega was not present, but Rodrigo Ranjel and the Gentleman of Elvas of the De Soto Expedition had met and recorded the Cayas of a site on the upper Ouachita, not far from present Hot Springs, Arkansas, called Tanico. U.S. DE SOTO EXPEDITION COMMISSION (52, 54, 57, 61) tentatively placed the Cayas in the Tunica group, unrelated linguistically to any other Indians. Nuttall's Indian hunting and war paths are annotated in note 37 *infra*.

[34]Little Rock, here already well known geographically, would become not only a town but the capital of Arkansas Territory under "a bill of assurances" of November 20, 1821, subscribed to by the owners and proprietors of the land site, William Russell, Henry W. Conway, Robert Crittenden, William Trimble, Robert C. Oden, Thomas P. Eskridge, and Joseph Harden. Arkopolis failed as the town name, except on some early maps. TERR. PAPERS, XIX, 357–64.

[35]Edmund Hogan, who entered Missouri public life as a justice of the peace at Cape Girardeau, Louisiana (Missouri) Territory in 1806, was settled in Arkansas (later Pulaski) County by the first week in October, 1815. He had been a member of the Georgia legislature and was elected successively to the Missouri and Arkansas territorial legislatures. His removal as brigadier general of militia, for which he had been chosen by Secretary of War John C. Calhoun, by Acting Territorial Governor Robert Crittenden, would be urged in 1823. His death from stabbing by Judge Andrew Scott, formerly of the Arkansas Territorial Supreme Court, was reported June 4, 1828, by the *Arkansas Gazette*. TERR. PAPERS, XIII, 548; XIV, 476, 806; XV, 88; XIX, 206n.

There are a few families living on both sides, upon high, healthy, and fertile land; and about 22 miles from Hogan's, there is another settlement of nine or ten families situated towards the sources of Saline creek of the Washita, which enters that river in 33° 27';[36] this land, though fertile and healthy, cannot be compared with the alluvions of the Arkansa; notwithstanding which, I am informed, they were receiving accessions to their population from the states of Kentucky and Tennessee. The great road to the south-west, connected with that of St. Louis, already noticed, passing through this settlement, communicates downwards also with the post of Washita, with the remarkable thermal springs near its sources, about 50 miles distant, and then proceeding 250 miles to the settlement of Mount Prairie on Saline creek of Red river, and not far from the banks of the latter, continues to Natchitoches.[37] The whole of this country, except that of the hot-springs, which is mountainous, consists either of prairies or undulated lands thinly timbered, and possessed of considerable fertility.

21ST.] For three or four nights past, we experienced frost sufficient to

[36]It empties into the Ouachita below the point in Bradley County where it is joined by Eagle Creek.

[37]The Indian traces, some of which would become roads after the Louisiana Purchase, were many: from Saint Louis along the Mississippi to Cape Girardeau, thence southwestward along the Ozark Escarpment to Walnut Ridge in N.E. Arkansas, on to Little Rock, present Hot Springs, thence southwestward to Nuttall's "post of Washita," or Fort Miró, named for Esteban Rodríguez Miró, governor of Spanish Louisiana, 1782–91, which had been changed to the town name Monroe, seat of Ouachita Parish, La., the year before Nuttall's arrival. Others came down from Osage River at its mouth on the Missouri River and from the mouth of Kansas River along the present western borders of Missouri and Arkansas. All had as their trading goal the post of Natchitoches on Cane River, now the seat of Natchitoches Parish, La., founded 1714 by the French, who proved to be far more aggressive Indian traders than the Spaniards at Nacogdoches west of the Sabine, or even at the Spanish post of Los Adaes, founded 1717 at present Robeline, only fourteen miles from Natchitoches. The French supplied guns, ammunition, and other goods to the large Caddoan population along Red River, as well as to the Osages and eastward-ranging Plains tribes. Cf. Herbert Eugene Bolton, ed., *Athanase de Mézières and the Louisiana-Texas Frontier, 1768–1780*, 2 vols., I, 37–38, 71–75; John R. Swanton, *Indian Tribes of the Lower Mississippi Valley and Adjacent Coast of the Gulf of Mexico*, Bureau of American Ethnology, *Bulletin 43*.

Nuttall's Mount Prairie settlement, subsequently a historical puzzle, was at the upper end of the Great Bend of the Red River, present Red River County, Arkansas, with modern Ogden in its center. It appears in a sketch map sent by William Rector, surveyor general of the territories of Illinois, Missouri, and Arkansas, with his letter to Josiah Meigs, commissioner of the General Land Office, from Saint Louis, April 14, 1819. Nuttall's Saline Creek and Rector's Saline Landing are conclusive. TERR. PAPERS, XIX, 62–67.

destroy most of the early grape, plum, popaw, and red-bud bloom. At 6 o'clock this morning, the thermometer was down to 22°. In the distance of two miles we arrived at the younger Mr. Curran's,[38] nearly opposite to whose house appeared gentle hills, presenting along the bank of the river beds of slate dipping about 45° to the north-west. About two miles above, commence on the right bank of the river, the first hills, or rather mountains, being not less than 4 or 500 feet high, and possessing a dip too considerable to be classed with the secondary formation. Their character and composition refer them to the transition rocks, and, as far as I have had opportunity to examine, they appear, at all events, generally destitute of organic reliquiae. Similar to what we had already examined, they are a stratum of slate made up of the detritus of more ancient rocks, and frequently traversed with crystalline quartzy veins. I cannot, in fact, perceive any difference betwixt this rock and that of the greater part of the Alleghany mountains in Pennsylvania and Virginia, and particularly those which are of like inconsiderable elevation. About eight miles from Mr. Curran's, appeared again, on the left, very considerable round-top hills, one of them, called the Mamelle, in the distance, where first visible, appeared insulated and conic like a volcano.[39] The cliffs bordering the river, broken into shelvings, were decorated with the red cedar (*Juniperus virginiana*), and clusters of ferns.

After emerging as it were from so vast a tract of alluvial lands, as that through which I had now been travelling for more than three months, it is almost impossible to describe the pleasure which these romantic prospects again afforded me. Who can be insensible to the beauty of the verdant hill and valley, to the sublimity of the clouded mountain, the fearful precipice, or the torrent of the cataract. Even bald and moss-grown rocks, without the aid of sculpture, forcibly inspire us with that veneration which we justly owe to the high antiquity of nature, and which appears to arise no less from a solemn and intuitive reflection on their vast capacity for duration, contrasted with that transient scene in which we ourselves only appear to act a momentary part.

[38]Lemuel R. Curran would become sheriff of Pulaski County in August, 1819. His appointment and replacement in 1821 because of his death are noted in TERR. PAPERS, XIX, 793.

[39]The Mamelle, at the mouth of the Maumelle (a corruption) took its name from its breastlike form.

Many of the plants common to every mountainous and hilly region in the United States, again attracted my attention, and though no way peculiarly interesting, serve to show the wide extension of the same species, under the favourable exposure of similar soil and peculiarity of surface. To me the most surprising feature in the vegetation of this country, existing under so low a latitude, was the total absence of all the usual evergreens, as well as of most of those plants belonging to the natural family of the heaths, the rhododendrons, and the magnolias; while, on the other hand, we have an abundance of the arborescent *Leguminosæ,* or trees which bear pods, similar to the forests of the tropical regions. Here also the *Sapindus saponaria,* or soap-berry of the West Indies, attains the magnitude of a tree.[40]

On the banks of the river, near the precise limit of inundation, I met with a new species of *Sysinbrium,*[41] besides the *S. amphibium,* so constant in its occurrence along the friable banks of all the western rivers. This plant, which is creeping and perennial, possesses precisely the taste of the common cabbage (*Brassica oleracea*), and, from its early verdure, being already in flower, might perhaps be better worth cultivating as an early sallad, than the *Barbarea americana,* or winter sallad.

22D.] From Mr. Blair's,[42] at which place and in the neighbourhood Mr. D. spent the remainder of the day, I proceeded down the river about eight miles, in order to examine the reported silver mine of that place. My route along the banks of the river lay through rich and rather open alluvial lands, but, in many places, not free from transient inundation.

The pretended silver-mine is situated about one mile below White Oak bayou or rivulet. The search appears to have been induced by the exposure

---

[40] *Sapindus saponaria* = *S. Drumondii* H. and A.

[41] Sysinbrium (*Sisymbrium*), misspelled in Peter Simon Pallas, *Reise,* II, 740 (1774), lost several species to the genus *Rorippa,* marsh cress, by transfer, including the Old World *Sisymbrium amphibium* L., which became *Rorippa amphibia* (L.) Besser, first correctly reported from North America in 1930, George J. Goodman tells me. Nuttall described from the area (Torrey and Gray, *Flora of North America,* I, 73–74 [1838]) three new species under the genus *Nasturtium: obtusum, sessiliflorum,* and *sinuatum,* subsequently transferred to *Rorippa.* His plant *supra,* "creeping and perennial," is most logically *Rorippa sinuata* (Nutt.) Hitchc.

Barbarea americana, not used as a published name until 1900, by Rydberg, for a plant from Montana, evidently refers to a species of *Barbarea,* winter cress.

[42] Jessee Blair was in Pulaski County at this time, whereas a number of other Arkansas Blairs were not.

of the rocks in the bank of the river, which present indeed an appearance somewhat remarkable. The dip of the strata, about 45° to the north-west, and the whole texture of the rock, is similar to that which we have already noticed. The principal and lowest stratum, is a dark coloured, sandy, but fragile slate-clay; the upper beds are a fine-grained, siliceous sandstone, containing grains of mica, and occasionally traversed with veins of quartz. In one of these veins, about a foot in breadth, were abundance of rock crystals, scattered over with round masses or imperfect crystals of a white and diaphanous talc, collected into radii, each plate forming the segment of a circle.

I was for some time unable to ascertain the character of the pretended ore of silver, as the whole concern lay abandoned. I observed, however, that the slags of their furnace betrayed a considerable proportion of iron in their operations, and at length I discovered a heap of what appeared to have been the ore, containing pyrites, some of the crystals of which were cubic, like those so common around Lancaster (Pennsylvania), in the chlorite slate. Whether these pyrites did indeed contain silver or not, I could not absolutely determine, though nothing extraordinary could reasonably have been expected from their very common appearance and unequivocal character. On showing these specimens to the neighbours, they informed me, that the pyrites was the ore in question, while others asserted it to be sulphur, and considered the siliceous matrix as the silver ore. It did not, however, to the microscope betray the smallest metallic vestige which could be taken for silver.[43] Like all the rest of this rock, it indeed contained abundance of magnetic iron-sand, which on the disintegration of the stone, appeared scattered along the strand of the river. Upon the whole, I am inclined to believe that some imposition had been practised upon the ignorance and credulity of those who were enticed into this undertaking. Monsieur Brangiere is the person who first made the experiment, or attempted to bring the project into execution.

Ever since the time of Soto, reports concerning the discovery of precious metals in this territory have been cherished; we see them marked

---

[43]This is Nuttall's first mention of his "pocket microscope," which he had been using on the flora and paleontological specimens he had encountered almost from the moment of his departure from Lancaster, Pa., half a dozen months before. It became a casualty to Osage thieving later in his overland journey.

Distant View of the Mamelle. Plate 1 in Nuttall's original of 1821

upon the maps, and although the places are easily discoverable, the gold and silver they were said to afford has entirely vanished like a fairy dream. It is indeed averred that about 60 dollars woth of silver were obtained from this rock, but that it was relinquished in consequence of the labour exceeding the profits. A furnace and several temporary sheds proved that some earnest attempts had been made, either really or fictitiously, to obtain silver. If any silver was obtained, it may be considered as connected with the magnetic iron-sand, which at St. Domingo and in India is found occasionally mixed with gold and silver.[44]

Du Pratz, after animadverting on the visionary reports of the wealth of this territory, himself adds; "I found, upon the river of the Arkansas, a rivulet that rolled down with its water, gold-dust." "And as for silver mines, there is no doubt but that they might be found there, as well as in New Mexico, on which this province bordered."[45]

Near to these hills reported to afford silver, I observed two low aboriginal mounds, though the situation did not appear favourable to the residence of the natives.

23D.] Mr. D. remained nearly the whole day at J. Piat's, where a second family also resides, as well as a third on the opposite side of the river, and several others in the vicinity.[46] About a quarter of a mile above Piat's I amused myself in sketching a view of the romantic hills that border the river, and which are not less than 5 to 800 feet high, with the strata inclined about 45° to the south-east.

[44]Spaniards in the sixteenth and seventeenth centuries extrapolated precious-metals discoveries in New Mexico and Arizona to embrace also the Arkansas River country, as did Bénard de La Harpe, the Frenchman, in the first quarter of the eighteenth century. But the U.S. House of Representatives, Committee on Commerce and Manufactures, referred in more positive terms in 1804 to "masses of virgin silver and gold that glitter in the veins of the rocks which underly the Arkansas." These surmises proved untrue. What underlay the Arkansas was coal. Rich deposits of lead and zinc, the former in eastern Missouri, and a combination of both in southwestern Missouri, southeastern Kansas, and northeastern Oklahoma, were real but outside the Arkansas strata. Cf. SCHOOLCRAFT [2], 246–62; JAMES, E. [1], in THWAITES [1], XVII, 183–255; GIBSON [2], 9–24.

[45]Hist. Louisiana, p. 219, London Edition. —NUTTALL. [He quotes from the 1764 (second London) edition of *Histoire de la Louisiane* (1758), which is more paraphrase than translation.]

[46]Drope could have been visiting with James, John, or Jacob Pyeatt, all of whom appear in the territorial records of the time, along with Andrew, Henry, and Peter Pyeatt, who together appear to have been the bulk of the residents of Pyeattstown a dozen miles above Little Rock. James Miller, the hero of the Battle of Lundy's Lane in the War of 1812 and first territorial governor of Arkansas, 1819–24, lived here. The town no longer exists.

In the afternoon I crossed the river, and ascended to the summit of these lofty cliffs of slaty and siliceous sandstone, where, from an elevation of about 600 feet, I obtained a panorama view of the surrounding country, checquered with low mountains running in chains from the north of west to the south of east. The meanders of the river appeared partly hid in the pervading forests of its alluvial lands, still fertile and expansive. To the west, the lofty, conic, and broken hill called the Mamelle now appeared nearly double the elevation of that on which I stood, probably more than 1000 feet in height. Two miles above, it presented the appearance of a vast pyramid, hiding its summit in the clouds. In this direction opened an extensive alluvial valley, probably once the bed of the river, which from hence makes a general curve of about 20 miles towards the north. These mountains appear to be connected with the Mazern chain of Darby, as they continue from hence towards the sources of the Pottoe of Arkansa, and the Little river, and Kiamesha of Red river.[47]

Amidst these wild and romantic cliffs, and on the ledges of the rocks, where, moistened by springs, grew a cruciferous plant, very closely allied, if not absolutely the same, with the *Brassica napus* or the Rape-seed of Europe, and beyond all question indigenous.[48]

24TH.] After taking a second sketch of the Mamelle mountain, from a different point of view, I proceeded to join the boat, and crossed a poor and rocky Pine hill. Here the sandstone is scarcely slaty, and, as usual, more or less ferruginous. Crossing the bayou Palame (or rather rivulet), I joined the boat at Mr. Gozy's,[49] in whose neighbourhood there were also two other families. This evening we proceeded nearly to the termination of Grand island, which is four miles in length.

25TH.] About a mile below Grand island, on our left, the hills again

[47]Here and earlier Nuttall had been looking westward at the Ouachita Mountains, part of the time from the elevation of Mamelle (now Pinnacle) Mountain, stretching from Little Rock to the present Oklahoma border and beyond. North and west of Little Rock were the Ozarks. The highest elevations in both mountainous areas are under three thousand feet.

[48]*Brassica Napus* L. (old generic name), turnip, and *B. Rapa* L. (old generic name), bird's rape, both Eurasian, were early introduced into North America, but two months later Nuttall would collect near the Kiamichi a plant he assigned to his new genus and species, *Streptanthus maculatus* Nutt., similar to the *Brassica*.

[49]Both John and Aaron Goza were established in this area by the year 1818. TERR. PAPERS, XIX, 12, 17, 20.

Mamelle. Plate 2 in Nuttall's original of 1821

come in upon the river, presenting the most romantic cliffs. In one place particularly, an unbroken fasçade not less than 150 feet of slaty sandstone presents itself, the lamina of which, about 12 or 18 inches in thickness, dipping to the south-east, are elevated at an angle of near 80° from the horizon, and altogether resemble the basis of some mighty pyramid. In four miles further we passed the outlet of Fourche La Fève, said to proceed in a western direction for 200 miles, and to take its sources in the mountains of the Pottoe.[50] A north-western range of hills here in the whole distance border the river, the strata of which, still lamellar, dip north-north-east, and are inclined about 45°. This evening, at Mr. Montgomery's, the Cadron hills appear before us, at the distance of about six miles.[51]

26TH.] A strong north-west wind arose in the night, accompanying a rise in the river of two and a half feet, and a current of the velocity of four or five miles per hour.

On the 27th we arrived at the Cadron settlement, containing in a contiguous space about five or six families. Mr. M'Ilmery, one of the first, is at present the only resident on the imaginary town plot. A cove of rocks here affords a safe and convenient harbour, and a good landing for merchandize.[52]

No village or town, except Arkansas, has yet been produced on the banks of this river, though I have no doubt, but my remarks may ere long be quoted and contrasted with a rising state or more condensed population. Town-lot speculations have already been tried at the Cadron, which is yet but a proximate chain of farms, and I greatly doubt whether a town of any consequence on the Arkansa will ever be chosen on this site. Some high

[50]Fourche la Fave, the source of Nimrod Lake, empties into the Arkansas below Bigelow in Perry County. HEMPSTEAD (840) has Francis Lefave settling in what became Pulaski County "as early, probably, as 1807." Leon, his brother, was still living at "an advanced age of near 90 years" in 1911. Cf. note 28 *ante*.

[51]Richard Montgomery, of the several recorded Montgomerys, seems most likely.

[52]Cadron, at a point slightly south of the mouth of Cadron Creek, west of modern Conway in Faulkner County. John McIllmurray had come to the upper settlements of Arkansas (Arkansas County) as early as 1813, for which he was appointed justice of the peace (TERR. PAPERS, XIV, 650). Nuttall's estimates of the Cadron Settlement in what follows are probably accurate, but five years earlier there had been "perhaps 40 or 50 families at, near to, and above Cadron Creek," mostly on public lands. William Russell, deputy surveyor, to William Rector, principal deputy surveyor, April 20, 1814, in TERR. PAPERS, XIV, 756–57.

and rich body of alluvial lands would be better suited for the situation of an inland town, than the hills and the rocks of the Cadron. Modern cities rarely thrive in such romantic situations. There is scarcely a hundred yards together of level ground, and the cove in which Mr. M'Ilmery lives is almost impenetrably surrounded by tiresome and lofty hills, broken into ravines, with small rills of water. It is true, that here may be obtained a solid foundation on which to build, without danger of dislocation by the perpetual changes and ravages of the river, but in an agricultural settlement something more is wanting than foundations for houses.

The Cadron was at this time in the hands of four proprietors, who last year commenced the sale of town-lots to the amount of 1300 dollars, and the succeeding sale was appointed to take place in the approaching month of May.

What necessity there may be for projecting a town at this place, I will not take upon myself to decide, but a house of public entertainment, a tavern, has long been wanted, as the Cadron lies in another of the leading routes through this territory. It is one of the resorts from St. Louis, and the settlements on White river, as well as to the hot springs of the Washita,[53] and the inhabitants of Red river. From Arkansas to this place, about 150 miles by land, there is a leading path which proceeds through the Great Prairie.

To those southern gentlemen who pass the summer in quest of health and recreation, this route to the hot springs of the Washita, which I believe is the most convenient, would afford a delightful and rational amusement.

In the course of the day I amused myself amongst the romantic cliffs of slaty sand-stone, which occupy the vicinity of the Cadron. Here I found vestiges of several new and curious plants, and among them an undescribed species of *Eriogonum,* with a considerable root, partly of the colour and taste of rhubarb.[54] The *Petalostemons,*[55] and several plants of the

[53]Hot Springs has fulfilled Nuttall's ideas of its value as an American spa. Located 52 miles s.w. of Little Rock, it is now a national park, and the adjoining Hot Springs, seat of Garland County, is a notable health resort.

[54]*Eriogonum longifolium* Nutt., discovered at its eastern limit of distribution by Nuttall.

[55]*Petalostemum multiflorum* Nutt. (many-flowered) got its name later from a prairie clover Nuttall collected on Red River; others may have been *P. candidum* (Willd.) Michx., *P. pulcherrimum* Heller, and *P. purpureum* (Vent.) Rydb., all of which have an Arkansas range.

Cadron Settlement. Plate 3 in Nuttall's original of 1821

eastern states, whi-ch I had not seen below, here again make their appearance. The *Cactus ferox*[56] of the Missouri, remarkably loaded with spines, appears to forbode the vicinity of the Mexican desert.

The dip of the strata is here south-east, and the mountains, generally destitute of organic remains, pass off in chains from the north of west to the south of east.

28TH.] The river still continued rising. This morning I walked out two or three miles over the hills, and found the land, except in the small depressions and alluvion of the creek, of an inferior quality, and chiefly timbered with oaks and hickories thinly scattered. Ages must elapse before this kind of land will be worth purchasing at any price. Still, in its present state, it will afford a good range of pasturage for cattle, producing abundance of herbage, but would be unfit for cotton or maize, though, perhaps, suited to the production of smaller grain; there is not, however, yet a grist-mill on the Arkansa, and flour commonly sells above the Post, at 12 dollars per barrel. For the preparation of maize, a wooden mortar, or different kinds of hand or horse-mills are sufficient. Sugar and coffee are also high priced articles, more particularly this year. In common, I suppose, sugar retails at 25 cents the pound, and coffee at 50. Competition will, however, regulate and reduce the prices of these and other articles, which, but a few years ago, were sold at such an exorbitant rate, as to be almost proscribed from general use. There is a maple in this country, or rather, I believe, on the banks of White river, which has not come under my notice, called the sugar-tree (though not, as they say, the *Acer saccharinum*),[57] that would, no doubt, by a little attention afford sugar at a low rate; and the decoctions of the wood of the sassafras and spice bush (*Laurus benzoin*),[58] which abound in this country, are certainly very palatable substitutes for tea.

It is to be regretted that the widely scattered state of the population in this territory, is but too favourable to the spread of ignorance and bar-

---

[56]*Cactus ferox* Nutt., not Willd. = *Opuntia missouriensis* DC. = *Opuntia polycantha* Haw., one of the prickly pears, here out of range; more likely *O. compressa* (Salisb.) Macbr.

[57]*Acer saccharum* Marsh. is represented in Arkansas, but perhaps *A. barbatum* Michx., the southern sugar maple, is our best candidate.

[58]Respectively, *Sassafras albidum* (Nutt.) Nees and (for Laurus benzoin) *Lindera Benzoin* (L.) Blume, spicebush.

barism. The means of education are, at present, nearly proscribed, and the rising generation are growing up in mental darkness, like the French hunters who have preceded them, and who have almost forgot that they appertain to the civilized world. This barrier will, however, be effectually removed by the progressive accession of population, which, like a resist-less tide, still continues to set towards the west.

Contiguous to the north-eastern, or opposite declivity of the chain of hills, which flank the settlement of Mr. M'Ilmery, I observed in my ramble, a considerable collection of aboriginal tumuli, towards the centre of which, disposed in a somewhat circular form, I thought I could still discern an area which had once been trodden by human feet;—but, alas! both they and their history are buried in impenetrable oblivion! their existence is blotted out from the page of the living! and it is only the eye which has been accustomed to the survey of these relics, that can even distinguish them from the accidental operations of nature. How dreary is this eternal night which has overtaken so many of my fellow-mortals!—a race, perhaps brave, though neither civilized nor luxurious, and who, like the retreating Scythians pursued by Darius, made, perhaps, at last, an obstinate resistance around their luckless families, and the revered tombs of their ancestors!

Besides these tumuli scattered through the forests, there are others on the summits of the hills, formed of loose stones thrown up in piles. We have no reason to suppose, that these remains were left by the Arkansas; they themselves deny it, and attribute them to a people distinct and governed by a superior policy.

29TH and 30TH.] Still at Mr. M'Ilmery's, during which time the weather has been cold and stormy.

The United States have now ordered the survey of all the alluvial and other saleable lands of the Arkansa, which are to be ready for disposal in about two years from the present time. One of the surveyors, Mr. Pet-tis,[59] was now laying out the lands contiguous to the Cadron into sections. Another surveyor is also employed in the Great Prairie, and proceeding, at this time, from the vicinity of Arkansas to this place. The poorer and hilly lands, generally, are not yet thought to be worth the

[59]Otherwise unidentified.

expense of a public survey. Some of these surveys, however, extend as far to the north as the banks of White river. Mr. P. obtains three dollars per mile, for surveying the river lands, which are extremely difficult, from the density and extent of the cane-brakes, and the multiplicity of lagoons or portions of the deserted channel of the river, which, as we have had already occasion to remark, are still continually forming.

These fine cotton lands have not altogether escaped the view of speculators, although there is yet left ample room for the settlement of thousands of families, on lands, which, except the few preemption rights, will be sold by the impartial hand of the nation, at a price as reasonable as the public welfare shall admit of, which has heretofore been at the rate of two dollars the acre, and as no lands on this river are now surveyed and offered for sale, but such as are considered to be of the first and second rate, there can consequently be no room left for imposition, and though there is, indeed, a considerable proportion of inundated land unavoidably included, yet in general, as I understand from the surveyor, there will be in almost every section, a great portion of elevated soils.

The preemption rights, as they are called, are a certain species of reward or indemnification for injuries sustained in the late war, and afforded to such individuals only, as had made improvements in the interior of the territories, prior to the year 1813. Such individuals, if able to pay, are entitled to one or more quarter sections, as the lines of their improvements may happen to extend into the public lines when surveyed, of one or more such plots or fractional sections of land. These rights have been bought up by speculators, at from 4 or 500 to 1000 dollars, or at the positive rate of from 3 to 10 dollars the acre, including the price of two dollars per acre to the United States; a certain proof of the growing importance of this country, where lands, previous to the existence of any positive title, have brought a price equal to that of the best lands on the banks of the Ohio, not immediately contiguous to any considerable town. The hilly lands, which have not been thought worthy of a survey, will afford an invaluable common range for all kinds of cattle, while the alluvial tracts are employed in producing maize, cotton, tobacco, or rice. I must, here, however, remark by the way, that there exists a considerable difference in the nature of these alluvial soils. They are all loamy, never cold or argillaceous, but often rather light and sandy; such lands, however, though inferior for maize, are still well adapted for cotton. The richest soils here produce 60 to 80 bushels of maize per acre. The inundated lands, when properly banked so as to exclude and introduce the water at pleasure by sluices, might be well employed for rice, but the experiment on this grain has not yet been made, on an extensive scale, by any individual in the territory, although its success, in a small way, has been satisfactorily ascertained. Indigo is occasionally raised for domestic use, but would require more skill in its preparation for the market. Indeed, as yet, the sum of industry calculated to afford any satisfactory experiment in agriculture or domestic economy, has not been exercised by the settlers of the Arkansa, who, with half the resolution of the German farmers of Pennsylvania, would ensure to themselves and their families comfort and affluence.

After the most diligent inquiries concerning the general health of this country, I do not find any substantial reason to alter the opinion which I have already advanced. I am, however, firmly persuaded, that the immediate banks of the Arkansas, in this respect are to be preferred to the prairies, and I can only account for this remarkable circumstance, by the unusual admixture of common salt, or muriate of soda, in its waters, which prevents it from becoming dangerously putrid in the neighbouring ponds and lagoons; and I would farther recommend its use to the inhabitants in preference to any fountain water, however convenient. The pellucid appearance of the water, in most of the lagoons which have come under my notice, is, in all probability, attributable to this circumstance.

I was indeed informed that instances of the ague were known at some seasons, but that this disease had been principally confined to those who were destitute, through indolence or accidental poverty, of the proper means of nourishment, and who, after its commencement, neglected the aid of medicine.[60] A better proof, than the general healthy appearance of the inhabitants, and the total absence of doctors, whose aid must of course be unnecessary, need not be adduced in favour of the prevailing salubrity of the banks of the Arkansa.

From Mr. M'Ilmery, I learn that there exists very considerable tracts of fertile land, along the banks of La Feve's creek, which proceeds in a

[60]Ague was an acute fever induced by malarial infection, mosquito-borne, not fully understood until the beginning of the twentieth century.

south-west direction towards Red river for about 200 miles, deriving its source with Little river of the latter, as well as with another contiguous stream of the Arkansa, called Petit John, and likewise with the Pottoe.[61] It is also said to be navigable near 100 miles, and possessed of a gentle current.

From Mr. Pettis, the surveyor, I obtained two small specimens of the oil-stone, or hone of the Washita. It is a siliceous slaty rock, of a conchoidal and sometimes splintery fracture, bordering on hornstone; some of it is as white as snow, and it splits so evenly as to afford hones without any additional labour. Occasionally it appears divided by ferruginous illinations, presenting muscoid ramifications in relief, but scarcely discolouring the surface. It feebly absorbs oil or water, and then becomes somewhat diaphanous. It is infusible by the common blowpipe.[62]

31ST.] This evening we proceeded to David M'Ilmery's, about three miles above the Cadron, who lived about a mile and a half from the bank of the river, at the head of a small alluvial plain or prairie, apparently well calculated for a superior farm. While passing through this prairie, I observed five deer feeding, and passed almost without disturbing them.

Wild cats of two kinds, both striped and spotted, as well as panthers, bears, and wolves (black and grey), are in considerable abundance in this country. The bison (improperly called buffaloe) is also met with occasionally in the distance of about a day's ride towards the Washita.[63]

---

[61]The area of Rich Mountain (2,681 feet) in western Arkansas, above Mena, Polk County, gives rise to Fourche la Fave River, the Ouachita, Mountain Fork (of Oklahoma), and the Kiamichi (of Oklahoma) but not the Poteau, which rises in the Petit Jean Mountain area of eastern Scott County. Little River rises in the Kiamichi Mountains area of Le Flore County, Oklahoma. The Petit Jean rises near Hartford, Sebastian County, Arkansas, and joins Dutch Creek near Danville, in Yell County.

[62]For a further account of this mineral, which appeared to be undescribed, see a note in the Essay on the Geological Structure of the Valley of the Mississippi, which I published in the first part of the second volume of the Journal of the Academy of the Natural Sciences of Philadelphia. —NUTTALL. [Novaculite (whetstone), which Schoolcraft (*A View of the Lead Mines of Missouri*, 1819) had examined the year before Nuttall's arrival, noting a quarry which was then shipping the stone as far as New Orleans.]

[63]The cats Nuttall saw were probably representatives of *Lynx rufus floridanus*, the bobcat, inasmuch as we have no records of the appearance of *Felis pardalis*, the ocelot, or of *Felis onca*, the jaguar, in this range. His wolves were representatives of *Canis latrans* in its subspecies *C.l. frustror*, coyote, common in the N.W. half of Arkansas, whereas *Canis lupus*, the wolf proper, is without recorded observation historically in the Gulf Southwest, including Arkansas and E. Oklahoma. HALL AND KELSON, II, 849.

The inhabitants were just beginning to plough for cotton, an operation here not very laborious, except when breaking up the prairies, as the soil is friable and loamy.

In a small prairie adjoining, where a second family were residing, a single tree of the bow-wood (or *Maclura*) existed, having a trunk of about 18 inches diameter. [64]

April 1st.] The Arkansa after a sudden rise had now commenced again to fall; its inundations being chiefly vernal, taking place from February to May, are less injurious than those of the Missouri and Mississippi, which occur in mid-summer, and are consequently unavoidably injurious to the advancing crops. This circumstance also tends to prove, that no considerable branch of this river derives its source within the region of perpetual snow, which dissolves most in the warmest season of the year, and that its inundations are merely the effect of winter rains; its rising and falling, from the same cause, is also much more sudden than that of the Missouri.

About eight miles from the Cadron, we passed Mr. Marsongill's, pleasantly situated on the gentle declivity of a ridge of hills, which commence about a mile from the river. [65] Three miles further, we passed Mr. Fraser's, the commencement of the Pecannerie settlement. [66] Here, at the distance of more than 12 miles, the hills of the Petit John appear conspicuous and picturesque. In three miles more, seven or eight houses are seen, situated along either bank of the river, and sufficiently contiguous for an agreeable neighbourhood.

From the Cadron upwards, the falls of the rivulets afford conveniences for mills. A grist-mill did not, however, as yet exist on the banks of the Arkansa, though a saw-mill had been recently erected.

2d.] Mr. D. proceeded about eight miles above Fraser's, and remained the rest of the afternoon nearly opposite to the bayou or rivulet of point Remu, from whence, on that side, commences the Cherokee line. [67] Here

[64]*Maclura* (monotypic) is Nuttall's genus: *M. pomifera* (Raf.) Schneid., Osage orange, or bois d'arc.

[65]The Massingales of that spelling and Massongale, Massingill, and other variants, had settled in the area as early as 1818. TERR. PAPERS, XIX, 13.

[66]William Frazer appears in the records for this area as of 1818. The Pecannerie Settlement was eleven miles upstream on the Arkansas from the mouth of Cadron Creek in present S.E. Conway County.

[67]Point Remove, in present Conway County in the area of Morrilton, was the starting

the hills again approach in gentle declivities, presenting beds of black slaty siliceous rock (grauwacke slate), inclined about 60° south-east. Both banks of the river in this distance are one continued line of farms. Some of the cabins are well situated on agreeable rising grounds; but the nearer, I perceive, the land is to the level of inundation, the greater is its fertility. The highest grounds are thin and sandy, so much so, that occasionally the Cactus or prickly-pear makes its appearance.

3D.] Still opposite point Remu. On this side of the river, where Mr. Ellis now resides, an agreeable site for a town offers, but the landing is bad.[68] A few miles back there are not less than 14 families scattered over the alluvial land. There were also a number of families settled along the banks of the Remu. Adjoining Mr. Ellis's there was a small sandy prairie, over which I found Cactus's and the *Plantago gnaphaloides* abundantly scattered.[69] I am informed that there are considerable quantities of this poor and sandy land, though not in any one place very extensive, and immediately surrounded with richer lands which have been, and are yet skirted by the overflow. With slight banking, these lands, not too deeply submerged, will one day be considered the best for all kinds of produce, but more particularly maize and rice.

4TH.] A storm of wind sprang up during the night from the south-west, and continued so as to retard us, after proceeding with difficulty about six miles, in which distance we arrived at the house of Mr. Tucker,[70] situated at the base of a lofty ridge of broken hills, not less than 6 or 700 feet high, presenting an alternation of terraces and cliffs, and continuing in a north-west direction nearly the same height for about eight miles. This range is known by the same name as that of the contigu-

---

point in the land description contained in the Cherokee Treaty of July 8, 1817, ceding certain Cherokee lands east of the Mississippi River in exchange for the Arkansas reserve. The line ran north from Point Remove to the White River, thence westward. The treaty, one of twenty-five cessions by the Cherokees between 1791 and 1819, was contributory to the ongoing hostility between the Osages and the Cherokees, the former having been induced in 1808 by United States treaty commissioners Pierre Chouteau, Capt. Eli B. Clemson, and Lt. Reazen Lewis to give up their Arkansas holdings. KAPPLER, II, 29, 51, 73, 90, 95, 124, 125, 141 ff.; TERR. PAPERS, XIX, 89n.

[68]William Ellis's association with the mail route from Arkansas Post north and westward suggests his identification here. TERR. PAPERS, XIX, 379, 385.

[69]*Plantago gnaphaloides* Nutt. = *P. purshii* R. and S.

[70]The Tuckers along the Arkansas were many in early territorial days, so that this one, whether William or John, must remain obscure.

ous rivulet, the Little John, some Frenchman probably who first discovered it. At the south-east end I found the ascent very steep, and which, like most considerable chains, was at this extremity the highest and most precipitous. From the summit a vast wilderness presented itself covered with trees, and chequered with ranges of mountains, which appeared to augment and converge towards the north-west. To the east a considerable plain stretches out, almost uninterrupted by elevations. From the south-west I could enumerate four distinct chains of mountains, of which the furthest, about 40 miles distant, presented in several places lofty blue peaks, much higher than any of the intermediate and less broken ridges. I thought that this ridge tended somewhat towards the Mamelle, whose summit at this distance was quite distinct, though, at the lowest estimate, 40 miles distant. To the north-east the hills traverse the river, and are in this quarter also of great elevation, affording sources to some of the streams of White river, and to others which empty into the Arkansa. Over the vast plain immediately below me, appeared here and there belts of cypress, conspicuous by their brown tops and horizontal branches; they seem to occupy lagoons and swamps, at some remote period formed by the river. As it regards their structure, the lower level of the hills was slaty, the tabular summits a massive, fine-grained sandstone, containing nodules of iron ore. In one place I also saw one of those gigantic tessellated zoophytic impressions,[71] which indicate the existence of coal. The dip of the sandstone is inconsiderable, and to the north-west. Towards the southern extremity of the ridge which I ascended, there are several enormous masses of rocks so nicely balanced as almost to appear the work of art; one of them, like the druidical monuments of England, rocked backwards and forwards on the slightest touch. On the shelvings of this extremity of the mountain, I found a new species of *Anemone*.[72]

As we proceeded in the boat, towards the level of the river, and about a mile below the entrance of the Petit John, we could perceive a slaty and

[71] A Strobilaria, more commonly considered as a species of Phytolite. —NUTTALL.

[72] John Torrey and Asa Gray (*Flora of North America*) were not always kind to Nuttall's genera and species, many of his species being reduced to varieties, "alterations made by persons far less experienced than himself," Jeannette E. Graustein (*Thomas Nuttall, Naturalist*, 352) points out. Here, however, his new species of *Anemone*, listed by T. & G. Fl. No. Am. 1: 12. 1838, as *Anemone caroliniana* Walt. var. *heterophylla*, which they noted from his manuscript, now is accepted by many as *Anemone heterophylla* Nutt. or *A. decapetala* Ard. var. *heterophylla* (Nutt.) Britt. & Rusby.

partly horizontal bed of matter, in which there were distinct indications of coal.

5TH.] We passed the outlet of the Petit John, a rivulet about 200 miles long, deriving its source with the Pottoe and other streams in the Mazern mountains. Here the hills turn off abruptly to the south, and for four or five miles border the rivulet, which, for some distance, keeping a course not very far from the Arkansa, approaches within 10 miles to the southeast of the Dardanelle settlement.[73] At the distance of about five miles from the first Cherokee village, called the Galley, Mr. D. and myself proceeded to it by land. The first two or three miles presented elevated and rich alluvial lands, but in one or two directions bordered by the backwater. At length we arrived at the Galley hills, a series of low and agreeable acclivities well suited for building. Here the Cherokees had a settlement of about a dozen families, who, in the construction and furniture of their houses, and in the management of their farms, imitate the whites, and appeared to be progressing towards civilization, were it not for their baneful attachment to whiskey. Towards the level of the river a darkish bed of slate-clay appeared, having a dip of not more than 10 to 15°; beneath which occurred a slaty sandstone, containing a little mica, and somewhat darkened apparently by bitumen. It likewise abounded with organic reliquiae, among which were something like large alcyonites, sometimes the thickness of a finger, but flexuous instead of rigid, and collected together in considerable quantities; also, a moniliform fossil allied to the Icthyosarcolite of Desmarest, though not very distinctly, being equally flexuous with the above, and fragments resembling some species of turrilites, but no shells of any other description, besides these, were visible.

The insects which injure the morel cherry-tree so much in Pennsylvania, I perceive, here occasionally act in the same way upon the branches of the wild cherry, (*Prunus virginiana*).[74]

[73]Dardanelle, of the present same name, on the south bank of the Arkansas, named for the Dardenne family, Toussaint, the father, of Fort de Chartres near Kaskaskia, Ill., and the son, Jean Baptiste, who had a grant during the Spanish regime before 1800 on the north bank of the Arkansas.

[74]Chokecherry. But *Prunus virginiana* L. was commonly applied in Nuttall's time to another species, the black cherry, *Prunus serotina* Ehrh., as well. The latter has a large distribution in Arkansas. Cf. Rogers McVaugh, "A Revision of the North American Black Cherries," *Brittonia*, 7 (1951), 279–315, esp. note 5, 287–88, 289–91.

6TH.] This morning the river appeared rapidly rising to its former elevation, being nearly bank full, almost a mile in width, and but little short of the Mississippi in magnitude. The current was now probably four or five miles in the hour, and so difficult to stem, that after the most laborious exertions since day-light, we were still in the evening five miles below the Dardanelle, having made only about 10 miles from the Galley. We have had the low ridge, which originated this fanciful name, in sight nearly the whole day. On the same side of the river, but more distant, a magnificent empurpled mountain occupies the horizon, apparently not less than 1000 feet high, forming a long ridge or table, and abrupt at its southern extremity. From its peculiar form it had received the name of the Magazine or Barn by the French hunters.[75] It strongly resembles the English mountain in the north of Yorkshire, called Pendle-hill, familiar to me from infancy, and by which all the good wives in the surrounding country could foretel the weather better than by the almanac.

Along either bank the lands are generally elevated and fertile, and pretty thickly scattered with the cabins and farms of the Cherokees, this being the land allotted to them by congress, in exchange for others in the Mississippi Territory, where the principal part of the nation still remain.

I was considerably disappointed in learning that Mr. D. had relinquished the idea of proceeding to the garrison, with whom I had entertained the hope of continuing my passage, without interruption or additional delay.[76]

7TH.] Both banks of the river, as we proceeded, were lined with the houses and farms of the Cherokees, and though their dress was a mixture of indigenous and European taste, yet in their houses, which are decently furnished, and in their farms, which were well fenced and stocked with cattle, we perceive a happy approach towards civilization. Their numerous families, also, well fed and clothed, argue a propitious progress in their population. Their superior industry, either as hunters or farmers, proves the value of property among them, and they are no longer strangers to avarice, and the distinctions created by wealth; some of them are pos-

[75]Magazine Mountain, 2,823 feet in elevation, highest in Arkansas, is in Logan County.

[76]The garrison here refers to Fort Smith, at this time commanded, as it had been from its founding, by Maj. William Bradford. FOREMAN [1], 48–50.

sessed of property to the amount of many thousands of dollars, have houses handsomely and conveniently furnished, and their tables spread with our dainties and luxuries.

They say, that their language is perfectly distinct from that of every other spoken by the aborigines.[77] Yet the Delawares, according to Mr. Heckewelder, considered them as their descendants.[78]

The following notice of them occurs in La Vega's history of the incursion of Ferdinand de Soto, as early as the year 1541. Seven days' journey from Cutifachiqui, which is stated to be 430 Spanish leagues, or 860 miles from the bay of Apalache, and in a direction of from south-west to north-east, De Soto arrived in a province called Chalaque (evidently the same people now called Cherokees, as they call themselves Chalakee).[79] The country they then occupied was said to be sterile, and affording but little maize, that they fed upon spontaneous roots and herbs, which they sought in the wilds, and upon the animals of the forest, hunted with bows and arrows. In their manners they were gentle, and went habitually

[77]Charlevoix also remarks, "I cannot find out to what language the Cherokees belong, a pretty numerous people, who inhabit the vast meadows between the Lake Erie, and the Mississippi," and adds that the Iroquois make war with them. Hist. Journal, p. 115, London Ed. —NUTTALL. [The Cherokees, of the Iroquoian linguistic family but detached from that group, were not related linguistically to the Delawares, who were Algonquian. The Iroquois domination of the Delawares in Pennsylvania in the eighteenth century, however, explains a presumed kinship.]

[78]John Gottlieb Ernestus Heckewelder (1743–1823), Moravian missionary to the Indians of Ohio, was the author of historical and linguistic works on the Indian tribes of the Northeast from 1797 to a time shortly before his death, of which his Delaware place names for the states of Pennsylvania, New Jersey, Maryland, and Virginia was published posthumously (1833). His many vocabularies, grammars, and papers on Indian dialects are represented in the manuscript holdings of the American Philosophical Society, Philadelphia. To his work and that of his contemporary and friend Peter Stephen Du Ponceau, together with the deposit by Thomas Jefferson of items surviving from his own extensive collection of Indian vocabularies at the American Philosophical Society in 1817, may be traced in part the burst of interest in Indian languages and history by intellectuals, of whom Nuttall and Rafinesque were two. Cf. John F. Freeman, comp., *A Guide to Manuscripts Relating to the American Indian in the Library of the American Philosophical Society* (Philadelphia, 1966); for Heckewelder and Du Ponceau see the bibliography appended to the present volume. The loss of many of Jefferson's vocabularies is covered in EDGERTON, 29–30.

[79]Purchas's Pilgrims, vol. IV, p. 1539. —NUTTALL. [Chalaque, John R. Swanton believes, does not signify Cherokee but a Siouan people possibly related to the Catawba. Chalaque = "people of a different language." Moreover, there is no reason to believe the Cherokees were as far south as they were represented in the middle of the seventeenth century. SWANTON [1], 49, 50, 53, 198–99.]

naked. Their chief sent as a present to De Soto a couple of deer skins, and their country abounded with wild hens (probably the Prairie hen, *Tetrao cupido*). In one town they made him a present of 700 of these birds, and he experienced the like liberality in several other of their towns.[80]

They were acquainted with this country prior to their removal, but never laid any claim to it. It was merely the resort of their renegadoes and wandering hunters. The number who have now emigrated hither are about 1500. The unsettled limit of their claim in this country, has been the means of producing some dissatisfaction, and exciting their jealousy against the agents of government. One of their principal chiefs had said, that rather than suffer any embarrassment and uncertainty, he would proceed across Red river, and petition land from the Spaniards.[81] The Cherokees, with their present civilized habits, industry, and augmenting population, would prove a dangerous enemy to the frontiers of the Arkansa Territory. As they have explicitly given up the lands which they possessed in the Mississippi Territory, in exchange for those which they have chosen here, there can be no reason why they should not immediately be confirmed, so as to preclude the visits of land speculators, which excite their jealousy. A serious misunderstanding will probably

[80] *Tetrao cupido* (Linnaeus) = *Tympanuchus cupido cupido* (Linnaeus), the heath hen of the N.E. coastal area of the United States, extinct since about 1930, had no historic range in the De Soto itinerary. But the greater prairie chicken, *Tympanuchus cupido americanus* (Reichenbach), did. James Mooney believed that the hens received by the De Soto expedition were turkeys, if *gallinhas*, set down by the Gentleman of Elvas in Portuguese, and *gallinas* in the Spanish of Frederico Ranjel, may be so equated (*pavo*, "turkey," did not become current in Spanish until after the De Soto travels). For the etymologically inclined, *Meleagris gallopavo silvestris* Vieillot, the eastern nominate species of the turkey, may be suggestive. MOONEY, Part 1, 24.

[81] Cf. notes 10 and 67 *ante.* "Renegadoes and wandering hunters" here refers principally to the emigrant Cherokees who, under Chief Bowl of the detached Cherokee towns at Chickamauga, Tenn., had massacred migrants moving westward at Muscle Shoals in 1794, then fled across the Mississippi to the Saint Francis in present Arkansas. Their depredations ranged as far south as Red River in ensuing years. The Bowl led them into Mexican Texas in 1824, where, on Angelina River, they were attacked by troops from the Republic of Texas in 1839 and the Bowl was killed. Other "renegadoes" who had operated with the Cherokees under the Bowl in Arkansas were Delawares, Shawnees, Koasatis, Creeks, and Choctaws, but separate operations by white renegades on and south of Red River were common. Territorial Governor James Miller to the Secretary of War, June 20, 1820, in TERR. PAPERS, XIX, 194; George Gray, Indian Agent at Sulphur Fork Agency of Red River, to John C. Calhoun, secretary of War, April n.d., 1824, TERR. PAPERS, XIX, 664–65. FOREMAN [1], 175 ff.

arise at their ejectment from the south side of the river, which has, I believe, been concluded on by the government. Although the power of the natives is now despised, who can at this time tell, what may grow out of this nation of the aborigines, who, by wisely embracing the habits and industry of the Anglo-Americans, may in time increase, and become a powerful and independent nation, subject by habit to a monarchial form of government.

We find mention, as already remarked, of the Cherokees (under the name of Chalaque) by Garcilasso de la Vega, who found them living near the Apalachian mountains, and speaks in contempt of their poverty and population. At this time, however, they amount to between 12 and 13,000 souls, and are in a promising way of advancing beyond all the other aborigines in strength and population. From examining the oldest histories and maps, it appears that a portion of this nation also occupied the sea-coast of South Carolina, where, according to a tradition still extant, they first saw the white people approach in ships, near to the present site of the city of Charlestown. They requested, say they, a small portion of land, which was readily granted, but at length encroached upon us, until we had to cross the mountains, and now even the banks of the Missis-sippi.[82]

Arriving in the afternoon at Mr. Raphael's,[83] who keeps a store for the supply of the Cherokees, I hastened to examine the neighbouring ridge of rocks, which originated the name of the Dardanelle, or as it is here more commonly called Derdanai, both by the French and Americans.[84] The fires which commonly take place among the dry herbage, and which had

[82]No historical record exists for the presence of the Cherokees in the Carolina coastal area, but their control of the entire Allegheny region from the headwaters of the Kanawha and Tennessee rivers southward nearly to present Atlanta is undisputed. They had num-bered 20,000 in 1800. Nuttall's estimate of 1819 is close to the census of eastern Cherokees at 16,542 in 1838, with some 6,000 in the West to be added. Return J. Meigs counted just over 2,000 western Cherokees in 1816. MOONEY, 31, 34, 39, 81, 103; Meigs to Wm. H. Crawford, February 17, 1816, in TERR. PAPERS, XV, 121–22.

[83]Mr. Raphael here could be one of the French-speaking Rapieux, for whom we have Louisiana territorial mentions in 1805 at the village of Saint Ferdinand de Florissant, now a suburb of Saint Louis, Mo., Jean and Joseph being two. HOUCK [1], II, 3, 68, lists among French Canadians at San Fernando de Florissant in 1794 Louis and Joseph Rapieux, *dit* Lamare (Lamère).

[84]Named for Jean Baptiste Dardenne, whose Spanish land grant was across the Arkan-sas (left bank).

but recently been in action, prevented me from making any botanical collections, and I amused myself by ascending the ridge, which, at the first approach, appeared to be inaccessible. At length I gained the summit, which, at the highest point on the bank of the river, might be about 300 feet. The rock was a massive sandstone, with the laminae elevated towards the south-east, at an inclination of near 60°, and, in many places intricately traversed with seams of ferruginous matter, presenting, by their numerous intersections, an almost tessellated or retiform appearance. In some specimens, the interstices were perfectly rhomboidal, and separated into rhombic fragments. Several enormous and romantic blocks were scattered along the margin of the river, and on some of them small trees were growing. From the summit opened another sublime view of the surrounding country. Again to the south and south-west, I could distinguish three of the four chains of mountains, which were visible from the high hills of the Petit John, and still, to my surprise, distinctly appeared the Mamelle, though, by water, near upon 100 miles distant, and not less than 60 by land, which would appear to argue an elevation more considerable than that which I had at first imagined. The Magazine mountain to the west, though, at first, apparently so near, is not less than 10 miles distant, looking, if any thing, more considerably elevated than the Mamelle, and probably not less than 1200 feet high. In this point of view, it appears isolated, gradually descending into the plain, and accumulating in magnitude to the north-west; it here descends rather more abruptly, though the highest point is still to the south, where it appears to rise in broken fasçades unconnectedly with the auxiliary ridge.[85]

8TH.] From the Cherokees I understood that there still exists some portion of the Natchez, who live with the Choctaws, near Mobile river. It would be interesting to learn, what affinities their language possesses with that of the existing nations. The Chetimachas of bayou Placquimine, said by Du Pratz to speak the same language, and to be a branch of the same people, might also afford some information concerning the Natchez and their connections.[86]

[85]Magazine Mountain, indeed, rises 2,300 feet above the floor of the Arkansas Valley and, as earlier noted, has a total elevation of 2,823 feet.

[86]For the Natchez, refer to Chapter II, note 26. The Chitimachas, neighbors to the Natchez in Louisiana, were unrelated to them linguistically, speaking their own distinct tongue. Like the Natchez, who massacred Chopart and his French garrison at Fort

In the evening, we crossed to the right-hand cliff of the Dardanelle, where Mr. D. again renewed his trade with the Indians and their retailers. I embraced this opportunity to make one of my usual rambles, and found an extraordinary difference in the progress of vegetation here, exposed to the south and sheltered from the north-western wind. Proceeding leisurely towards the summit of the hill, I was amused by the gentle murmurs of a rill and pellucid water, which broke from rock to rock. The acclivity, through a scanty thicket, rather than the usual sombre forest, was already adorned with violets, and occasional clusters of the parti-coloured Collinsia. The groves and thickets were whitened with the blossoms of the Dogwood (Cornus florida). The lugubrious vociferations of the whip-poor-will; the croaking frogs, chirping crickets, and whoops and halloos of the Indians, broke not disagreeably the silence of a calm and fine evening, in which the thermometer still remained at 70°; and though the scene was not finished in the usual style of rural landscape, yet to me it was peculiarly agreeable, when contrasted with the dull monotony of a gloomy and interminable forest, whose solitude had scarcely ever been cheered by the voices or habitations of men.

9TH.] In the forenoon, I proceeded to Mr. Webber's,[87] along the hills of the Dardanelle, which border the right bank of the river, opposite to which, a contiguous ridge and similar cliffs also appear, forming, as it were, a wide chasm traversed by the river. The approach of these hills to either bank, like vast portals, probably originated the name of this place. Walking along the margin of the continued precipice which bordered the river, I observed a brownish animal quickly retreating into its burrow, which in size appeared to be little short of that of a mole. On rolling away

---

Rosalie in 1729, the Chitimachas earlier had killed Saint Cosmé, in 1706, soon after the beginning of French settlement near the mouth of the Mississippi. Le Page du Pratz, the author of *Histoire de la Louisiane*, was present at their subsequent surrender.

[87]Walter Webber, a headman of the Western Cherokees and a trader on the south bank of the Arkansas at Dardanelle (present Yell County), was reported by Capt. John R. Bell, of the Long Expedition in 1820, to be distancing the government trading post at Spadre Bluff, a few miles up the Arkansas. Webber would lead a war party of Cherokees against the trading post on the Neosho River operated by Col. A. P. Chouteau and Joseph Revoir, the French-Osage mixed blood, in 1821, ending in the death of Revoir. Webber's post burned in 1824, after which he traded at Nicksville, halfway between the Three Forks and present Van Buren, thereafter at Webber's Falls in present Muskogee County, Okla., to his death in 1834. AM. ST. PAPERS, INDIAN AFFAIRS, II, 329; TERR. PAPERS, XIX, 105–107; FOREMAN [1], 53, 227–28.

a fragment of rock, I succeeded in discovering that the object of my pursuit was an enormous spider, no less than four inches from the extremity of one foot to that of the other, and two inches from head to tail, covered with long brown hair; the eyes six in number and minute, the mouth not discoverable, but in the place of jaws, as in the Monoculi, two of the six pair of feet, of a strong cartilaginous texture, very short and retracted together, each terminated by a simple hooked claw, and internally lined with a row of minute teeth for mastication. In fact, it entirely resembled those gigantic tropical spiders, which we see exhibited in museums.[88]

The rocks, like many others which we had now seen, are still arenilitic, and apparently destitute of organic remains. From the enormous dislocated masses and gaping chasms which here border the precipice, I am strongly inclined to believe, that this ridge had, at some period, been convulsed by an earthquake.

In the course of my inquiries concerning minerals, I was told of the existence of a silver mine, somewhere along the banks of White river, but though the opinion is a very prevalent one, it is necessary to receive it with caution. Fragments of pyrites, as usual, have been shown to me for precious ores, and the true statement of their value, so contrary to sanguine expectation, is often treated as an imposition to conceal their importance.

Mr. Walter Webber, a metif, who acts as an Indian trader, is also a chief of the nation, and lives in ease and affluence, possessing a decently furnished and well provided house, several negro slaves, a large, well cleared, and well fenced farm; and both himself and his nephew read, write, and speak English. Yesterday, while passing along the bank of the river, I observed with pleasure the fine farms and comfortable cabins occupied by the Indians, and found them very busily employed felling trees, and clearing their grounds preparatory to the seed-time. The failure, however, of last year's crops, in consequence of the dry weather, was severely felt, and more particularly in consequence of the arrival among them of many ill-provided families of emigrants from the old nation.

In the evening, the brother of their late principal chief Tallantusky, arrived here, accompanied by his wife and two or three other Indians.[89]

[88]What Nuttall saw was one of the tarantula (Theraphosidae) family, possibly of the genus *Aphonopsema*.

[89]Tahlonteskee, principal chief of the Arkansas Cherokees, had migrated west with

He last year took leave of the old nation in the Mississippi territory, and embarked with the emigrants, who are yet far from forming a majority of the nation. Being a half Indian, and dressed as a white man, I should scarcely have distinguished him from an American, except by his language. He was very plain, prudent, and unassuming in his dress and manners; a Franklin amongst his countrymen, and affectionately called the "beloved" father. Sensible to the wants of those who had accompanied him in his emigration, he had confidently expected a supply of flour and salt from Mr. Drope, all of which articles had, however, been sold below, excepting a small quantity reserved for the chief himself. He could have sent, he said, some of his people down to the mouth of the river, to purchase maize and flour, but that it would interrupt them in preparing their fields for the ensuing crop. Mr. D., who had in the Mississippi territory become acquainted with Jolly, the chief, tells me that his word is inviolable, and that his generosity knew no bounds, but the limitation of his means.

11TH.] Returning from my rambles to-day, chiefly in quest of insects, I picked off my skin and clothes more than 50 ticks (*Acarus sanguisugas*), which are here more abundant and troublesome than in any other part of America in which I have yet been.[90] Many of the same kinds of insects, common to the banks of the Missouri, and, indeed, to most parts of the United States, are also found in this territory.

From the hills in the vicinity of Mr. Webber's, I obtained a fine view of the Magazine mountain, and now found that it was connected with a range of others, proceeding for many miles a little to the north of west. The side which here presents itself, appeared almost inaccessibly precipitous.

15TH.] This afternoon, I had again the pleasure of seeing the brother

---

three hundred of his tribesmen in 1809. He took a leading part in the guerilla warfare between the Cherokees and Osages, including the massacre of Osages at Claremore Mound, the site of Osage Chief Clermont's village, in the autumn of 1817. AM. ST. PAPERS, INDIAN AFFAIRS, II, 97–98, 125–26; *Niles' Weekly Register*, XIII, 80; FOREMAN [1], 34n., 51–52.

John Jolly, Tahlonteskee's brother, who emigrated with a party of 331 Cherokees to Arkansas in February, 1818, assumed the chieftainship of the western Cherokees on Tahlonteskee's death in the spring of that year. Return J. Meigs to John C. Calhoun, February 19, 1818, in FOREMAN [1], 65.

[90]*Acarus sanguisugas* = *Acarus americanus* Linn., 1758 = *Amblyomma americanum* Koch, 1844, the lone star tick, abundant in Arkansas.

Magazin Mountain. Plate 4 in Nuttall's original of 1821

of the late governor Lewis, now Cherokee agent, whom I had first met with at fort Mandan, on the Missouri.[91] From him I learn, that the progress of civilization among the Cherokees, is comparatively modern; that Nancy Ward, called by way of eminence and esteem "the beloved," first introduced among them the domesticated cow. From her have sprung several men of distinction in the nation, by whose influence and example the condition of their Indian brethren has been ameliorated. Her advice and council borders on supreme, her interference is allowed to be decisive even in affairs of life and death.[92]

From the civilized Cherokees, with whom alone I could conveniently hold converse, I found it extremely difficult to acquire any knowledge, either of the traditions, opinions, or ancient customs of their nation. The humiliating details of former poverty, ignorance, and superstition, tended to wound the feelings of those, who, besides the advantages, had also imbibed the pride and luxury of Europe. If the Cherokees had only discarded their superstitions, and retained their social virtues, besides acquiring habits of industry, we might indeed congratulate them on the change of their condition; but, unfortunately, with the superior intelligence, conveniences, and luxuries of civilization, have also been acquired that selfish attachment to property, that love of riches, which, though not really intrinsic, have still the power to purchase sinister interest, and separate the condition of men, and hence arises that accumulation of laws

[91] Reuben Lewis (1777–1844), only brother of Meriwether Lewis, had been co-host with his partner in the Missouri Fur Company, Manuel Lisa, to Nuttall, John Bradbury, the English naturalist, and Henry Marie Brackenridge, of Philadelphia, at Fort Mandan, the company fur-trading post on the Upper Missouri, in 1811. After a summer and autumn of collecting, Nuttall had gone downriver with Lewis, Lisa, and their other partner, Andrew Henry, to Saint Louis, arriving October 21. GRAUSTEIN, 70, 71, 74.

Lewis, as a subagent for Indian Affairs, was present at the signing of the Osage Treaty of November 10, 1808, at Fire Prairie (near present Kansas City) ceding Osage lands between the Missouri and Arkansas rivers. He succeeded Maj. William L. Lovely as agent for the Cherokees on the Arkansas July 11, 1817, after the latter's death. He had previously traded with both the Cherokees and Osages in Arkansas. TERR. PAPERS, XIV, 242–44; XV, 54, 291; Edwin C. Bearss, "In Quest of Peace on the Indian Border: The Establishment of Fort Smith," *Arkansas Historical Quarterly*, Vol. XXIII, No. 2 (Summer, 1964), 129–30.

[92] James Mooney noted Nuttall's statements in the present tense about Nancy Ward but doubted she still lived in 1819. Apparently a half-blood, she possibly was the daughter of a British officer and a Cherokee woman, sister of Attakullaculla, principal chief at Great Echota, present Monroe County, Tenn. Her biography is more fully developed in MOONEY, 202–204.

and punishments, from which the patriarchal state of those we call savages was so happily exempt. No legal snares were laid for the heedless; no gallows erected for the guilty; no contest arose for wealth or power. Every tribe was but a single family; their aged chief and his venerable associates were as fathers, governors, and advisers. No one was rich while the others were poor; and they considered nothing of value that was not essentially useful. As their frugal wants were almost spontaneously supplied, they were strangers alike to poverty and affluence; they boasted not of possessions; and were habitually hospitable to strangers. Scarcely sensible of want, they were alive to friendship and undissembled passions. Their pride, confined to personal excellence, was always checked by the emulation of superior worth, sanctioned and acknowledged by the approbation of the aged.

Almost unrestrained by artifice or moral education, we should, perhaps, expect the man of nature to become the prey of passion, like the irrational creation. Yet so nicely balanced, in every situation, is the proportion of good and evil allotted to humanity, that one stage of society has but little advantage over another. Nature is not a cruel demon, nor delights in the accomplishment of destruction. Those who are fed by her frugal bounties are but seldom hurried into excess; indeed, the nations of America were stigmatized with apathy, so great was their command of the social passions, and their magnanimity under suffering. But the dire hatred which they bore their enemies, was a lasting proof of the strength of their affections, and mutual attachment. They felt for each other as members of the same family, as sons of the same father; a band of brothers mutually bound to defend and revenge the cause of each other, by a just and undeviating system of retaliation.

Their affection for those, whom time or casualty removed from the social circle, was as great and sincere, as extravagant demonstration could possibly declare. Among the Cherokees and others, the dead were not only accompanied by the choicest things which they had valued in life, but even, if a chief or father, interred in the house which had been his habitation, and which was thenceforth devoted to ruin and desolation. So awful even was the inanimate body then considered, that all who had immediately attended the interment, or touched the corpse, refrained from the company of their wives and families, for the space of seven days and nights.

In no part of North America have we ever met with that kind of irrational adoration called idolatry. All the natives acknowledged the existence of a great, good, and indivisible Spirit, the author of all created being. Believing also in the immortality of the soul, and in the existence of invisible agencies, they were often subjected to superstitious fears, and the observance of omens and dreams, the workings of perturbed fancy. By these imaginary admonitions, they sometimes suffered themselves to be controlled in their most important undertakings, relinquishing every thing which was accidentally attended by any inauspicious presage of misfortune.

As among the Asiatics, and other imperfectly civilized nations, the condition of the female sex bordered upon degradation. Considered rather as objects of pleasure and necessity, than as rational companions, several of them often lived together in the house of the same husband. However custom might have tolerated this habit, we are happy to find that civilization tends to its abolition. Polygamy among the Cherokees, without any legal restraint, will, in time, be spontaneously abandoned, as their conjugal attachment appears to be strong and sincere.

Marriage among the Cherokees, as with most of the natives, was formerly consummated with very little ceremony. When a young man became enamoured, it was the custom modestly to declare his desire to marry through the medium of some female relative, who exclusively conferred with the mother, the father never interfering. If the mother agreed, and thought well of the proposal, it was immediately made known. If not, she put off making a direct answer by a reference to her brother or eldest son. Consent being obtained of the mother, the bridegroom without much further conference with the bride, was then told where she lay, and thenceforward admitted to her bed.

From some cause or other, it appears, that the women of the Cherokees frequently made use of means to promote abortion, which at length became so alarming, as to occasion a resort to punishment by whipping.

In all stages of society regulations have existed, either as controling customs, or written laws, whereby the conduct of men with each other was limited and restrained. A system of equity was established, more or less strictly according with justice, as influenced by exterior circumstances; thus life was claimed for life, and objects wrested from the weak or unsuspecting, restored by the interference of moral power vested in superiors and rulers. Among the Cherokees and other Indians of North America, the conviction of natural justice went so far as frequently to draw no distinction of punishment betwixt manslaughter and murder. Governed also by the idea of a general fraternity existing throughout a tribe of people, the brother of a murderer, or even his nearest relative was not secure from the fatal avenger, in the absence of the principal. In consequence of this, it sometimes happened that the brother became the executioner of his brother or nearest relative, who had committed a murder, in order to save himself from vengeance. He who had taken away the life of another, either by malice or accident, was also occasionally suffered to redeem it, by obtaining and presenting to the injured party, a scalp or a prisoner of the enemy, as they were satisfied in any way to obtain life for life.

An institution, I believe unparallelled in the policy of the northern natives, except among the Cherokees and Creeks (and which has been quoted by Mr. Adair in order to prove an affinity with the Jews),[93] was the existence of a town of refuge, inhabited by the supreme chief, in which no blood was suffered to be shed, and into which those who had committed manslaughter and other crimes were suffered to enter on excusing themselves or professing contrition.

With the inequality of fortune which civilization has introduced among the Cherokees, we find also a severity in their legal punishments, to which they were formerly strangers. Out of their salaries now received

---

[93]James Adair was the author of *The History of the American Indians* (London, 1775). The myths, religion, and social and cultural institutions of the Cherokees have been subjects of intensive investigation since Nuttall's day, the bibliography for which is now large. Mooney's work, frequently cited in the present notes, is memorable. But even as Nuttall was writing, a singular expression of a cross-fertilization between white and Cherokee cultures was about to take form in Sequoyah's syllabary of the Cherokee language, the matrices for which were punched in Boston sometime between 1821 and 1823 (they may be seen in the Division of Manuscripts of the Bizzell Memorial Library, University of Oklahoma, Norman, where they were placed by the editor of the present volume).

from government, they appropriate a certain sum towards the support of a police, whose duty it is to punish those who are guilty of crimes against the public. A man who has for the first time been convicted of horsesteal-ing, receives a punishment of 100 lashes, and for the second offence 200, thus increasing the punishment for every additional offence. For stealing a cow 50 lashes were inflicted, and so on, in proportion to the value of the property stolen.

Mr. John Rogers, a very respectable and civilized Cherokee,[94] told me that one of the regulators happening to have a relation who had been repeatedly guilty of theft, and finding him incorrigible, he destroyed his eye-sight with a penknife, saying, "as long as you can see you will steal, I will therefore prevent your thefts by the destruction of your sight." Dis-satisfied with this system of punishment, many of the poor renegadoes fled from the bosom of the Cherokee nation, and came to the banks of the Arkansa and Red river. The same punishment for theft will now, how-ever, probably be established also in this territory.

The former preparation of the warrior, among the Cherokees, was more calculated to inspire fortitude under suffering than courage in the field. The chief was ever attentive to the admonition of dreams and omens. They sung the songs of war, and imposed upon themselves the most rigid fasts and mortifying ablutions, at all seasons of the year, in order to obtain a favourable omen for their departure. Day after day these privations and voluntary sufferings were continued with fearful austerity, and those who might express a wish for relaxation were desired to leave the society.

The arrival of the Cherokees in this country did not fail, as might have been foreseen, to excite the jealousy of the Osages, within whose former

[94]John Rogers was an intermarried Cherokee and a chief under John Jolly. He ap-peared in Arkansas as early as 1816 and had emigrated with thirty-one Cherokees on October 18, 1817, from Tennessee to claim Arkansas lands provided the Cherokees in exchange for certain holdings ceded east of the Mississippi. They arrived on the Arkansas seven months later, on April 18, 1818. Rogers would later operate the salt works on the Grand (Neosho) at present Salina, Mays County, Oklahoma, after Sam Houston, who had acquired them in 1830, departed for Texas. By his contemporaries Rogers was said to be white (Governor Joseph McMinn to the Secretary of War, November 11, 1817, in FOREMAN [1], 64), but, regardless of race, in most documents he is referred to as a Cherokee and a chief.

territory they had now taken up their residence. Major Lovely, the first agent appointed to reside among the Cherokees of the Arkansa, on his arrival held a council with the Osages at the falls of the Verdegris, and about 60 miles distant from their village.[95] Some quarrel, however, about two years ago arising between the two nations, the Osages way-layed 12 or 14 of the Cherokees and killed them. On this occasion, the Cherokees collected together in considerable numbers, and ascended the river to take revenge upon the Osages, who fled at their approach, losing about 10 of their men, who either fell in the retreat, or becoming pris-oners, were reserved for a more cruel destiny. The Cherokees, now forgetting the claims of civilization, fell upon the old and decrepid, upon the women and innocent children, and by their own account destroyed not less than 90 individuals! and carried away a number of prisoners. A white man who accompanied them (named Chisholm), with a diabolical cruelty that ought to have been punished with death, dashed out the brains of a helpless infant, torn from the arms of its butchered mother! Satiated with a horrid vengeance, the Cherokees returned with exultation to bear the tidings of their own infamy and atrocity.[96]

[95]Lovely, who before the Revolution had lived in the home of James Madison's father, was appointed Indian agent to the Cherokees of Arkansas in 1813. With characteristic enthusiasm he set about reshaping boundaries on the Arkansas and White rivers, for which he was reprimanded by Superintendent of Indian Affairs William Clark. He urged a government factory for the Arkansas River Cherokees in 1816 (it became a reality in 1818) and negotiated in the same year what became known as Lovely's Pur-chase from the Osages, as a vast extension of the Cherokee domain in western Arkansas and eastern Oklahoma. His unauthorized purchase was confirmed by a treaty between the United States and the Osages, signed September 25, 1818, nineteen months after his death on February 24, 1817. TERR. PAPERS, XV, 50–52, 121–22, 173; Stephen H. Long to Thomas A. Smith, January 30, 1818, in TERR. PAPERS, XIX, 6 and 6n.; *Arkansas Gazette*, September 23 and 30, 1828; KAPPLER, II, 96–100, 116–17.

[96]The principal battle described above took place at Claremore Mound, N.E. of present Tulsa, in the autumn of 1817, when some six hundred Cherokees and allied Choctaws, Delawares, and Shawnees from east of the Mississippi and Western Cherokees and Cad-dos, Koasatis, Tonkawas, and Comanches in Arkansas attacked Clermont's Osage vil-lage in the absence of its chiefs and warriors, who were hunting on the Plains. Nuttall's account of John D. Chisholm's part in the massacre is the most vivid of several contem-porary statements. It may have been achieved from Major Bradford at Fort Smith, after Nuttall's arrival there. His broad details of the event conform to those in JAMES [1] in THWAITES [1], XVII, 19–23.

Chisholm, one of eleven whites on the expedition, had established a claim to Arkansas lands by or before 1796, and apparently from associating and trading with the Eastern and Western Cherokees had become a headman among the latter as early as 1809. He and

It appears, to me, to have been the duty of the superintendent of Indian affairs to have apprehended that white man, and delivered him over to the government for trial and punishment. Without some interference of this kind, and indeed a cognizance of the conduct of every white man found permanently dwelling among the Indians, it will not be possible for a traveller or a merchant to go amongst these people without incurring the greatest personal risk, as their revenge is but too often indiscriminate in its object; neither can the security of the frontier settlements ever be rendered certain, until these wanton and unprovoked cruelties of the whites, and their piratical wars, be prevented.

Two or three families of the Delawares are now living with the Cherokees, who appeared to be very poor, and addicted to intoxication. Another remnant of these unfortunate people, once so considerable, is also about to be transferred from the state of Ohio to the banks of the Arkansa, where, it is to be hoped, they will enjoy amidst domestic tranquillity the superior advantages of civilization.

17TH.] My rambles to-day were rewarded with the discovery of a new genus, of the class Tetradynamia or Cruciferae, allied to *Ricotia* and *Lunaria*. In the evening I visited Mr. Rollins, the agent for Indian trade, who treated me with politeness and hospitality.[97]

James Rogers, son of John Rogers, were "deputies" of the chiefs and headmen and were given power of attorney in signing the Cherokee Treaty of July 8, 1817, at Calhoun, near present Dayton, Tenn., where Treaty Commissioners Andrew Jackson, Joseph McMinn, and David Meriwether rewarded him with one thousand dollars "under the table." *Niles' Weekly Register*, XIII, 80, 312; KAPPLER, II, 96ff.; JACKSON [1], II, 305; TERR. PAPERS, XIII, 401–12; XIV, 472, 528; XIX, 429–30, 482–83.

[97]Nuttall's rambles (on foot) had carried him upstream a dozen miles from Dardanelle to Illinois Bayou, on the left bank of the Arkansas, where Isaac Rawlings was operating the U.S. Trading Factory temporarily as he carried forward the construction of the more permanent factory at Spadre Bayou, completed some four months later, in September, 1819.

The Arkansas River had not had a government factory since the closing of the Arkansas Post factory in 1810, a short five years after it was opened in 1805. The arrival of the Cherokees in force on the upper river seemed to promise good business for the enterprise. Rawlings did not remain long at his post, however, being replaced by Matthew Lyon on May 20, 1820.

PEAKE, 275; Thomas L. McKenney to Rawlings, September 25, 1819, in TERR. PAPERS, XIX, 106; MORRIS, 40–41; AM. ST. PAPERS, INDIAN AFFAIRS, II, 505.

CHAPTER VIII.

---

*Pass several inconsiderable rivulets, and obtain sight of the Tomahawk
mountain and the Gascon hills—Mulberry creek—that of Vache Grasse—
Lee's creek—prairies—Sugarloaf mountain—Arrive at the garrison of
Belle Point—a change in the vegetation—The Maclura or Bow-wood—
The garrison—Cedar prairie—Rare plants.*

20TH.] This morning I left Mr. Webber's, in a perogue with two
French boatmen, in order to proceed to the garrison, about 120 miles
distant by water. We proceeded nearly to Charbonniere creek,[1] 24 miles
from the place of departure. Ten miles from Webber's we passed the
outlet of Piney creek,[2] so called from the pine-hills by which it is bordered. Eight miles further we came to Rocky creek,[3] opposite to the outlet
of which, a ledge of rocks nearly traverses the Arkansa, and presents a
considerable obstruction in the navigation at a low stage of water. The
current even at this time broke with a considerable noise.

21ST.] About six miles above Rocky creek we passed the Charbonniere, so called from the occurrence of coal in its vicinity; we also observed the outlet of Spadrie creek,[4] on the borders of which there are
considerable tracts of fertile land, well supplied with springs, and occupied by the Cherokees. The rocks which occasionally border the river,
of very inconsiderable elevation, are composed of slaty sandstone, dipping
about 25°, sometimes towards the north-west, and at others to the south-
east, or in opposite directions, and also exhibiting indications of coal. The

[1]Charbonnière Creek, in Logan County, Ark., flows north into the Arkansas. It gets
its name from the coal, semianthracite and bituminous, which underlies the area, notably
north of the Arkansas. In what follows, Nuttall gives streams and other landmarks
between his starting point at Webber's trading post and the Charbonnière.
[2]Now Pine Creek, flowing in S.E. Johnson County into Dardanelle Reservoir.
[3]Rock Creek, now Shoal Creek, in Logan County.
[4]Spadre Bayou flows southward in Johnson County, emptying into Dardanelle Reservoir opposite the Charbonnière at the old village of Spadra (Spadre).

Charbonniere rock, in particular, about 50 feet high, presents beds of a slaty sandstone, with a dip of scarcely 20°, and inclined in opposite directions so as to form a basin, in which there are indications of coal. A lofty blue ridge appears to the south, called by the French hunters the Cassetete or Tomahawk mountain, and about eight miles from hence enters the creek of the same name,[5] beyond which we proceeded eight miles of a 12 mile bend, making a journey of about 28 miles in the course of the day, and encamped in view of another lofty ridge of mountains. We saw, as we proceeded, no less than 13 deer and a bear.

22D.] Four miles from Allmand creek[6] the Cassetete mountain appears very distinct, and somewhat resembles the Magazine; being a long ridge abrupt at either end. Another range also was visible at a considerable distance, called the Gascon hills. We were detained awhile by a thunderstorm, but proceeded, notwithstanding, about 30 miles, and encamped on an island just below the outlet of Mulberry creek, on the banks of which, before the arrival of the Cherokees, there was a considerable settlement on a body of excellent land.[7] It now constitutes the Cherokee line of demar-

[5]Cassetête (Tomahawk) Mountain is modern Short Mountain, rising five hundred feet above the surrounding terrain. It gives its name to Short Mountain Creek, in Logan County.

[6]Allmand (*Allemand,* French for "German") Creek is apparently lost without further trace among names of physical features, as are also the Gascon Hills.

[7]Mulberry River on the east and Mulberry Creek a few miles from it on the west, in Franklin and Crawford counties, empty into the Arkansas. The old settlement of Mulberry lies between the two streams. It possessed a blockhouse, used for defense against Osage retaliatory raids against Cherokee settlements downstream from it on the Arkansas. Osage-Cherokee warfare, rather than Cherokee treaty provisions, caused whites to leave Mulberry periodically, although some families did remove in 1819, after the execution of the Cherokee treaty with the United States of February 27, as noted by Nuttall and, later, by U.S. Factor Matthew Lyon at Spadre Bayou. Journal of April 8, 1821, reproduced in TERR. PAPERS, XIX, 343–45.

Nuttall's "Cherokee line of demarkation" refers to a supposed western boundary, which, however, was left open-ended by the Cherokee Treaty of July 8, 1817, from which the Cherokees were to receive north of the Arkansas lands compensating the tribe "acre for acre" for lands relinquished east of the Mississippi. No western line was established until surveys, made more or less arbitrarily by the General Land Office in January and February, 1825, placed it at Table Rock on the Arkansas S.W. of Fort Smith, running N. 1 mile and 70 chains, thence N. 53° E. 132 miles and 31 chains to White River opposite the mouth of Little North Fork. Relevant papers for the General Land Office, War Department (Indian Office), and the Territorial Government of Arkansas are indexed in TERR. PAPERS, XV, XIX, and XX. Graphic representation appears in Charles C. Royce, *Land Cessions in the United States,* Bureau of American Ethnology, *18th Annual Report,* Part II, Plate 6, Area 143.

kation, and they made free to occupy the deserted cabins and improvements of the whites without any compensation received either from them or the government. The bend, which we continued this morning, of 12 miles extent, is surrounded on the right hand side with an amphitheatre of lofty cliffs, 3 to 400 feet high, having a highly romantic picturesque appearance. Nearly continuing to Mulberry creek, a fine stretch of about eight miles opens to view, affording an ample prospect of the river; its rich alluvions were now clothed in youthful verdure, and backed in the distance by bluish and empurpled hills. The beauty of the scenery was also enlivened by the melody of innumerable birds, and the gentle humming of the wild bees, feeding on the early blooming willows,[8] which in the same manner line the picturesque banks of the Ohio. The Arkansa, in its general appearance throughout this day's voyage, bears, indeed, a considerable resemblance to that river. It is equally diversified with islands, and obstructed in its course by gravelly rapids; two of them which we passed to-day, could not have a collective fall of less than 10 or 12 feet each.

The sandstone beds still present very little dip, and by contrary inclinations produce the appearance of basins or circumscribed vallies.

23D.] Two miles above Mulberry creek we passed two islands nearly opposite to each other, and a settlement of three or four families situated along the left bank of the river, on a handsome rising ground, flanked by a continued ridge of low hills. The dawn of morning was again ushered in by the songs of thousands of birds, re-echoing through the woods, and seeking shelter from the extensive plains, which every where now border the alluvion.

We proceeded about 32 miles, and experienced a scorching sun from noon till night, when at length the sky became obscured by clouds portentous of thunder. My thermometer when exposed to the sun rose to 100°. Nearly opposite Vache Grasse creek we passed a rapid over which there is scarcely more than 12 inches water, in the lowest stage.[9] No hills now appear on either hand, and a little distance in the prairie, near Vache Grasse, stands the last habitation of the whites to be met with on the banks of the Arkansa, except those of the garrison.

[8]Salix caroliniana [Michx.] —NUTTALL. [*Salix nigra* Marsh. is possibly what he saw.]

[9]Vache Grasse Creek drains central Sebastian County, S. of the Arkansas.

Not far from Lee's creek, Perpillon of the French hunters,[10] a low ridge again comes up to the border of the river, in which is discoverable the first calcareous rock on ascending the Arkansa. From hence also the prairies or grassy plains begin to be prevalent, and the trees to decrease in number and magnitude. Contiguous to our encampment commenced a prairie of seven miles in length, and continuing within a mile of the garrison. The river, now presenting long and romantic views, was almost exclusively bordered with groves of cotton-wood, at this season extremely beautiful, resembling so many vistas clad in the softest and most vivid verdure, and crowded with innumerable birds, but of species common to the rest of the United States.

24TH.] This morning we passed the hills of Lee's creek, which for a short distance border the Arkansa; and about noon arrived at the garrison, which comes into view at the distance of about four miles, agreeably terminating a stretch of the river. Rising, as it were, out of the alluvial forest, is seen from hence, at the distance of 35 miles, a conic mountain nearly as blue as the sky, and known by the French hunters under the name of Point de Sucre, or the sugar loaf.[11]

I met with politeness from major Bradford the commander of the garrison,[12] but was disagreeably surprised to be given to understand, that I

[10]So named after some Frenchmen, and not Papillon, as called by Pike.—NUTTALL. [Lee Creek, Nuttall's identification, has stuck. It enters the Arkansas from the N.E. between Van Buren and Ft. Smith. THWAITES [1], XIII, 197n. identifies it mistakenly as River au Millieu from Lt. James Biddle Wilkinson's sketch map (formalized in Pike's Map No. 3 in *The Journals of Zebulon Montgomery Pike, with Letters and Related Documents*, ed. by Donald Jackson, I, II, 17n.). But Wilkinson had River au Millieu entering the Arkansas below Vache Grasse Creek, clearly too far downstream.]

[11]An extended elevation in Le Flore County, Okla., variously given as 2,550 to 2,570 feet.

[12]Maj. William Bradford had been successively a captain and a major of infantry in the War of 1812, and from August 20, 1814, had been retained as a captain with the brevet rank of major in the crack Rifle Regiment, ascending to major of that regiment in November, 1818. In the chain-of-command order from Acting Secretary of War George Graham for the creation of a military post athwart the contested ground between Osages and Cherokees "at, or as near to, as circumstances will admit, the point where the Osage boundary crosses the Arkansaw river," issued July 30, 1817, Gen. Andrew Jackson, commanding the Southern Department of the Army at Nashville, relayed instructions to Brig. Gen. Thomas A. Smith, commanding the Ninth Department at Belle Fontaine, Missouri Territory. Smith, himself commandant of the Rifle Regiment from 1799, chose perhaps naturally another Rifle Regiment officer, Bradford, for the task of setting up this westernmost post. HEITMAN, I, 238; BEARSS, 123–53.

could not have permission to proceed any higher up the river without a special credential from the secretary of state, authorizing me to hold that intercourse with the natives, which I might deem necessary in further pursuing my journey. It appeared to me, however, sufficiently obvious, that the governor of the territory must be empowered to permit an intercourse, civil and commercial, with the Indians, and liberty to travel through their country by their concurrence. And, indeed, all difficulty was removed by a reference to the recent regulations, which empowered the commanders of the garrisons optionally to permit such intercourse; and I am happy to add, that this measure, which referred me to the hospitality of the major, was, apparently, as gratifying to him as to myself.[13]

At the benevolent request of the commander, and agreeably to my intentions of exploring the natural history of the territory, I resolved to spend a few weeks at the garrison, and make it the depot of my collections. It is with a satisfaction, clouded by melancholy, that I now call to mind the agreeable hours I spent at this station, while accompanied by the friendly aid and kind participation of Dr. Russel,[14] whose memory I have faintly endeavoured to commemorate in the specific name of a beautiful species of *Monarda*.[15] But relentless death, whose ever-withering hand delights to pluck the fairest flowers, added, in the fleeting space of a few

[13] Bradford was asserting the provisions in Article 5 of the Cherokee treaty of February 27, 1819, prohibiting white intrusion and settlement on Indian lands (it referred to "an act [Chap. 13] to regulate trade and intercourse with the Indian tribes" passed in 1802). But Nuttall must have known something of the Arkansas territorial extent under the Act of March 2, 1819 (3 STAT. 493–96) creating the territory. It would have left much discretion to the territorial governor, nominally at least the superintendent of Indian Affairs for an area which embraced not only present Arkansas but most of present Oklahoma s. of 36°30'. John C. Calhoun, Secretary of War, to Governor James Miller, September 29, 1819, in TERR. PAPERS, XIX, 102. The broad question of Indian sovereignty was referred to but was not an issue in the U.S. Supreme Court decision in 1970 (397 U.S. 620), which contains succinct historical summaries of both the Cherokee and the Choctaw presence in Arkansas and Oklahoma.

[14] Dr. Thomas Russell (1793–1819), the young post surgeon, was a native of Salem, Mass., and had been educated at Brown University and at the Medical School of the University of Pennsylvania, from which he took his M.D. in 1814. At the latter he presumably had courses with Benjamin Smith Barton, John Redman Coxe, and Caspar Wistar, all of whom had strong avocational botanical interests (Nuttall named the genus *Wisteria* [more euphonious than *Wistaria*, he said] for Wistar). Russell had been an army doctor since his graduation. GRAUSTEIN, 123, 142.

[15] *Monarda russeliana* [Nutt.] —NUTTALL.

short days, another early trophy to his mortal garland; and Russel, the only hope of a fond and widowed mother, the last of his name and family, now sleeps obscurely in unhallowed earth! Gentle Reader, forgive this tribute of sympathy to the recollection of one, whom fully to know was surely to esteem, as a gentleman, an accomplished scholar, and a sincere admirer of the simple beauties of the field of nature.

27TH.] Yesterday I took a walk of about five miles up the banks of the Pottoe, and found my labour well repayed by the discovery of several new or undescribed plants. In this direction the surface of the ground is gently broken or undulated, and thinly scattered with trees, resembling almost in this respect a cultivated park. The whole expanse of forest, hill, and dale, was now richly enamelled with a profusion of beautiful and curious flowers; among the most conspicuous was the charming Daisy of America,[16] of a delicate lilac colour, and altogether corresponding in general aspect with the European species; intermingled, appears a new species of *Collinsia*, a large-flowered *Tradescantia*, various species of *Phlox*, the *Verbena aubletia*, and the esculent *Scilla*.[17] From a low hill, the neighbouring prairie appeared circumscribed by forests, but the mountains of the Pottoe were not visible. The soil, even throughout the uplands, appeared nearly as fertile as the alluvions, and affords a most productive pasture to the cattle.

[16] *Bellis integrifolia* Michx. —NUTTALL. [= *Astranthium integrifolia* (Michx.) Nutt., since Nuttall concluded that this plant was not congeneric with *Bellis* and therefore described the genus *Astranthium* Nutt. for it.]

[17] *Collinsia violacea* Nutt., of the figwort (Scrophulariaceae) family. Nuttall had honored his friend Zaccheus Collins (1764–1831), the Quaker merchant and Philadelphia philanthropist, a decade earlier by naming the genus *Collinsia* Nutt. for him, the genus being erected to accommodate a new plant, *Collinsia verna* Nutt., which he found on his foot journey from Pittsburgh to Le Boeuf in 1810 and which continued to be one of his favorites to the end of his days. GRAUSTEIN, 45.

Tradescantia L., of the spiderwort (Commelinaceae) family, may be in this range either *T. Ernestiana* Anders. and Woodson or *T. ozarkana* Anders. and Woodson.

Phlox has many representatives in this range: *P. divaricata* L. and *P. pilosa* L. are abundant; *P. glaberrima* L. and *P. paniculata* L. occur here; and *P. bifida* Beck and *P. bifida* var. *cedaria* (Brand) Fern. are present but infrequent.

Verbena aubletia = *V. canadensis* (L.) Britt.

Scilla L. is an Old World genus, English bluebell or harebell. Nuttall's reference is to the plant known as *Scilla esculenta*, now known as *Camassia scilloides* (Raf.) Cory, the eastern camass or wild hyacinth.

On the 28TH, a slow rise in the river was perceptible, produced by the Canadian, or similar branches, and communicating a chocolate-red colour to the stream.

In the course of the day, I walked over the hills bordering the Pottoe, about six miles, in order to see some trees of the yellow-wood (*Maclura*), but they were scarcely yet in leaf, and showed no indications of producing bloom. Some of them were as much as 12 inches in diameter, with a crooked and spreading trunk, 50 or 60 feet high. Its wood dies yellow, and scarcely differs from the Fustick of the West Indies. From appearances, those few insulated trees of the Pottoe, are on the utmost limit of their northern range, and, though old and decayed, do not appear to be succeeded by others, or to produce any perfect fruit.[18] The day was so warm, that at 9 o'clock in the evening, the thermometer still stood at 75°.

The soil, wherever there is the slightest depression, is of a superior quality, and thickly covered with vegetable earth. The trees appear scattered as if planted by art, affording an unobstructed range for the hunter, equal to that of a planted park.

On the 29th, I took an agreeable walk into the adjoining prairie, which is about two miles wide and seven long. I found it equally undulated with the surrounding woodland, and could perceive no reason for the absence of trees, except the annual conflagration. A ridge of considerable elevation divides it about the centre, from whence the hills of the Pottoe, the Cavaniol, and the Sugar-loaf, at the distance of about 30 miles, appear partly enveloped in the mists of the horizon. Like an immense meadow, the expanse was now covered with a luxuriant herbage, and beautifully decorated with flowers, amongst which I was pleased to see the Painted Cup[19] of the eastern states, accompanied by occasional clusters of a white flowered *Dodecatheon* or American primrose.[20] The numerous rounded

[18]*Maclura* Nutt. (monotypic), Osage orange, or bois d'arc, originally of Arkansas and Texas, has been introduced and naturalized as far north as N.E. New York. Meriwether Lewis had sent slips of the "Osage Apples" to Thomas Jefferson from Saint Louis before the Lewis and Clark Expedition got under way. Pierre Chouteau propagated them in the Saint Louis area much earlier. Lewis to Jefferson, March 26, 1804, in JACKSON, D. [2], 170–71.

[19]*Euchroma coccinea* (Bartsia coccinea, Lin.). —NUTTALL. [Better *Castilleja coccinea* (L.) Spreng.]

[20]*D. Meadia* L. and var. *brachycarpum* (Small) Fassett are present in Arkansas and E.Oklahoma.

elevations which chequer this verdant plain, are so many partial attempts at shrubby and arborescent vegetation, which nature has repeatedly made, and which have only been subdued by the reiterated operation of annual burning, employed by the natives, for the purpose of hunting with more facility, and of affording a tender pasturage for the game.

May 1ST.] The river still continued rising, and also red and turbid from an admixture of the clay of the salt formation.

The garrison, consisting of two block-houses, and lines of cabins or barracks for the accommodation of 70 men whom it contains, is agreeably situated at the junction of the Pottoe, on a rising ground of about 50 feet elevation, and surrounded by alluvial and uplands of unusual fertility. The view is more commanding and picturesque, than any other spot of equal elevation on the banks of the Arkansa.[21] The meanders of the river to the eastward, backed by the hills of Lee's creek, are visible for more than six miles. The basis of the fort is a dark-coloured slaty micaceous sandstone, the lamina of which, nearly horizontal, and occasionally traversed by calcareous illinitions, are about four to six inches in thickness, and denudated for some hundreds of yards by the washing of the current, which, in an elevated stage, roars and foams with great velocity. About three or four miles up the Pottoe, this rock is underlayed by a bituminous slate-clay, indicative of coal, beneath which, no doubt, would be found calcareous rock; neither this nor the sandstone, however, present any organic remains.

3D.] To-day, accompanied by Doctor Russel, and another gentleman of the fort, I rode to Cedar prairie, lying about 10 miles south-east of the garrison, and presenting an irregular or undulating surface. I here found a second species of that interesting plant, which my venerable friend,

[21]Maj. Stephen Harriman Long (1784–1864), of the Corps of Topographical Engineers, who had been ordered by Gen. Thomas A. Smith to accompany Major Bradford and select the site for a post at the Osage line in Arkansas, preceded Bradford and most of his detachment on the ascent of the Arkansas River from Arkansas Post in mid-October, 1817. Returning downstream from the Falls of the Verdigris, Long chose the site called Belle Pointe by the French hunters at the junction of the Poteau with the Arkansas. He identified it as "Camp Smith" in his report of January 30, 1818, to Smith (his report of December 3, 1817, has not been found). Bradford and his detachment found Long's smaller party at the future site of Fort Smith on Christmas Day, 1817, while Long explored southward to Red River. By the time Nuttall arrived eighteen months later, the post was fully operative. TERR. PAPERS, XIX, 4–10; BEARSS, 143–46.

Cavaniol Mountain. Plate 5 in Nuttall's original of 1821

William Bartram,[22] called *Ixia coelestina*;[23] the flowers of this species are also of a beautiful blue, and white at the base. The whole plain was, in places, enlivened with the *Sysirinchium anceps*,[24] producing flowers of an uncommon magnitude; amidst this assemblage it was not easy to lose sight of the azure larkspur,[25] whose flowers are of the brightest ultramarine; in the depressions also grew the ochroleucous *Baptisia*,[26] loaded with papilionaceous flowers, nearly as large as those of the garden pea.

From this prairie, and more particularly from a hill which partly traverses it, the mountains of the Pottoe appeared quite distinct, the Sugar-loaf on the east, and the Cavaniol, about three miles apart, on the west side of the river; the latter is to all appearance much the highest, and presents a tabular summit.[27] The extensive and verdant meadow, in every direction appeared picturesquely bounded by woody hills of different degrees of elevation and distance, and lacked nothing but human occupation to reclaim it from barren solitude, and cast over it the air of rural cheerfulness and abundance.

7TH.] The Pottoe and the Arkansa were now at their utmost elevation, and their waters of a pale or milky colour, in consequence of being swelled

[22]Nuttall had met William Bartram (1739–1823) through Benjamin Smith Barton soon after he arrived from England on April 23, 1808. The distinguished son of John Bartram, whom Linnaeus considered the greatest "natural botanist" in the world and George III named Botanist Royal for the British Colonies in America, William was himself an able botanist, ornithologist, and compiler of a pharmacopoeia. His *Travels* (1791), not only in English but in German, French, and Dutch translations, was of great eminence. At the Bartram family home and gardens on the Schuylkill within present Philadelphia, Nuttall, a frequent guest, learned many of his early botanical lessons. GRAUSTEIN, 19–20.

[23]*Ixia coelestina* was one of two species Nuttall saw in western Arkansas and eastern Oklahoma. To accommodate them, he described the genus *Nemastylis*, but *N. coelestina* (Bartr.) Nutt., from the original *Ixia coelestina*, proved to be a different plant, which has become *Sphenostigma coelestinum* (Bartr.) Foster. Nuttall's plant then became known as *Nemastylis Nuttallii* Pickering, and his second of the genus is *N. geminiflora* Nutt. (The unraveling is George J. Goodman's, from R. C. Foster, Contr. Gray Herb. No. 155:26–44. 1945.)

[24]*Sisyrinchium anceps* Cav. = *S. angustifolium* Mill., one of the blue-eyed grasses of the iris (Iridaceae) family.

[25]*Delphinium azureum* [Michx.]. —NUTTALL. [= *D. carolinianum* Walt.]

[26]*Baptisia *leucophaea*. —NUTTALL. [Indigo, cream-colored. Editor's asterisk added to indicate Nuttall's naming of the species.]

[27]Cavanal Mountain, 2,400 feet in elevation, in Le Flore County, Okla., is lower than Sugar Loaf's 2,570 feet.

by the northern streams. The sand-bars and beaches were entirely submerged, and the river still also continued augmenting on the 8TH.

On the 9th, I again rode out to Cedar prairie, accompanied by the
Doctor, and one of the soldiers, whose intention was to hunt. Several deer
were discovered, but all too shy to be approached. We spent the night
about the centre of the first portion of the prairie, which is divided into
two parts by the intersection of s small wooded rivulet; and though the
evening was mild and delightfully tranquil, the swarms of musquetoes,
augmented since the recent freshet, would not permit us to sleep.

It is truly remarkable how greatly the sound of objects, becomes absorbed in these extensive woodless plains. No echo answers the voice, and
its tones die away in boundless and enfeebled undulations. Even game
will sometimes remain undispersed at the report of the gun. Encamping
near a small brook, we were favoured by the usual music of frogs, and
among them heard a species which almost exactly imitated the lowing of a
calf. Just as night commenced, the cheerless howling of a distant wolf
accosted our ears amidst the tranquil solitude, and the whole night we
were serenaded with the vociferations of the two species of whip-poor-
will.

The dawn of a cloudy day, after to us a wakeful night, was ushered in
by the melodious chorus of many thousands of birds, agreeably dispersing
the solemnity of the ambiguous twilight.

Amongst other objects of nature, my attention was momentarily arrested by the curious appearance of certain conic hillocks, about three feet
high, generally situated in denudated places, and covered over with minute pebbles; these on closer examination proved to be the habitations of
swarms of large red ants, who entered and came out by one or two common apertures.

On the wooded margin of the prairie, the doctor and myself were
gratified by the discovery of a very elegant plant, which constitutes a new
genus allied reciprocally to *Phacelia* and *Hydrophyllum*.[28]

---

[28]I have given it the trivial name of *Nemophila*, as, in this country, it now constitutes
the prevailing ornament of the Shady woods. —NUTTALL. [Here specifically *Nemophila
phacelioides* Nutt.]

CHAPTER IX.

Journey to Red river—Prairies and mountains of the Pottoe—Pass the divid-
ing ridge—Kiamesha river—Arrival on the banks of Red river—The
murder of a Cherokee; attempts to obtain redress—Wild horses—Charac-
ter, geological structure, and rare vegetable productions of the prairies—
Return to the garrison at Belle Point.

May 16TH.] This morning I left Fort Smith with major Bradford and
a company of soldiers, in order to proceed across the wilderness, to the
confluence of the Kiamesha and Red river. The object of the major was to
execute the orders of government, by removing all the resident whites out
of the territory of the Osages; the Kiamesha river being now chosen as the
line of demarkation.[1]

On this route we again proceeded through Cedar prairie, and, after
traversing two tiresome ridges of sand-stone hills, scattered with oaks and
pines, we encamped in the evening near to the base of the Sugar-loaf
mountain, having travelled about 25 miles in a south-west direction.
After passing the two ridges and crossing two brooks, one of them called
James' Fork, we kept westwardly towards the banks of the Pottoe, and
found the whole country a prairie, full of luxuriant grass about knee high,
in which we surprised herds of fleeting deer, feeding as by stealth.

The Cavaniol, now clear of mist, appeared sufficiently near to afford
some more adequate idea of its form and character. A prominent point
which appears on its summit, is, I am told by the Cherokees who accom-

[1]The Kiamichi (from French *kamichi*, "horned screamer") rises at Rich Mountain at
the present Arkansas-Oklahoma border and flows between Winding Stair and Kiamichi
mountains, through Le Flore, Pushmataha, and Choctaw counties, emptying into Red
River below Fort Towson (1824). The Osages would not relinquish their claims to lands
in this area until the Treaty of June 2, 1825. What Bradford and the Indian Office were
preparing for was the relocation of the Choctaw Indians of Mississippi (which had become a state in 1817) in much of present southwestern Arkansas and present eastern-
western Oklahoma south of the Canadian "to its source," in the language of the Treaty of
Doak's Stand, October 18, 1820. KAPPLER, II, 153–54, 211–14.

Nuttall's itinerary,

CANADA

LAKE SUPERIOR

MICHIGAN

TERRITORY

LAKE MICHIGAN

LAKE HURON

LAKE ONTARIO

LAKE ERIE

NEW YORK

Detroit

Erie

Cleveland

PENNSYLVANIA

Harrisburg

Philadelphia

Pittsburgh

IOWA

River

River

Mississippi

ILLINOIS

OHIO

INDIANA

Cincinnati

Ohio *River*

VIRGINIA

Kansas *River*

Independence

St. Louis

Louisville

KENTUCKY

Richmond

Grand *River*

Mississippi River

MISSOURI

Verdigris *River*

Bogie's Trading Post

Ft. Smith

White River

TENNESSEE

Tennessee River

NORTH CAROLINA

Little Rock

River

Hot Springs

ARKANSAS

Arkansas Post

SOUTH CAROLINA

River

MISSISSIPPI

ALABAMA

GEORGIA

Charleston

Savannah

Vicksburg (Walnut Hills)

Natchez

TEXAS

LOUISIANA

FLORIDA TERRITORY

New Orleans

Gulf of Mexico

From H. S. Tanner's map in Nuttall's first edition, 1821

panied us, a mound of loose stones, thrown up either as a funeral pile or a beacon by the aborigines. The natives and hunters assert that subterraneous rumblings have been heard in this mountain. The Sugar-loaf, covered to its summit with trees and shrubs, is composed of sandstone, and appears now accompanied by three other less elevated conic eminences, all mutually connected at the base by saliant ridges. From what I perceive, I am inclined to consider the Cavaniol as a continuation of the same chain, proceeding west by north. From the garrison to the encampment of this evening, indications of coal are sufficiently obvious in the bituminous shale and carbonaceous reliquiae.[2]

17TH.] The day was delightfully clear and warm, and the whole aspect of nature appeared peculiarly charming. In the morning our party fell in with a favourite amusement, in the pursuit of two bears, harmlessly feeding in the prairies, which, being very fat, were soon overtaken and killed. We proceeded about 20 miles; towards evening passing the Pottoe, which was quite fordable, notwithstanding the late fresh. Our course was principally south-south-west, and this evening, after crossing the Pottoe, more westwardly. We were again in full view of the two picturesque mountains, the Cavaniol and Point Sucre; the latter yet appeared somewhat conic, and scantily wooded, but covered with thickets like the Alleghany mountains. Our route was continued through prairies, occasionally divided by sombre belts of timber, which serve to mark the course of the rivulets. These vast plains, beautiful almost as the fancied Elysium, were now splendid of which were the azure Larkspur, gilded Coreopsides, Rudbeckias, fragrant Phloxes, and the purple Psilotria. Serene and charming as the blissful regions of fancy, nothing here appeared to exist but what contributes to harmony.[3]

[2]The expedition on leaving Fort Smith had passed over present Massard's and Long prairies, W. of Cedar Prairie, which lies S.E. of Fort Smith. It crossed over into present Oklahoma at present Gap Creek.

Nuttall's itinerary, chronology, and scientific findings have been so thoroughly treated by Samuel Wood Geiser that no effort will be made to duplicate them, except in outline. See GEISER, "Thomas Nuttall's Botanical Collecting Trip to the Red River, 1819," *Field and Laboratory,* Vol. XXIV, No. 2 (April, 1956), 43–60. My accompanying map is based on Geiser's on p. 44. Nuttall's (inaccurate) map has only historical interest and is not, therefore, reproduced as H. S. Tanner drew it for him, but appears in the present edition redrawn.

[3]The campsite was in the valley of Caston Creek near present Victor, after crossings of Gap, Nail, Sugarloaf, and Morris creeks and the Poteau.

18TH.] To-day, in a journey of about 25 miles, we passed several very rocky pine ridges but over which a loaded wagon had been dragged as far as the Kiamesha, accompanied by a family of emigrants, who had been obliged to remove from the settlement of Mulberry creek, on the arrival of the Cherokees. At breakfast time, we were regaled with the wild honey of the country, taken from a tree which the guide had discovered for us. Our course was still to the south of south-west, in which direction we twice crossed the meanders of a branch of the Pottoe, called Fourche Malin. About 2 o'clock we passed the dividing ridge of the Pottoe and Kiamesha, nearly the height of the Alleghany in Pennsylvania, very rocky, and thinly scattered with pines and oaks; the rock sandstone, and destitute of organic remains. This ridge forms part of the principal chain called Marzern mountains by Darby.[4] In the rivulets and ravines I was gratified by the discovery of a new shrubby plant allied to the genus Phyllanthus. After crossing the mountain, we proceeded, at first, a little east of south, to clear the subsidiary ridges, afterwards westwardly, the mountains passing north-west; we then came upon an extensive prairie cove considerably diversified with hills and groves of trees.[5] To the west continued a proximate chain of piney hills, with remarkable serrated summits, known by the familiar name of the Potatoe hills, and to the northwest backed by a more distant and more lofty chain equally piney. On the summit of the dividing ridge, we observed a pile of stones in the bison path that we travelled, which, I was informed, had been thrown up as a monument by the Osages when they were going to war, each warrior casting a stone upon the pile. Discovering herds of Bison in the prairie, the soldiers immediately commenced the chase, and the bulls, now lean and agile, galloped along the plain with the prodigious swiftness, like so

[4]The Fourche Maline rises in Latimer County, flowing eastward originally as a tributary to the Poteau but now into Wister Lake in Le Flore County. William Darby (1775–1854), perhaps the greatest of the early United States geographers, author of *A Geographical Description of the State of Louisiana . . . Being an Accompaniment to the Map of Louisiana* (1816, 1817) and *The Emigrant's Guide to the Western and Southwestern States and Territories* (1818), had designated the Mazerns, now Winding Stair Mountain. He had explored parts of the southern Louisiana Purchase, 1804–1809. His original spelling was "Masserne chain." Here for Nuttall's new shrubby plant he described both genus and species later as *Lepidanthus phyllanthoides* Nutt., now *Andrachne phyllanthoides* (Nutt.) Muell. Arg.

This was the Great Cove or Prairie of the Kiamichi, and the party's campsite must have been 4 miles E. and 2 s. of present Talihina. GEISER, 48.

many huge lions. The pendant beard, large head hid in bushy locks, with the rest of the body nearly divested of hair, give a peculiar and characteristic grace to this animal when in motion. We discovered them in a state of repose, and could perceive the places where they had been gratifying themselves by wallowing or rolling in the dust. The bison, entirely distinct from the buffalo of Europe, notwithstanding the surmises of Doctor Robertson, can scarcely be domesticated.[6] The male, infuriate and jealous in his armours, gores every thing which falls in his way, and becomes totally unmanageable.

Perhaps no animal employs a greater diversity of diet than the bear; the common American species feeds upon fruits, honey, wasps, and bees; they will turn over large logs in quest of other insects, and are also destructive to pigs and fawns, by which means the hunters, imitating the bleat of the latter, will sometimes decoy them within gunshot.

Panthers are said to be abundant in the woods of Red river, nor are they uncommon on the banks of the Arkansa. A somewhat curious anecdote of one of these animals was related to me by our guide. A party of hunters in the morning missed one of their dogs from the encampment, and after a fruitless search were proceeding on their route, when one of the other dogs obtaining a scent, discovered to the hunters, dead beneath a tree, the dog which had strayed, together with a deer and a wolf in the same condition. It appeared, that the panther, having killed a deer, and eat his fill, got into a tree to watch the remainder, and had, in his own defence, successively fallen upon the wolf and the dog as intruders on his provision.

19TH.] This morning we set out late in consequence of the rain, which had continued throughout the night. We proceeded a little west of south, along the hills and prairies which divide the three principal branches of the Kiamesha, skirting the south side of the bare serrated hills already noticed scattered with pine and post-oak, in order to shorten the distance which we should have been obliged to make by keeping more into the level prairies. In this course we passed a number of little rivulets of torrents with rocky beds. The hills abounded with a kind of slaty petrosilex, which, as well as the slate-clay with which it alternates, appears destitute of organic remains. Some of the fragments were greenish, and appeared to be of the

---

[6]The Eurasian *Bison bonasus,* rare in Nuttall's time, was primarily forest-dwelling and somewhat larger than the American *Bison bison,* from which it also exhibited several physiological differences.

same character with the hone-slate of the Washita. At the junction of its three branches, the Kiamesha is hemmed in by very lofty ridges, partly covered with pine and oak. On one of the most conspicuous summits we had observed, for many miles, a beacon of the Osages, being a solitary tree fantastically trimmed like a broom. Our path now became difficult and obstructed by fallen rocks; that which we had pursued in the earlier part of the day was one of those, which, from time immemorial, had been trodden out by the bison. We still continued in a south-south-west direction, along the rocky valley of the Kiamesha, which this evening we crossed. The wooded hills prevailed on either hand without any prospect of termination, and strongly resemble the mountains of the Blue ridge, at Harper's Ferry, in Virginia.[7]

20TH.] This morning we proceeded four or five miles before breakfast through a pathless thicket, equally in difficulty to any in the Alleghany mountains. The hills now approached the river in cliffs and inaccessible acclivities, and we concluded to leave the impassable windings of the river by the first gap of the mountain. Having now left the almost impenetrable barriers of the river, we proceeded along a blind bison trace, but at length descended into a rocky ravine, scarcely passable for goats, but which at length we cleared, after being some hours dispersed from each other, and came again into hilly open woods, near the head of Field's cove and creek, deriving its name from an outlaw who here sought refuge from justice. This cove was a kind of hilly prairie land interspersed with small plains, presenting rocky terraces where most elevated, and covered with herbage. Lofty wooded hills, scarcely inferior to those of the river, hemmed in this cove on either hand. I am informed that the sources of all the rivers in this part of the Arkansas territory, however, closely locked betwixt mountains, present extensive prairies or plains, where they divaricate to their sources.

Our course was a little west of south, and the distance we travelled probably 20 miles. We calculated upon arriving at Red river on the succeeding evening, being somewhere about 30 miles distant. The woods

[7]The route taken was generally w.s.w., with an evening campsite 2 miles west and ½ mile south of present Tuskahoma. The days' marches, which were substantial, were on horseback. In addition to Major Bradford and Nuttall, the party consisted of half a dozen soldiers, James Rogers (interpreter) and his brother Lewis, sons of the Cherokee headman John Rogers. AM. ST. PAPERS, INDIAN AFFAIRS, II, 557.

were now disgustingly infested with ticks, though free from musquetoes. [8]

21ST.] We continued about five miles over dreary and rocky pine hills,
without the good fortune of a bison trace, when, after taking a frugal
breakfast, our hunters again surprised a herd of Bison lying down, but
which were quickly roused into an active gallop. Deer were uncommonly
abundant, and scarcely timid, or conscious of the aim of their destroyers.
At length getting rid of the pine hills, we proceeded through a shrubby
prairie, but, by continuing too much to the westward, again came inadvertently to the Kiamesha, and were obliged to leave it some miles directly
behind us, in order to keep clear of the swampy alluvions and ponds by
which it was bordered. We now continued south-east, about 20 miles,
over hilly woods covered with dwarfish post and black oaks, which having
been burnt were extremely difficult to penetrate, lashing and tearing every
thing with which they came in contact; we had also to encounter the
additional embarrassment of ponds and wet prairies. [9]

The rock was still sandstone, containing appearances indicative of coal.
For the last two days I was busily employed in collecting new and curious
plants, which continually presented themselves.

22D.] This morning we kept two or three miles to the south-east, and
on turning to the south, had the good fortune to enter upon a beaten path,
recognised by our guide, which, in the distance of about three miles,
brought us to Mr. Styles's, where we had the gratification of obtaining
milk and butter for breakfast. This was the emigrant whose traces we had
discovered, and who had encountered the Mazern mountains with a
loaded wagon, women, and children, among whom was the mother of his
wife, blind, and 90 years of age! Mr. Styles had chosen the margin of the
prairie for his residence, at a short distance from whence commences the
usual bushy hills. [10] After breakfast we continued our route, parallel with
Red river, over an extensive prairie to the confluence of the Kiamesha.
The people appeared but ill prepared for the unpleasant official intelli-

[8]The rocky ravine was probably Peal Creek, after which the party pursued Cedar
Creek, camping between its two forks.
[9]The course on May 21 had been E.S.E., with crossings of Rock and Possum creeks,
after which the party moved S. and E., crossing the head of Spencer Creek, camping on its
headwaters, not far distant from the future location of Spencer Academy (GEISER, 50).
[10]William Styles, Sr., only newly arrived, was one of the white intruders of whom

gence of their ejectment. Some who had cleared considerable farms were thus unexpectedly thrust out into the inhospitable wilderness. I could not but sympathise with their complaints, notwithstanding the justice and propriety of the requisition. Would it had always been the liberal policy of the Europeans to act with becoming justice, and to reciprocate the law of nations with the unfortunate natives![11]

A flagrant act of injustice to the Indians now, however, came to our knowledge. It was, no doubt, the hopes of employing the present opportunity of gaining redress, which had instigated the journey of the two civilized Cherokees (Messrs. Rodgers), who had accompanied us; one of whom acted as the state interpreter. The information which we obtained concerning this affair gives it almost an incredible air of atrocity. It appears, that about three months ago, one of the Cherokees, returning from hunting in this quarter, saw some horses in the possession of two brothers named Gibbs, which he recognised to have belonged to Monsieur Vaugin, of the Arkansa, and which had been stolen by these renegadoes. For fear he should convict them of the theft, they treacherously took an opportunity of way-laying the Indian, and shot him dead with a rifle. The same two brothers, this very evening, inadvertently passed by our camp, but in the absence of the major and the Cherokees, and though our circumstantial knowledge of this horrid fact was purely accidental, yet such is the self-condemning nature of guilt, that no sooner had they learnt who we were, than they rushed into the adjoining cane-brake, and effected their escape into the neighbouring province of Texas. A party, indeed, went out

---

Major Bradford was instructed to request removal, but two years later, in 1821, he was still occupying his illegal holding. TERR. PAPERS, XIX, 388. Here the party was about four miles from the future site (1824) of Fort Towson. This day, May 22, they visited the Red River settlements on both sides of the Kiamichi and after camping on Red River for the night continued their work the following day.

[11]In the government, the left hand did not always know what the right hand was doing. Only the month before, on April 14, 1819, William Rector, surveyor general for the U.S. Land Office in the territories of Illinois, Missouri, and Arkansas, had forwarded to Josiah Meigs, commissioner of the General Land Office in Washington, his surveyors' map showing plats only a few miles east of the Red River settlements, between the Kiamichi and Little River, and eastward along the Little River drainage. TERR. PAPERS, XIX, 62–67. A year and a half earlier, on January 30, 1818, Major Long, reporting to Brig. Gen. Thomas A. Smith at Belle Fontaine, had described "a considerable village of Choctaws, Shawnees, and a few Delawares and Creeks" above Red River, with settlers coming in from Indiana, Kentucky, Tennessee, and Illinois Territory, aggregating, he thought, perhaps three thousand. TERR. PAPERS, XIX, 4–10.

instantly in pursuit of them, but were obliged to return in consequence of the darkness of the night, and the extreme difficulty of the way. Orders for their apprehension were left with the magistrate of the district, accompanied by a reward from the Cherokees. They returned after an absence of three weeks, when an attempt was made to bring them to justice by two hunters armed with rifles; and one of the brothers, who had not actually committed the murder, in the act of warning the other, was shot dead by one of the hunters, whom he had formerly injured in the most indelicate manner. With this revenge, though not sufficiently discriminate, I afterwards learnt, that the Cherokees had expressed themselves satisfied, as it accorded probably with their own ideas of diverging retaliation. [12]

The change of soil in the great Prairie of Red river now appeared obvious. It was here that I saw the first calcareous rock charged with shells, &c. since my departure from the banks of the Ohio. Nothing could at this season exceed the beauty of these plains, enamelled with such an uncommon variety of flowers of vivid tints, possessing all the brilliancy of tropical productions.

After passing through a swamp, we crossed the Kiamesha in boats, and swam our horses. [13] Five or six miles from Styles's we, at length, obtained sight of Red river, appearing here scarcely more than 100 yards wide, passing to the south-east, with the water very red and turbid. I was told that the river was here 1100 miles from its confluence by the meanders, or 900 above Natchitoches.

Here, for the first time, I saw the *Maclura* (or Bow wood) in abundance, but almost a month past flowering, at least with the staminiferous plant.

We found in this country two poisonous species of Coluber, or common snake, one of them very small, and finely marbled with vivid colours. [14] The other frequents waters, and is called the water-mockasin, and

[12]By June 1, 1819, John Fowler, U.S. factor at Sulphur Fork (present Miller County, Ark.) had named two white traders, Musick and Williams, operating forty miles upstream on the Red from his factory, for actions paralleling those described by Nuttall. Williams had previously been expelled from the Arkansas River. Fowler to John Jamison, Indian agent at Natchitoches, June 1, 1819, TERR. PAPERS, XIX, 75–76.

[13]It will be noted that Nuttall has passed over May 23, but we know that the party had continued the visitations begun on May 22, leaving the left bank of the Kiamichi late in the day on May 23 for the right bank, visiting settlers there until nightfall.

[14]The eastern coral snake, *Micrurus fulvius*.

poisonous black-snake; it is nearly black, two or three feet long, and thick in proportion, the head triangular and compressed at the sides.[15] Both of them were furnished with the mortal fangs.

24TH.] To-day we continued to the Horse-prairie, 15 miles above the mouth of the Kiamesha.[16] In our way we proceeded for about three miles through the fertile alluvion of Red river to Mr. Varner's, where we break-fasted, and at length arriving at our destination on the banks of Red river, we remained there the whole of the following day. This prairie derives its name from the herds of wild horses, which till lately frequented it, and of which we saw a small gang on our return. It is very extensive, but flat, and in some places swampy. In these depressions we saw whole acres of the *Crinum americanum* of the West Indies, besides extensive glaucous fields of a large leaved and new species of *Rudbeckia*.[17] The *Sus tajassu* or Mexican hog,[18] is not uncommon some distance higher up Red river. A great part of the skin of one of these animals was shown me by Mr. Varner; so that we need not go to Mexico, in order to account for the head of this animal which was found in one of the saltpetre caves of Kentucky. That a continual intercourse was also kept up by the natives of the east and west sides of the Mississippi, is evident from the authority of Du Pratz, who tells us that the Mobilian or Chicasaw language was even spoken by the natives of Red river.[19]

On the banks of Red river, nearly on a level with the water, as it appeared at the present depression, I noticed a dark greenish-grey sand-stone, resembling trap, and occasionally interspersed with pebbles of agate, jasper, and chalcedony; the cement of this curious conglomerate proved to be calcareous spar.

26TH.] To-day we prepared to return by the route which we had come.

[15]*Agkistrodon piscivorus.*

[16]When Nuttall says "above the mouth of the Kiamesha," he means along the Red and upstream of that river. Martin Varner, with whom the party breakfasted May 24, would be a petitioner two years later (1821), attempting to retain his holding against the Choc-taws. TERR. PAPERS, XIX, 388.

[17]Crinum americanum = *Hymenocallis liriosme* (Raf.) Shinners; Rudbeckia = *R. maxima* Nutt.

[18]*Sus tajacu* Linn. is here the familiar Texas subspecies of the collared peccary, *Tayassu tajacu angulatus* (Cope).

[19]To Le Page du Pratz's linguistic finding about the Chickasaw lingua franca in the lower Mississippi drainage may be added that of Albert S. Gatschet and Cyrus Thomas, of the Bureau of American Ethnology. HODGE, I, 261. John R. Swanton's attribution to

Knowing that we should arrive early at Mr. Styles's, and spend the remainder of the day there, I delayed about two hours behind the party, for the purpose of collecting some of the new and curious plants interspersed over these enchanting prairies. It was not, however, my fortune ever again to overtake the party.[20] Deceived by the continued traces of two strangers who had accompanied us, I passed the place of rendezvous, and was, in fact, so much engaged as to travel along no less than seven miles below Mr. Styles's, which I ascertained by enquiring at another house, to which accident had directed me. Night began to approach, and I had proceeded but about three miles on my return when the sun set. By pursuing a new path which now opened, I had the good fortune to arrive at the house of Mr. Davis, contiguous to Gates's creek, which I had crossed.[21] Here I was kindly requested to remain for the night, as the path from hence was even difficult to trace by daylight. Four guns were fired at major Bradford's camp as signals to me, which were answered by Mr. Davis, but unfortunately they were never heard.

27TH.] It was scarcely day-break when I arose, impatient to join my companions; but now my horse was not to be found, and it was not until we had made two or three unsuccessful searches, that he was at length discovered two miles on the path I had yesterday travelled. By this time it was near eight o'clock, and nine when I arrived at the major's camp, where I found they had departed about half an hour. It is unnecessary to pourtray my apprehensions on this occasion; not a moment was to be lost, and I offered one of Mr. Styles's sons two dollars to accompany me for a few hours to find their trace, and, if possible, to overtake them. We travelled as fast as possible for about 10 miles through a horrid brake of

---

the Choctaw language may be qualified by the realization that Chickasaw and Choctaw languages, both Muskhogean, are practically identical. SWANTON, Bureau of American Ethnology, *Bulletin 103*.

[20]By the time for the return to Fort Smith, Bradford had given notice of removal to some two hundred families, according to his original instructions, from a line drawn from the source of the Kiamichi (at the present Arkansas-Oklahoma border) to the Poteau on the north, and from the source of the Kiamichi south to Red River. The notification of settlers east of the Red River settlements to and including those at Pecan Point (on Red River in present southern McCurtain County, Oklahoma) was left to other hands. AM. ST. PAPERS, INDIAN AFFAIRS II, 557.

[21]Both Daniel and John Davis were on the disputed lands at this time, as were William and Charles Gates, who had given their name to Gates Creek. TERR. PAPERS, XIX, 387–89.

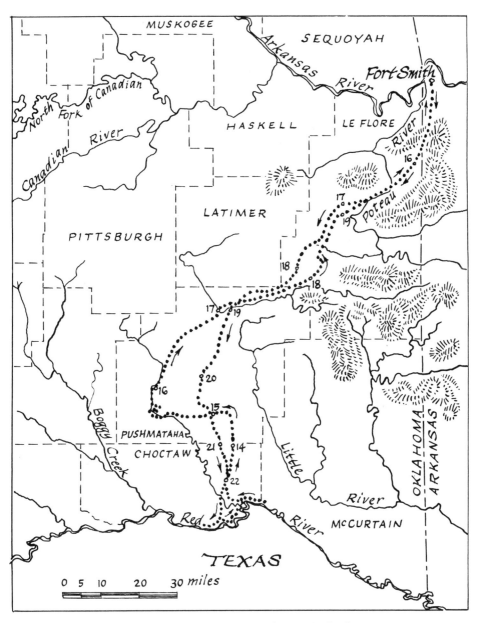

The Bradford-Nuttall expedition to Red River

scrubby oaks, but all to no purpose, and, after firing a gun, which was neither heard nor answered, we returned again, as I dared not to venture alone and unprepared through such a difficult and mountainous wilderness. My botanical acquisitions in the prairies, proved, however, so interesting as almost to make me forget my situation, cast away as I was amidst the refuse of society, without money and without acquaintance; for calculating upon nothing more certain than an immediate return, I was consequently unprovided with every means of subsistence.

I was informed by the hunters, that these prairies, partially divided by groves and strips of timber, bordering the water courses, continued with little interruption to the hot springs of the Washita, to which, from hence, there is a plain and direct road. The surface of these woodless expanses was gently undulated, and thickly covered with grass knee high, even to the summits of the hills, offering an almost inexhaustible range to cattle. The flowers, which beautify them at this season of nature's vigour, communicated all the appearance of a magnificent garden, fantastically decked with innumerable flowers of the most splendid hues. The soil appears to be universally calcareous, with the limestone nearly white and full of shells, among which there was abundance of a small species of gryphite, and in the more compact beds some species of terebratulites. This calcareous rock, different from the mountain limestone, often contains uncemented or loose shells immersed in beds of friable clay, and is more analogous to that of South Carolina and Georgia, than that of St. Louis and the Ohio.

Along the further edge of the prairie, relative to Red river, there were, in the distance of 10 miles, five or six families settled, or rather encamped, upon the lands of the United States, which have not yet been surveyed or offered for sale.

June 1ST.–5TH.] I still remained at the house of Mr. Styles, without any very obvious prospect of regaining fort Smith. On the 4th I walked over the adjoining prairie to a more considerable hill than any which I had yet visited, near Red river. Its north-western declivity was thinly wooded; here I found the limestone more compact than usual, containing also smaller shells, but still presenting scarcely any perceptible dip. The summit was scattered with coarse quartzy and petrosiliceous pebbles, originating from the disintegration of a ferruginous conglomerate, of which large masses still lay on the surface compact. A similar overlay, though much more abundant, and continuous, occurs over the calcareous rock of South Carolina and Georgia.

The singular appearance of these vast meadows, now so profusely decorated with flowers, as seen from a distance, can scarcely be described.[22] Several large circumscribed tracts were perfectly gilded with millions of the flowers of *Rudbeckia amplexicaulis,* bordered by other irregular snow-white fields of a new species of *Coriandrum.* The principal grasses which prevail are *Kaeleria cristata* of Europe, *Phalaris canariensis* (Canary birdseed), *Tripsacum dactyloides,* which is most greedily sought after by the horses, *Elymus virginicus* (sometimes called wild rye), a new *Rotbolia,* one or two species of *Stipa* and *Aristida,* with the *Agrostis arachnoides* of Mr. Elliott, and two species of *Atheropogon.* The common Milfoil, and sorrel (*Rumex acetocella*), are as prevalent, at least the former, as in Europe. In these plains there also grew a large species of *Centaurea,* scarcely distinct from *C. austriaca;* and along the margin of all the rivulets we met with abundance of the Bow-wood (*Maclura auran-*

---

[22]For the fifteen species observed or mentioned in what follows, these notes may be used in explication:

Rudbeckia amplexicaulis Vahl., black-eyed Susan. Nuttall gave later to the new species of *Coriandrum* the name *Coriandrum americanum,* which became *Biflora americana,* closely allied to Coriandrum. *Koeleria cristata* (L.) Pers., June grass, is native to both Eastern and Western Hemispheres. *Phalaris canariensis* L., canary, or birdseed, grass, is adventive from Europe, but recent distribution maps give it no occurrence in Arkansas, nor are there any specimens from either Arkansas or Oklahoma in the Bebb Herbarium. Nuttall [3] seems to indicate that he doubted his identification and therefore described *Phalaris occidentalis* Nutt., from "fort Smith on the Arkansas to Red River," which has since been considered as identical with *Phalaris caroliniana* Walt., a common native grass in the area. *Tripsacum dactyloides* L. is gama grass, and *Elymus virginicus* L. is wild rye. His *Rotbolia* became *Rottboellia R. campestris* Nutt. = *Manisuris cylindrica* (Michx.) Kuntze. For *Stipa* L. as genus, Nuttall later listed [3, 145] three species, which on present known distribution can be narrowed to *S. avenacea* L., black oat grass, in this range, and from others not listed, *S. comata* Trin. & Rupr., needlegrass; to which another in-range genus and species may be added, *Muhlenbergia capillaris* Lam., long awned grass. *Aristida* L. received on this trip *A. purpurea* Nutt., purple triple awned grass, collected by the author during his stay with Styles on Red River. *Agrostis arachnoides* Ell. = *A. Elliottiana* Schultes, bent grass. For *Atheropogon* he later listed [3, 150] *A. apludoides* Muhl. = *Bouteloua curtipendula* (Michx.) Torr., side-oats grama, and *A. olygostachyum* Nutt. = *Bouteloua gracilis* (HBK.) Lag., blue grama. Common European milfoil (*Achillea Millefolium* L.) may have been present here, but the greater likelihood is that he saw the North American phase (*Achillea lanulosa* Nutt.), which he described much later. Similarly, the Old World sorrel, *Rumex Acetosella* L. may be found in Arkansas and Oklahoma, but he may possibly have seen the American native *Rumex hastatulus* Baldw. His *Centaurea* became *Centaurea americana* Nutt.

tiaca), here familiarly employed as a yellow dye, very similar to fustic.

6TH.] To-day I went five or six miles to collect specimens of the *Centaurea*, which, as being the only species of this numerous genus indigenous to America, had excited my curiosity. All the lesser brooks and neighbouring springs were now already dried up, and the arid places appeared quite scorched with the heat. Still there prevailed throughout these prairies, as over the sea, a refreshing breeze, which continued for the greatest part of the day. The swarms of musquitoes, which prove so troublesome along the banks of the Mississippi and the Missouri are here almost unknown, and never met with except on the immediate alluvial borders of the rivulets.

In my solitary, but amusing rambles over these delightful prairies, I now, for the first time in my life, notwithstanding my long residence and peregrinations in North America, hearkened to the inimitable notes of the mocking-bird (*Turdus polyglottus*). After amusing itself in ludicrous imitations of other birds, perched on the topmost bough of a spreading elm, it at length broke forth into a strain of melody the most wild, varied, and pathetic, that ever I had heard from any thing less than human. In the midst of these enchanting strains, which gradually increased to loudness, it oftentimes flew upwards from the topmost twig, continuing its note as if overpowered by the sublimest ecstasy.[23]

On the 8th I went down to the Red river settlement, to inquire concerning some company, which I had heard of, on my returning route to the Arkansa; and, on conferring together, we concluded to take our departure on Sunday next, a day generally chosen by these hunters and voyagers on which to commence their journeys. In our way to this settlement we crossed Gates's and Lemon's creek and another smaller brook. The width of the prairie to the banks of Red river might be about five miles, and the contracted alluvial lands, which by the crops of corn and cotton appeared to be exceedingly fertile, were nearly inhabited to their full extent. The wheat planted here produced about 80 bushels to the acre, for which some of the inhabitants had now the conscience to demand three dollars and a half per bushel, in consequence of the scarcity of last season. Along the

[23]*Turdus polyglottos* (Linn.), the eastern mockingbird, has become *Mimus polyglottos polyglottos* (Linn.). Nuttall was almost equally captivated by the scissor-tailed flycatcher, which he had seen at Fort Smith and again above the mouth of the Kiamichi. NUTTALL [6], I, 275–76.

borders of this part of Red river a chain of low hills appears, on which I observed large dislocated masses of a ferruginous conglomerate, inclined towards the river, and incumbent on the usual calcareous rock.

These people, as well as the generality of those who, till lately, inhabited the banks of the Arkansa, bear the worst moral character imaginable, being many of them renegadoes from justice, and such as have forfeited the esteem of civilized society. When a further flight from justice became necessary, they passed over into the Spanish territory, towards St. Antonio, where it appears encouragement was given to all sorts of refugees. From these people we frequently heard disrespectful murmurs against the government of the United States. There is, indeed, an universal complaint of showing unnecessary and ill-timed favours to the Indians. It is true that the Osages and Cherokees have been permitted, almost without molestation, to rob the people on this river, not only of their horses and cattle, but even occasionally of their household furniture. It does not appear from experiment, that the expensive forts, now established and still extending, possess any beneficial influence over the savages which could not be answered by the interference of the territorial government.

It is now also the intention of the United States government, to bring together, as much as possible, the savages beyond the frontier, and thus to render them, in all probability, belligerent to each other, and to the civilized settlements which they border. To strengthen the hands of an enemy by conceding to them positions favourable to their designs, must certainly be far removed from prudence and good policy. To have left the aborigines on their ancient sites, rendered venerable by the endearments and attachments of patriotism, and surrounded by a condensed population of the whites, must either have held out to them the necessity of adopting civilization, or at all events have most effectually checked them from committing depredations. Bridled by this restraint, there would have been no necessity for establishing among them an expensive military agency, and coercing them by terror.

14TH.] According to our appointment, my traveling companions called upon me, and, although about the middle of a Sunday afternoon, it was not possible to persuade them to wait for Monday morning. So, without almost any supply of provision, I was obliged to take a hasty departure from my kind host and family, who, knowing from the first my destitute situation, separated from pecuniary resources, could scarcely be prevailed upon to accept the trifling pittance which I accidentally possessed. I shall always remember, with feelings of gratitude, the sincere kindness and unfeigned hospitality, which I so seasonably experienced from these poor and honest people, when left in the midst of the wilderness.

The evening was pleasant, and, after proceeding about eight miles through oak thickets in a path of the hunters, we reposed without further trouble by a brook, beneath the shade of the forest, and under the serene canopy of a cloudless sky.

15TH.] My companions, three in number, appeared to be men of diligence and industry, and were up by break of day.[24] The object of their journey was the recovery of horses stolen from them by the Cherokees. After proceeding about six miles from the place of departure, the trace or path could no longer easily be followed, as we now began to enter upon the pine hills scattered with loose rocks. Our first object was to have entered Field's cove; we got, however, too far to the east, and crossed a considerable brook of the Kiamesha. All ignorant of the country, except myself, we had taken the precaution to mark down the reported bearings and distances, from the information of Mr. Styles. Our proper course was now north-north-east, but the man who took the lead, embarrassed by the accumulation of the mountains, which appeared in succeeding ridges for 40 miles before us, and too confidently considering the proposed route impracticable, kept towards the west in direct opposition to our proper course, so that on the 16th, about noon, we obtained sight of Field's cove, which we ought now to have left, and crossing the Kiamesha, much too low down, found it running nearly due west, and very low. Our labour and distance was thus doubled, and we passed and repassed several terrific ridges, over which our horses could scarcely keep their feet, and which were, besides, so overgrown with bushes and trees half-burnt, with ragged limbs, that every thing about us, not of leather, was lashed and torn to

[24]GEISER (46n.) had Amos Kuykendall and Captains James Bryan and Nathaniel Robbins, of the Red River settlements, as Nuttall's companions on the return journey. All of them had lost horses to the Cherokees or Caddos, according to a grand-jury presentment in Hempstead County in April, 1820, and presumably were going into the organized portion of Arkansas Territory to lodge formal complaints. TERR. PAPERS, XIX, 196.

pieces. We now relinquished the mountains, and kept up along the banks of the Kiamesha, by a bison path, frequently crossing the river, which was almost uniformly bordered by mountains or inaccessible cliffs. Having killed a fat bison bull, we encamped at an early hour in a small prairie, in order to jerk or dry some of the beef for our future subsistence, it being now all the provision on which we had to depend. [25]

All the rock we saw since our departure from Mr. Styles', consisted of a fine-grained sandstone, with no inconsiderable dip, and, as far as visible, destitute of organic remains.

In a lake, about a mile from the Kiamesha, where we crossed it at noon, grew the *Pontederia cordata, Nymphoea advena, Brassenia peltata,* and *Myriophyllum verticillatum,* all of them plants which I had not before seen in the territory, and which I have found chiefly confined to the limits of the tide water. [26] In a northern bend of the Kiamesha, about 30 miles from its mouth, I am informed, there exists a very copious salt spring.

17TH.] We still continued up the Kiamesha, over pine hills, and through a succession of horrid, labyrinthine thickets and cane-brakes, meeting, to our disappointment, very little prairie. At length, we arrived at the three main branches of the river: Jack's creek to the south, Kiamesha to the east, and a third rivulet to the north. To the entrance of Jack's fork, as it is called, the Kiamesha continues hemmed in with lofty pine hills. From hence the mountains diverge; the highest chain still continuing on one side to border the main stream, while, to the north, we came in sight of the "Potatoe hills." In this extensive cove, covered with grass, and mostly a prairie of undulated surface, I had the satisfaction to find, as I had also done at noon, the *Ixia coelestina* of my venerable friend, Wm. Bartram. [27] Instead of sandstone, we now found a predominance of slaty petrosiliceous rock breaking in rhombic fragments, nearly of the same nature as the honeslate of the Washita, and alike destitute of organic reliquiae.

[25]The travelers were on the east side of the Kiamichi, possibly near modern Moyers on the route of the St. Louis and San Francisco Railroad.

[26]*Pontederia cordata* L., pickerelweed; Nymphaea advena is, rather, *Nuphar advena* (Ait.) Ait. f., yellow pond lily; *Brassenia* peltata = *Brasenia Schréberi* Gmel., purple wen-dock; *Myriophyllum verticillatum* L., water milfoil, out of range; more likely *M. heterophyllum* Michx. or *M. pinnatum* (Walt.) BSP.

[27]Ixia coelestina becomes *Nemastylis Nuttallii* Pickering, as noted in Chapter VIII, note 23, *ante.*

18TH.] We continued across the great cove of the Kiamesha, towards the dividing ridge of mountains which separates the waters of the Arkansa and Red river, and which had been visible to us on the very day after our departure. We now kept a course rather too much south of east, and encamped on the banks of a creek that appeared to issue from a conspicuous gap in the mountains. The prairie, though in many places open and hilly, was still divided by small torrents, now generally dry, and lined with thickets, laced with thorns and green briers. Towards the middle of this fertile cove, we passed over a large tract formed like a lake, and, except a southern outlet towards the Kiamesha, surrounded with low hills. In one of these rich alluvial bottoms, we saw abundance of tumuli. On the hills of the prairies of Red river, I also saw them of stone, and containing, according to custom, fragments of earthen pots.[28] All the hills in this cove, which abound with pine, present slaty rocks of the petrosilex already mentioned, apparently forming partial beds, alternating with a soft slaty or shale rock, which occasionally exhibits balls of argillaceous iron ore, and the fibrous mineral production which has been called cone coralloid.

To-day we came very near losing our horses, for, while reposing at noon, though as usual hobbled, the torments of the large flies which appear at this time of the day and in the evening, became so extreme, as to excite them to run away, and with some difficulty we traced them for five or six miles, through woods and prairies, to the banks of the Kiamesha, into which they had rushed for alleviation. We here also found, by the bell, a horse which had been lost by some hunters. In consequence of this unexpected delay, we did not proceed more than about 20 miles.

19TH.] We continued across the cove towards the mountains, and began the ascent, but totally missing the gap, arrived at length, with much difficulty, upon one of the highest summits of the dividing ridge. Towards the Pottoe, the descent was altogether impracticable: for miles we could perceive nothing but one continued precipice of the most frightful elevation. After proceeding, however, with difficulty for about three

[28]Nuttall and his companions were pursuing a route close to the Kiamichi on its right bank, but their route was east of the one Nuttall and Bradford had taken on the way to Red River. The Indian archaeological remains encountered were among the scores of stream-shelf sites in eastern Oklahoma, of which that near Spiro in northern Le Flore County is most striking. GRIFFIN-ORR, 239–55.

miles along the summit of the mountain, high as any part of the Blue ridge, through thickets of dwarf oaks (*Quercus chinquapin, Q. montana,* and *Q. alba*),[29] none of them scarcely exceeding the height of a man; we began the descent, which we still found extremely steep and broken, and, after toiling four or five hours in the mountains, had, at last, the unexpected satisfaction of entering upon, and pursuing the wagon trace, so recently trod by the major's party. We now clearly saw, a little to the north-west, the right gap of the mountain which we ought to have sought.[30]

In the course of the afternoon, we passed over three pine ridges, and two creeks, and then re-entering the prairie, proceeded before night about ten miles from the mountain, which, as well as the lesser ridges, consisted of sandstone.

20TH.] This morning we passed the Pottoe, and proceeded along the trace, some distance beyond the Sugar-loaf mountain. The prairies were now horribly infested with cleg flies, which tormented and stimulated our horses into a perpetual gallop. In the evening, we encamped in the valley of the third oak ridge that separated us from Cedar prairie.

21ST.] Passing the fourth ridge, I again entered Cedar prairie, and before noon arrived at the garrison, where I had been long expected, and was very cordially welcomed by the Doctor and the Major.

To the end of the month, I now remained at the garrison.

[29]*Quercus chinquapin* Pursh = *Q. prinoides* Willd., chinquapin oak, dwarf chestnut oak; *Q. montana* Willd. = *Q. prinus* L., chestnut oak, rock chestnut oak; *Q. alba* L., white oak; but it is more likely that, instead of the two latter, Nuttall saw *Quercus stellata* var. *Margaretta* (Ashe) Sarg., dwarf post oak, sand post oak.

[30]Having mistaken Bohannon Creek for Buzzard's, which would have led to the gap in the Winding Stair Mountains on the eighteenth, the party reached one of the highest crests in the chain, 2,428 feet. Finally descending, they were at the fork of Holston reek when they found Major Bradford's return tracks. GEISER, 53.

CHAPTER X.

Continue my voyage up the Arkansa—Geological remarks—Pass several lesser rivulets, and the outlet of the Canadian and the Illinois—Salt springs—Obstructions in the navigation—Indications of coal—Pass Grand river, and enter the Verdigris.

JULY 6TH.] Having obtained accommodation in the boat of Mr. Bougie, agent for Mr. Drope, I left the garrison in order to proceed to the trading establishment, at the confluence of the Verdigris, by the course of the river about 130 miles distant.[1] The day being very warm we did not proceed more than 10 miles, having delayed our departure until near noon. Eight miles from the garrison we had another conspicuous view of the Cavaniol.

Among three or four other new plants afforded me by examining the sand-beaches, was a *Portulaca*, apparently the same with *P. pilosa* of the West Indies; its taste was almost as disagreeably bitter as the succulent *Stapelias* of Africa.[2] On these sand-flats we also saw abundance of deer, brought to the river in search of water, as well as to escape the goading of insects; and it is customary for them to remain for hours licking the saline efflorescences which are deposited upon the alluvial clay. We encamped four miles below Skin bayou,[3] and our party amused themselves by searching for turtle's eggs, which the females deposit in the sand at the depth of about eight or ten inches, and then abandon their hatching to the

---

[1]Joseph Bogy *père*, whom we met in Chapter VI, note 16, was by now a partner with William Drope, originally a New Orleans cotton merchant and long a resident also of Arkansas Post. Bogy had built his trading post on the Verdigris at Three Forks some time after 1806, when the Choctaws had robbed him of merchandise he was carrying to the Osages des Chênes. MORRIS, 36–37; JOHNSON, 273–74.

[2]*Portulaca pilosa* L. = *P. parvula* Gray, one of the purslanes, or it could have been *P. mundula* I. M. Johnston.

[3]Skin Bayou = Big Skin Bayou, which empties from the N. into the Arkansas E. of Wilson Rock.

genial heat of the sun. They are spherical, covered with a flexible skin, and considered wholesome food.

7TH.] The river land on both sides appears to be of a good quality, and generally elevated above inundation. The depression of the forest also begins to be obvious. About half a league below Skin bayou occur low cliffs of cark-coloured grauwacke slate, resembling sand-stone, which continue for about a mile along the right hand bank. The rock is entirely similar to that of the garrison (or Belle Point, as the situation is called), equally horizontal, and probably underlaid by coal. The under stratum was singularly undulated in short and broken waves, while the upper was almost perfectly horizontal. Not far from the place of our encampment, on the left, we passed the Swallow (or Hirundel), rocks, a projecting cliff, about 150 feet high, adorned with bushes of cedar, in the centre of which there appears to be an entrance into a cavern, and several other fretted excavations scattered over with clusters of martin nests.[4] The rock consists of two beds; the upper a lighter coloured ferruginous and laminated sand-stone, excavated with appearances similar to nitre caves; the lowest bed, with a more considerable dip (about 10° to the south-east), consists of thinner greenish grey lamina, containing a little mica, and exhibiting the usual zoophytic carbonaceous impressions, indicative of coal. The river bars now abound in gravel, which is principally petrosiliceous. After passing Cajou creek,[5] on the left, about two miles, we encamped near a bar, to avoid the visits of the musquetoes, our progress to-day being about 24 miles.

8TH.] Four miles further we again obtained a view of Point de Sucre and the Cavaniol. On Sambo island,[6] about 12 miles from our departure this morning, we stopped to dine; and here on a bar of gravel I found a new species of the Mexican genus *Stevia*, and never saw it afterwards in any other locality.[7] To the taste it was quite as bitter as many of the

[4]Swallow or Hirundel Rocks = modern Wilson Rock.

[5]Cajou Creek is possibly modern Cache Creek, emptying into the Arkansas from the s. in Le Flore County.

[6]Sambo Island = San Bois Island in Haskell County, near the mouth of Little San Bois Creek.

[7]*Stevia callosa* = *Palafoxia callosa* (Nutt.) T. and G., one of the Composites, one of fourteen species (nine of which Nuttall named specifically or by genus) on which he delivered papers to the Academy of Natural Sciences of Philadelphia, 1821–22, subsequently published in the *Journal* of the academy. GRAUSTEIN, 157.

Eupatoria. This plant, and the *Portulaca* already mentioned, appear to have been recently, and almost accidentally, disseminated from the interior. The cane still continues abundant, and the alluvial lands are extensive and fertile, with a basis of sandstone, which two miles below appears in the same dark and ferruginous rocky mass as near Skin bayou. On some of our party going out a hunting, we concluded to spend the remainder of the day on the island.

9TH.] This morning we crossed the river to the mouth of Sambo creek, and went out into the neighbouring prairie to hunt for bison; but after walking about nine miles, going and returning, were not fortunate enough to find any game. The grass was now so loaded with honey dew as to give our mocasins and pantaloons the appearance of being soaked in oil, seeming totally inexplicable as the produce of aphides, and rather attributable to some vitiation in the proper juices of the plant, taking place apparently at the ultimate period of vegetative vigour, and being more or less copious in proportion to the prevailing degree of heat. The cane brake which we here crossed by a hunting path, was about half a league wide, and flanked by low hills, whose declivities gently subside into the adjoining prairie, of about 20 miles in circuit, and five in width. Here the Cavaniol and Sugar-loaf mountains appeared, at least the latter, not more than 15 or 18 miles distant, towards the south-east. We proceeded about five miles above the creek, and spent the night on the margin of a sand bar, according to our usual custom, to avoid the musquetoes.

10TH.] I went out this morning on the second bar we arrived at, which continued uninterruptedly for about five miles; we found a few Chichasaw plums, with natural orchards of which every beach abounds, but this year, in consequence of the late frosts, they were generally destitute of fruit. The current of the Arkansa was here unusually rapid; on the right hand side the water was clear, but on the left, red and muddy. The clear water issued from the Illinois river, to which we were now contiguous.[8] Among the scattered boulders and gravel of the bar, there were fragments of limestone and petrosilex, containing organic remains, also pebbles of chalcedony; we likewise saw specimens of coal, accompanied by the usual carbonaceous, tesselated vegetable, or zoophitic remains.

[8]The Illinois River empties into the Arkansas from the north in Sequoyah County, one mile S.E. of Webber's Falls.

One of the masses of chalcedony contained chrystalline illinitions of coal.—About breakfast time, we passed the mouth of the rivulet or brook, called by the French Salaiseau, from some hunters having here killed a quantity of bison, and salted the beef for traffic.[9] Major Bradford, who explored this stream, informed me, that the uplands as well as the prairies along this creek, were uncommonly fertile, and well watered by springs, and that the upper side of the creek presents a calcareous soil. Here, for the first time, near the Arkansa, we meet with the hazel (*Corylus americana*), and the American raspberry (*Rubus occidentalis*). In consequence of the rapidity of the current, we only proceeded about 12 miles.

11TH.] After ascending about six miles, we passed the outlet of the Canadian, 60 miles below the confluence of Grand river, or the Six Bull, a navigable river of considerable magnitude. Its main south branch sources with Red river, while another considerable body keeps a western course through the saline plains, where it becomes partially absorbed in the sands of the desert, but afterwards continues towards Santa Fe or the Del Norte. The Canadian, like Red river, always continues red and muddy, and is often impotably saline; 100 miles from its mouth, its banks are said to abound with selenite, disseminated through beds of red clay.[10] Above the confluence of this stream, the Arkansa, where deep, appears clear, green, and limpid. The alluvial lands now begin to be somewhat narrower, though neither hills nor cliffs approach the bank. This morning, however, we again observed a horizontal ledge of the grauwacke slate. About four miles above the Canadian, we passed the river Illinois, on the right, a considerable stream of clear water, as are all

[9]Sallisaw Creek empties into the Arkansas from the N. in Sequoyah County, N. of Laine.

[10]The Canadian empties into the Arkansas below the corners of Haskell and Sequoyah counties. Its source is in Colfax County, N.Mex., on the eastern flank of the Sangre de Cristo Mountains.

The Red, which constitutes along its south cutbank the border between Oklahoma and Texas to a point just E. of the 100th meridian, receives at that point Buck Creek and is extended by its own south fork, known historically as Prairie Dog Town Fork, which in turn has the tributaries Mulberry, Tule, and Palo Duro (S.) creeks, and Tierra Blanca and Blanco creeks farther W. For the history of past errors relating to the Red, see GITTINGER, 203n; FOREMAN [2], xx–xxii; FOREMAN [3], 298–310.

Nuttall's "another considerable body" of the Canadian is the North Canadian, emptying originally into the Canadian in southern McIntosh County, Okla., but now into

the other rivers flowing into the Arkansa from the north.[11] A few miles from its mouth, its banks present salt springs similar to those of Grand river, and scarcely less productive; indeed, most of the streams on this side the Arkansa are said to afford springs of salt water which might be wrought with profit. On the south side, the salines commencing about the Canadian, occur in the red clay formation, forming as it were a belt which extends to the third Red fork, or saline rivulet of the Arkansa. The salines on the north, appear rather in connection with the coal formation, at least, they do not belong to the same series as those on the south side of the river.[12]

This afternoon, two of the hunters went out and brought in the most part of the meat of a fat bison, whose track they had followed from the bar.

About four miles above the Illinois, we came to a cascade of two or three feet perpendicular fall. In endeavouring to pass it, our boat grounded upon the rocks, and we spent several hours in the fruitless attempt to pass them, but had at last to fall back, and attempt it again in the morning, which we then (on the 13th) effected by the assistance of the wind without much difficulty, by passing further into the shute. At this season, in

---

Lake Eufaula. It is formed in Woodward County, Okla., from Wolf Creek and Beaver River, which in turn has as tributaries in Cimarron County, Okla., Currumpa and Cienequilla creeks, heading in N.E. New Mexico.

Not the North Canadian but another stream, the Salt Fork of the Arkansas, rising in Comanche County, Kansas, and emptying into the Arkansas in the S.E. corner of Kay County, Okla., is the one which flows through the Salt Plains.

Nuttall shared a common misconception about the extent and sources of the Red, the boundary, Americans hoped, between the United States and Spain to the Rocky Mountains. A year hence, on July 24, 1820, Maj. Stephen Harriman Long, having earlier failed to "ascend the Platte to its source," as directed by John C. Calhoun, secretary of war, assumed the second part of his task, to "return to the Mississippi by way of the Arkansas and the Red." To Capt. J. R. Bell he entrusted the Arkansas descent, while he undertook exploration of the Red. Encountering a tributary of the Canadian, his men pursued it and on August 4 were on the Canadian proper, which they mistook for the Red. After a long descent they discovered their error but too late. JAMES, E. [1], in THWAITES [1], XVII, 63, 85–86, 94–95, 139, 170.

[11]Illinois River, not to be confused with Illinois Bayou met *ante* opposite Dardanelle Rock, rises in N.W. Arkansas but flows mostly in present Oklahoma.

[12]The salt springs on the Neosho or Grand, about which we will learn more from Nuttall subsequently, provided the equipment, when abandoned, for a salt works operated by Mark Bean and his partner, named Sanders, near the Illinois, seven miles above its mouth. It was about to begin production as Nuttall passed by on the Arkansas. Captain J. R. Bell in JAMES, E. [1], in THWAITES [1], XVII, 286.

which the water is far from being at its lowest ebb, no boats drawing more than from 12 to 18 inches water, could pass this rapid without lightening, and it appears to form one of the first obstacles of consequence in the navigation of the Arkansa.[13]

The variety of trees which commonly form the North American forest, here begin very sensibly to diminish. We now scarcely see any other than the smooth-barked cottonwood, the elm, box-elder (*Acer Negundo*), curled maple (*Acer dasycarpon*), and ash, all of them reduced in stature. From hence the forest begins to disappear before the pervading plain. To-day we were favoured with a fine south-east breeze, and sailed along with rapidity. Early in the afternoon we passed Bougie's island, near to which, and in two other places, the hills, of about 300 feet elevation, approach the river; the rocks being still a slaty sandstone. Elk and deer now appeared common on the sand beaches, being obliged to come to the river for water, as the springs in the prairies are at this season nearly all dried up. We continued to pass several rapids, with the water curling over beds of gravel. According to the common estimate, we proceeded to-day 45 miles, and in the evening were only two leagues from our destination.[14]

14TH.] This morning we passed a low ledge of rocks on our left, apparently the usual dark-coloured slaty sand-stone, and which has received the name of the Charbonniere, from the appearances of coal which it exhibits. On this side, the prairie approaches the immediate bank of the river, and presents a very unusual open prospect. We again passed three or four difficult rapids, within the short distance which remained to complete our present voyage, but presently after saw the outlet of Grand river, (or the Six Bulls as it is called by the French hunters), and now entered the Verdigris, where M. Bougie and Mr. Prior had their trading houses.[15]

[13]The falls on the Arkansas would later be known as Webber's, from the Cherokee headman Walter Webber, who would have his trading post and farm there.

[14]Most of the landmarks here noted (in present Muskogee County) have given way to the McClellan-Kerr Arkansas River Navigation Project, the inland waterway from the mouth of the Arkansas to the Port of Catoosa, east of Tulsa.

[15]The mouth of the Grand or Neosho is slightly west of present Fort Gibson (1824), in Muskogee County. The mouth of the Verdigris, also in Muskogee County, is s.e. of the former settlement of Wybark. Here the confluences of the two rivers are scarcely a quarter of a mile apart. Above the former are Lakes Fort Gibson and Hudson and Lake O' The Cherokees and, above the last, Lake Oologah, all developed by dams.

The Three Forks area was a busy place in the summer of 1819. It supported four

The water of both these rivers was quite pellucid; while that of the Arkansa was now whitish and muddy, from the partial influx and augmentation of some neighbouring streams.

principal trading posts: those of Joseph Bogy and William Drope, whom we have met earlier; Capt. Nathaniel Pryor, Samuel Richards, Samuel Rutherford, of Virginia, and Hugh Glenn, of Cincinnati (who the following year would become post sutler at Fort Smith); Joseph Revoir, agent for A. P. Chouteau of Saint Louis; and Capt. Henry Barbour, of New Orleans, and George W. Brand, of Tennessee. RAND, 149; FOREMAN [4], 152–53; DRUMM, 255–56; FOREMAN [5], 35–47.

CHAPTER XI.

Character of the surrounding country of the Verdigris river—Remarks on the Osage Indians

14TH.] This morning, accompanied by Mr. Prior, I walked over a portion of the alluvial land of the Verdigris, the fertility of which was sufficiently obvious in the disagreeable and smothering luxuriance of the tall weeds, with which it was overrun. This neck of land, situated betwixt Grand river and the Verdigris, is about two miles wide, free from inundation, and covered with larger trees than any other I had seen since leaving Fort Smith. Among them were lofty scarlet oaks, ash, and hackberry, and whole acres of nettles (*Urtica divaricata*),[1] with whose property of affording hemp, the French hunters and settlers have been long acquainted. Contiguous to the lower side of Grand river, there was a thick cane-brake, more than two miles in width, backed by the prairie, without the intervention of hills.[2] As is common in large alluvions, so in this of the Verdigris, a second terrace or more elevated bottom succeeds the first, beyond which, occur thinly timbered hills. We then enter upon the great western prairies, or grassy plains, separated from each other by small rivulets, exhibiting belts of trees along their margin. About eight miles from the Arkansa, commences the great Osage prairie, more than 60 miles in length, and, in fact, succeeded by a continuation of woodless

---

[1] Urtica divaricata L. = Urticastrum divaricatum (L.) Ktze. = *Laportea canadensis* (L.) Wedd., wood nettle.

[2] Lt. James B. Wilkinson, descending the Arkansas in 1806 from the Pike Expedition, encountered an Osage village near where Nuttall now found himself and later recommended the creation of a post which in 1824 became Fort Gibson, established by Col. Matthew Arbuckle. PIKE I, Map 3; II, 15–17. Washington Irving departed Fort Gibson in 1832 for the tour on the prairies with the Englishman Charles Joseph Latrobe, Indian Commissioner Henry L. Ellsworth, and the young Count Albert-Alexandre de Pourtalès, all of whom were impressed with the natural surroundings. IRVING, 109–16; POURTALES, 77–80. George Catlin in 1834 described the Three Forks grasses and flowers, and the perfume of the latter, in extravagant terms. CATLIN II, 36.

plains to the banks of the Missouri.[3] Mr. Prior informed me, that in the first hills below, not far from the Arkansa, on the east side, and about six miles distant, there is calcareous rock. On entering the prairie, I was greatly disappointed to find no change in the vegetation, and indeed, rather a diminution of species. The *Amorpha canescens*,[4] which I had not heretofore seen, since leaving St. Louis and the Missouri, and a new species of *Helianthus*, however, instantly struck me as novel.[5]

Leaving the path to the Osage village, we visited the rapids of the Verdigris, which are situated five miles above its embouchure. This obstruction is occasioned by a ledge of rocks, which traverse the river, now bare, except about three or four yards, over which the water foamed in a small cascade. The stream was quite pellucid, and along the ledge we saw great numbers of buffaloe-fish, as well as gars (*Esox osseus*),[6] accompanied by several other smaller kinds. While viewing the surrounding objects, my attention was attracted to a beautiful green-striped lizard, resembling, except in the colour and larger size, the *Lacerta vittata*.[7]

If the confluence of the Verdigris, Arkansa, and Grand rivers, shall ever become of importance as a settlement, which the great and irresistible tide of western emigration promises, a town will probably be founded here, at the junction of these streams and this obstruction in the navigation of the Verdigris, as well as the rapids of Grand river, will afford good and convenient situations for mills, a matter of no small importance in the list of civilized comforts.[8] From the Verdigris to St. Louis, there is an Osage trace, which reduces the distance of those two places to about 300 miles, and that also over a country scarcely obstructed by mountains.[9]

[3]Nuttall's "great Osage prairie" begins at the present town of Okay and runs N.W. in Wagoner, Tulsa, and Osage counties, characterized principally as prairie-plains and sandstone hills. MCREYNOLDS, maps at 396.

[4]*Amorpha canescens* Pursh, leadplant, of the Leguminosae (pulse family).

[5]*Helianthus petiolaris* Nutt., one of the sunflowers which Nuttall would subsequently name, as he would also *H. silphoides* Nutt., both from the Arkansas.

[6]Here, rather, *Lepisosteus osseus*, the long-nosed gar.

[7]The Lacertidae are true Old World lizards, of which *L. vivipara* is abundant in England. We cannot be sure what he saw in this range.

[8]Urban development often disregards the logic of natural setting and even water resources. Modern Muskogee, in the county of that name, lying south of the Arkansas below Three Forks, and Tulsa, much upstream on the Arkansas, emerged, respectively, from the agency for the Five Civilized Tribes (Cherokee, Chickasaw, Choctaw, Creek, and Seminole) and great oil strikes beginning in 1905.

[9]See map, p. 164.

The low hills contiguous to the falls of this river, and on which there exist several aboriginal mounds, were chosen by the Cherokees and Osages to hold their council, and to form a treaty of reciprocal amity as neighbours. This first friendly interview with the Cherokees, was soon after broke through by jealousy, and accompanied on both sides with the most barbarous revenge. Scarcely any nation of Indians have encountered more enemies than the Osages; still they flatter themselves, by saying, that they are seated in the middle of the world, and, although surrounded by so many enemies, they have ever maintained their usual population, and their country. From conversations with the traders, it appeared, that they would not be unwilling to dispose of more of their lands, provided that the government of the United States would enter into a stipulation, not to settle it with the aborigines, whom they have now much greater reason to fear than the whites. The limit of their last cession proceeds in a north-east direction from the falls of the Verdigris, and enters the line which was run from Fire prairie, on the Missouri, to Frog bayou, about 60 miles from the Arkansa; but, as it would appear, through a culpable oversight, the saline of Grand River was omitted, on the supply of which the whole territory so much depended for salt.[10]

Limestone appears to exist along the banks of the Verdigris, not many

[10]Nuttall's description of the Osage Treaty cession of September 25, 1818, is reasonably accurate. The resulting loss of the then principal salt source in the Three Forks area at a point west of the Grand, or Neosho, five miles N.E. of present Mazie in Mayes County, Okla., to the Osage domain was evidently mentioned to Nuttall by Major Bradford at Fort Smith (see Bradford to John C. Calhoun, March 28, 1819, in TERR. PAPERS, XIX, 57–58). This great saline lay well within the western boundary (the Verdigris) agreed to by the Osages in their meeting with William L. Lovely, agent for the Cherokees, in 1816 covering what subsequently became known as Lovely's Purchase. The ultimate line of the cession, however, was made to run from the lower falls of the Verdigris to the "upper saline" on the east bank of the Neosho where Salina now stands. Thus from 1816 to 1818, the date of the United States treaty with the Osages, this saline remained under Osage title. The latter treaty provided a north boundary running from the lower falls of the Verdigris to the old Osage north–south line of 1808 from Fire Prairie to Frog Bayou on the Arkansas, at a point twenty leagues above the latter. Thus both of the great salines mentioned above fell back into the Osage domain. We shall hear more of the first saline in Nuttall's subsequent account. Of salines, however, there was in that era an abundance: three on the Illinois within fifteen miles of its mouth, one of which would be operated by Bean and Sanders; Captain Pryor's, a few miles above Union Mission on the E. bank of the Grand (Governor Miller to the Secretary of War, May 27, 1822, in TERR. PAPERS, XIX, 439); on the N. side of the Arkansas, a short distance above the mouth of the Canadian; and at Chouteau's Old Trading House on the E. bank of the Verdigris at the lower falls.

miles above the falls, as large rolled fragments charged with shells were scattered along the shores. The slaty sandstone, also, which forms the falls, dipping about 10° to the north-west, exhibits, in some of its beds, organic impressions, resembling a very serpentine caryophyllite, and traversed with calcareous sparry illinitions.

15TH.] The first village of the Osages lies about 60 miles from the mouth of the Verdigris, and is said to contain 7 or 800 men and their families. About 60 miles further, on the Osage river, is situated the village of the chief called White Hair.[11] The whole of the Osages are now, by governor Clarke, enumerated at about 8000 souls. At this time nearly the whole town, men and women, were engaged in their summer hunt, collecting bison tallow and meat. The principal chief is called by the French Clarmont, although his proper name is the Iron bird, a species of Eagle.[12] The right of governing is commonly hereditary, but not always directed by primogeniture. Talia,[13] the son of the last chief, being considered too young at the decease of his father, the rule was conferred on Clarmont, son of the chief of White Hair's village, on the Osage river, and his behaviour as regent for many years, secured to him the undivided controul of the village. Like most of the rulers among the aborigines, he neither affects nor supports any shadow of pomp or distinction beyond that of his office as supreme commander, and leader of the council.

[11] Perhaps half the Great and Little Osages had remained on the Osage and Marmaton rivers in Missouri in 1802 under Chief White Hair. The other half had gone southwest to the Three Forks with the Chouteau trading firm. Nuttall's White Hair (*Paw-Hiu-Skah*) was the second of that name. The first had been active in the late eighteenth century and was present (and took a white wig, hence his name) when Little Turtle and the Miami Indians defeated Gen. Arthur St. Clair in the Northwest Territory in 1791. He died in 1808, White Hair II in 1833. FOREMAN [1], 20 n.

[12] Clermont, whose Osage name, according to Mathews, was *Gra-Món*, or Arrow-Going-Home, was also the second of his name and chose for himself the appellation Maker-of-Towns. The first Clermont appears in Francisco Cruzat's report of November 15, 1777, to Bernardo de Gálvez on the tribe of Big Osages, with eight hundred warriors, living at the confluence of the Osage and Missouri rivers. Clermont II's place on Osage River was usurped when he was young by White Hair. In the migration of his followers to the Three Forks he had as regent exercising his powers *Cashesegra*, called Big Track or, by the Osages, Makes-Tracks-Going-Far-Away. Clermont II would live until 1828. HOUCK [1], I, 144; PIKE, II, 16–17, 254, 289; FOREMAN [1], 136. The last of the line of Clermonts, or *Gra-Móns*, still possessing a buckskin shirt decorated with Cherokee scalps, was living in 1936. MATHEWS, 418–19.

[13] Tallai, or *Ta-Eh-Ga-Xe*, Buck-Making-Horns, was *Gra-Món*'s second-in-command, the latter being undeniably Grand *Hunkah*, or Chief. MATHEWS, 416.

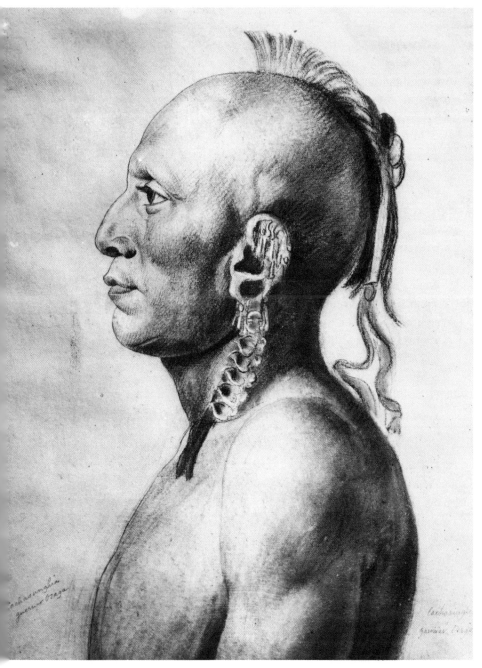

Cachasunghia [Cashesegra], by C. B. J. F. de Saint-Mémin

Payouska [Paw-Hiu-Skah, White Hair I], by Saint-Mémin
Courtesy The New-York Historical Society, New York City

His influence is, however, so great as to be prudentially courted by all who would obtain any object with the village. He appeared to be shrewd and sagacious, and no way deficient in Indian bravery and cunning.

The Osages at this time entertained a considerable jealousy of the whites, in consequence of the emigration of the Cherokees to their frontiers; they considered it as a step of policy in the government to overawe them, and intended to act in concert with the establishment of the garrison. This consideration, as well as the power and wealth of the whites, which have been witnessed by their chiefs on their deputation to Washington, has, within these two years back, had a salutary tendency to restrain their pretensions. Still the white hunters and trappers are frequently insulted and chastised by them. And, on the other hand, we have surely no just reason to expect from the Indians an unstipulated license to rob their country of that game, which is necessary to their convenience and subsistence. [14]

From the Osage interpreter, of whom I made the inquiry, I learned, that, in common with many other Indians, as might be supposed from their wandering habits and exposure to the elements, they are not unacquainted with some peculiar characters and configurations of the stars. Habitual observation had taught them that the pole star remains stationary, and that all the others appear to revolve around it; they were acquainted with the Pleiades, for which they had a peculiar name, and remarked the three stars of Orion's belt. The planet Venus they recog-

[14]From the earliest period of the Spanish regime in the Mississippi Valley, the Osages, their warlike customs, and their raiding were subjects of observation by Spanish colonial officials. Athanase de Mézières (BOLTON, I, 194–95) called the Osages appearing at Natchitoches in 1770 to trade "haughty and bold." Joseph Bogy *père*, as early as 1769, was carrying northward reports of Osage depredations in lower Louisiana. FOREMAN [1], 16n. As everyone agreed, they got along badly with their neighbors: Kadohadachos and other Caddoans on and south of Red River, Quapaws of the lower Arkansas River, Kansa on the Missouri and Kansas rivers, Omahas farther up that stream, Pawnees of the Platte and Loup rivers, Apaches and Comanches of the Great Plains, and the ever-pressing immigrant Cherokees now occupying much of their former domain. The sophistication of the latter, sharpened by long association with whites east of the Mississippi, often put the Siouan Osages at a severe disadvantage, as in the negotiations over Lovely's Purchase, later (1818) in the treaty cession to Gen. William Clark, which failed to achieve for these woodland and prairie warriors what they most desired, a white buffer land between themselves on the west and the now often raiding Cherokees on the east. Their customs and beliefs are seen to good advantage in Nuttall's account and in MATHEWS, TIXIER, WILKINSON (in PIKE, II), CORTAMBERT, and FLINT [2].

nised as the Lucifier or harbinger of day; and, as well as the Europeans, they called the Galaxy the heavenly path or celestial road. The filling and waning of the moon regulated their minor periods of time, and the number of moons, accompanied by the concomitant phenomena of the seasons, pointed out the natural duration of the year.

The superstitions of the Osages differ but little from those which have so often been described, as practised by the other natives. The importance of smoking, as a religious ceremony, is such as to be often accompanied by invocations for every aid or necessary of life. Before going out to war they raise the pipe towards heaven or the sun,[15] and implore the assistance of the Great Spirit to favour them in their reprisals, in the stealing of horses, and the destruction of their enemies, &c. &c. They are acquainted with the value of wampum, know the destructive effects of guns and gunpowder, and the fascinating, but deleterious qualities of spiritous liquors. Their minds have not been deluded into a belief in sorcery, which, from its supposed fatality, is by many of the eastern Indians punished with death. At their festivals, as among most of the other natives, the warriors recount their actions of bravery, and number them by throwing down a stick upon the ground for every exploit, or striking at a post fixed for the purpose. On such occasions, they sometimes challenge each other with a mutual emulation, to recount a like number of warlike deeds. Yet this ostentation is rarely suffered to degenerate into insult or envious combat; vulgarity is unknown amongst the aborigines of America; and the crest-fallen warrior, superceded by a competitor, only seeks an equal share of honour in the claims of patriotism, in the wars of his nation.

After scalping, the greatest feat of the Indian warrior is the stealing of horses from the enemy, which they effect with notorious dexterity. The bad effects, which may be easily anticipated to arise from this thirst for martial fame, is a perpetual and obstinate continuance of war upon the slightest pretext; to which may also be added, their inability often, or unwillingness to distinguish betwixt public and personal wrong. Instead

---

[15]The Naudowessies [Dakota], and, as we are told by La Hontan [*Nouveaux voyages de Mr le baron Lahontan, dans l'Amérique Septentrionale* (La Haye, 1703)], the Hurons, smoked to the sun and the four cardinal points of the compass, which, according to Sir William Jones, is the characteristic ritual of the Tartars. —NUTTALL.

of punishing offenders against the peace, and thus endeavouring to keep up a good understanding with their neighbours, the friends of the incendiary, who has hurried his nation into war, hearken perhaps with indulgence to his misrepresentations, and thus too often effectually prohibit the application of salutary punishment. In fact, the want of legal restraint, and of an efficient government, in spite of all our admiration of patriarchal rule, have proved the ever baneful means of aboriginal depopulation. It is this anarchy which has so often prevented their common union against the encroachment of foreigners, and deprived them, in a great degree, of the advantages and comforts of public security and civilization. The most tyrannical oligarchy, as we have seen in the example of the Mexicans, the Peruvians, and the Natchez, would have been less injurious in its effects on their society, than this paternal form of government, which, unfortunately, however natural and virtuous in its principle, proves, by its lenity, insufficient to check a vicious populace.

CHAPTER XII.

———————

An excursion up Grand River to visit the Osage salt works—Geological observations—Return across the prairie; its general appearance and phenomena.

17TH.] To-day I proceeded with two young men in a canoe up Grand river, with an intention of visiting the salt works. We found the water of this stream very clear, and the channel little inferior in breadth to some parts of the Arkansa; also full of rapids, and now so shallow as to admit of no vessel drawing more than 12 inches of water. The islands are very numerous and small, and the bars and bends, except by the predominance of gravel, resemble the Arkansa on a reduced scale. The gravel is entirely composed of lime-stone and chert. In the distance of about seven miles we found the first ridge terminating on the borders of the river to be calcareous. Below this, and about two or three miles from the mouth of the river, the usual dark-coloured slaty sandstone prevails. In the course of the day we killed several large buffaloe fish, which are very abundant in all the shallow and gravelly ripples, apparently a *Cyprinus*,[1] and very palatable when fried in oil. The boney gar (*Esox osseus*), and the large grey catfish, are also sufficiently common. We proceeded about 30 miles.

18TH.] The morning was fine, and we embarked at sunrise. About eight o'clock we passed a bend called the Eagle's nest, a mile above which, and its island, a fasçade of calcareous rock appears, inlaid with beds of whitish hornstone. While examining these cliffs, I recognised as new, a large shrub, and to my great surprise found it to be a simple-leaved *Rhus*, scarcely distinct from the *R. Cotinus* of the south of Europe and of our gardens.[2] Hills and cliffs, but partly hid in woods, were now of frequent

———

[1]The buffalo fish, one of the family Cyprinidae, or soft-finned, freshwater fishes, here specifically *Megastomatobus cyprinella*.

[2]The American smoke tree, *Cotinus americanus* Nutt. (1849), gave way to *Cotinus obovatus* Raf., 1840, monotypic. LITTLE [2] notes it as one of Oklahoma's rarest trees.

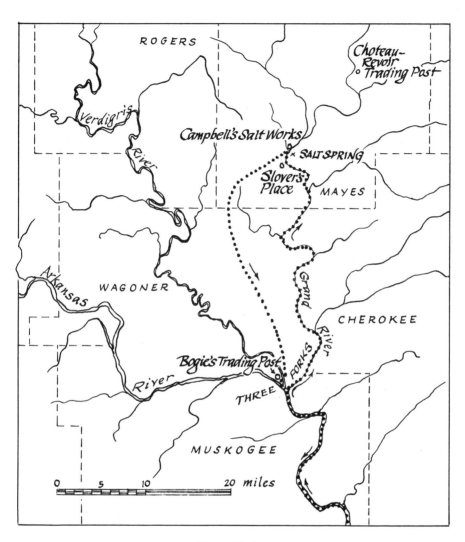

Three Forks

occurrence along the river bank. The neighbouring thickets abounded with game, amongst which two bears made their appearance. The gravel bars were almost covered with *Amsonia salicifolia*,[3] with which grew also the *Sesbania macrocarpa* of Florida.[4]

This evening I arrived at Mr. Slover's, two miles below the saline. The farm which this hunter occupied was finely elevated and productive, and apparently well suited to the production of small grain. Up to this place, which is said to be 50 miles from the Arkansa, the cane continues to be abundant. In this elevated alluvion I still observed the Coffee-bean tree (*Gymnocladus canadensis*),[5] the over-cup white oak (*Quercus mac-rocarpa*),[6] the pecan (*Carya olivoeformis*),[7] the common hickory, ash, elm; and below, in places near the margin of the river, the poplar-leaved birch (*Betula populifolia*).[8]

Mr. S. informed me, that on the opposite side of the river, and two miles from hence, another strong salt spring breaks out through the in-cumbent gravel; and that there are other productive springs 25 miles above.[9]

19TH.] This morning, I walked with Mr. Slover to see the salt works, now indeed lying idle, and nearly deserted in consequence of the murder of Mr. Campbell, by Erhart, his late partner, and two accomplices in their employ. Melancholy as were the reflections naturally arising from this horrid circumstance, I could not but congratulate myself on having escaped, perhaps a similar fate. At the Cadron, I had made application to Childer's, one of these remorseless villains, as a woodsman and hunter, to accompany me for hire, only about a month before he had shot and bar-barously scalped Mr. Campbell, for the purpose of obtaining his little

[3] *Amsonia Tabernaemontana* var. *salicifolia* (Pursh) Woodson, willow-leaved amsonia of Apocynaceae (dogbane family).

[4] Called by many botanists *Sesbania exaltata* (Raf.) Cory, of the Leguminosae (pulse family).

[5] *Gymnocladus* canadensis = *G. dioica* (L.) K. Koch.

[6] *Quercus macrocarpa* Michx., mossy-cup oak, bur oak.

[7] * *Carya* olivaeformis = *C. illinoensis* (Wang.) K. Koch.

[8] *Betula populifolia* Marsh., gray birch, which, however, has no Oklahoma range (LITTLE [2]); but *Betula nigra* L., river birch, is present in the Oklahoma-Arkansas area.

[9] "Opposite side" here must mean on the east (left) bank of the Grand, or Neosho, since Campbell's was on the west. The other productive springs "25 miles above," again on the east bank, seem to be at the location of the Chouteau-Revoir trading site at present Salina.

property, and in spite of the friendship which he had uniformly received from the deceased.[10]

But to return to the subject. We proceeded two miles, along the hilly and woody skirts of the river, and through the adjoining prairie to the saline, which appeared to be a gravelly, alluvial basin, of about an acre in extent, and destitute of all vegetation. A small fresh water brook, now scarcely running, passed through this area, and the salt water, quite pellucid, issued copiously to the surface in various directions. In one place it boiled up out of a focus of near six inches diameter, emitting fetid bubbles of sulphuretted hydrogen, which deposited a slight scum of sulphur. All the springs are more or less hepatic, which circumstance is attributable to a bed of bituminous and sulphuretted slate-clay, visible on the margin of the stream, and, probably, underlaid by coal, through which the water rises to the surface. In the adjoining heights, a coarse-grained sandstone occurs, answering the purpose of mill-stones; the stream then contracts at the entrance of a ledge of slaty rocks, and, about a half mile from its immediate outlet, the water is perfectly fresh. The only well dug upon the premises for the salt water, was about five feet deep, and quarried through a bed of dark-coloured limestone, containing shells and nodules of black hornstone, similar to the chert of Derbyshire. This salt appears to be concomitant with a coaly or bituminous formation. No marine plants appear in this vicinity, as at Onondago, where we meet with the Salicornia of the sea marshes. When the works were in operation, 120 bushels of salt were manufactured in a week, and the water is said to be so strong, that after the second boiling, it became necessary to remove the lye. No mother water, or any thing almost but what is volatile, appears mixed with this salt, which is of the purest whiteness on the first boiling, and only takes about 80 gallons of water to produce a bushel. Hitherto these springs have been unaccompanied by any fossil remains of quadrupeds.[11]

[10]The men charged with the murder of Johnson Campbell were his partner, David Earheart, John Bounyon, and William G. Childers. The crime had occurred about May 1, 1819, at the Campbell Salt Works, on the west bank of the Grand, five miles N.E. of present Mazie. Timothy Flint, who talked with the men after they had been apprehended, wrote that "they were imprisoned, and undoubtedly would have been executed but they contrived in a few days to escape." FOREMAN [1], 56; FLINT [2], 195.

[11]Nuttall's description of this saline is more detailed, and more immediate, than any others we have. Amos Stoddard, first U.S. civil administrator of Upper Louisiana in 1804, and later in the same year of Lower Louisiana, wrote that the spring had a "foun-

This forenoon I was disagreeably surprised by a slight attack of the intermittent fever, which was also beginning to make its appearance in the family of Mr. Slover. In the spring, they were likewise affected by the influenza, which prevailed in the Osage village, and induced several pulmonary consumptions. No medicines being at hand, as imprudently I had not calculated upon sickness, I took in the evening about a pint of a strong and very bitter decoction, of the *Eupatorium*, the *E. perfoliatum* or Boneset, not being to be found in the neighbourhood.[12] This dose, though very nauseous, did not prove sufficient to operate as an emetic, but acted as a disphoretic and gentle laxative, and prevented the proximate return of the disease.

20TH.] This morning I left Mr. Slover's, and proceeded, by compass, across the Great Osage plain, towards the mouth of the Verdigris. My course was south by west, the distance being about 30 miles. Twenty miles of this route was without any path, and through grass three feet deep, often entangled with brambles, and particularly with the tenacious "saw-brier" (*Schrankia horridula*).[13] The honey upon the grass, as at Sambo prairie, was so universally abundant, that my mockasins and pantaloons were soaked as with oil.[14] Several insulated eminences, appearing almost artificial, served to diversify the cheerless uniformity of the extensive plain, still wrapt in primeval solitude. Not even a tree appeared, except along the brooks of Grand river and the Verdigris, which rivers, for 25 or 30 leagues, are not more than 12 to 15 miles apart. About a mile from the base of one of those prominent hills, insulated like an aboriginal mound, and towards which I was directed to proceed, passed the path to the Indian village, and the outlet of the Verdigris. It was evening when I

---

tain or bason at its source of about forty feet in diameter. It then suddenly disappears under a rock of about forty yards in extent, the cap of which is flat and smooth." STODDARD, 401. It had first been worked by Bernard R. Mouille under a grant from Cherokee Agent William Lovely in 1815 but had been acquired by Campbell and Earheart by 1817. TERR. PAPERS, XV, 50 and note 73.

[12]The "decoction" was from one of the several species of the genus *Eupatorium* which occur in the area.

[13]*Schrankia horridula* Chapm. = *Schrankia microphylla* (Dryand.) Macbride, limited to the S.E. United States. The only species of the genus in this area is *S. Nuttallii* (DC.) Standl.

[14]Honeydew, here encountered for the second time, is secreted by sapsucking insects (aphids, whiteflies, scale insects, plant lice, and plant hoppers) and consists of water, amino acids, and sugars (sucrose, fructose, glucose, and melezitose).

arrived at this hill, which had been a prominent object in view, ever since my outset this morning. From its summit, the wide and verdant plain appeared visible for 40 miles. Proceeding about four miles from this eminence, much fatigued, I lay down to sleep in the prairie, under the clear canopy of heaven;—but alone, and without the necessary comforts of either fire, food, or water. The crickets, grashoppers, catidids, and stocking-weavers, as they are familiarly called, kept up such a loud and shrill crepitation, as to prove extremely irksome, and almost stunning to the ears. Every tender leaved plant, whether bitter or sweet, by thousands of acres, were now entirely devoured by the locust grashoppers, which arose before me almost in clouds. I slept, however, in comfort, and was scarcely at all molested by musquetoes. The next day, after spending considerable time in botanizing, I arrived at the trading houses.

CHAPTER XIII.

Interviews with the Osages—Occasional observations on their manners and habits, &c.—Sickness in the encampment.

24TH.] Last evening, as well as this morning, we were waited upon by two of the Osage chiefs from the village, one of whom was Tálai, their hereditary ruler. Some of the inferior chiefs were begging tobacco, like earnest and genuine mendicants. It is to be regretted, that the man of nature should sink so low by intercourse with the civilized world, and by the acquisition of what were once to him merely artificial wants. Surrounded by a fertile country, the Indian, without ever being either rich or independent, finds it difficult to obtain subsistence, trespasses upon his neighbours, lives in insecurity, and in implacable enmity with those of his own race. A stranger to our ideas of honour, he destroys his enemies by the meanest stratagems, and levels, in his revenge, all distinctions of age and sex. Such is the general character of the Osages, and such even that of the Cherokees, after all their external approaches towards civilization.

To give my Reader some idea of the laborious exertions which these people exercise to obtain a livelihood, I need only relate, that the Osages had now returned to their village from a tallow hunt, in which they had travelled not less than 300 miles up the Arkansa, and had crossed the Saline plains, situated betwixt that river and the Canadian. In this hunt, they say, that 10 villages of themselves and friends (as the Kansas, who speak nearly the same language) joined for common safety. They were, however, attacked by a small scout of the Pawnees, and lost one of their young men who was much esteemed, and, as I myself witnessed, distractingly lamented by the father, of whom he was the only son. They say, the country through which they passed is so destitute of timber, that they had to carry along their tent poles, and to make fire of the bison ordure.

The activity and agility of the Osages is scarcely credible. They not uncommonly walk from their village to the trading houses, at the mouth of the Verdigris, in one day, a distance of about 60 miles.

The Osages, in their private conversations, do not appear still to be on an amicable footing with the Cherokees. One of their chiefs insisted on the hunting boundary being established betwixt the two nations, so that either party might be punished, by robbery and plunder (or confiscation as we term it), who should be found transgressing the limits assigned. Aware of the strength of their enemies, they have been led to seek the alliance of other Indians, and have recently cultivated the friendship of the Outigamis (now called Sauks and Foxes) of the Mississippi. In a recent council, held at the village of the Verdigris, these people were presented with 100 horses by the Osages. Sensible of this liberality, the Outigamis pledged themselves to prove their active allies, whenever necessity should dictate it to them. These gifts, however great, are not difficult to replace, as they now, this hunt, obtained more than 300 horses, which they had either caught wild, or stolen from the Pawnees, their enemies.[1]

27TH.] This morning, Clarmont, accompanied by some of the lesser chiefs, arrived from the lower village, on their way to the garrison, where they were to hold a council with the Cherokees. There was some degree of urbanity, though nothing at first very prepossessing, in the appearance of Clarmont. He wore a hat ornamented with a band of silver lace, with a sort of livery or regimental coat, and appeared proud of the artificial distinctions bestowed on him by the government. He asked, familiarly, if I had ever heard of him before, and appeared gratified at my answering in the affirmative. I am told, however, that, of late years, his influence at *home* has been greatly superceded by that of Ta-lai, the true hereditary chief. Ta-lai was now also present, but destitute of any exterior decorations, though on his way to the general council; I did not consequently recognise him until pointed out to me. In excuse for laying aside the

---

[1]The four bands of the Pawnees—Chaui, Skidi, Pitahauerat, and Kitkehahki—living on the Platte and Loup Fork in east-central Nebraska, often came down in small groups to visit their Caddoan kinsmen on and south of Red River. These movements put them in the Osage hunting range, with resulting encounters with the big Siouans. More often, however, it was the small expedition of Pawnees bent on horse stealing that produced conflict with the Osages. Cf. HYDE [1], *passim*.

honourable distinctions of the government, he said, there was no necessity, he thought, of parading the medal, his people knew him to be the
chief, and the major could not be ignorant of his station. This natural
unassuming behaviour, which we so seldom witness in life, surprised and
prepossessed me in favour of this legitimate chief. His aspect was uncommonly benign, and bespoke the man of candor and benevolence.

Last summer a general council of the natives, friendly disposed towards
the Osages, took place at their village; amongst them were Shawnees,
Delawares, Creeks, Quapaws, Kanzas, Outigamis, &c. Their ostensible
object was not known; it would appear, however, that they had been
invited by the Osages, who on this occasion gave away more than 300
horses. The Outigamis told them in an unlimited manner, that they
would be always ready at the first notice, to join them at any time, against
any nation. With the Creeks they were dissatisfied, and alledged that they
had undervalued their hospitality by bringing spoons in their pockets,
which was probably turned into a sinister omen.[2]

Preparatory to undertaking a warlike expedition, the Osages, in common with many other of the aborigines, practised rigid fasts, which were
frequently continued from three to seven days together, forming, with
other privations and inflictions, a kind of penance, by which they disci-
plined themselves for disasters, and supplicated the pity and favour of
heaven. Their invocations to the Good Spirit, and their lamentations, are
incessant. About sunrise the whole village re-echoes with the most plain-
tive tones of distress, uttered at the doors of their lodges, or at the tombs of
those whom they loved and esteemed while living. Indeed, all their affec-

---

[2]So far as is known, Nuttall's account of the 1818 council called by the Osages at their
village near present Claremore is the only surviving record of this event. The list of tribes
represented suggests an unlikely alliance, even against the Cherokees, for the Osages had
committed offenses against all of them in the preceding decade and would commit more.
A second council was to have taken place a few weeks before Nuttall's meeting with the
Osages:

"I have also understood," Major Bradford wrote the secretary of war from Fort Smith,
March 28, 1819, "that a large council of Indians is to be held in the month of June at a
place called Salt Plains lying between the waters of Red River and Arkansas at a distance
about three hundred miles west of here. The Council will be composed of Great and
Little Osages, Aropohoos, and a number of the Sox, Sieux, and Kansas now in the Osage
Nation. The Iotans [Ietans = Utes, but here more probably another Shoshonean tribe,
the Comanches] which are much the most numerous tribe west of this will also attend."
TERR. PAPERS, XIX, 59.

tions, uncontrolled by the mask of affectation, are sincere and ingenuous. Of the sincerity of their conjugal attachment, notwithstanding the coldness of temper which has been alleged against the aborigines generally, I have witnessed, among them and others, many unequivocal proofs. The expression of affection, perhaps, as in other societies, where it is so studiously concealed, is more tender and assiduous on the part of the female. A few days ago we were near upon witnessing something tragical, in the conduct of an Indian woman, who had been several years married to a French hunter, living with the Osages. Soon after Mr. Bougie's arrival, intoxication taking place in the camp, a quarrel ensued between the husband of this woman and another of the French hunters. Their altercation filled her with terror, and she gave way to tears and lamentations, not doubting but that the antagonist, who was the aggressor, intended the death of her husband, as threats among the Indians are the invariable preludes to fatal actions. When, at length, they began to struggle with each other, without any more ado, she seized upon a hatchet, and would instantly have dispatched the man who fought with her husband, if not prevented by the bystanders.

That curious species of polygamy, which prevails among some other Indian nations, is likewise practised by the Osages, by which, the man who first marries into a family, from that period possesses the controul of all the sisters of his wife, whom he is at liberty either to espouse himself, or to bestow upon others. The maid, as amongst the Quapaws and others, is distinguished from the matron by the method she employs in braiding her hair into two cylindric rolls, which are ornamented with beads, silver, or wampum, and inclined to either side of the head near the ears. After marriage the hair is unloosed and brought together behind. This is one of those little arbitrary distinctions which is quite as invariable as the general costume of the people who employ it.

A practise no less notorious among the young men of the Osages, and the natives generally, is the careful extraction of the marks of pubescence from every part of the body. These Indians even pluck out their eyebrows, shave their heads, and leave only a small scalp upon the crown. Of this, two locks left long, are plaited and ornamented with silver, wampum, and eagle's feathers. The tonsure and ears, as well as the eye-lashes, are painted with vermillion on ordinary occasions, but blackened to express

grief or misfortune. Sometimes, apparently out of fancy, they fantastically decorate their faces with white, black, or green stripes. The use of
calico or shirts is yet unknown among them, and their present fashions
and mode of dress have been so long stationary, as now to be by themselves
considered characteristic. In their dress, fairish tawney red colour, and
aquiline features, they resemble the Outigamis.[3]

The Osages are more than usually superstitious. With them an ominous dream is often sufficient to terminate the most important expedition.
After performing an exploit, instead of pursuing their success, scarcely
any consideration can deter them from instantly returning to bear the
welcome intelligence to their band. Their communion with each other is
so frank, that nothing can remain a secret. In this way their intentions of
war and plunder are long anticipated, however sudden and secret may be
their actual operations. They are no strangers to dissimulation, when it
will answer their purpose in their intercourse with others, but falsehood
among their friends or fellows would be looked upon as unnatural and
unpardonable. They entertain unconquerable prejudices against hunters.
While in the village, or in their company abroad, the stranger is sure to be
protected and treated like themselves in every particular; but if he is found
in their country as a foreigner, and pursuing a different interest from their
own, he can scarcely be distinguished from an enemy and an intruder, and
must calculate on meeting with chastisement accordingly. To be found
upon their war-paths is likewise considered criminal. These particular
routes which they pursue in quest of their enemies, are recognised by
beacons, painted posts, and inscribed hieroglyphics, commonly set up
near the boundaries of their range; and those whom they chance to find in
this direction, are at best considered as ambiguous friends, and trespassers
on the neutral character which is expected to be maintained.

The miserable fate which, last autumn, befel Mr. M'Farlane (who is

---

[3]The Outigamis = Fox Indians, who, with their kinsmen, the Sauks, of the Algonquian linguistic family, originally of Wisconsin, were so warlike that they were in
frequent conflict with the French of the early period. They often joined the Sioux in war.
Depleted by 1780, they amalgamated with the Sauks. In 1805, Lewis and Clark estimated them at 1,200. Attempts to retain a new homeland in Illinois gave rise to the Black
Hawk War of 1831–32. After sojourns in Iowa, Missouri, and Kansas, most Sauks and
Foxes were removed in 1869 to Indian Territory, present Oklahoma, where more than
1,000 still live, in eastern Lincoln and eastern Pottawatomie counties. Early in the
nineteenth century they were known to range as far west as Santa Fe. WRIGHT, 222–28.

mentioned by Wilkinson, in his descent of the Arkansa, as then taken prisoner by the Osages) is a sufficient proof the danger of intruding on their war-path.[4] The Osages had taken this hunter into custody near to a Pawnee village, with whose inhabitants they were at war, and were about to proceed with him to their own town on the Verdigris. He was, however, very desirous of returning to the village for his son who remained behind, to which the Indians at last consented, and two of them offered to accompany him back towards the Pawnees; but after proceeding some distance they seized upon him, put out his eyes, and then goaded him along for several miles with sharpened canes, thus protracting his death by torture, until one of them, through compassion, put an end to his existence by the tomahawk. Although this fact was now well known in the territory, and not denied by the Osages, no steps had been taken to avenge the death of this unfortunate hunter. The Osages indeed disavowed the deed as that of their nation, but contented themselves by saying, that the action had been committed by two bad men, who were beyond their control.[5] The property of the white hunter generally, whom they discover in their country, without special permission, is considered as an indisputable perquisite; and after perhaps (as I have heard related) breaking his gun in pieces, and flogging him with the ram-rod, they will turn him out into the wilderness nearly naked, and leave him to perish, unless, like a prisoner, he consents to adoption or affiliation, when every thing is again restored to him, and he is received as one of their people.

28TH.] To-day I accompanied one of the hunters about 9 or 10 miles over the alluvial lands of Grand river, which were fertile, and covered in great part with cane. The river lands are no less extensive and luxuriant betwixt the Verdigris and Arkansa, and would apparently support a condensed settlement; but the prairies will only admit of settlements along

[4]Charlevoix remarks, "Every one is an enemy found in the warrior's path," p. 155. —NUTTALL. [P. F. X. de Charlevoix, S.J., *Journal of a Voyage to North America*, 2 vols. (London, 1761), I.]

[5]Wilkinson (in PIKE II, 17 & n.) reported that in his descent of the Arkansas he had met an Osage war party December 29, 1807, and "received from them a man by the name of M'Farlane, who had been trapping on the Potoe." He was James McFarlane, already a veteran in the area. He was later commissioned to regulate trade with the Osages on the Arkansas. In private undertakings Meriwether Lewis, who died in October, 1809, left a debt of $718.45 to McFarlane. JACKSON, D. [2], 471, 473n.

their borders, in consequence of the scarcity of wood and water. Coal, however, in this country appears abundant, as fragmenta are to be seen commonly deposited along the borders of the rivers.

On the 30th and 31st an irregular remittent fever began to show itself in our camp, with which myself and five or six others were affected. With me it came on towards evening, unaccompanied by any sensible chill, but attended with the most excruciating head-ache and violent heat.[6]

August 2D and 3D.] These two days in succession I experienced the same fever, but now more moderate, and preceded by chills.

4TH.] Last evening the chiefs of the Osage village arrived from fort Smith, without effecting an interview with the Cherokees, who, under the pretext of attending to their harvest, had postponed the meeting until the month of September. The chiefs, not without reason, appeared to be considerably perplexed and disappointed at the conduct and apparent evasion of the Cherokees.

Yesterday, whilst I lay sick, some Indian contrived to rob me of the only penknife in my possession, and my pocket microscope. I immediately suspected the thief to have been a fellow who had the same morning, out of amusement, mounted my coat and hat, but he constantly denied the theft, and suffered himself to be searched by the soldier of police, who is generally some trusty warrior appointed by the chief to keep order in the camp or village, and to punish offenders in a summary way.

The chiefs addressed the Indians present concerning the theft, and seriously admonished those who had the articles to give them up. Tálai reproved the Indians in general terms for their injustice, which he asserted to be the means by which they had made themselves so many enemies. "Why will you," says he, "steal things which are useless to you, and which are, at the same time, of importance to others. To-day, while we were travelling, we heard the report of a gun, which might, indeed, have been that of white people, who are our friends, but it might likewise have been some party of those enemies by which we are everywhere surrounded, who could so easily have destroyed a handful of old and almost defenceless chiefs. How much better, my friends, would it be if we could learn to do right and be honest. We should then have friends instead of enemies; but as long as we violate justice, we shall continue to live in fear

---

[6]Nuttall was now a victim of malaria at a more advanced stage than he yet knew.

and shame. When did the white people steal from us? yet you have both plundered and killed those who have always been your friends and bene-factors. This evening we arrived here fatigued and hungry, and the white people have fed us. We ought to return this kindness by presents of provi-sion; but, instead of that, the Osages sell their tallow, and corn, and meat, give nothing, and come and eat of that which they have sold. The Osages are always a bad people, and so have many enemies."

The candour of this speech surprised us, although it well accorded with the honest and benevolent character of the speaker. I am told that he was quite assiduous in attempting the reform of the village, and inculcating amongst them the necessity and advantage of maintaining peace with their neighbours. It is gratifying to learn that this chief, Tálai, whose example so well accorded with the just principles which he preferred, was now gaining the ascendancy over Clarmont, whose conduct had always been tinctured by rapacity. Tálai, indeed, well deserved the chief medal of the nation.

It is, I think, to be regretted, that the Indians should not be made sensible of the impropriety and illegality of executing summary and un-limited punishment upon the citizens of the United States, who are found travelling or hunting in their country. Ought they not rather to be taught that the government would be ever willing and ready to do them justice, by punishing their own citizens, rather than submitting them, in this way, to the cruel pilfering, and castigation of savages! If the frontier garrisons are not capable of effecting this beneficial purpose, for what were they established? but could not even this be better executed by the governor and the militia of the territory, than by the arbitrary commander and the soldiers of a garrison?

This morning, about day-break, the Indians, who had encamped around us, broke into their usual lamentations and complaints to the Great Spirit. Their mourning was truly pathetic, and uttered in a peculiar tone. Amongst those who first broke forth into lamentation, and aroused the rest to their melancholy orisons, was the pious Tálai. The commenc-ing tone was exceedingly loud, and gradually fell off into a low, long continued, and almost monotonous base. To this tone of lamentation was modulated, the subject of their distress or petition. Those who had experi-enced any recent distress or misfortune, previously blackened their faces with coal, or besmeared them with ashes. This lamentation and abasement, in unison with oriental customs, recalled to mind the penance of the Jews, their "sackcloth and ashes," and Jeremiah their weeping prophet.[7]

4TH.] Last evening two very handsome young men of the Osages arrived from the village, with some tallow to barter, and while Mr. Bougie and the rest of the camp were amusing themselves at cards, these Mercuries contrived to carry off a small brass kettle, and endeavoured, though ineffectually, to hook off a musquetoe bier, after which they took the advantage of the night to make their escape. They appeared to have been very well satisfied with the trader, but could not postpone their dexterity at thieving, which being scarcely considered as a dishonourable action, is rarely punished further than by the restitution of the articles.

On the evening of the 5th, we were visited by another of the Osages, bringing the usual commodities of the season, tallow, dried bison meat, and sweet corn, being dried while in the milk, and thus forming an agreeable ingredient in the soup of the prepared bison beef. It is a dish which the Indians, from time immemorial, have been accustomed to prepare, and consider a luxury coeval with their annual festival of the "Green-corn Dance."[8]

[7]"The Osage wail with a religious purpose; it is a prayer in which they expose before the Master of Life their pains and their needs . . . the warriors who are to take part in an expedition tearfully beseach the Evil Spirit. They hope to be spared, through fasting and prayers, the death which threatens them. . . . This song of tears . . . has its fixed rules; the men begin their loud praying before daylight, but the women are allowed to sing only when the men have finished." TIXIER, 164–65.

The Frenchman from Clermont-Ferrand was incomplete in his categories, but he wrote more succinctly than his predecessors or immediate successors about Osage daily songs and *wí-gi-es* (recitatives) until Francis La Flesche and Alice Fletcher, with sure linguistic command, recorded them in extenso in our century. What PIKE (I, 295), BRADBURY (63–64), BRACKENRIDGE (61–62), and Nuttall witnessed was memorable enough, but back of group and individual chanting was an elaborate structure, poetical, alliterative, and not infrequently with the suggestion of rhyming, sometimes running in certain rites to fourteen hundred lines, the condensed wisdom of a people in practical and cosmic affairs—all of it unwritten. The Homeric analogy is obvious. Chanting to Wahkonda, the great spirit, occurred, in La Flesche's words, "at dawn, when they saw the reddened sky signaling the approach of the sun, men, women, and children stood in the doors of their houses and uttered their cry for divine help; as the sun reached midheaven they repeated their prayer; and their supplications again arose as the sun touched the western horizon." LA FLESCHE [I], 47–49; see also LA FLESCHE [2], *The Rite of Vigil*, and LA FLESCHE [3], *The Child-Naming Rite*.

[8]Corn culture had been a feature of Osage life for some time. Pierre Chouteau noted in

In the morning, I was informed, that this Indian wished to exchange a horse with me, for the mare which I had purchased of Mr. Lee; I desired them to tell him, that I requested to have nothing to say to him; knowing him, by report, to be a consummate thief and rascal; but, as he insisted on the subject, I went to see the animal offered me in exchange, and was truly surprised at the impudence and knavery of the demand. The horse which he proffered, was not worth possession, as lean as Rosinante. It may easily be supposed that I rejected his offer, which was nothing better than an insult. My mare was at this time feeding across the Verdigris. The Indian said no more, concluded his barter with the trader, and left us; but instead of proceeding directly towards the village, by the usual route, he kept down the Verdigris. I now suspected that he was intent on thievery, and two of us directly followed him by land, and two by water. We saw him and his wife now crossing the river, and then walking hastily across the beach; by the time we came up with him, he had seized my horse, loaded it with his baggage, and would in a minute or two more, with all the dexterity of an Arab, have carried him off, and so by force and robbery have effected the exchange he so much desired. Daring villains seldom want excuses; he pretended, that the man of whom Mr. Prior bought the horse, had told him to bring it away, and leave the one he offered in its stead. His first depredation, this morning, was stealing a case of razors, which being discovered in his shot pouch, were taken from him; these he said, he only wanted to shave his head, and would then have returned them.

Circumstanced as we were, it was not politic to chastize him, as he would probably, out of revenge, have lurked about a week, in order to have stolen my horse. After some persuasion, and, above all, a hint that if his conduct were made known at the garrison, from whom I had received permission to proceed up the country, he need not expect the restitution of his wife and three children, from the hands of the Cherokees, if that was to be his line of conduct; he now began to speak in a submissive tone, and

---

1815 that the tribe and its divisions avoided conflicts between buffalo hunting on the Great Plains and spring and summer planting and harvesting seasons (M. P. Leduc to Frederick Bates, December 30, 1815, TERR. PAPERS, XV, 98–99). LA FLESCHE [1], 134–37, in the Rite of the Buffalo Bull Gens, recites the life symbols of red, blue, speckled, and yellow corn. PIKE (II, 34) was struck by the large production of corn by Osages, the work being done by women.

ordered his squaw to unpack my horse. I was still, however, mortified to find that it was necessary, prudentially, as suggested by the trader, not only to desist from administering punishment, but even to bestow a present upon the villain by way of encouragement. Such is the indulgent method of dealing with Indians employed by the traders!

As among most other nations of the aborigines, the principal labour, except that of hunting, devolves upon the women. Accustomed to perpetual drudgery, they are stouter and lower in stature than the men. They appear scarcely to inherit the same condition. Considered almost as slaves and creatures of appetite, their lives are always secured as prisoners. It is to their industry and ingenuity, that the men owe every manufactured article of their dress, as well as every utensil in their huts. The Osage women appear to excel in these employments. Before the Cherokees burnt down their town on the Verdigris, their houses were chiefly covered with hand-wove matts of bulrushes.[9] Their baskets and bed matts of this material, were particoloured and very handsome. This manufacture, I am told, is done with the assistance of three sticks, arranged in some way so as to answer the purpose of a loom, and the strands are inlaid diagonally. They, as well as the Cherokees and others, frequently take the pains to unravel old blankets and cloths, and re-weave the yarn into belts and garters. This weaving is no modern invention of the Indians. Nearly all those whom De Soto found inhabiting Florida and Louisiana, on either side of the Mississippi, and who were, in a great measure, an agricultural people, dressed themselves in woven garments made of the lint of the mulberry, the papaw, or the elm; and, in the colder seasons of the year, they wore coverings of feathers, chiefly those of the turkey. The same dresses were still employed in the time of Du Pratz.[10] These feather

---

[9]The massacre of the inhabitants and the burning of the Osage village at Claremore Mound in the autumn of 1817, previously noted. PIKE (II, 31–32) gives a detailed account of the construction and measurements of these more or less permanent dwellings covered with rush mats. Rectangular, some of them extended nearly one hundred feet in length. "With neatness and a pleasing companion, they would compose a very comfortable and pleasant summer habitation," Pike permitted himself to observe. TIXIER (159–60) describes the lodge used by the Osages on buffalo hunts as being similar to the mat lodge but floored and covered with buffalo skins.

[10]"Many of the women wear cloaks of the bark of the mulberry tree, or of the feathers of swans, turkies, or India ducks. The bark they take from mulberry shoots that rise from the roots of trees that have been cut down; after it is dried in the sun, they beat it to make

mantles were, within the recollection of the oldest men, once used by the Cherokees, as I learnt whilst among them. There is, therefore, nothing extraordinary in the discovery of these garments around the bodies which had been interred in the nitre caves of Kentucky. Presents of these "mantels" as they are called by Purchas, now superceded by European blankets, were perpetually offered to Soto, throughout the course of his expedition, and are still made use of by the natives of the north-west coast. Nor is there any thing in this invention beyond the common ingenuity of man, guarding himself against the inclemencies of climate. To assert that all men were of the same race, because they had all invented a somewhat similar clothing, is quite as futile, as the same conclusion would be in consideration of their all being born naked.[11]

The principal food of the present Indians, who inhabit the west side of the Mississippi, is the bison, which they prepare in a very commodious way, without the use of salt, by cutting it up into broad and thin slices, which are dried on a scaffold over a slow fire, and afterwards folded up in the manner of peltries, so as to be equally portable. The tallow is rendered into skins or cases, like the utriculi, or leathern bottles of the ancients, the whole animal being skinned through the aperture of the neck. In this way, they also collect with convenience the honey and bear's oil, which is the produce of their forests.

From the general absence of religious ceremony, and the unostentatious character of devotion among the Indians, it has always been a difficult matter to inspire them with any thing like correct ideas of the

---

all the woody part fall off, and they give the threads that remain a second beating, after which they bleach them by exposing them to the dew. When they are well whitened, they spin them about the coarseness of packthread, and weave them in the following manner: they plant two stakes in the ground, about a yard and a half asunder, and having stretched a cord from one to the other, they fasten their threads of bark double to this cord, and then interweave them in a curious manner into a cloak, of about a yard square, with a wrought border around the edges." Du Pratz, Hist. Louisiana, p. 363. Lond. Ed.

According to Adair also, the Choctaws formed blankets of the smaller feathers of the turkey. "They twist the inner end of the feathers very fast into a strong double thread of hemp, or the inner bark of the mulberry tree of the size and strength of coarse twine, and they work it in the manner of fine netting." Adair's History of the American Indians, p. 423. —NUTTALL.

[11]See Archaeologia Americana, vol. i p. 320, &c. in which there is an attempt to prove that the ancient inhabitants of the western states originated from the Malays. —NUTTALL.

Christian religion. As we have already remarked, they are not, however, void of superstition, such as a belief in the warnings of dreams, the observance of omens, the wearing of amulets, and the dedication of offerings to invisible or miraculous agents, supposed to be represented in the accidental forms of natural objects. But these objects, calculated to inspire a momentary homage, are never addressed for any thing beyond temporal favours.[12]

Although they generally believe in the immortality of the soul, they have no steady and distinct conception of a state of reward and punishment. The future state, believed to be but little different from that which they now enjoy, is alike attainable by every hunter, and every warrior. It is on a conviction of this belief, that the implements of war, and the decorations and utensils employed by the living, are entombed with the dead. Their jealousy of the whites, and suspicion of sinister designs, render them cold and cautious in the adoption of Christianity, and it has ever been those who have said the least on religion, and who, like the Society of the Friends and the Moravians, have preached rather by their benevolent example, and by the introduction of useful arts, that have made the most durable and favourable impression on the minds and morals of the natives.

To show how little can be anticipated among the Osages, by the inculcation of the mere dogmas of Christianity, may be seen by the following anecdote. Mr. Bougie, informed me, that last winter, while accidentally engaged in reading the New Testament, two or three young men, of the Osages, coming into his store, enquired of him what was in that book. He answered, that it informed him of the descent of God upon the earth, who was seen by men, conversed with them, and wrought miracles. If that was

[12]Unequipped linguistically, most travelers and traders among the Dhegiha Siouan tribes, of which the Osages were one, had to depend upon mixed-blood interpreters for even a rudimentary understanding of Indian religious concepts. What Nuttall here describes would be undertaken in larger measure by Thomas Say of the Long Expedition a year later, but still inconclusively. The systematic unfolding of Osage religious understanding would wait upon the investigations of J. O. Dorsey in "Osage Traditions," *Bureau of American Ethnology, Sixth Annual Report*, 373–97; "A Study of Siouan Cults," B.A.E., *Eleventh Annual Report*, 351–544; and the work of Francis La Flesche previously cited. What emerges is Wakanda, the Supreme Being, but with varying manifestations, as in the Osage concept of the sun as Wakanda of the day and the moon as the Wakanda of the night, among many.

true, they asked, why did he not come down now among men as he did then? To which Mr. B. replied, because the world was now so wicked. They looked at one another, held their hands to their mouths, as they always do in token of surprise, and, smiling, said, "the book may tell you so, but we don't believe it."

Independent of some resemblance in language, discoverable betwixt the aborigines of North America, and the Tartar tribes of the Russian empire, there is, likewise, something very similar in their habits and morals. They are equally erratic and unsettled in their abode, and have ever been so, according to Herodotus, for thousands of years. The Hamaxobii,[13] of that author, still live in their travelling houses, and occupy the same country without any sensible diminution or increase of numbers. Both people are separated into numerous bands or tribes, characterised by a diversity of language, acknowledging no other rule than that which is patriarchal, and no other alliance than fraternity. They are alike insensible to the wants and comforts of civilization. They know neither poverty nor riches; vice nor virtue. Their simple condition appears to have perpetually partaken of that of the first family of the human race, and they have been alike exempt from the luxuries of ephemeral grandeur, and the mournful vicissitudes of fortune. Happy equality, which knows neither the sins of ambition, nor the crimes of avarice!

The picture of the Samoyades,[14] drawn apparently by a careful hand, might almost pass for that of the North American Indians. Alike they acknowledge the existence of a supreme and invisible Being, the author of all things. The sun and moon they also adore as superior beings of the creation. They both in their invocations address the four quarters of the earth. Their priests or elders administer to them charms when sick or unfortunate in hunting. They submit with apathy (or resignation) to misfortunes, and express no violent passions. Their insensibility is such, as to prevent all surprise or curiosity at the sight of novelties. They fear, but do not adore bad spirits. Unacquainted with laws, and governed by customs, they acknowledge no ruler beyond the senior of the common family or tribe. To religious ceremonies they are strangers. Anticipating

[13]Hamaxobii = ʽΑμαεόβιοι = Scythians.
[14]Vide Pinkerton's collection of Voyages and Travels, vol. 1, in loco. —NUTTALL.

the contingencies of a future state of existence, they also inter with the warrior his bow and arrows. They allow polygamy, but avoid consanguinity in marriage. Their wives are purchased (to evince their esteem), and the marriage, consummated at an early age, is no longer binding than the continuance of mutual friendship and affection. Their names are taken from the animals of the forest, or the phenomena of nature. Their hair is coarse, lank, and black, and they have little or no beard, or marks of pubescence on other parts of the body, and, whenever it does appear, it is carefully eradicated. Such is the character, and such the manners of those Asiatics, inhabiting the very same parallel as that which includes the most proximate and occidental point of the North American continent, the same parallel, which in both continents afford the *Ovis Ammon,* or wild sheep, the reindeer, the white wolf, the chacal, the silver fox, the sable, and the ermine.[15]

---

[15]The Asiatic origin of the American Indian, hypothesized in Nuttall's time, has been archaeologically established in ours. Perhaps the strongest exponent of the Asiatic origin concept was Benjamin Smith Barton in his *New Views of the Origin of the Tribes and Nations of America* (Philadelphia, Printed for the Author by John Bioren, 1797, 2d ed. 1798), a work undoubtedly familiar to Nuttall.

CHAPTER XIV.

—————

Journey by land to the Great salt river of the Arkansa—Proceed across the prairies to the Little North Fork of the Canadian—Detailed by sickness—Continue up the Little North Fork, arrive at Salt river, and afterwards at the Arkansa—Molested and pursued by the Osages—Arrive again at the Verdigris, and proceed to the garrison—Conclusion of the treaty between the Osages and Cherokees.

August 11TH.] To-day I left the trading establishment of the Verdigris to proceed on a land journey up the Arkansa, accompanied by a trapper and hunter named Lee, who had penetrated across this country nearly to the sources of Red river, and followed his present occupation for upwards of eight years.[1] We crossed the river, and proceeding through the alluvion, entered the prairie, over which we continued in a westwardly course, encamping in the evening upon the banks of a small creek, about 12 miles from our place of departure. The prairies or grassy plains which we entered upon a mile from the river, exhibited the same appearance as below, and on the opposite side of the river. The rock of the hills, like those of the prairies near the garrison, consisted of a ferruginous sandstone. To the south of our encampment, we had in view a low ridge of hills very abruptly broken into fantastic contours. In these prairies, I found a second species of *Brachyris*, pungently aromatic to the taste, and glutinous to the

[1]Lee, otherwise unidentified, was one of the many trapper-hunters who had operated quietly westward from the Red River settlements and the Three Forks for a decade or more before Arkansas became a territory. The pace was now accelerating, with the granting of some two hundred licenses by the territory before the close of 1819. TERR. PAPERS, XIX, 128; John Maley Journal, Silliman Papers, *passim*.

Nuttall says nothing here or later of his intent to advance westward to the Rocky Mountains, perhaps because his effort would prove abortive. Eight months before, he had written his patron Zaccheus Collins from Arkansas Post that "my intention is to proceed up the Canadian river to the mountains either by land or by water . . ." (GRAUSTEIN, 139). He would return, he said, by way of the Red. His presently chosen route would avoid the circuitous course imposed by the Great Bend of the Arkansas, in present Kansas.

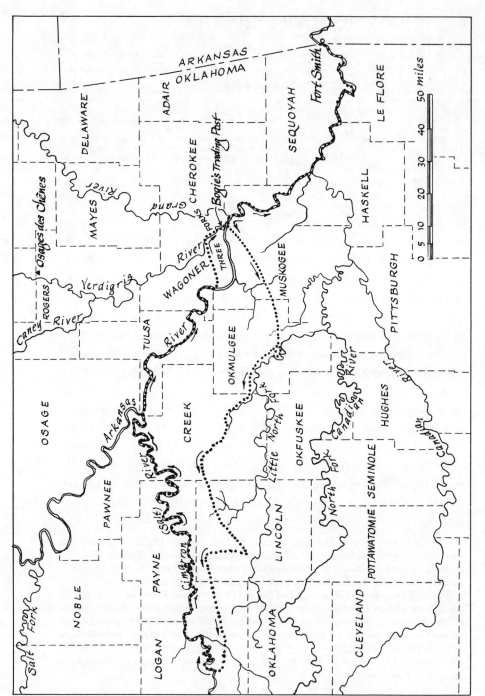

Nuttall's thrust towards the Rocky Mountains

touch; its aspect is that of *Chrysocoma*.[2] Our route was directed towards the Salt river, or the first Red river of the Arkansa, called by Pike the Grand Saline, and about 80 or 90 miles distant from our encampment.[3]

12TH.] We continued our journey about sunrise, proceeding over the plain in a south-west direction. About 10 miles from the brook of our last night's encampment we passed another, but destitute of running water, which is at this season of the year exceedingly scarce. The Arkansa, several miles to our right, appeared to make an extensive sinus to the north-west, as is designated in Pike's map, where it is continued up to the 100th degree of longitude, the dividing line from the possessions of Spain. We found the prairies full of grass about knee deep, although all the gullies and smaller streams were perfectly dried up; it was only when we arrived at a brook or rivulet that we could obtain a draught of water, and that always stagnant, and often putrid. The day being oppressively hot and thirsty, I very imprudently drank some very nauseous and tepid water, which immediately affected my stomach, and produced such a sickness, that it was with difficulty I kept upon my horse, until we arrived at the next creek for shelter, where we encamped and remained for the rest of the afternoon. Our horses were still tormented with the clegs or green-headed flies of the prairies, which goaded them without intermission.

About 10 o'clock this morning, we crossed the trace which the Osages had made, going out to hunt in a body of 2 or 300 men and their families. Its direction was south, or towards Red river. Two or three miles further we crossed their returning track. We were no way anxious to meet the Indians, as they would, probably, rob us of our horses, if not of our baggage, and ill-treat us besides, according to the dictates of their caprice and the object of their party.——To-day we came about 20 miles.

[2]The *Brachyris* (Nuttall's genus) became *B. dracunculoides* DC., but Nuttall later transferred it to his new genus as *Amphiachrys dracunculoides* (DC.) Nutt., which = *Gutierrezia dracunculoides* (DC.) Blake in FERNALD, broomweed.

[3]The travelers were trending W.S.W. past modern Muskogee to strike Grave Creek, a tributary of Deep Fork, S.E. of modern Okmulgee and would pursue Deep Fork, then Little Deep Fork, westward to strike the Cimarron (Nuttall's Salt river or "first Red river of the Arkansas") near modern Guthrie. Pike's Map 3 (PIKE, I, 324) gave a nearly straight north–south trend to the Cimarron which would have defeated Nuttall's objective, but it seems probable that Lee, less the cartographer than the *voyageur*, knew that the river would take them on an economical route into S.E. Colorado, and ultimately to a point near Raton, N.Mex.

13TH.] We were again on our way soon after sunrise, and still continued through plains destitute of timber. After proceeding about four miles, we passed another insignificant brook, and about six miles further a second of the same magnitude. We observed very little game. Yesterday, Mr. Lee pointed out to me the burrow of a badger, about the size of those made by the prairie wolf. Still proceeding, a little to the north of west, about 10 miles further, we came to a considerable rivulet of clear and still water, deep enough to swim our horses. We kept for about two miles through the entangled thickets, by which it was bordered, in search of a ford. Both above and below it was bordered by wooded hills, which appeared almost to shut up our course, and terminate the prairies. This stream was called the Little North Fork (or branch) of the Canadian, and emptied into the main North Fork of the same river, nearly 200 miles distant, including its meanders, which have been ascended by the trappers of beaver.[4] Having encamped, without crossing the rivulet, towards evening, I was about to bathe, but was sufficiently deterred by the discovery of a poisonous water snake, lurking a few yards from the spot I had chosen. No change yet appears in the vegetation; and the superincumbent rock continues arenaceous. No mountains or picturesque prospects present themselves to amuse the eye. Occasionally, indeed the monotonous plain is diversified by the view of low and broken ridges, often presenting isolated hills, deserted by the more friable materials with which they were once surrounded, and now presenting the fantastic appearance of artificial tumuli, and piles of ruins. In the course of the day we passed three or four of these hillocks, of considerable elevation. About six miles from our encampment, to the right, there are two of them nearly together, and two also which are separated from each other, nearly opposite to the others on the left. The Indians remark them in the regulation of their routes, and, on some of them, they have made elevated interments. This fondness for burying in high places has not subsided among the aborigines, and, probably, gave rise to the erection of artificial hills over the remains of the dead. Blackbird, the chief of the Mahas, was interred, at his particular request, on the summit of a hill which overlooked the village; and both the Mahas

---

[4]Little Deep Fork. The Deep Fork proper rises at small Belle Isle Lake in north Oklahoma City.

and the Arikarsees made choice of the summit of a neighbouring ridge for their general place of sepulture.[5]

The day was very warm, though occasionally relieved by a breeze from the south-west; and the dazzling light of the prairies proved oppressive and injurious to the eyes. We passed a place where the Indians appeared to have been killing numbers of deer, though not recently.

14TH.] We remained to-day on the banks of the Little North Fork, to recruit our horses, that of my companion being from the first totally unfit to travel from a large wound upon its back. I now experienced a relapse of the remittent fever, attended with delirium. Being about 3 o'clock in the afternoon when it came on, I was exposed to a temperature of between 90 and 100°. It was with difficulty that I could crawl into the shade, the thin forest being every where pervious to the sun, so that I felt ready to burn with heat; by forcibly inciting a vomit, I felt relieved. Mr. Lee, profiting by our delay, began to trap for beaver, and the last night caught four of these animals. Scarcely any thing is now employed for bait but the musk or castoreum of the animal itself. As they live in community, they are jealous and hostile to strangers of their own species, and following the scent of the bait, are deceived into the trap.

15TH.] At night I again experienced an attack of the fever, without any preceding chill, and attended with diarrhoea. It continued 36 hours, the paroxysm being only divided for a short space by an intermediate chill. The heat of the weather continued excessive; and the green blow-flies, attracted by the meat brought to our camp, exceeded every thing that can be conceived. They filled even our clothes with maggots, and penetrated into the wounds of our horses, so as to render them almost incurable.

16TH.] Still at the same encampment, and still afflicted with the fever.

17TH.] This morning, at the suggestion of my companion, for the purpose of trapping, we went about five miles lower down the rivulet. In

[5]Blackbird was principal chief of the Omahas from 1770 until his death, along with half his tribe, from smallpox introduced into his village by the great contagion of 1801. Blackbird Hills, overlooking the Missouri on the N.E., also overlook Blackbird's Omaha village of the time and later, on Omaha Creek, S.W. of the river in Dakota County, Nebr. FLETCHER AND LA FLESCHE (p. 82 and map at p. 89) consider the Lewis and Clark account of the horse burial apocryphal (*Original Journals*, I, 106). Descriptions come down to us also from BRACKENRIDGE, 229–30; IRVING [3], 161–65; and from CATLIN, II, Plate 117); but Thomas Say's account of March, 1820, in JAMES, E. [1], in THWAITES [1], XIV, 315–21), is the most nearly complete.

proceeding this short distance, I fainted with the effort, and was near falling off my horse. All the remainder of the day and the succeeding night, I experienced the fever under the exposure of a burning sun and sultry air. Shade was not to be obtained, and the night brought with it no alleviation but darkness.

In the evening Mr. Lee suggested the propriety of our returning to the Verdigris, before I became so weak as to render it impossible; but the idea of returning filled me with deep regret, and I felt strongly opposed to it whatever might be the consequences.

18TH.] To return, was again urged to me in plainer terms than before. I therefore complied, on the condition of trying the event of one or two days longer, and that then, if no better, I would return. I remarked to him, however, that these small distances from one trapping place to another, would, at this hot season, be far less difficult for me to accomplish, than to enter back again upon the prairies.

19TH.] We proceeded to another place of encampment, through ponds and dry gullies, crossing the prairies from point to point, for about 10 miles, instead of a supposed five or six, until it became dark, when, not finding the place where Mr. Lee had deposited his baggage, we stopped in a very eligible situation, compared with the rest of the wilderness through which we had been toiling. The preceding night we had experienced a slight rain, and had reason to suspect it again, but we lay down unprepared; and about midnight were caught in a thunder storm of great violence, and continued till daylight under pelting torrents of rain.

20TH.] Mr. Lee now said nothing more about returning, as his horse was become incapable of carrying either himself or his baggage. We had no method left of proceeding, at present, but by making double journeys, and employing my horse to convey the whole. The flies still continued to annoy us, filling our blankets, linen, and almost every thing about us with maggots. To compensate, however, in some measure, for these disgusting and familiar visitors, we had the advantage of the bee, and obtained abundance of excellent honey, on which, mixed up with water, I now almost entirely subsisted, as we had no other food but venison, and were without either bread or vegetables.

21ST.] We again proceeded five or six miles further over stoney hills, with great fatigue, and again encamped on a branch of the Little North

Fork. Lee was now in a great dilemma about our falling into the way of the Indians; he observed to-day their general encampment quite contiguous.

The fever had now rendered me too weak to bear any exercise; and it was become impossible to find any thing which would suit my feeble appetite. In the commencing coolness of the weather, I had, however, a reasonable hope of recovery.

23D.] We continued about three miles further up the banks of the rivulet, and again encamped amidst gloomy prospects.

24TH.] To-day, Mr. Lee having contrived to place a great part of his baggage upon his own horse, we proceeded about 10 miles, alternately along the borders of the rivulet and over the bases of the adjacent hills, which we had now the satisfaction to find more open and less rocky. We passed by three or four enormous ponds grown up with aquatics, among which were thousands of acres of the great pond lily (*Cyamus luteus*),[6] amidst which grew also the *Thalia dealbata,* now in flower, and, for the first tine, I saw the *Zizania miliacea* of Michaux. At length we gained sight of the prairies, which were doubly interesting after being so disagreeably immured amidst thickets and ponds. In our way we struck across the desiccated corner of the pond; here the *Ambrosias* or bitter weeds were higher than my head on horseback, and we were a considerable time in extricating ourselves from them. Clearing the thicket, we ascended a hill of the prairie, and continued across it to the first creek, where we encamped.

26TH.] While Mr. Lee was absent this morning examining the beaver traps, which he had set, to my surprise I observed, on the opposite side of the creek, an Indian busily examining our horses; after viewing them a few minutes, he chased them down the creek in a gallop towards our encampment, and after looking at me also with caution, instantly disappeared without paying me a visit. I need not say, how unwelcome this intelligence was to my cautious companion, who had not now to learn the rapacity of the savage hunters, having nearly lost his life, and all his

---

[6]*Cyamus luteus* = *Nelumbo lutea* (Willd.) Pers. The other species that follow are *Thalia dealbata* Roscoe, one of the erect aquatic herbs; *Zizania miliacea* Michx. = *Zizaniopsis miliacea* (Michx.) Doll. & Aschers., southern wild rice; and *Ambrosia trifida* L., giant ragweed.

property, last autumn, by falling in with the Cherokees near the banks of the Canadian. We delayed not a moment to leave our encampment, expecting nothing more certain than an unfriendly visit or clandestine theft. My own situation was indeed extremely critical, as I could not possibly walk, and even required assistance to get on and off my horse: thus to have had it stolen would have been to leave me to perish without hope. As we passed along, something which I imagined to be an Indian, dodged near us twice, from amidst the high grass, like some unfriendly animal of the forest, and slunk from our observance. This evening I felt extremely unhappy, and became quite delirious; when reclined, it was with difficulty that I could rise; a kind of lethargy, almost the prelude of death, now interposed, affording an ominous relief from anxiety and pain.

27TH.] Three days were now elapsed since I had been able to taste any kind of food, and to add to the miseries of sickness, delirium, and despondence, we experienced as many days of unremitting gloom, in which the sun was not visible even for an hour.

30TH.] Being a little recovered, we now ventured out some distance into the prairie hills; but, after travelling a few miles without much pain, my mind became so unaccountably affected with horror and distraction, that, for a time, it was impossible to proceed to any convenient place of encampment. This evening my companion killed two bison, the first we had seen on the route, but neither of them were fat, or any thing like tolerable food. I here spent a night of great misery and delirium, and felt exceedingly cold from the sudden decrease of the temperature.

31ST.] We moved onwards a few miles, but encamped at an early hour.

September 1ST.] We proceeded about 10 miles over wooded hills, with the expectation of soon arriving at the Salt river, which we imagined to lie before us, either to the west or south-west, but were entirely deceived, and my companion now appeared to be ignorant of the country. We saw nothing far and wide but an endless scrubby forest of dwarfish oaks, chiefly the post, black, and red species.[7]

[7]The travelers had been in the Cross Timbers for much of the time since leaving the Arkansas, but at their present location they were beginning to experience the densest growth in this *Quercus-Andropogon* (mixed oak and bluestem grass) zone, as it is identified by the U.S. Geological Survey (*National Atlas of the United States*, plates 90–91), extending N.E. from the Brazos in six states. Captain R. B. Marcy's exploring expedition

2D.] We now travelled about 15 miles nearly north, in the hope of arriving, at any rate, on the Arkansa, and passed through oak thickets, like those of Red river, for most part of the day. The land was poor and hilly, but abounded with clear and cool springs, issuing through rocks of a fine grained sandstone. We found the small chinquapin oak by acres, running along the ground as in New Jersey. The *Portulaca* resembling *P. villosa*, [8] which I had seen below in a solitary locality, Mr. Lee picked up for me to-day, growing in arid rocky places, where the soil had been nearly washed away. The general aspect of the vegetable kingdom still, however, continued nearly the same.

3D.] We continued on about 26 miles through the same kind of deeply undulated country, abounding with clear grit springs, but the land poor, and covered with scrubby oak, except occasional prairie openings and narrow valleys. At length we arrived on the banks of a small clear brook dammed up by the beaver, where we obtained a ford. Towards evening, greatly fatigued, and with our course directed more towards the west, we observed clouds of sand to arise at a distance, which we were satisfied must originate from the beach of some neighbouring river, and, in about an hour after, we came upon the rocky bank of the First Red Fork or Salt river, which, though very low, was still red and muddy, bordered with an extensive beach similar to the Arkansa, and not greatly differing from it apparently in point of magnitude. Along the argillaceous banks I observed saline incrustations, and, on tasting the water, I found it to be nauseous and impotably saline. Our horses, however, naturally fond of salt, drank of it with the utmost greediness. Though gratified by the sight of this curious stream, which we had so tediously sought, I now lamented the loss of the fine spring water lately afforded us by the barren hills. This extensive stream constitutes the hunting boundary of the Pawnees and Hietans. Its first view appeared beautifully contrasted with the broken and sterile country through which we had been travelling. The banks of cotton-wood (*Populus monilifera*),[9] bordered by the even beach, resembled a verdant garden in panorama view. A few days journey to the west,

thirty years later would describe it rather fully (FOREMAN [6], 202, 390 n.), as Josiah Gregg had done in 1844 (GREGG [1], 360–61; GREGG [2], I, 68).

[8] Noted in Chapter X, note 2.

[9] *Populus* monilifera Ait. = *P. deltoides* Marsh. var. *missouriensis* Rehd. The moving sand hills immediately following are in the vicinity of modern Dover, Okla.

Mr. Lee informs me, that there are extensive tracts of moving sand hills, accompanied by a degree of sterility little short of the African deserts.

4TH.] We continued a few miles up the banks of this saline stream, crossing it from point to point. But the following day (5th) we concluded on leaving it, studying our safety from the Osages, whose traces became now more and more evident. We pursued our course along the sand beaches of the river, now oppressively hot, and about noon turned out into a shade. Here, unfortunately, while Mr. Lee was busied about his beaver traps, his horse got into a mirey gully, and could not be extricated. In this dilemma, no resource for proceeding remained for my companion, but to construct a canoe, and so descend by water. From the general diminution and deterioration of the forest, it was not even an easy matter to find a tree of sufficient size for this purpose. The largest timber was the cotton-wood (*Populus angulata*).[10] After an unexpected and irksome privation, I was now again gratified by the taste of fresh water, which we found in a small stagnant rivulet contiguous to our encampment.[11]

On the 8th, my companion launched his canoe, which so exactly answered his purpose that it would have sunk with any additional loading. Although I had now so far recovered as to possess a little appetite, we were, for several days, destitute of any kind of food, except the tails of the beaver, the flesh of this animal being now too lean and musky to be eaten. The game appeared to be driven out of the country by the approach of the Indians. I still continued my route along the beaches of the river, which proved almost insupportably hot, and I severely felt the want of fresh water, though it now, from necessity, became possible for me to swallow this tepid brine, which always proved cathartic. As we proceeded, the river appeared continually bordered by sandstone hills, like the Arkansa. Amongst several other new plants, I found a very curious *Gaura*,[12] an

[10]*Populus* angulata = *P. deltoides* var. *missouriensis* Rehd. (var. angulata [Michx. f.] Sarg.).

[11]The farthest west the two travelers could have gone along the Cimarron was probably near the site of modern Guthrie in Logan County, Okla., for on the return they would strike the mouth of the river on the Arkansas in four days and a half, say 90 miles, following the meanders of the Cimarron. Any calculus is, however, hazardous, for they had moved, according to Nuttall, 56 miles from the time they had left Little Deep Fork on the way west until they arrived on the Cimarron, during which journey Lee was not at all sure of his route, as our map shows.

[12]This and succeeding species are (*Gaura*) an undescribed evening primrose, possibly

undescribed species of *Donia*, of *Eriogonum*, of *Achyranthes*, *Arundo*, and *Gentian*. On the sandy beaches grew several plants, such as the *Uralepsis aristulata (Festuca procumbens*, Muhlenberg), an *Uniola* scarcely distinct from *U. spicata* and *Sesuvium sessile*, which I had never heretofore met with, except on the sands of the sea coast.

9TH.] About noon we arrived at the entrance of the Arkansa, and were once more gratified with the taste of fresh water. Here the stream, now at its lowest depression, was almost colourless, and scarcely any where exceeding the depth of three feet. We travelled down it 9 or 10 miles, and saw the ascending smoke of the general encampments of the Osages, whom, if possible, we wished to avoid. By the multitude of traces upon the sand, it was easy to perceive that the whole village and its accompaniments were in motion.[13]

10TH.] We still saw the smoke of the Osage fires in all directions, and hourly expected a discovery. As I passed along contiguous to the river, now alone, one of the Indians saw me in the wood, but did not venture to come up, dodged out of sight, and then ran along with haste towards his encampment. This wolfish behaviour, it may be certain, was not calculated to give me any very favourable anticipation of our reception. I could not help indeed reflecting on the inhospitality of this pathless desert, which will one day perhaps give way to the blessings of civilization. The

---

G. parviflora Dougl. *forma lachnocarpa* Weath.; *Donia ciliata* Nutt., which the author later transferred to his new genus *Prionopsis* as *P. ciliata* Nutt. of the Compositae = *Haplopappus ciliatus* (Nutt.) DC. in FERNALD; the *Eriogonum* became *E. annuum* Nutt. of the Polygonaceae (buckwheat family); *Achyranthes lanuginosa* Nutt. = *Tidestromia lanuginosa* (Nutt.) Standl., which has not since been collected so far east in Oklahoma, George J. Goodman tells me; *Arundo* he subsequently named *Calamagrostis gigantea* Nutt. = *Calamovilfa gigantea* (Nutt.) Scribn.; the *Gentian* Nuttall identified as *Lisianthus glaucifolius* = *Eustoma grandiflorus* (Raf.) Shinners, prairie gentian (his prairie-rose gentian *Sabatia campestris* Nutt. remains entirely his); *Uralepsis aristulata* Nutt. = *Triplasis purpurea* (Walt.) Chapm., purple sand grass; (*Festuca procumbens* Muhl. *nomen nudum est* and is unrelated to *Uralepsis aristulata*, but upon it Nuttall based his new genus and species *Diachroa procumbens* Nutt., which = *Leptochloa fascicularis* (Lam.) Gray); he named his *Uniola U. multiflora* Nutt., still, however, convinced of its similarity to *Uniola spicata* L., which = *Distichlis spicata* (L.) Greene, while *Uniola multiflora* Nutt. became *Distichlis stricta* (Torr.) Rydb., salt grass; *Sesuvium sessile*, from a specimen Goodman thinks was Nuttall's when Rafinesque described it in 1838, became *Sesuvium verrucosum* Raf., the only species of this genus known in Oklahoma (Rafinesque, New Flora of N. Am., Pt. 4:16 1836 [1838]).

[13]Nuttall and Lee had begun the descent of the Arkansas at present Keystone Lake and continued to a point opposite present Sand Springs, where the Osages were encamped.

scenery was not without beauty; wooded hills of gentle slope every where bordered the river; and its islands and alluvions, still of considerable extent, are no way inferior to the lands of the Ohio.[14]

11TH.] To-day, with all our caution, it became impossible to avoid the discovery of the Indians, as two or three families were encamped along the borders of the river. They ran up to us with a confidence which was by no means reciprocal. One of the men was a blind chief, not unknown to Mr. Lee, who gave him some tobacco, with which he appeared to be satisfied. About the encampment there were a host of squaws, who were extremely impertinent. An old woman, resembling one of the imaginary witches Macbeth, told me, with an air of insolence, that I must give her my horse for her daughter to ride on; I could walk;—that the Osages were numerous, and could soon take it from me. At last, the blind chief invited us to his camp to eat, but had nothing to offer us but boiled maize, sweetened with the marmalade of pumpkins. When we were about to depart, they all ran to the boat, to the number of 10 or 12, showing symptoms of mischief, and could not be driven away. They held on to the canoe, and endeavoured to drag it aground. Mr. Lee tried in vain to get rid of them, although armed with a rifle. At length, they got to pilfering our baggage; even the blind chief, who had showed us a commendatory certificate which he had obtained at St. Louis, also turned thief on the occasion. We had not got out of the sight of these depredators, before another fellow came after us on the run, in order to claim my horse, insisting that it was his, and I could no way satisfy his unfounded demand, but by giving him one of my blankets.

Mr. Lee, as he descended, now observed two men on the shore, who hid themselves at his approach, and began to follow him as secretly as possible. They continued after us all the remainder of the day, till dark. We knew not whether they intended to kill or to rob us; and, endeavouring to elude their pursuit, we kept on in the night, amidst the horrors of a thunder storm, the most gloomy and disagreeable situation I ever experienced in my life. In consequence also of the quicksands and the darkness, it was with the utmost difficulty that I could urge my horse to take the

[14]They had moved east on the Arkansas to the site of present Tulsa, where the river turns almost abruptly south to present Jenks, the banks bordered by forested hills and headlands.

river, which it was necessary repeatedly to cross. In one of these attempts, both myself and it were on the point of being buried before we could extricate ourselves. Dressed in leather, I came out of the water drenched and shivering, almost ready to perish with cold. After some persuasion, I prevailed upon Lee to kindle me a handful of fire, by which I lay alone for two or three hours, amidst the dreary howling of wolves, Mr. Lee not wishing to trust himself near such a beacon. Nothing, however, further molested us, and, after cooking and eating a portion of a fat buck elk, which my companion had contrived to kill in the midst of our flight, we continued our journey by the light of the moon. After proceeding about 20 miles father down the Arkansa, unable to keep up with Lee and his boat, at noon we agreed to part. I took with me some small pieces of the boiled elk, with a portion also uncooked, and furnished myself, as I thought, with the means of obtaining fire, but, when evening arrived, I was greatly mortified to find all my attempts to obtain this necessary element abortive. My gun was also become useless, all the powder having got wet by last night's adventure.

14TH.] Fatigued with the sand-beaches, as hot and cheerless as the African deserts, I left the banks of the river; and, after travelling with extreme labour through horrible thickets for three miles, in which the *Ambrosias* were far higher than my head on horseback, I, at length, arrived amongst woody hills, and a few miles further came out, to my great satisfaction, into the open prairies, from whence, in an elevated situation, I immediately recognised the Verdigris river.[15] At night, though late, I arrived on its wide alluvial lands, lined with such an impenetrable thicket, that I did not attain the bank, and had to lie down alone, in the rank weeds, amidst musquetoes, without fire, food, or water, as the meat with which I had been provided was raw, and spoiled by the worms.

15TH.] With all the advantage of day-light, it was still difficult to penetrate through the thicket, and ford the river. Towards evening, I again arrived at the trading establishment of Mr. Bougie, an asylum, which probably, at this time, rescued me from death. My feet and legs were so swelled, in consequence of weakness and exposure to extreme heat

---

[15]Nuttall had apparently left the Arkansas at a point north of present Haskell in Muskogee County, to ride eastward to the trading posts at Three Forks.

and cold, that it was necessary to cut off my pantaloons, and at night both my hands and feet were affected by the most violent cramp.

I remained about a week with Mr. Bougie, in a very feeble state, again visited by fever, and a kind of horrific delirium, which perpetually dwelt upon the scene of past sufferings. I now took the opportunity of descending to the garrison with an engagée, but continued in a state of great debility, my hands and feet still violently and frequently affected with spasms.

In about five days slow descending, from the feebleness of my invalid companion, we arrived at the garrison.

The Indian councils now pending betwixt the Osages and Cherokees filled the fort with a disagreeable bustle. The Osages, according to the stipulation of the treaty signed at St. Louis, were assembled to receive their prisoners from the hands of the Cherokees. The captives, chiefly female, were, however, kept back, and they wished to retain them on the score of adoption.[16] Tálai and Clarmont insisted on their compliance with the treaty; and the government agents now ordered the Cherokees to produce the prisoners in 10 days. The 11TH day, however, arrived without any appearance of the Cherokees, excepting five of their hunters. The chiefs of the Osages were exceedingly mortified. Captain Prior told them to demand of the commander the liberty of seizing upon the five Cherokees in the fort as hostages. To this the chief, called the Mad Buffalo,[17] objected, saying, "if we take these Cherokee prisoners to our village, the warriors, and those who expected the return of their own people, would say, who are these strangers and enemies? we wanted our own captives, not Cherokees, and so they would instantly kill them."

In the evening the Osage chiefs left the fort, and proceeded towards

[16]After months of mutual reprisals following the Cherokee slaughter of Osages at Claremore Mound in November, 1817, the two tribes and the Cherokee allies agreed to peace at a council held in Saint Louis October 6, 1818 (AM. ST. PAPERS, INDIAN AFFAIRS, II, 172). Representatives of the two tribes were to meet at Fort Smith the next spring for an exchange of prisoners, principally Osage, in the hands of the Cherokees. It was not until midsummer, 1819, however, that the Cherokees agreed to meet the Osages at the fort the first week of August. When Clermont and other headmen arrived there, they found that the Cherokees had postponed the return of prisoners to September, at which time they hedged again but yielded on the insistence of Major Bradford. Restoration of Osage captives was only partial by the middle of the month. FOREMAN [1], 72–74.

[17]Son of Clermont II, the Maker-of-Towns.

Tooan Tuh, Spring Frog, of the Cherokees
McKenney and Hall

their village; but next morning the Cherokees began to assemble, and the Osages were sent for to receive their prisoners, now arrived. Tálai and Clarmont sent the lesser chiefs, and remained behind, but the Cherokees insisted on the presence of the whole, and after a second message they came as desired.

Tikitok, one of the principal Cherokees, a very old and venerable looking man, presided on the occasion, and every appearance of friendship and satisfaction, accompanied by the usual smoking, prevailed on either side.[18] The prisoners, after some little talk, were now produced, and given up according to the treaty. There was, however, a chief sitting next to Tikitok, who undertook to propose, that the prisoners should be permitted to use their own will, and go to either party as they should chuse, but this unfair and equivocating proposal was not made known to the Osages, some private conversation with the Cherokees putting a stop to it. It appeared that, in the interval of captivity, one of the young women had contracted marriage with a Cherokee of her own age. Their parting was a scene of sorrow; the Cherokee promised to go to the village, and ask her of her father, she also plead with the chiefs to stay, but Clarmont, unmoved by her tears and entreaties, answered, "your father and mother lament you; it is your duty to go and see them. If the Cherokee loves you, he will not forget to come for you." In this way terminated the treaty of peace between the Osages and Cherokees, in September, 1819.[19]

[18]Takatoka, the old Cherokee headman, was called by his people "the beloved man." In common with so-called peace chiefs of various tribes, he represented the voice of moderation. FOREMAN [1], 74n.

[19]Since this period, as might readily be foreseen, hostilities have again commenced between these restless and warlike tribes, who can perhaps never be prevailed upon to live in friendship, as they will be perpetually transgressing each other's hunting bounds. At a recent date (1821), 400 Osage warriors appeared before the garrison of Belle Point, on their way against the Cherokees, accompanied by a party of the Sauks and Fox Indians, and killed four Quapaws hunting in the neighbourhood. Such is the effect of the imprudent and visionary policy of crowding the natives together, in the hopes of keeping them at peace. —NUTTALL.

[Failure of the Cherokees to deliver all their Osage prisoners led to many reprisals and, equally, Cherokee countermeasures: In February 1820, a war party under Mad Buffalo killed three Cherokee hunters on the Poteau; thereafter, while the Osages were relating their exploits at Capt. Nathaniel Pryor's trading post a mile and a half above the mouth of the Verdigris, they were surrounded by a superior force of Cherokees but escaped through a ruse developed by Pryor; in retaliation, the Cherokees broke into Pryor's warehouse and made off with 150 pounds of beaver pelts. In April, 1820, Arkansas Territorial Governor James Miller could not persuade the Cherokees to surrender four Osage prisoners still in their hands, nor would the Osages deliver up the "murderers" of the Cherokee hunters. In the spring of 1821, Mad Buffalo and some 400 Osages made a sally against Fort Smith in search of ammunition preparatory to attacking the Cherokees farther east, but, failing, they killed four Quapaws on the Poteau nearby. NILES' REGISTER, June 30, 1821; FOREMAN [1], 74–96.]

CHAPTER XV.

Proceed from the garrison to the Pecannerie settlement—Hot-springs of the Washita—Phenomena of the seasons.

In consequence of sickness, and an extreme debility, which deprived me of the pleasure of my usual excursions, I remained at the garrison until the 16th of October. A nervous fever had now for ever separated me from the agreeable company of Dr. Russel, and amongst my associates in affliction were numbered two missionaries, who had intended to proceed to the Osages. One of them, (Mr. Viner), after the attacks of a lingering fever, paid the debt of nature![1]

From July to October, the ague and bilious fever spread throughout the territory in a very unusual manner. Connected apparently with these diseases, was one of an extraordinary character. It commenced by slight chills, and was succeeded by a fever, attended with unremitting vomitings, accompanied with blood, and bloody fœces. Ejecting all medicine, it became next to impossible to administer internal relief. The paroxysms, attended with excruciating pain, took place every other day, similar to the common intermittent. One of the soldiers who descended with us, was afflicted in this way for the space of six days, after which he recovered. On the intermitting days he appeared perfectly easy, and possessed a strong and craving appetite. I was credibly informed that not less than 100 of the Cherokees, settled contiguous to the banks of the Arkansa, died this season of the bilious fever.[2]

---

[1]The United Foreign Missionary Society of New York had sent Epaphras Chapman and Job P. Vinall in 1819 to select mission sites in Missouri Territory. On the ascent of the Arkansas River they stopped at Fort Smith and held council with the Osage Indians looking to a mission among the latter. But both missionaries contracted a disease, from which Vinall died in September. Chapman, helped by Nathaniel Pryor, chose the future site of Union Mission five miles N.E. of Mazie, Mayes County, Okla., finally occupied February 18, 1821. FOREMAN [7], 42; *Arkansas Gazette,* July 8, 1820; MORSE, 214ff.

[2]Two diseases, malaria and yellow fever, were raging at the time. Nuttall's account of

On the 3d of November, I at length got down in a perogue of the garrison as far as Major Wilborne's[3] in the Pecannerie settlement. Here, though the bilious fever and ague had been unusually prevalent, no instance of mortality had taken place.

In this settlement there was a succession of heavy rains down to the month of September. Above, we had experienced no rain beyond the month of June. Perhaps the unusual prevalence of rain, on the banks of the Arkansa, might have been conducive to the extraordinary sickness of this season. As a proof of the locality of this rain, the river was now so exceedingly low, that no boats drawing more than 10 or 12 inches of water could possibly navigate it from the Dardanelles to the Verdigris. All along the banks, the clay and pebbles of the beaches were whitened with an efflorescence of salt (muriate of soda), deposited from the water of the red freshes. We also remarked that all the sandstone rocks, scattered confusedly on the borders of the river, blacken by exposure, and assume a metallic tinge, probably arising from an admixture of manganese.

The Pecannerie, now the most considerable settlement in the territory, except Arkansas, derived its name from the Pecan nut-trees (*Carya olivoeformis*), with which its forests abound; in a few years it will probably form a county, containing at this time about 60 families, all, in regard to circumstances, living in a state of ignorance and mediocrity of fortune: many of them indeed were renegadoes from justice who had fled from honest society, to seek refuge in these fertile alluvial forests, where, indulging themselves in indolence, they become the pest of their more industrious and honest neighbours, and are encouraged in their dishonest practices by the laxity of the laws, and the imperfect manner in which they are administered. Thus the settlement was now oppressed by gangs of

---

symptoms above is for the latter. His stay at Fort Smith was at Major Bradford's invitation of the preceding spring, to remain there for the winter. GRAUSTEIN, 148, note 29.

[3]Curtis Wilborne, a major of territorial militia as well as a trader and trapper, had been a Pulaski County magistrate at the Pecannerie Settlement until mid-August, 1819. He would be killed at the mouth of l'Eau Bleu on Red River, November 17, 1823, by Osages led by Mad Buffalo, son of Clermont II, and Little Eagle. Antoine Barraque, Wilborne's partner, escaped, but of the party of seven hunters four were killed and two wounded. Mad Buffalo and Little Eagle were subsequently tried in federal court and convicted but were pardoned March 29, 1825, by President John Quincy Adams. TERR. PAPERS, XIX, 569–70, 691–93, 737–38, 808; XX, 17; FOREMAN [1], 163.

horse thieves, who carried their depredations even among the neighbour-ing savages.[4]

The soil throughout this settlement, after three or four years working, is found to be extremely favourable for the growth of cotton, as appeared by the crops of the present year, but the price was fallen to 3 dollars per cwt. in the seed, with little or no demand, so that the settlers, for want of a market, were really indigent, and most of them lived in a very poor and uncomfortable manner. The alluvial lands, here about two miles wide, are flanked by a range of wooded hills, and a somewhat broken country of considerable fertility.

A number of families were now about to settle, or rather take pro-visionary possession of the land purchased from the Osages, situated along the banks of the Arkansa, from Frog bayou to the falls of the Verdigris; a tract in which is embraced a great body of superior alluvial land. But, to their disappointment, an order recently arrived, instructing the agent of Indian affairs to put the Cherokees in possession of the Osage purchase, and to remove them from the south side of the river. It appeared, from what I could learn, that the Osages, purposely deceived by the interpreter, at the instigation of the Shoutous, had hatched up a treaty without the actual authority of the chiefs, so that in the present state of things a war betwixt the Cherokees and the Osages is almost inevitable, unless the latter relinquish the banks of the Arkansa, as Messrs. Shoutou [Chou-teau] wish them. The Osages in a recent council said, they would have no objection to dispose of their lands, provided the whites only were allowed to settle upon them.[5]

---

[4]The Pecannerie Settlement lay eleven miles upstream from the mouth of Cadron Creek in present s.e. Conway County, Ark.

[5]The acceptability of Lovely's unauthorized purchase of 1816 to the Osages, who were relinquishing this vast tract, was based not on the idea that the immigrant Cherokees in Arkansas Territory would thereby achieve a hunting domain on the Cherokee western flank but on the idea that whites settling there would form a buffer between the Cherokees and the Osages. That the Osages had misunderstood the extent of their cession is confirmed in Maj. Stephen H. Long's report of January 30, 1818, to Brig. Gen. Thomas A. Smith. They subsequently acceded to much of the cession made in Lovely's Purchase in the formal treaty cession with the United States of September 25, 1818, signed with Superintendent of Indian Affairs William Clark at Saint Louis (TERR. PAPERS, XV, 454–55, XX, 4–7). The United States kept the ceded area out of white settlement and relinquished none of it to the Cherokees until the Cherokee Treaty of 1828.

I understand that the hot springs of the Washita are situated about a mile from that river, contiguous to the bank of a brook. At the springs, a ridge of between five and six hundred feet, from whence smoke had been seen to issue, appears, by the massive rocks that fill this stream, to have been broken through, or undermined by its torrents. Many thermal springs, besides those employed by visitors, are seen boiling out of the side of the hill, and mingling with the cool water of the brook. The principal fountain, issuing from amidst huge masses of black rocks, apparently bituminous and calcareous slate in thick laminae, has a stream of near a foot in diameter at its orifice, and hot enough to boil eggs or fish; a steam arises from it as from water in a state of ebullition, attended with a considerable discharge of bubbles. It is only after mixing with the cool water of the brook, at some distance from this spring, that it becomes of a temperature in which it is possible to bathe. There is, however, a kind of rude inclosure made around the spring, as a steam bath, which often probably debilitates, and injures the health of ignorant and emaciated patients. Major Long, who visited these springs in the month of January, found their temperature to vary from 86° to 150° of Fahrenheit.[6] Hunter and Dunbar ascertained the temperature of five different springs, to be at 150°, 154°, 140°, 136°, and 132°.[7] The water, as near Onondago, in the state of New York, at the tepid baths of Natlock in Derbyshire, and in many parts of Italy, charged with an excess of carbonic acid, holding lime in solution, deposits a calcareous tufa, which incrusts leaves, moss, or any

[6]Long's observations at Hot Springs were for January 1, 1818. After locating the site for the future Fort Smith in December, 1817, we may recall, he went south to Red River and stopped on his northward return at the springs. Nuttall could have gained knowledge of Long's observations from the latter's report to the secretary of war of January 20, 1821, or orally from one or more members of the Long Expedition after their return east in 1821, while Nuttall was preparing his book (cf. GRAUSTEIN, 154–57). James incorporated the Long data in a footnote (THWAITES [1], XVII, 46–47), not published until 1823.

[7]William Dunbar (1749–1810), plantation owner near Natchez of Scottish birth, had early come to Thomas Jefferson's attention and on the latter's recommendation had become a member of the American Philosophical Society, to which he made frequent scientific contributions. Jefferson appointed him and George Hunter in 1804 to explore parts of the Red, Black, and Ouachita rivers. An abstract of his manuscript "Journal of a voyage..." appeared in Jefferson's message to Congress (*Doc. 113*, 9 Cong., 1 sess., February 19, 1806, AM. ST. PAPERS, Class II, INDIAN AFFAIRS, I, 731–43), but Nuttall may have seen the full manuscript journal, since it had been deposited at the American Philosophical Society in 1817 (A.P.S., *Documents Relating to the Purchase and Exploration of Louisiana*, Part II, 95–147).

other substance which it meets in its course, to the great surprise of the ignorant, who commonly pronounce them petrifactions. Indeed, the exploring party of the Washita assert, that a mass of calcareous rock, 100 feet perpendicular, had been produced by this aqueous deposition. Eruptions of argillaceous mud in small quantities have also been observed, which in time become considerably indurated.

Among the more remarkable features of the autumnal season in this country, is the aspect of the atmosphere, which in all directions appear so filled with smoke, as often to render an object obscure at the distance of 100 yards. The south-west winds at this season are often remarkably hazy, but here the effect is greatly augmented by the burning of the surrounding prairies, annually practised by the savages and whites, for the benefit of the hunt, as the ground is thus cleared of a heavy crop of withered grass, prepared for an early vegetation in the succeeding spring, and also assisted in its growth by the stimulating effects of the alkaline ashes. Indeed, ever since the beginning of September, the prairies had appeared yellow and withered, with a prevailing mass of dying vegetation. The autumnal Asters and Solidagos, are but a faint gleam of the midsummer splendour of these flowery meadows. Throughout this territory, there are no grasses nor other vegetables of consequence in agriculture (except the cane), which retain their verdure beyond the close of September. 'Tis true, that in the sheltered alluvions, verdure may be protracted, and it is here that the cattle, left to nature, now seek their food, and, as the winter advances, finally repair to the sempervirent cane brake. That delightful and refreshing verdure one naturally expects to see in a garden, regales not the eye of the Arkansa farmer beyond the vegetating period assigned by nature. From the month of September to February (except in the lowest and richest alluvions), every enclosure, in common with the prairies, appears a dreary waste of withered herbage, with the exception of the biennial turnip, the radish, and the cabbage, which still retain their freshness. The month of February, however, scarcely closes before vegetation again commences, and the natural meadows, thickets, and alluvions, in March, are already enamelled with the flowers of May.

The aridity of the autumnal atmosphere, which becomes more and more sensible as we advance towards the west, or recede from the ocean, may be perceived to modify many of the natural productions of the country, and deserves to be studied by those who reside on the spot. Amongst the *Cucurbitaceae*, every species of melon, which attain such enormous bulk and perfection east of the Mississippi, are here often of diminutive size, notwithstanding the heat of the climate; and by the increasing dryness of the air, the plants, full of young fruit, wither and prematurely die. The diminution of the forest, and at length its total disappearance, is also, in all probability, attributable to the same source of infertility.[8]

The natural phenomena of the seasons appear no less corroborative of a distinction of climate betwixt the eastern and western territories. From the Pecannerie settlement eastward, heavy rains were experienced for most part of the summer down to the beginning of September; while from the garrison upwards, scarcely any rain except the slightest flying showers had fallen since the month of June. It might, indeed, be reasonably conjectured, that the further any country was removed from the ocean, the great reservoir of rains, and the more it was elevated above that level, the more it would have to depend upon the winter or rainy season for irrigation; and that, in such a country, rain can hardly be expected in the summer, especially if the temperature be elevated. Facts bear out these conjectures, for the higher we ascend toward the great platform of the Andes, the more arid becomes the climate; and at length, approaching the mountains, nothing is to be seen but a barren and desert region, tantalized with numerous streams, which flow only in the winter, and then with such force and velocity, as to tear up frightful ravines, and, sweeping away thousands of acres of friable materials, which to a considerable depth constitute the more ancient incumbent soil, leave behind, upon the denuded plains, colossal masses insulated in the most fantastic forms, so as to appear like piles of artificial ruins. Such is the appearance of the saline plains of the Arkansa, and many extensive tracts towards the sources of the Missouri, from Fort Mandan westward to the basis of the Northern Andes.

[8]Nuttall sensed and partly described the ecological succession, from dense forest and high rainfall in the Ozark and Ouachita regions of eastern Oklahoma, to parklands and lower rainfall west of that zone, and finally to bunch grasses and cacti in the High Plains. But he was not far enough west to confirm the succession, whereas twenty-five years later Josiah Gregg, who had witnessed it all from Van Buren to the Cimarron, could do so. GREGG [1], 359–64. Modern records show 84.47 inches of rainfall (1957) in the Ouachitas and as little as 8 inches for the High Plains on the west. MORRIS AND MCREYNOLDS, Plate 4.

CHAPTER XVI.

Cadron settlement—Arrive at Arkansas—Continue to the Mississippi—The wandering fanatics—Pirates—Natchez—stratification of its site, and remarks on its agricultural productions—The Choctaws—Fort Adams— Point Coupé—Baton Rouge—Opulent Planters—New Orleans.

ON THE EVENING of the 18th of December, I again arrived at the Cadron,[1] where four families now resided. A considerable concourse of travellers and some emigrants begin to make their appearance at this imaginary town. The only tavern, very ill provided, was consequently crowded with all sorts of company. It contained only two tenantable rooms, built of logs, with hundreds of crevices still left open, notwithstanding the severity of the season.

Every reasonable and rational amusement appeared here to be swallowed up in dram-drinking, jockeying, and gambling; even our landlord, in defiance of the law, was often the ring-leader of what it was his duty to suppress. Although I have been through life perfectly steeled against games of hazard, neither wishing to rob nor be robbed, I felt somewhat mortified to be thus left alone, because of my unconquerable aversion to enter this vortex of swindling and idleness.

From the 18th to the 27th we had frosty nights; and on the 28th a fall of snow that continued throughout the day, and which still (*January* 3d) remained on all northern exposures; considerable sheets of ice, near three quarters of an inch in thickness, now began to invade the still water of the river, but were generally broken up by evening.

In one of the beds of grauwacke slate, which form the picturesque cliffs of the Cadron, I observed articulations of a species of orthoceratite, appar-

[1]Or Quadrant, a name applied to the neighboring creek by the French hunters, probably in commemoration of some observation made there by that instrument, to ascertain the latitude. —NUTTALL. [Cadron, as earlier noted (Chapter VII, note 52), was at a point slightly south of the mouth of Cadron Creek, west of modern Conway, in Faulkner County.]

ently belonging to the genus Raphanister of Montfort.[2] Above this bed, and forming the summit of the hills, occurs a massive laminated sandstone of a grey colour and inconsiderable dip.

On the 4th of January, 1820, after waiting about a month for an opportunity of descending, I now embraced the favourable advantage of proceeding in the boat of Mr. Barber, a merchant of New Orleans, to whose friendship and civility I am indebted for many favours.[3]

5TH.] This morning we again passed the outlet of the river called La Feve's Fork, coming in on our right. It sources with the Pottoe, the Kiamesha, Little river of Red river, and with the Petit John forms an irregular and acute triangle, affording a large body of good land, and, as well as the latter, is said to be navigable near 200 miles, including its meanders. Its entrance is marked by a concomitant chain of hills and cliffs, which border the Arkansa, and proceed in a north-westerly direction. For about a mile and a half, these hills, of grauwacke slate, present the appearance of an even wall coming up to the margin of the river, and owe this singular aspect to their almost vertical stratification. Their summits are tufted with pine, and the opposite alluvial point, which was sandy, and to appearance scarcely elevated above inundation, possessed also a forest of similar trees.

This evening we again arrived at Piat's, and in view of the pyramidal Mamelle; its extraordinary appearance, elevation, and isolation arises from the almost vertical disposition of its strata, which are probably of the same nature as those we passed to-day near the Petit John. Not far above inundation, on the same side of the river, three miles above Piat's, these vertical rocks form a very curious and crested parapet.

6TH.] This evening we arrived at Mr. Daniel's, an industrious farmer,

---

[2] A fossil cephalopod. The genus Raphanister had been noted by Nuttall in Pierre Denys de Montfort's *Histoire naturelle, générale et particulière des Mollusques* (Paris, 1802). But no species of *Orthoceras* occurs in North America; hence most of our species have been assigned to *Michelinoceras* Foerste 1932. SHIMER, 537; see also Adolf Naef, *Die Fossilen Tintenfische*.

[3] Henry Barbour, mentioned earlier in these notes, was in partnership with George W. Brand as a trader with bases at Arkansas Post and New Orleans as well as Three Forks. MORRIS, 43; FOREMAN [7], 75. In December, 1820, John James Audubon would ascend the Arkansas to Arkansas Post, where, on seeing his old Pittsburgh acquaintance Barbour, he would be told that on Barbour's last ascent to the Osage villages he "fell in with Nuttall the Botanist and had him on board for 4 Months" (CORNING, I, 70).

and provided with a rough-looking, but comfortable winter cabin. About two miles from hence, Mr. D., who lives upon a confirmed Spanish right, had erected a grist mill.[4] Saw-mills were also about to be built at the Cadron, and two or three other places. The establishment of a town was now contemplated also at the Little Rock, by colonel Hogan, and some others. They had not, however, sufficient capital, and no doubt expected to derive some adventitious wealth from those speculators who were viewing various parts of the newly-formed territory.[5]

7TH.] We again arrived at the lower end of the Eagle's-nest bend, from whence commenced the uninhabited tract of 60 or 70 miles.

8TH.] To-day we passed seven bends, making about 28 miles. The water at this, its lowest stage, appears to be perfectly navigable for the larger boats from the Little Rock to the Mississippi. By the cane which occurs in all the bends, and indeed by the apparent elevation, there are here great bodies of good land, free from inundation. The soil in some of the banks consists of an uncommonly rich dark Spanish brown loam.

9TH.] This forenoon we passed the fourth Pine Bluff, at the base of which we observed abundance of earthy iron ore, in flattened, contorted, and cellular masses, scattered about in profusion; much of it appeared to be pyrites, other masses more or less argillaceous and siliceous. Here, on the portions of the high bank which had sunk down by the undermining of the current, we saw the wax-myrtle of the Atlantic sea-coast.[6]

10TH.] This evening we arrived near to the termination of the second Pine Bluffs, which continue along the river for nearly two miles. We passed through seven bends of the river, and came about 27 miles. The frost was now succeeded by mild and showery weather, and the bald eagles (*Falco leucocephalus*) were already nestling, chusing the loftiest poplars for their eyries.[7]

[4]Wright Daniel, whom Nuttall had met on his ascent of the Arkansas the previous spring (Chapter VII, note 32), was one of hundreds of claimants to Arkansas lands under Spanish or French grants, after the Louisiana Purchase. Their claims were reviewed by commissioners appointed by the General Land Office, who denied most of them, and those judicially examined and approved under the Act of May 26, 1824, were subsequently thrown out by United States courts. AM. ST. PAPERS, PUBLIC LANDS, VI, 129–35, 329–30; TERR. PAPERS, XXI, 24–25.

[5]For Little Rock and Edmund Hogan's association with it, see Chapter VIII, notes 34, 35.

[6]Wax myrtle in this range is *Myrica cerifera* L.

[7]*Falco leucocephalus* L. = *Haliaeetus leucocephalus leucocephalus* (Linnaeus).

11TH.] Soon after breakfast we came again in sight of the houses of the French hunters Cusot and Bartolemé, and found also two families from Curran's settlement encamped here, and about to settle. I here obtained two fragments of fossil shells, apparently some species of oyster, one of which was traversed with illinitions of crystallized carbonate of lime, and contained specks of bovey coal, from which I concluded them to have been washed out of the Bluffs above. Besides these I was also shewn a small conch-shell, not apparently altered from its natural state, and probably disinterred from some tumulus. Some time after dark we arrived at Mr. Boun's, a metif or half Quapaw, and interpreter to the nation, who lived at the first of the Pine Bluffs. Two or three other metif families resided also in the neighbourhood.[8]

On the 12th we arrived at Monsieur Dardennes', and to-day experienced a keen north-western wind. Water froze the instant it touched the ground.

13TH.] The weather still freezing. In the evening we passed Mr. Harrington's, a farmer in very comfortable circumstances. Betwixt Morrison's and this place, the river makes two cuts, through two bends of about eight miles each.

14TH.] This evening we arrived at the residence of the late Mr. Mosely, and about 20 miles below Harrington's. His estates were said to be worth not less than 20,000 dollars, which had all been acquired during his residence in this territory. A proof that there is here also scope for industry, and the acquisition of wealth.[9]

About noon we landed at one of the Quapaw or Osark villages, but found only three houses constructed of bark, and those unoccupied. In the largest of them, apparently appropriated to amusement and superstition, we found two gigantic painted wooden masks of Indians,[10] and a consid-

[8]Mr. Boun is Michel Bonne, cf. Chapter VII, note 22.

[9]Samuel Moseley, an Indian trader on the Arkansas, had been active and had a trading license even before William L. Lovely's time as Cherokee agent, the latter reported to William Clark in August, 1814. Clark's promulgation of Missouri territorial laws on the Arkansas fell to Moseley two years later. He was sometime partner in the Indian trade (principally among the Osages) with Reuben Lewis, brother of Meriwether Lewis. TERR. PAPERS, XV, 54, 181–82.

[10]The Tuscaroras also wear masks at set times, for the purpose, as they pretend, of driving away evil spirits, and accompany these ceremonies by the sacrifice of two white dogs. —NUTTALL. [BOSSU [1], 63, noted masks and figures, similarly, between 1751

erable number of conic pelt caps, also painted. These, as we learnt from
an Indian who came up to us from some houses below, were employed at
festivals, and worn by the dancers, a custom which was also probably
practised by the Natchez, in whose temple Charlevoix observed these
marmosets. At the entrance of the cabin, and suspended from the wall,
there was a female figure, with a rudely carved head of wood painted with
vermillion. Being hollow, and made of leather, we supposed it to be
employed as a mask for one of the musicians, having in one hand a
pendant ferule, as if for the purpose of beating a drum. In the spring and
autumn the Quapaws have a custom of making a contribution dance, in
which they visit also the whites, who live in their vicinity, and the chief
alms which they crave is salt or articles of diet.

On the 15th we again arrived at the post of Osark, or as it is now not
very intelligibly called, Arkansas, a name by far too easily confounded
with that of the river, while the name Osark, still assumed by the lower
villagers of the Quapaws, and in memory of whom this place was first so
called, would have been perfectly intelligible and original.[11]

In the evening we had a storm of melting snow and hail, which, on the
following morning was succeeded by a northwest wind, accompanied by a
severe frost. The river was now, however, beginning to rise and assume a
muddy tinge from the influx of the lagoons, and lower rivulets. A more
extensive fresh cannot now be expected before the commencement of
milder weather, and the thawing of the river towards its sources. The
oldest settlers affirm, that the Arkansa had not, during their knowledge of
it, ever been so low as before the present rise. The Ohio and Mississippi
also continued too low for the navigation of the steam-boats.

16TH.] This morning we observed the newly appointed governor, general Miller, going up to the town from his boat, which appeared to be very

---

and 1762; cf. DORSEY [3], 393, 515; BUSHNELL, 111. The Quapaws were, and are,
little studied, possibly because their numbers were small after 1804; hence their religious
practices and fetishes can only be inferred from kindred tribes or tribal neighbors.]

[11]Here even Nuttall is to be counted among those who wished to "change the name of
Arkansas." *Aux Arcs*, from the French = Place of the Arkansas Indians, in M.
Pénicaut, *Relation* (MARGRY, V, 402); hence modern Ozark. La Salle's *Acansa* (1680)
and Joutel's *Acansas* (1687), with many subsequent variations among the French and
Anglo-Americans, began by 1700 (Pénicaut) to give way to *Arkansas* (notable in Zebulon Montgomery Pike a century later) and inevitably to *Arcs* and *Arks* as abbreviations for
the Indians we now know as Quapaws.

handsomely and conveniently fitted up, bearing for a name and motto "I'll try," commemorative of an act of courage for which the general had been distinguished by his country.[12]

On arriving in the town, we found the court engaged in deciding upon the fate of a criminal, who had committed a rape upon the unprotected, and almost infant person of a daughter of his late wife. The legal punishment, in this and the Missouri territory, for this crime, castration! is no less singular and barbarous, however just, than the heinous nature of the crime itself. The penitentiary law of confinement, so successfully tried in the states of Pennsylvania and New York, for every crime short of murder, is an improvement in jurisprudence, which deserves to be adopted in every part of the United States. It often reclaims the worst of the human race, learns them habits of industry with which they had been unacquainted, and corrects those vices which perhaps ignorance and parental indulgence had fostered. There is certainly a flagrant want of humanity in the multiplicity of sanguinary and stigmatizing punishments. To sacrifice all that portion of the community to infamy, who *happen* to fall beneath the lash of the law, is incompatible with the true principles of justice. Maim a man, or turn him out with the stigma of infamy into the bosom of society, and he will inevitably become a still greater scourge to the world, in which he now only lives to seek revenge by the commission of greater but better concealed crimes.[13]

Interest, curiosity, and speculation, had drawn the attention of men of education and wealth toward this country, since its separation into a terri-

---

[12]James Miller (1776–1851), of New Hampshire, was approaching his appearance before the Arkansas Territorial Assembly February 10, 1820, for which he was "late," his appointment having been made by President James Monroe on March 3, 1819 (the *Arkansas Gazette*, Vol. 1, No. 1 [November 20, 1819], noted his acceptance). Nuttall correctly called him general, from the brevet rank of brigadier general dating from July 25, 1814, when Miller responded at Lundy's Lane (near Niagara Falls) to his commanding officer's inquiry about silencing an English battery with, "I'll try, Sir." By a resolution of Congress November 3, 1814, he was accorded a gold medal for his services in the War of 1812. Miller's presence in Arkansas was sporadic to 1825, when he resigned the governorship. Most of his duties fell to Secretary and Acting Governor Robert Crittenden. HEITMAN, I, 710–11; TERR. PAPERS, XIX, 50, 118–19, 138–41.

[13]Pennsylvania derived its concepts of (solitary) penal confinement not from Cesare Beccaria (1764) or Jeremy Bentham's hedonistic calculus but from its own Quakers. The system was widely influential in Europe and largely employed there to 1876. New York in Nuttall's time did not confine prisoners in solitary quarters during the day.

tory; we now see an additional number of lawyers, doctors, and mechanics. The retinue and friends of the governor, together with the officers of justice, added also essential importance to the territory, as well as to the growing town. The herald of public information, and the bulwark of civil liberty, the press, had also been introduced to the Post within the present year, where a weekly newspaper was now issued.[14] Thus, in the interim of my arrival in this country it had commenced the most auspicious epoch of its political existence.

17TH and 18TH.] I again paid a visit to the prairie, which, as well as the immediate neighbourhood of the town, is in winter extremely wet, in consequence of the dead level, and argillaceous nature of the soil. The interesting plants and flowers which I had seen last year, at this time, were now so completely locked up in the bosom of winter, as to be no longer discernible, and nearly disappointed me in the hopes of collecting their roots, and transplanting them for the gratification of the curious.

On the 19th, I bid farewell to Arkansas, and proceeded towards the Mississippi, in the barge of Mons. Notrebé, a merchant of this place,[15] and the day following, without any material occurrence, arrived at the confluence of the Arkansa, a distance of about 60 miles. The bayou, through which I came in the spring, now ran with as much velocity towards White river, as it had done before into the Arkansa, its current and course depending entirely upon the relative elevation of the waters of the two rivers with which it communicates. The large island, thus produced, possesses extensive tracts of cane land, sufficiently elevated, as I am told, above inundation, as does also the opposite bank of the Arkansa. About 12 miles above the mouth, the site first chosen for the Spanish garrison, and which was evacuated in consequence of inundation, was pointed out to me. A house now also stands on the otherwise deserted spot, where once were garrisoned the troops of France, at the terminating point of the river.[16] We now found ourselves again upon the bosom of one of

[14]The *Arkansas Gazette,* published at Arkansas Post, 1819–21, and at Little Rock thereafter, thrives into our own day.

[15]Frederick Notrebe, earlier noted, carried on trading activities between Arkansas Post and New Orleans regularly, and apparently in substantial volume. He was busy buying cotton for William Drope's and his own account on the Arkansas between December 4, 1819, and January 15, 1820, for shipment to New Orleans. JOHNSON, 274.

[16]Many subsequent historians have stumbled (as I nearly did) on this informed, spe-

the most magnificent of rivers, which appeared in an unbroken and meandering sheet, stretching over an extended view of more than 12 miles, and decorated with a pervading forest, only terminated by the distant horizon.

21ST.] I now embarked for New Orleans in a flat boat, as the steam boats, for want of water, were not yet in operation.[17]

Not far from this place, a few days ago were encamped, the miserable remnant of what are called the Pilgrims, a band of fanatics, originally about 60 in number. They commenced their pilgrimage from the borders of Canada, and wandered about with their wives and children through the vast wilderness of the western states, like vagabonds, without ever fixing upon any residence. They looked up to accident and charity alone for support; imposed upon themselves rigid fasts, never washed their skin, or cut or combed their hair, and like the Dunkards wore their beards. Settling no where, they were consequently deprived of every comfort which arises from the efforts of industry. Desertion, famine, and sickness, soon reduced their numbers, and they were every where treated with harshness and neglect, as the gypsies of civilized society. Passing through Ohio, Indiana, and Illinois, they at length found their way down the Mississippi to the outlet of White river and the Arkansa. Thus ever flying from society by whom they were despised, and by whom they had been punished as vagabonds, blinded by fanatic zeal, they lingered out their miserable lives in famine and wretchedness, and have now nearly all perished or disappeared. Two days after my arrival in the territory, one of them was found dead in the road which leads from the Mississippi to Arkansas. If I am correctly informed, there now exists of them only one man, three women, and two children. Two other children were taken

cific statement in Nuttall's writing, which makes clear that the first (French) fort of 1686 called Arkansas Post was near the mouth of the Arkansas; the second, made necessary by flooding of the first, was three leagues (nine miles) upstream from it, according to Philip Pittman (1770); and the third, replacing the second also because of flooding, was on the left (north) bank beginning sometime between 1776 and 1781, and from it Nuttall had just departed. Cf. MATTISON, 131–32; PITTMAN, 82; Former Spanish Commandant to William Clark, June 5, 1816, TERR. PAPERS, XV, 178–79.

[17]Henry Miller Shreve's *Washington*, the second steamboat plying the Mississippi after Robert Fulton's and Robert R. Livingston's *New Orleans* (1811), dated from 1816. Not every steam vessel on the river had its shallow draft, ideal for the treacherous stream, as Mark Twain would discern fifty years later. Winter ice upstream from the mouth of the Arkansas halted shipping often.

from them in compassion for their miserable situation, and the man was but the other day seized by a boat's crew descending the river, and forcibly shaved, washed, and dressed.

Down to the year 1811, there existed on the banks of the Mississippi, a very formidable gang of swindling robbers, usually stationed in two parties at the mouth of the Arkansa, and at Stack island. They were about 80 in number, and under the direction of two captains. Amongst other predatory means of obtaining property, was that of purchasing produce from boats descending the river, with counterfeit money. Clary and his gang of the Arkansa, had, some time in the autumn of 1811, purchased in this way some property from a descending flat boat. The owner, however, before leaving the shore, discovered the fraud, and demanded restitution, but was denied with insolence; and they proceeded, at length, so far as to fire upon his boat. These circumstances being related to the companies of several other flats who very opportunely came up at this time, and 12 of them being now collected, they made up a party to apprehend this nest of pirates. It was nearly night when they landed, and were instantly fired upon by the robbers. They at last arrived at the house which they occupied, broke it open, and secured Clary and two others who had attempted to hide themselves. A court martial was held over them, which sentenced Clary to receive a number of lashes from the crew of each boat, and the two other delinquents were condemned to confinement, and to work the boat in the place of two of the boatmen who were wounded. These men, on arriving at Natchez, were committed to prison, but no one appearing against them, they were of course acquitted. Clary confessed, that he and his crew had, within the week previous to his apprehension, bought and transmitted up the Arkansa, with counterfeit money, 1800 dollars worth of produce. It was also known that he had been a murderer, and had fled to the banks of the Mississippi from justice. The Stack island banditti have never been routed, and some of their character were still found skulking around Point Chicot and the neighbouring island, always well supplied with counterfeit money. [18]

[18]A century earlier, in 1719–20, the last year of John Law's Mississippi Bubble, the French government was preparing to move several hundred convicts to the lower Mississippi (FOREMAN [1], 142). Athanase de Mézières half a century later described deserters from French and Spanish armies and fleeing criminals working in bands at the mouth of

22D.] This morning we were visited by three Choctaws in quest of whiskey. Their complexions were much fairer than most of the Indians we meet with on the Mississippi. Two of them were boys of about 18 or 19, and possessed the handsomest features I have ever seen among the natives, though rather too effeminate. About 20 miles below the Arkansa, in the Cypress bend, we saw the first appearance of *Tillandsia* or Long Moss.[19]

On the 24th, we arrived at Point Chicot, which is included in the Arkansa territory; the boundary being the Big Lake, about 20 miles below.[20] From one of the settlers, living a few miles below Point Chicot, I learn, that on the eastern side of the Mississippi, the high lands are here from 15 to 20 miles distant. The reaches and bends, in this part of the river, are hardly less than six miles in length. Toward the centre of the bends considerable bodies of cane appear, indicative of an elevation above the usual inundations; it is, however, probable that these tracts are narrow, and flanked at no great distance by lagoons and cypress marshes subject to the floods. Many bends indeed presented nothing but Cypress and black ash.

From the Chicasaw Bluffs downward, along the banks of the Mississippi, we perceive no more of the Tulip tree (*Liriodendron tulipifera*), and but little of the *Platanus*, greatly reduced in magnitude, compared with what it attains along the Ohio. The largest tree of the forest here is that which is of the quickest growth, the Cottonwood poplar (*Populus angulata*).[21]

27TH.] The whole country, generally speaking, along the river, appears uninhabited, though vast tracts of cane land occur in the bends. I am, however, informed that the cane will withstand a partial inundation. Since we left Point Chicot the river presents us with several magnificent views, some of 8, some of 12, and even 15 miles extent; but the absence

---

the Arkansas (BOLTON, I, 166). Increased traffic on the Mississippi after the Louisiana Purchase and settlement thrusts had not reduced the problem in Nuttall's day.

[19] *Tillandsia usneoides* L., Spanish moss.

[20] Point Chicot lies opposite Greenville, Miss., 45 miles by water from the Arkansas boundary.

[21] *Liriodendron Tulipfera* L. (old generic name) is not out of range here, even though Nuttall may not have seen it. *Platanus occidentalis* L., the eastern sycamore, varies with terrain. *Populus angulata* Ait. = *P. deltoides* Marsh., but the cottonwood species he saw may well have been *P. heterophylla* L., which, like the former, grows to great size.

of variety, even amidst objects of the utmost grandeur, soon becomes tiresome by familiarity. As above the Arkansa, the river still continues meandering. The curves, at all seasons washed by a rapid current, present crumbling banks of friable soil more or less mixed with vegetable matter. By the continued undermining and removal of the earth, the bends are at length worn through, the former tongue of land then becomes transformed into an island, and the stagnation and partial filling of the old channel, now deserted, in time produces a lake. Some idea of the singular caprice of the Mississippi current may be formed, by taking for a moment into view the extraordinary extent of its alluvial valley, which below the Ohio is from 30 to 40 miles in width, through all which space it has from time to time meandered, and over which it will never cease to hold occasional possession. On the opposite side of all the bends there are what are called bars, being platforms of sand formed by the deposition of the siliceous matter washed out of the opposite banks by the force of the current. These sand flats, sometimes near a mile in width, are uniformly flanked by thick groves of willows and poplars, the only kind of trees which survive the effects of the inundation to which these bars are perpetually subject.

28TH.] This morning we passed the settlement called the Walnut Hills, a situation somewhat similar to that of Natchez, consisting, however, of a cluster of hills of 150 or 200 feet elevation, laid out in a chain of agreeable farms.[22] The banks, along the river, though not near so elevated as those of the Chicasaw Bluffs, are still far enough above the reach of inundation, and present a stratification and materials entirely similar: the same friable ferruginous clays, and also one or two beds of lignite, the lower about a foot in thickness, very distinct at this low stage of the water, and about three feet from its margin. The declivity for near half a mile back presents innumerable slips parallel with the river, and in one of the ravines large masses of sandstone were washed out towards the river.

In the evening we arrived at a small town called Warrington, containing two inns and as many stores.[23] The land appeared low, but was se-

[22]Walnut Hills became the site of Vicksburg, Miss., laid out in 1811. Here Spain had created Fort Nogales, replaced by the U.S. Fort McHenry in 1798, honoring Secretary of War James McHenry, abandoned 1803.

[23]Rather Warrenton, county seat of Warren County, Miss., later giving way to Vicksburg.

cured from inundation by a levee or embankment carried out for two or three miles below the town. Out of its small quota of population, 37 individuals last summer died of the yellow-fever, said to have been introduced by the steam-boat Alabama. The gloomy mantling of the forest communicated by the *Tillandsia usneoides* or long moss, which every where prevails, is a never-failing proof of the presence of an unhealthy humidity in the atmosphere. The stagnating lagoons and bodies of refluent water also largely contribute to the unhealthiness of the climate. The vast extent and depth of this inundation is sufficiently evident by the marks along the banks of the river, which in places exhibited a rise of 50 feet above the present level!

29TH.] To-day we passed the grand Gulf or eddy, near to which enters Big Black river.[24] Here again the friable hills of the high land make their appearance on the borders of the river, on and around which there are settlements. At the base of the hills loose heaps of sandstone lie scattered. A thin stratified bed of the same was now also visible. In high water a violent and dangerous eddy sweeps along these rocks. On the declivity of this hill we see the first trees of the *Magnolia grandiflora*. The small palmetto (*Sabal minor*) commences about Warrington.[25] The distance to high land on the opposite or western side of the river is said to be little less than 30 miles.

30TH.] This morning we came to what is called the Petit Gulf, where another cluster of hills appears scattered with settlements. Here the banks present nothing but friable materials, still also similar to the Chicasaw Bluffs. Beds of very white sand, intimately mixed with argillaceous earth, appear in prominent cliffs. One of the houses which we visited is apparently built upon an aboriginal mound, and there are two others about a mile distant, in which have been found bones and potsherds. Last evening we passed bayou Pierre, 30 miles up which stream, and 15 by land, is situated the thriving town of Gibsonport.[26]

31ST.] To-day we arrived at the well known and opulent town of

[24]Grand Gulf lies below the mouth of Big Black River, which constitutes the border between Warren and Claiborne counties, Miss. Petit Gulf lies w.s.w. of modern Rodney.

[25]*Sabal minor* (Jacq.) Pers., dwarf palmetto.

[26]Now Port Gibson, 2,800 pop., in Claiborne County, Miss.

Natchez, situated on the summit of a hill which forms part of the same range and primitive soil as the Petit Gulf. The port was crowded with flat-boats, produce bearing a reduced price in consequence of the low rate of, and small demand for, cotton.[27]

The cliffs of Natchez appear more elevated than those of the Petit Gulf. The lands, of an inferior soil, are also remarkably broken and deeply undulated. The crumbling precipice, of about 150 feet elevation, is continually breaking, by the action of springs and rain-water, into gullies and frightful ravines; the whole visible matter which composes the hills consisting of clays, ferruginous sand, and quartzy gravel. A few years ago, the undermining of current swept down a considerable part of the bank with several houses upon it. From the irregularity in the thickness of this ancient maritime alluvion, arises the great difference of depth at which water is here obtained. In the same vicinity water has been found at 35, and then again at 110 feet from the surface.

The day after my arrival I waited upon Saml. Postlethwaite, Esq., related by marriage to the late Mr. Dunbar. From Mr. P. and his amiable lady, I met with every attention and kindness which friendship, hospitality, and politeness could have possibly dictated.[28]

To my enquiries concerning the horticulture and agriculture of Natchez, Mr. P. informed me, that the peach and fig, as well as the pear and quince, succeed extremely well. The apple trees also, introduced

[27]Natchez, originally part of French Louisiana, was first settled 1720 by three hundred colonists under the auspices of John Law's Mississippi Company, under a monopoly for Lower Louisiana granted by the French crown. It was the site, at the foot of modern South Broadway, of the French Fort Rosalie, annihilated by the Natchez Indians in 1729; and it gave its name to the Natchez Trace, begun by the U.S. Army commanded by Gen. James Wilkinson in 1801, completed 1803, running N.E. over an old Indian trail to the site of Nashville, Tenn., a distance of 550 miles. It had been incorporated as a city in 1803, although it had been the territorial capital until 1802, when it lost the honor to Washington, 6 miles east. Its best early description is that of 1766 by Capt. Harry Gordon of the British army. GORDON, 479–80.

[28]Samuel Postlethwait, as he signed himself in most surviving documents, had married Ann, the daughter of William and Dinah Clark Dunbar. William Dunbar (1749–1810), of a titled Scottish family, scientist, member of the American Philosophical Society of Philadelphia on Thomas Jefferson's nomination, had settled at The Forest, a plantation nine miles S.E. of Natchez in 1792. On Jefferson's appointment he and George Hunter had ascended the Ouachita to Hot Springs in 1804 and under Jefferson's plans would have ascended the Red sometime in the period 1805–1806 but for the opposition of Spanish colonial officials, who indeed turned back Thomas Freeman. ROWLAND, 385–86.

from Kentucky, afforded nearly equal success. The cherry, the gooseberry, and the currant, though thriving, scarcely produce at all. The pomegranate, and the myrtle, grow and fruit almost as in their native climate. The orange and lemon require some shelter from the prevailing winter. Grapes attain to tolerable perfection, but the clusters are often blighted, apparently by the humidity of the atmosphere. The kernels of dates which have been planted, germinate and grow with considerable vigour. The olive, which so many years ago was introduced by the first French settlers, and said, by Du Pratz, to have succeeded, is now entirely lost.

Cotton, which constitutes the staple commodity and wealth of this country, has, like all other crops, a considerable tendency to impoverish the soil; before the settlement became so much condensed, and land so advanced in value, no method of improving the worn out lands was ever thought of. Such fields were then left waste, and new lands still continually cleared. Of late years some attention has been paid towards renovating the soil, by plowing in the herb of the cotton, after being thrashed to pieces as it stands in the field. A much more convenient and expeditious method, however, is that which Mr. P. has practised, who employs a loaded harrow or a roller armed with knives, which divides the plant also into much smaller pieces. The seed, which forms three-fourths of the crop in weight, being very oleaginous, would likewise return to the soil a considerable share of nourishment, as appears by the experiment of applying it to maize, which, thus treated, grows as luxuriant as when manured with gypsum. The seed of the cotton also, when scalded, and mixed with a little salt, forms a nourishing and agreeable food for cattle.[29]

Of late years, a prevailing disease has injured the crops of this plant. From what I learn, it appears to be of the same nature as that which destroys the grapes, and depends apparently upon the state of the atmosphere, progressing with more or less rapidity in proportion to its humidty. The disease in question attacks the extremity of the peduncle, appearing, at first, like a moist or oily spot, which is succeeded by a

---

[29]The properties of cottonseed were subjects of Dunbar's investigations, from which Postlethwait undoubtedly had obtained the information he was in 1820 discussing with Nuttall. Stubble mulch would wait a century and a half for Edward H. Faulkner's *Plowman's Folly* (1944), least applicable, however, to cotton culture.

sphacelous state of the integuments, and an abortion of the capsule.[30]

Although we perceive but little attention paid to science or literature in this territory, it does not by any means appear to be destitute of public patronage, as there is a very handsome endowment in lands appropriated by the state for the building and support of a college. Some difficulty, now nearly obviated, as I understood, had been the means of retarding the progress of the institution.[31] The inhabitants of Natchez, generally speaking, as in most of the southern states, live in ease and affluence.

To my enquiries concerning the aboriginal Natchez, Mr. P. said, he was inclined to believe them now extinct, as some years ago he had heard that only two or three individuals of them then remained. Their first flight, after the cruel defeat and massacre which took place in their fort, was across the river, to what is now called Sicily island, a body of land at this time settled, of about five miles in width, partly insulated by the overflows of the Tensaw, and rising into a hill considerably above the reach of inundation. The unfortunate Natchez were not, however, suffered to remain in peace, and being again routed by the French and their Indian allies, were, on the verge of extermination, driven to seek refuge among the neighbouring Indians. From my friend, Mr. Ware, of the Mississippi Territory, I learn, that there still exists a small village of the Natchez on the banks of the Tallipoosee, in Alabama, governed by a chief, named Coweta, who joined the United States against Lower Creeks in the late war.[32]

[30]Fusarium rot, affecting cotton bolls in the high rainfall area of Mississippi, was probably the disease here noted, rather than the boll weevil (*Anthonomus grandis*), which did not enter the United States until 1892.

[31]The reference is to Jefferson College at Washington, second territorial capital of Mississippi (from 1802) and first state capital (from 1817 but succeeded by Columbia and Jackson, 1822). Congress on March 3, 1803 (2 STAT. 229–35) granted thirty-six sections of Mississippi territorial land plus two Natchez lots and one outlot of thirty acres to the college. Title to the Natchez properties was cloudy, the thirty-six sections were not located by the U.S. Land Office before Mississippi attained statehood in 1817, and lands ultimately granted by Congress to the state (February 20, 1819) were sold at auction but unrealized because of nonpayment and bank failure.

[32]The Natchez were not entirely destroyed by the French, following the massacre at Fort Rosalie in 1729, as Nuttall indicates. The band which fled under pressure to Sicily Island, in present Catahoula Parish, w. of Tensas River, was decimated by the French and Choctaws in 1731, and the surviving captives were sent to Santo Domingo. A few members of the original tribe remained near their old tribal grounds east of Natchez. The third band retreated to Alabama, in the area bounded by Coosa and Tallapoosa rivers. CUSHMAN, 437–65; HODGE, II, 35–36.

Mr. P. informs me, that in digging, some time ago, into a neighbouring mound, to the depth of a few feet, fragments of a sword blade, and some other relics of European warfare, were found, together with beads and remains which appeared to have accompanied an aboriginal interment. From these circumstances, it would appear, that some courageous opponent of the French had made a desperate stand upon this sacred ground, in order to annoy his enemies, and to sell his life as dear as possible upon the tomb of his ancestors. I am the more inclined to hazard this opinion, not only from the circumstances related (of the broken fragments of European weapons, and the decorations of a warrior), but likewise from the assertion of the aged Illinois chief, made at Kaskaskia, who, on being interrogated as to the use and origin of the lofty mounds in that neighbourhood, answered, that his forefathers had employed them as situations of defence against their enemies the Iroquois.

Mr. Ware informs me, that aboriginal remains abound in the vicinity of Natchez. Twelve miles above the town there is a square fort of three or four acres area, furnished with several gateways, and erected on a commanding situation. About 12 miles below the town there is likewise a group of mounds.[33]

Considerable numbers of Choctaws appeared at this season straggling through the streets of Natchez, either begging or carrying on some paltry traffic, but chiefly for the sake of liquor. I am informed that civilization is making some advances among those who live in the nation, and who have consequently abandoned their ancient wandering habits. Those of them we see here are meanly dressed and of a swarthy complexion. Their ancient mode of exposing the dead upon scaffolds, and afterwards separating the flesh from the bones, is falling into disuse, though still practised, as Mr. Ware informs me, by the six towns of the Choctaws on the Pascagoula. They still entertain the same tradition of their origin which was current in the time of Du Pratz, though he believes them to have emigrated into the country which they now possess. The legend is, that they sprung out of a hill, situated contiguous to Pearl river, which, Mr. Ware

[33]Selsertown Mound N.E. of Natchez, measuring approximately 600 by 400 feet, is of the platform type, possibly dating from the Temple Mound I Period (A.D. 700–1700), and represents either the Coles Creek or the Woodland-Marksville cultures. Foster Mound, near Washington, and a number of mounds south of Natchez are among the scores of mound sites in Mississippi. WILLEY, I, 290–305.

tells me, they still visit and venerate.[34] The Creeks entertain a tradition of coming from the west side of the Mississippi, and that too at so recent a date, as to have heard of the landing of White people on the Atlantic coast soon after their arrival. The Seminoles, Utchis, and Yamasees are a portion of those more ancient people whom they found in possession of the country, and with whom they carried on an exterminating warfare. Indeed, many of the people of that country discovered by Soto, and some of them numerous and powerful, are now no longer in existence. Those whom he calls the Cutifa-chiqui, then goverened by a female, held a court equally as dignified as that of Powhatan in Virginia.[35]

The Choctaws possess in an eminent degree that thirst for revenge, which forms so prominent a trait in the disposition of the man of America. By far too indiscriminate in its object, murder and accidental death are alike fatal to the perpetrator, and scarcely any lapse of time, or concession short of that of life, is taken. It is but a few years ago, that two Choctaws in the town of Natchez, firing at each other, in the same instant, fell both dead on the spot: one of them, in defence of a life which he had forfeited; the other, in quest of revenge for the death of a relative.

By a recent treaty, effected through the influence of general Jackson, the Choctaws are now about to relinquish the east side of the Mississippi, and to exchange their lands for others in the territory of Arkansa, situated betwixt Arkansa and Red rivers, and extending from the Quapaw reservation to the Pottoe. In consequence of this singular but impolitic measure

[34]For the bone-picking ceremony see DEBO, 5. The ancient Choctaw mound Nanih Waiya, at the junction of Nanawaya Creek and the Bogue Chitto with Pearl River on the line between Neshoba and Winston counties, Miss., was the Choctaw pantheon.

[35]The Creeks, like the Choctaws, were of Muskhogean linguistic stock, and as a confederacy they formed the largest division of that family, occupying the larger part of Alabama and Georgia, centering on Coosa and Tallapoosa rivers and on Flint and Chattahoochie rivers. The confederacy in Nuttall's time counted fifty towns, embracing people of three related languages besides their own, Muskogees, Hitchitis, and Koasatis. The Yuchis, Natchez, and Shawnees were unrelated to them linguistically. The Yamasees, formerly of southern Georgia and Florida, later of South Carolina, were Muskhogean. The Yuchi town and province on Savannah River in De Soto's time and later was Cofitachiqui.

The Seminoles were basically separatist Creeks who had moved into Florida from southern Georgia. Like the Creeks, who engaged Gen. Andrew Jackson in a long war (1813–14), the Seminoles were at war with the United States from 1817 to 1818 and, over their removal in the Second Seminole War, from 1835 to 1842, before many were finally transported to Indian Territory, later Oklahoma.

of crowding the aborigines together, so as to render them inevitably hostile to each other, and to the frontier which they border, several counties of the Arkansa territory will have to be evacuated by their white inhabitants, who will thus be ruined in their circumstances, at the very period when the general survey of the lands had inspired them with the confident ·expectation of obtaining a permanent and legal settlement.[36]

February 4TH.] To-day we left Natchez, and in the distance of 15 miles passed Ellis's Cliffs,[37] another portion of re-entering high land, broken into a very picturesque landscape, decorated with pines and magnolias. These cliffs, no way essentially different from those above, present here, immediately above the carbonaceous bed, a very thick stratum of white sandy clay, so far indurated as to withstand the washing which has carried away the superincumbent soil.

In the course of the night we arrived at Fort Adams,[38] another spur of the high land; a term which can only be used in reference to the alluvion, as the apparent undulation is here nothing more than an adventitious subsidence or washing of the soil, the ravines and gullies being occasioned by its friable nature. Rock, however, appears at the base of the lofty hill, on which stands a block house of the late garrison. A tavern, a store, and two or three other houses are here established for the convenience of the interior.

7TH.] To-day we arrived at the settlement of bayou Sarah,[39] a mile up which stream is situated the town of St. Francisville, and passed a line of opulent plantations on the Louisiana bank of the river called Point

[36]Nuttall's account of his trip with Major Bradford from Fort Smith to the Red River in Chapter IX explained the approaching removal of the Choctaws, effectuated by the Treaty of Doak's Stand between the tribe and the United States, presided over by Gen. Andrew Jackson, October 18, 1820, eight and a half months after Nuttall's present journal entry. Lands in western Arkansas embracing what are now ten counties and parts of nearly ten more, would go to the Choctaws in exchange for their Mississippi domain, along with the vast tract in present Oklahoma bounded by the Red River on the south and the Canadian and Arkansas rivers on the north, westward to the source of the Canadian. KAPPLER, II, 133; AM. ST. PAPERS, INDIAN AFFAIRS, II, 229–31, 394–99.

[37]Ellis's Cliffs was fifteen miles downstream from Natchez.

[38]Fort Adams, minutely described by CUMING (328–29) ten years earlier, had been built by the United States on orders of Gen. James Wilkinson in 1798. It was thinly held, customarily by a platoon, after the Louisiana Purchase, to 1813. It was located at Loftus Heights in S.W. Wilkinson County.

[39]The settlement and the stream are in West Feliciana Parish, La., east of the Mississippi.

Coupee. From hence we begin to perceive the orange, though not very thriving. Sugar is also planted thus far, and appears to succeed. Mons. Poydras, a bachelor 80 years of age, owns and employs in this settlement betwixt 4 and 500 negroes, which, together with property in New Orleans, amounts to an estate of several millions of dollars. His plantations at Point Coupee are principally employed in the lucrative business of planting and making sugar.[40]

8TH.] We again obtained sight of the high land in the cliffs near Thompson's creek,[41] and, as usual, on the eastern side of the river. About three feet above the present level, we also observed the occurrence of the bovey-coal or lignite, overlaid by massive beds of ferruginous clays and gravel. This high land, without again approaching to the immediate margin of the river, continues at no great distance from hence to Baton-Rouge.

9TH.] Early this morning we passed the thriving town of Baton-Rouge, where a garrison has been established ever since its cession.[42] Not far from hence, the high lands or primitive soil terminates, beyond which, to the sea, the whole country is alluvial and marshy. Continued lines of settlements still present themselves on either bank, and cotton and sugar are the great articles of their agricultural opulence.

About 3 o'clock in the morning, we experienced a heavy squall from the north-east, accompanied by torrents of rain, and were in considerable

[40]At the north end of Fausse Rivière, the oxbow lake remaining from an early eighteenth century diversion of the Mississippi to a new bed eastward, Julien de Lalande Poydras (1746–1824) presided over Alma Plantation, one of his six large holdings on and around the original Pointe Coupée, the narrow neck of land between the lake and the river itself. He was in his seventy-third year and was president of the Louisiana State Senate at the time of Nuttall's visit, having been president of the Legislative Council of Orleans Territory in 1804 and president of the state's constitutional convention in 1812. His published poetry in French was famous but undistinguished, but his large philanthropies reach into our own day. Poydras Street and the bust in the Cabildo in New Orleans commemorate this early Louisianan.

[41]Thompson Creek is the boundary between East and West Feliciana parishes, La.

[42]Baton Rouge (French for Red Stick, an early-eighteenth-century Indian boundary point on the E. bank of the Mississippi River) had had a French fort from 1719, ceded 1763 to England but taken over by Spain as part of West Florida in 1779. At the second battle of Baton Rouge (the Spanish conquest in 1779 was the first), American settlers occupied the fort September 23, 1810. It came under formal United States control when Zebulon Montgomery Pike was placed in command in early January, 1811, and was garrisoned thereafter principally at the Pentagon, on the older fort site, built beginning 1819. TERR. PAPERS, IX, 927–28.

danger of losing the flat, with all our property and baggage. Ever since leaving Natchez, we have had weather like summer, and vegetation already advances.

10TH and 11TH.] We have in view an almost uninterrupted line of settlements on either hand which continue to New Orleans. These planters are nearly all of French or Spanish extraction, and, as yet, there are among them but few Americans. Their houses are generally built of wood, with piazzas for shade in the summer. Notwithstanding their comparative opulence, they differ little either in habits, manners, or dress from the Canadians. Dancing and gambling appear to be their favourite amusements. The men, as usual, are commonly dressed in blanket coats, and the women wear handkerchiefs around their heads in place of bonnets. The inhabitants do not appear to be well supplied with merchandize, and the river is crowded with the boats of French and Spanish pedlars, not much larger than perogues, but fitted up with a cabin, covered deck, and sails.

Another vast monopolizer of human liberty, along the coast (as the borders of the Mississippi are termed by the French), is general Wade Hampton,[43] who possesses upwards of 400 slaves, and has obtained at one crop 500 hogsheads of sugar, and 1000 bales of cotton, then collectively worth upwards of 150,000 dollars: in the United States an immense fortune, without any additional property, and equal to that of almost any English nobleman. But, with the means of being so extensively useful, I do not learn that either this gentleman or Mons. Poydras,[44] expend any adequate part of their immense property to public advantage. And, more than that, these unfortunate slaves, the engines of their wealth, are scarcely fed or clothed in any way bordering on humanity. Their common allowance of food, is said to be about one quart of corn per day! Thus miserably fed, they are consequently driven to theft by the first law of

[43]Wade Hampton (1751 or 1752–1835), a Virginian, became a colonel in the Revolutionary War; member for South Carolina in the U.S. House of Representatives, 1795–97, 1803–1805; brigadier general in 1809, succeeding Gen. James Wilkinson at New Orleans that year; major general commanding at Lake Champlain, 1813, where, on being superseded by General Wilkinson, he resigned, devoting himself to extensive plantation holdings in Richland County, S.C., later acquiring others on the lower Mississippi. At his death he was reputedly the wealthiest planter in the United States.

[44]Mons. P. has, I understand, endowed a place in New Orleans for the education of female orphans. —NUTTALL. [Poydras Female Academy, founded 1817.]

nature, and subject the country to perpetual depredation. How little wealth has contributed towards human improvement, appears sufficiently obvious throughout this adventitiously opulent section of the Union. Time appears here only made to be lavished in amusement. Is the uncertainty of human life so great in this climate, as to leave no leisure for any thing beyond dissipation? The only serious pursuit, appears to be the amassing and spending of that wealth which is wrung from the luckless toil of so many unfortunate Africans, doomed to an endless task, which is even entailed upon their posterity. "O slavery, though thousands in all ages have drank of thee, still thou art a bitter draught!"

An evil, however, which has been so long established, cannot be eradicated at a single blow. The abolition of domestic slavery must be a work of time. Let an age be chosen at which it shall cease to operate; say a limit of 28 or 30 years. Let the negroes be sent into the civilized world with the rudiments of education, and the means of obtaining a livelihood. After acquiring their freedom, it is highly probable, that they would still continue to seek the employment of their former masters, and the neighbourhood in which they were born. The project of transporting the free negroes to the country in which they originated appears extremely rational, and ought to be promoted by every means in the power of the public. We are sensible that the negroes who remain in the society of the whites, must ever be subjected to the degradation of an inferior cast. They were not formed to mingle indiscriminately amongst us; but though they may be inferior to us in intellect and civilization, they were undoubtedly born to the possession of rational liberty.

In the contiguous country of Opelousa,[45] so called from the Indians who formerly lived in it, there are extensive and fertile prairies, where great herds of cattle are raised for the market of New Orleans. A year ago, about 12,000 head were sold on the banks of the Mississippi, at the rate of from 30 to 35 dollars each.

From hence to New Orleans, now 86 miles distant, the whole coast is defended from inundation by an embankment or trench of earth, thrown up with about the same labour as that which is bestowed upon a common

[45]Opelousa, from the name of the small Indian tribe of the Attacapan lingistic family living historically at or near Opelousas, the seat of St. Landry Parish, La.

ditched fence. In this simple way, millions of acres of the richest land, inexhaustible by crops, is redeemed from waste, and we have now the pleasure of viewing an almost uninterrupted line of opulent settlements continued from Baton-Rouge, to more than 50 miles below New Orleans.

Among the more common reptiles of this country, already beginning to appear abroad, I know of none more curious, than a kind of Cameleon lizard, of frequent occurrence, and in some measure related to that celebrated species, excepting that the colours which it assumes are only those with which it is familiar in nature; such as ash-colour in the vicinity of a pale object, dark brown upon the ground, or on the trunks of trees, and a bright green amidst verdant herbage.

17TH.] After another detention of two days by the prevalence of a strong south-west wind, we continued our voyage, and early this morning passed the great plantation of general Hampton, situated about 70 miles from New Orleans, at Ouma point, the name of a nation or tribe of Indians now nearly extinct, and who, with the remains of the Chetimashas, once living nearly opposite to bayou la Fourche, are at this time existing in a partly civilized state on the bayou Plaquemine.[46] The learned Peter S. Duponceau, Esq. informs me, that the language of the Chetimashas, a people said, by Du Pratz, to be a branch of the Natchez, appears to be radically distinct from that of the other aborigines of the southern states. From hence the banks of the river are lower, and the labour of keeping up the levees greater, though the rise of the river is slower, its width and uniformity of channel more considerable, and now almost destitute of islands or bars. The river is very probably influenced in this respect by the embankments, which are continued almost without interruption from Fort Adams nearly to Fort Placquemine.[47] We had

---

[46]Point Houma, slightly downstream on the Mississippi west bank from Donaldsonville, is in Saint James Parish. The Huma Indians, a detached group of the Choctaw tribe, ranged between this point and the vicinity of Houma, now the parish seat of Terrebonne. The Chitimachas and the Natchez appear in Chapter VII, note 86, *ante.* Du Ponceau was correct about their language. Far from disappearing, the Chitimachas recently counted sixty members at the Chitimacha Reservation, near the village of Charenton, on Bayou Teche; one hundred more are scattered in Louisiana and Texas. HANSEN, 419.

[47]Fort Plaquemine, sixty-six miles by water below New Orleans, was a Spanish post on the left bank commanding the lower Mississippi, occupied by the United States after

now in view a perpetual succession of the habitations of the richest planters, surrounded with groups of negro cabins. They are almost exclusively engaged in the planting of sugar, and possess establishments no way inferior to those of the West India Islands, some of them being valued at as much as 100,000 dollars, every thing included. As the settlements are chiefly in single lines along the bank of the river, the land is commonly sold by the measurement in front, running back about 40 arpents,[48] and have been disposed of at as much as 3000 dollars per arpent in front, or 75 dollars per arpent actual measurement.

Notwithstanding the fearful tyranny exercised over the slaves on these large plantations, the annals of this settlement are not without the remembrance of serious symptoms of revolt. About nine years ago, a party of negroes, equipped with arms, liberated themselves, after destroying their master with two or three other individuals who attempted to oppose them, and were not subdued until totally destroyed by the neighbouring militia. There were of them 300, who were routed near to Red Church, about twenty-four miles above New Orleans;[49] so that, betwixt the fears of inundation, the efforts of the enslaved Africans to emancipate themselves, and the fatality of the climate, the opulent planters of Louisiana possess no enviable advantage over the happy peasant, who dwells in the security which honest industry and salutary frugality afford him.

The excessive attachment to gambling which characterises the inhabitants of Louisiana, and the love of speculation, exhibited in the great and transitory influx of foreigners and citizens from the northern states, is now ostensibly checked by a species of taxation called license. Thus, every

---

the Louisiana Purchase. Not to be confused with Plaquemine, seat of Iberville Parish, or the bayou of the same name adjoining.

[48]The *arpent* of Paris is less than the English and United States statute acre, as 512 is to 605. The arpent is used in Louisiana, and other places in America inhabited by the French, as a measure of length; each arpent is equal to 29.1 Gunter's chain, very nearly; consequently, 40 arpents amounts to 116.4 Gunter, or 2660.8 yards. —Note by Mr. Darby. —NUTTALL.

[49]The revolt at Red Church, on the left (east) bank of the Mississippi, thirty miles above New Orleans, near modern Destrehan, Saint Charles Parish, the second week in January, 1811, was put down by a small force commanded by Gen. Wade Hampton January 10. The latter set the casualties at "fifteen or twenty" blacks killed (Hampton to Secretary of War William Eustis, January 16, 1811, in TERR. PAPERS, IX, 917–19). An earlier revolt had occurred at Alma Plantation, Julien Poydras's seat, in 1795 during the Spanish regime.

store-keeper pays an annual assessment of 110 dollars to the common-
wealth. Every pedlar 12 dollars. Every Pharo bank and Roulette table 500
dollars a year, and every Billiard table 40 dollars. In excuse for thus
tolerating the Pharo bank and the Roulette, the legislature affirm their
inability to check the evil by punishment.

18TH.] This morning we arrived at New Orleans, now said to contain
about 45,000 inhabitants, a great proportion of whom are of French
extraction and retain their mother tongue. The situation of the town,
which was begun in 1718,[50] is rendered unhealthy by the swamp which
circumscribes its western suburb, and which continues at all seasons totally impassable. A short canal crosses it, forming a communication with
the bayou St. John, and lake Ponchartrain, by which means a commercial communication is opened to Mobile, Pensacola, and the Alabama
territory.

In the neighbourhood of the city, and along the coast, the beautiful
groves of orange trees, orchards of the fig, and other productions of the
mildest climates, sensibly indicate our approach to the tropical regions,
where the dreary reign of winter is for ever unknown. But little pains as
yet have been taken to introduce into this country, though so thickly
settled, the ornamental and useful plants which it is calculated to sustain.
We yet neither see the olive, the date, nor the vineyard, notwithstanding
the adaptation of the climate to their culture. That the date itself would
succeed, an accidental example in the city renders probable. This palm,
which grows in Orleans street, has attained the height of more than 30
feet, with a trunk of near 18 inches in diameter, and has flowered annually for the space of several years. The period of inflorescence appears to be
about the commencement of April, but being only a staminiferous plant,
it has not consequently produced any fruit.

That fatal epidemic, the yellow fever, was last summer unusually
prevalent, and carried off probably 5 or 6000 individuals, a great part of
whom were, as usual, emigrants from the northern states, and different

[50]New Orleans, founded 1718 by Jean Baptiste le Moyne, Sieur de Bienville, governor under John Law's Company, had attained a population of just at eight thousand in
1800, at the close of the Spanish regime. But the Louisiana Purchase from France in
1803 resulted in a swift rise in population, greatly accelerated after the War of 1812.
Even a year made a startling difference, Paul Wilhelm, Duke of Württemberg, found in
1823. *Travels in North America, 1822–24*, 411.

parts of Europe. By what I can learn, the hospital in this place is very ill suited to the recovery of those patients who are hurried to it during the rage of this disease. They are crowded almost to contact; so that the contagion acquires force and fatality in the very institution formed for its recovery. Many, however, flock to this last refuge for the indigent and miserable, in a state which precludes all hopes of recovery.[51]

The expense of medical assistance, the difficulty of obtaining attendance, and the selfish and fearful supineness which seizes upon all classes at this awful season, serves to increase the fatal gloom which surrounds the unhappy stranger, thus often inhumanly abandoned by all society, and left, before the approach of the fatal moment, like a carcase to the vultures!

The scene of crowded graves which appals the eye in the general burying-ground, marked by boards, or covered tombs, inscribed with mournful remembrances; the hosts which are swept off, also, interred in forgotten crowds, and consigned to relentless oblivion, appeared thickly to chequer the whole surface of the earth, and warn the stranger, in no ambiguous phrase, of the fatal climate in which he sojourns. These crowds of sepulchres are not the slow accumulation of an age, as a section of these remains is frequently dug up and consumed, to give place to the renewed harvest of death.

The prevailing religion is that of the Catholics; though there is also a handsome church erected by the Presbyterians.[52]

Science and rational amusement is as yet but little cultivated in New Orleans. There are only three or four booksellers to supply this large city and populous neighbourhood. The French inhabitants, intermingled with the African castes in every shade of colour, scarcely exceed them, generally speaking, in mental acquirements. Every thing like intellectual improvement appears to be vitiated in its source, nothing exists to inspire emulation, and learning, as in the West Indies, has no existence beyond the mechanism of reading and writing. Something like a museum was

[51]Yellow fever, an acute infectious disease of viral character, is transmitted by any of several species of mosquitoes, in this zone by *Aëdes aegypti*. Beyond good nursing and supportive care there is no specific treatment yet known. The last major outbreak in New Orleans and other cities of the South occurred in 1905.

[52]That on Saint Charles Street between Gravier and Union streets, founded in 1819 and destroyed by fire in 1851.

begun in the city a few years ago, but by a protean evolution it has been transformed into a coffee-house for gambling. In another part of the city, an assemblage of specimens of the fine arts, busts, medallions, mosaics, and paintings, is also associated with the dice and bottle.[53]

The market, at this season, by no means dear, or bearing any thing like a reasonable proportion with the extravagant charges of the public entertainers, appeared to be tolerably well supplied, though singularly managed, and that entirely by negro slaves, who spread out the different articles in petty quantities, like the arrangement of an apple stall, charging, however, at the rate of about 100 per cent for the trouble. Superfine flour now sold at the low rate of six dollars per barrel; bacon and cheese at 10 cents the pound, salt butter at 25 cents; sugar at seven dollars per cwt.; coffee 25 to 30 dollars per cwt.; rice seven dollars per cwt. Fresh beef, however, and that by no means good, sold at 25 cents per pound. As in the West Indies, the principal market appears to be on Sunday in the forenoon. In the afternoon the negroes assemble in the suburbs of the city, and amuse themselves by dancing. When thus assembled by common friendship, if they have any reflection, they must be convinced of the efficient force which they possess to emancipate themselves; they are, however, strictly watched by the police, and the sole object of their meeting appears to be amusement.

Some idea of the extensive commerce carried on in the western states and territories with New Orleans, may be formed from the number of steam boats alone, now 75 in number, besides other craft and shipping, which navigate the Mississippi and its numerous tributary streams. But in consequence of the general and unfavourable fluctuation in the commerce of the United States, the number of these vessels is become greater than their actual employment will warrant. A majority also of the steam-boats have this year lain unemployed for more than six months, in consequence

[53]Nuttall, although only three years away from assuming his appointment to the Harvard faculty and the curatorship of the Boston Botanic Garden (the first week in March, 1823), reveals himself here as less the sophisticate than might otherwise be imagined. Paul Wilhelm of Württemberg found the New Orleans of this period enjoyable, notably for Théâtre Orléans, founded 1819, one of three French theaters, which Bernhard of Saxe-Weimar in 1825–26 praised for its productions. The American Theatre was similarly progressing. Elegant balls were being given regularly, and restaurant and hotel food was good and moderate in price. WÜRTTEMBERG, 34–35; SMITHER, *passim.*

of the extraordinary lowness of water; but the valuable staple produce of Louisiana, must always insure to its inhabitants a preponderating balance of wealth.[54]

[54]The river trade alone, depositing freight at New Orleans, would count 198 steam vessels in the year ending September 30, 1820, of a gross freight tonnage of 106,706 (HOUSE EXEC. DOC. 50 Cong., 1 sess., No. 6, Part II: Report on the Internal Commerce of the United States, 1887); MITCHELL, 933–63). For the following year 1,225 river flatboats would swell the tide, as flatboats had been doing for more than a generation.

Editorial Note to the Appendix

THOMAS NUTTALL'S UNDERTAKING up to this point offers a highly significant personal record, historically informative and rich in botanical and geographical findings. From many points of view it is pivotal to the story of the Near Southwest in the quarter century following the Louisiana Purchase. The Appendix which now follows is of a different, derivative character. In three of its four sections—the "Account of the Ancient Aboriginal Population" along the lower Mississippi, "The History of the Natchez," and "Observations on the Chicasaws and Choctaws"—the author is drawing almost exclusively on the published work of earlier explorers and writers. Any attempt to evaluate these materials in detail, much less to annotate them, as has been done for the *Journal*, would prove counterproductive.

The scholarship which has been expended on the De Soto Expedition, to take the first section, has been very large during the past 160 years. Hitherto unsuspected documents have emerged. The painstaking retracing (physically and geographically) of the De Soto itinerary required a fully staffed United States commission several years. The Indians of the lower Mississippi and the Gulf of Mexico have been examined in many linguistic and anthropological works, notably in the annual reports and bulletins of the Bureau of American Ethnology, as well as in the work of individual scholars. To all of these must be added the archaeological data which have been steadily accumulated since 1880.

The more profitable course, it seems to me, is to ask and answer several questions:

What impelled Nuttall to undertake these anthropological tasks and even to project a second volume devoted to "aboriginal antiquities of the western states" and "essays on the languages of the western Indians"?

Which historical and anthropological resources could he bring to bear on the De Soto Expedition and on the Natchez, Chickasaws, and Choctaws? Which important ones were missed by or unavailable to him?

How fully were Nuttall's Appendix findings accepted in his day and after?

To answer the first question: Whatever thoughts Nuttall had on the De Soto experience and the three Indian tribes he chose to treat in the Appendix could scarcely have been adjusted to the form of his *Journal*. These matters had to be extraneous, or appended, to the latter. And, after all, the journal form not only was the natural one for presenting his journey but was all but universally used in his time—even for many military reports.

More than this, however, was the pervasive interest of the American Philosophical Society in Indian antiquities and languages. From his election to the society in October, 1817, Nuttall had had access to its library, which included not only works on Indian history and antiquities but large manuscript holdings as well. He also had the opportunity to rub elbows with leading students of the Indian and to hear their papers—Peter S. Du Ponceau (1760–1844), elected to the society in 1791 and serving as vice-president at the time Nuttall was writing; John Pickering (1777–1846), elected in 1820, at about the time Nuttall arrived back in Philadelphia; Thomas Jefferson (1746–1826), elected 1779 and president of the society from 1797 to 1814; Albert Gallatin (1761–1849), elected 1791; J. G. E. Heckewelder (1743–1823), elected 1797; and others less prominent.

The list is a roster of the minds who shaped the approaches to American Indian ethnology and linguistics in their formative years. Du Ponceau and Pickering, it is now generally agreed, were two of the finest linguists of the first half of the nineteenth century (it was Du Ponceau who established the Osages as Siouan). Jefferson was scarcely an amateur, having produced one important work reflecting on Indian subjects in *Notes on the State of Virginia* (1784) and collected some forty vocabularies and grammars (many of which were lost by theft as his papers were en route to Monticello at the close of his presidency). Heckewelder was highly productive in Indian languages, and Gallatin, Jefferson's secretary of the treasury, was destined to fulfill Du Ponceau's search, as Clark Wissler put it, "for a Linnaeus to set up convincing principles of classification" for American Indians and their languages (1836).

Benjamin Smith Barton, Nuttall's friend and benefactor until his death in 1815, was in the background of all these developments. Nuttall could scarcely have forgotten his *New Views of the Origins of the Tribes and Nations of America* (1797). His learning continued to hover over the American Philosophical Society, to which he had been elected in 1789. Nor could Nuttall have escaped the purposeful drives of the Historical and Library Committee of the society, created in 1815, possibly on Thomas Jefferson's promptings to Du Ponceau. For the five years preceding Nuttall's return to Philadelphia, the committee had as its objectives (1) to collect historic documents and (2) to collect manuscripts recording Indian languages (WISSLER, 192). The first quarter of the nineteenth century was indeed a time of inquiry into Indian history, linguistic groupings, and culture, for the future of Indian life was already in doubt in many minds, Jefferson's among them.

Confronting the second question—Which historical and anthropological resources could Nuttall bring to bear on these subjects?—is largely a bibliographical matter. To save space, I identify here the works he drew upon by name of author in small capitals, as in the footnotes to the *Journal*. Full bibliographical details appear in the appended Sources Cited.

It is safe to say that, without PURCHAS, Nuttall could not have undertaken the first section, on the De Soto findings, just as he could have done little without a good knowledge of LE PAGE [2] in treating the Natchez, Chickasaws, and Choctaws, though clearly he had a not inconsequential reliance on ADAIR and CHARLEVOIX for the latter. Missing, particularly for the De Soto experience, are RANJEL, buried in OVIEDO until 1866, and BIEDMA, similarly unavailable to the author. The first was secretary to De Soto, and the second the king's factor.

Nuttall's knowledge of ELVAS, the third key figure in the De Soto explorations and second in importance, if that, only to RANJEL historically, was derived from HAKLUYT via PURCHAS. One of the puzzles here is that Nuttall seems to have been only minimally acquainted with Hakluyt, to whom we owe English versions (in 1609 and 1611) of ELVAS. He refers to GARCILASO, who was not on the expedition but recorded it fifty years later from informants, yet he could have known the text only from Spanish, in which he seems to have had no fluency, or French, which he seems to have been able to handle, from his references to VON HUMBOLDT. As the U.S. DE SOTO EXPEDITION COMMISSION shows (5–9), we had no English version before that of THEODORE IRVING

(1835) and no direct translation until VARNER (1951). Yet the inclusion of much Garcilaso de la Vega material in HERRERA, translation of whom in six volumes appeared in London, 1725–26, may remotely have been the source of Nuttall's familiarity with that overdramatized account.

Nuttall had, for the Indian tribes he chose to treat, TONTY in English translation; his friend BRACKENRIDGE; JONES; GOOKIN; COLDEN; DU PONCEAU; and HECKEWELDER, all of whom he either mentions or gives evidence of having examined. He apparently did not know DUMONT DE MONTIGNY, whose account parallels that of LE PAGE, unavailable then except in French; or that of BOSSU, although it had been translated (1771).

The answer to the third question which concerns us—How fully were Nuttall's Appendix findings accepted in his day and after?—is partly answered, for the lower Mississippi Indians, by the data which immediately precede this paragraph. The author's humanistic awareness was, from even the most critical standpoint, rather extraordinary. But he was not a descriptive or analytical linguist, in the sense in which those words can be applied to his contemporaries in the American Philosophical Society. Nor was he quite yet a historical researcher. He lacked the time, the money, and the willingness to separate himself from the area of natural science, specifically botany, to which he was fully committed, as he was secondarily to ornithology and geology.

But we would be badly mistaken if we did not know that Nuttall's was the dominant retracing of the western portion of the De Soto itinerary during the remainder of the nineteenth century, indeed almost down to the publication of its findings by the U.S. DE SOTO COMMISSION. It influenced GEORGE BANCROFT and BUCKINGHAM SMITH (perhaps more in J. C. Brevoort's map than in Smith's text), and, indeed, as the commission asserts, exerted a "most profound effect on later writers" (pp. 15, 26, 27, 46). But the commission in the end had to reject Nuttall's theory that the expedition had crossed the Mississippi at Chickasaw Bluffs (near present Memphis) for a site much downriver (pp. 234–37).

Even for Indian identification and linguistic relationships, Nuttall was much above the nonspecialist writers of his day. The ultimate correctives in this area are relatively recent, in the writings of SWANTON [1], [2], [3], [4]; MOONEY, GATSCHET, HODGE, DEBO, GIBSON [1], and BUSHNELL.

The proportions of the problem may be found in the analyses of linguistic and ethnological beginnings in Nuttall's day in EDGERTON and WISSLER. Is it too much to suppose, however, that the taxonomic skills the Arkansas traveler applied to the vast area of living plant species could have been applied with scarcely less success to the varieties of human inhabitants of North America in the first half of the nineteenth century? His contemporary in botanical exploration, RAFINESQUE, was bold enough to make the attempt a decade and a half later, driven as much by the anthropological ferment of the times as by his sometimes immodest ambitions.

APPENDIX

SECTION I

AN ACCOUNT OF THE ANCIENT ABORIGINAL POPULATION OF THE BANKS OF THE MISSISSIPPI, AND THE CONTIGUOUS COUNTRY.

THIS WILDERNESS, which we now contemplate as a dreary desert, was once thickly peopled by the natives, who, by some sudden revolution, of which we appear to be ignorant, have sunk into the deepest oblivion. In the abridged account of the great enterprise of Ferdinand de Soto by Purchas, begun in the year 1539, we read of numerous nations and tribes, then inhabiting the banks of the Mississippi, of whom, except the Chicaças, the Cherokees (called more properly Chelaques), and the small remnant of the Kaskaskias, and Tonicas, not an individual remains to reveal the destinies of tis compatriots. Their extinction will ever remain in the utmost mystery. The agency of this destruction is, however, fairly to be attributed to the Euopeans, and the present hostile Indians who possess the country. It is from these exterminating and savage conquerors, that we in vain inquire of the unhappy destiny of thie great and extinguished population, and who, like so many troops of assassins, have concealed their outrages by an unlimited annihilation of their victims.

As this part of the American history is very obscure and neglected, I shall probably be excused for introducing it at greater length than would otherwise have been necessary.

De Soto, after encountering considerable difficulty and hardship, in his progress through the interior of what then was called Florida, arrived, at length, amongst the Chicaças, who occupied pretty near the same country in which we find them at present. The principal object of the commander, and those who had embarked with him from the island of Cuba, of which he was governor, appears, as usual, to have been a search for the precious metals; and the natives, ever willing to rid themselves of those whom they feared and hated, kept perpetually instigating the adventurers to distant pursuits. The plain, on which we find them encamped, previous to their proceeding across the Mississippi (which did not at that time bear this name), and to which they had been conducted by their native guides, could have been no other than one of the Chicasaw Bluffs, or ancient crossing-places, and apparently the lowest. While busied here in providing boats for crossing, they were visited by a party of the natives who descended the river,[1] and declared to the governor (Soto), that they were the subjects of a great lord (or chief), whose name was *Aquixo*, who governed many towns, and a numerous people on the west side of the Great River (or Mississippi), and they came to inform him, that the chief with all his men would come to await his commands. The following day, the cazique[2] arrived with 200 canoes full of Indians, armed with their bows and arrows, painted and decorated with feathers of various colours, and defended with shields made from the skins of the bison; the warriors were numerously arranged from the head to the stern of the boats. The canoe of the cazique was furnished with a tilt over the stern, beneath which he sat, and gave his commands. The canoes of the lesser cheiftains were also equipped in the same manner. Approaching the bank, the cazique addressed the governor, saying, he came to visit, to honour, and obey him, inasmuch as he was the greatest lord upon the earth, and that he now waited his commands. The governor returned him thanks, and desired him to come on shore to hold some further communication. Without, however, attending to this request, the chief sent a present to the governor of three canoes loaded with fish, and loaves made of the pulp of persimmons.[3] Receiving this present, the governor again invited him to the shore, but without success. The cazique, baffled in his purpose of deceiving Soto, whom he found in readiness, began now to row off, on which, the governor instantly ordered the cross-bow-men to fire a volley at the natives, in which five or six of them fell. Still they retired in good

---

[1] Purchas's Pilgrims, vol. IV. p. 1546. —NUTTALL.

[2] This Peruvian title for chieftain is employed throughout the narrative, by Garcilasso de la Vega, the author of the history, and himself a descendant of the Incas, who chose to follow the fortunes of Soto, one of the conquerors of his country. —NUTTALL.

[3] Called Prunes by the Spaniards. —NUTTALL.

order, not a man deserting his oar, though his fellow warrior dropped at his side. They afterwards attempted several times to land, but as often fled to their canoes on the approach of the Spaniards. The canoes were very large and well made, being also decorated with tilts, plumes, paveses, and flags.

The river (Mississippi) de Soto found to be almost a mile broad. A man who stood still could scarcely be discerned from the opposite shore. The current was strong and deep, with the water always muddy, and continually charged with floating trees.

Having passed the Rio Grande (as he calls it), and travelled up the bank about three miles, he came to a great town of *Aquixo*, from whence the inhabitants had fled. They discovered a party of 30 Indians coming over the adjoining plain to reconnoitre their movements, but on perceiving the Spaniards they instantly fled. They were, however, pursued by the cavalry, who killed 10 of them, and took 15 prisoners. As the town to which Soto proceeded was situated near to the bank of the river, he left a detachment to bring up the boats, and proceeded with the rest of his armament by land, but finding it difficult to keep along the bank, which was obstructed by the entrance of creeks, left the boats exposed to the annoyance of the natives, but understanding which, he instantly dispatched a party of cross-bow-men to their defence. Here he broke up the boats, but saved the iron for future contingencies. The following day, he proceeded up the river in quest of the province called Pacaha, which he was informed lay contiguous to Chisca, where the Indians had told him of the existence of gold. On his way he passed through great towns of Aquixo, from all of which the inhabitants had fled at his approach. Here he was informed, by some of the natives whom they had taken, that three days journey further up the river there dwelt a great cazique named Casqui.[4] He crossed a small river upon a bridge, and the rest of the day, until

[4]The same apparently with Kaskaskia, spelled Kaskasquia by Father Charlevoix, and Caskaquia by Du Pratz. This band, as well as the Kahoquias, Tamaroas, Peorias, and Pimeteois, formed part of the Illinois nation, now nearly all extinct, though they could once enumerate as many as twenty thousand souls. They were found inhabiting the rivers which still retain their name, and have fallen before the Iroquois, and the Chicasa nations, with whom they waged war. Their name of Illinois, or Illinese of La Hontan, so much like Leni-Lenape, or that of the Delawares, and signifying, in common with that appellation, the *original* or *genuine men*, besides the tradition of their having come in company with the Miamies from the borders of Hudson's bay or the North Pacific, and

sun-set, they were continually wading in water either waist or knee deep. At length, they gained the dry land, and congratulated themselves, as they were under some apprehension of passing the night in that dismal situation. At noon they arrived at the first town of Casqui, and found the Indians unprepared for resistance. Here the Spaniards took many of both sexes prisoners, and considerable stores of garments[5] and skins, as well in the first town, as in a second, which was surprised by the cavalry, and lay about half a league distant. They found this country to be higher, drier, and more champaign than any part they had yet seen contiguous to the river; from which we are fully satisfied, that the country thus described, can be no other than the Little Prairie, and that chain of high lands which continues to New Madrid, in the vicinity of which, there are also many aboriginal remains. The neighbouring fields abounded with walnut trees, bearing round nuts with soft shells, and with leaves which they considered to be smaller than usual;[6] of these nuts the Indians had collected a store for use. Here they also found mulberries, and red[7] and grey plumbs.[8] The trees appeared as fruitful as if they had been protected in orchards, and the woods generally were very thin. De Soto continued travelling two days through the country of Casqui before he arrived at the town inhabited by the cazique; most part of the way was over champaign country, *filled with great towns, always within view of each other.* Soto sent an Indian to

---

their speaking nearly the same language, as related by Charlevoix,* appear as so many proofs of the common origin of these two people. It is also related by the same author (before their arrival in the country, which they so extensively occupied in the time of Soto's incursion, and in which they lived till the period of their approaching extinction), they had settled along the borders of the river des Moins, or Moingona, of the Mississippi, which gave name to one of their tribes. The friendship which they cultivated, about a century ago, with the Osages, and the Arkansas, who are the same people, and some incidental resemblances between them, lead us to believe them also commonly related by language and descent. —NUTTALL.

---

*Fifty years ago (1720) the Miamis were settled at Chicago, and were, at this time, "divided into three villages, one at the river St. Joseph, a second on Miami of Lake Erie, and the third called the Watanons of the Wabash." "There is scarcely a doubt," adds Charlevoix, "but that this nation and the Illinois were not long since one people, considering the affinity of their languages." *Charlevoix, Hist. Journ.* p. 114. —NUTTALL.

[5]These "mantels," as they are called by Purchas, were fabricated from coarse threads of the bark of trees and nettles. —NUTTALL.

[6]Probably Pecans (*Carya olivafaermis*). —NUTTALL.

[7]*Prunus chicasa?* —NUTTALL.

[8]*P. hiemalis.* —NUTTALL.

announce his arrival to the cazique, desiring his friendship and fraternity. To which he answered, by graciously bidding him welcome, and making an offer of his services to accomplish all that he requested. The chief also met him with a present of skins, garments, and fish. After which compliments de Soto found all the inhabitants of the towns peaceable and friendly, and their chiefs and elders coming out to congratulate him with presents. The cazique, attended by a numerous train of his people, respectfully awaited the approach of the governor, about half a league from the town.

Friendly compliments were again exchanged, and the cazique made an offer of his houses for de Soto to lodge in; he, however, excused himself from accepting this civility on prudential motives, and encamped in the adjoining fields.

The cazique went to the town, and afterwards returned again accompanied by many Indians singing. As soon as they arrived in the presence of the governor, they all prostrated themselves upon the ground. After which, the cazique besought him, as he was the son of the Sun, and a great lord, to restore two blind men to their sight, which he had brought along with him. The governor, however, excused himself, and referred him to the Supreme Being and author of health, and, on the occasion, had a cross set up for them to worship, in remembrance of Jesus Christ, who died thereon.

The governor now inquired of the chief the distance to Pacaha, and was told, that it was one day's journey; that at the termination of the country of Casqui, there was a lake like a brook, which ran into the Mississippi (or Rio Grande), and that he would send men before him to construct a bridge for his convenience in passing it. The same day the governor took his departure, he lodged at a town belonging to Casqui; the following, he passed some other towns, and came to the lake, which was half a crossbow shot over, deep, and running with a considerable current. The bridge, constructed of logs, was completed on his arrival. The cazique of Casqui attended upon the governor, accompanied by his people.

The cazique of Pacaha, it appears, was at enmity with the Casqui, and fled at the approach of Soto and his supposed allies, notwithstanding his endeavours to pacify them. Some of them, whom he took prisoners in an adjoining town, would have fallen victims to their natural enemies but for his interposition. In the town which they sacked, they found great store of woven garments, besides deer skins, lion skins (panther skins, in all probability), as well as bear and cat skins. They also found targets of bison hides.

De Soto, at length, entered into Pacaha, and took up his lodging in the town where the chief was accustomed to reside; which is described as large, walled, and defended with towers, through all which were cut loopholes for arms. The town was well supplied with maize, besides a promising harvest then in the field. Within from a mile and a half to three miles, were also other large towns, surrounded with enclosures of pickets. That now occupied by de Soto, was situated contiguous to a large lake, which filled a ditch thrown up nearly round the town. By a weir thrown over the outlet of the lake, abundance of fish were continually ready for the use and amusement of the chief, and with the nets which the Spaniards found in the town, they supplied themselves to their utmost satisfaction. Amongst them we readily recognize the *Silurus* or Cat-fish, which the natives called Bagres; those of the lakes were about the bigness of pikes, but in the river (Mississippi), they occasionally found some which weighed upwards of 100 lbs. There was another which they called the Pele-fish, destitute of scales, and with the upper jaw extended in front a foot in length, in the form of a peel or spatula.[9]

From this place, De Soto despatched a troop of 30 horse and 50 foot to the province of Caluça, to ascertain the practicability of proceeding to Chisca, where the natives, it may be remembered, had informed him of the existence of a mine of gold and of copper. The country over which they proceeded, for seven days, was an uninhabited dessert (probably in consequence of inundation), and they returned almost exhausted with famine and fatigue, existing almost entirely upon green plums, and stalks of maize, which they found in a poor town of six or seven houses.[10] From

[9]Of this singular fish, I received circumstantial accounts at the Post of Arkansa. It also exists in the Ohio, and is the *Platyrostra edentula* of Lesueur, described in the Journal of the Academy of Natural Sciences of Philadelphia, vol. i. part 2, pp. 227, 228, and 229, and allied to the *Polyodon* of Lacepède. The plain description of this very local and curious animal, affords additional evidence, if it were necessary, of the truth of the relations of Garcilassa de la Vega, notwithstanding the scepticism of some of the later French writers. —NUTTALL.

[10]This inundated country appears to be the Great Swamp, which commences below Cape Girardeau, said to be 60 miles long. —NUTTALL.

thence, towards the north, they learnt that the country was very cold and thinly settled, and so overrun with herds of bison, that it was scarcely possible to defend their maize from depredation; they also afforded the principal article of provision on which the natives subsisted.

Perceiving no possibility of supplying his troops in marching over this desert country, de Soto, from the information of the Indians, determined to change his course and proceed towards the south, where he had information of the existence of a great privince called Quigaute, affording abundance of provision. To this country the governor now directed his march, and, at length, arrived in the town usually occupied by the chief; by the way he received presents, of numerous skins and woven garments, but the cazique, justly afraid to meet the invaders of his country, absented himself from them. This town is recorded by La Vega, to have been the largest which they had yet seen in Florida.

According to their custom, the Spaniards took all the men and women whom they could conveniently seize as their prisoners. This arbitrary step produced the desired effect, and they now all came forward to prove their obedience to the mandates of the general. The cazique and his two wives were detained in the house of the governor, who made inquiry of them concerning the neighbouring country and its inhabitants. They said, that towards the south, down the river, there were large towns, and chiefs who governed extensive countries and numerous people; and that, toward the north-west, there was a province, contiguous to certain mountains, called Coligoa. To this place the governor and all his officers resolved to go, supposing that, as a mountainous country, it might, in all probability, afford mines of the precious metals. The country, which they had yet seen on the western borders of the Mississippi, was low and alluvial, and promised nothing but agricultural wealth, which had never entered into the sinister views of these El Dorado adventurers. The distance from Pacaha to Quigaute they considered to be about 200 miles.

They now proceeded for seven days through desolate forests, abounding in shoal lagoons, affording an abundance of fish. The Indians of Coligoa had never before seen Europeans, and at their approach fled up the river, near to whose banks their town was situated. The chief, however, and a number of both sexes, were taken prisoners by the orders of Soto. Presents of garments and deer skins were brought in to the governor, and among them were two robes of the bison,[11] which, within 10 or 12 miles of their town, were said to be abundant, and that the country was cold and thinly inhabited.[12]

Here our adventurers were again informed of a fertile and well inhabited country, called Cayas, still lying towards the south. From Quigaute to Coligoa, they supposed the distance to be about 80 miles. The soil here appeared to be extremely productive, and was planted with maize, kidney beans, and pumpkins. The chief of Coligoa provided them with a guide to Cayas, but did not accompany them in person. After a journey of five days, they came to a province called Palisema. The chief left his house for de Soto in a state of preparation, but did not wait an interview. A party of horse and foot were sent to detect him, but returned without success; they met with many people, but, in consequence of the roughness of the country, detained none of them as prisoners, except a few women and children. The town was small and scattered, and but ill supplied with maize. He afterwards proceeded to another town called Tatalicoya, and carried with him the chief, who conducted him in four days to Cayas. De Soto was disappointed by the scattered appearance of the population in this province, and imagined he had been deceived, but was informed, that the space inhabited was very considerable, and the land fertile. The town which they arrived in was called Tanico,[13] and was situated near to a river. The governor spent a month in the province of Cayas, which abounded with maize and pasturage for their horses. In the neighbourhood there was a lake of very hot and somewhat brackish water. Here the party provided themselves with salt, which they had long been in want of, and which they found the natives in the practice of using and fabricating from this water.[14]

From Cayas, de Soto proceeded to Tulla, but here he found the town abandoned at the news of his approach. The chief, however, came accompanied by 80 Indians, who brought with them a present of bison robes, which, at this advanced season of the year, proved very acceptable to the

[11]Called ox-hides. —NUTTALL.

[12]This mountainous country and province of Coligoa, was, in all probability, situated towards the sources of the St. Francis, or the hills of White river. —NUTTALL.

[13]The same people with the tunicas, called also Tonicas, by Charlevoix and Du Pratz. —NUTTALL.

[14]These are evidently the salt waters of the Washita. —NUTTALL.

party. La Vega greatly admired the decorum and propriety with which these natives behaved in their intercourse and addresses to the governor. Towards the west, de Soto was informed of a thinly inhabited country, but that towards the south-west, there were great towns, especially in a province called Autiamque, ten days' journey from Tulla, or about 160 miles, and a country well supplied with maize. To this place they proceeded, after dismissing the two caziques of Cayas and Tulla, with an intention of spending the winter which now approached, and which they expected would detain them for the space of two or three months. They proceeded five days over very rough mountains, and at length came to a town called Quipana,[15] situated between hills. Here awaiting in ambush, they succeeded in taking two Indians, who told them that Autiamque was six days' journey distant, and that there was another province towards the south, eight days' journey off, abounding in maize and well peopled, which was called Guahate; but, as Autiamque was nearer, the governor proceeded in that direction. After travelling three days, they came to a town called Anoixi; previous to entering, he surprised it by a troop of horse and foot, and took many men and women prisoners. Within two days after, they entered another town called Catamaya, and lodged in the adjoining fields. Two Indians came with a pretended message from the chief, to learn the intention of the Spaniards. Soto desired them to tell their lord, that he wanted to hold a conference with him. But the Indians never returned, nor any other message from the cazique. The following day they entered the town, which was deserted by its fearful inhabitants, and in it they found as much maize as they wanted. That day they lodged in a forest, and the following they arrived at Autiamque. Here they found abundance of Maize, French beans, walnuts, and prunes (or persimmons dried); they also took some of the natives busied in carrying off the provision which their wives had hidden. The surrounding country was open and well inhabited. The governor lodged in the best part of the town, and fortified his troops by a strong picket fence after the manner of the natives. Near to the town, there was a river (the Washita), which passed through the province of Cayas, and which was every where well peopled. They spent three months in Autiamque, and were well supplied with provision, amongst which La Vega enumerates conies (or hares), some of which

[15]Probably the same as the Quapaws. —NUTTALL.

were larger than those of Spain; these the natives caught by means of spring traps. The snow was here so considerable, that for one month they never left the town, except for firewood, and were obliged to follow the path which was beaten on purpose by the horsemen.

On the 6th of March, 1542, de Soto departed from Autiamque, and proceeded to Nilco, which the Indians said was contiguous to the Mississippi (or Rio Grande), from whence it was his determination to proceed to the sea, and procure a reinforcement of men and horses, as now he had but 400 men left out of the thousand with which he landed, and 40 horses, some of which were become lame. De Soto here experienced an irreparable loss in the death of John Ortiz, a Spaniard, who had accompanied the previous expedition of Pamphilo de Narvaez, being taken prisoner by the natives of the bay of Spirito Santo, in East Florida, amongst whom he had acquired much of the manners and language of the Indians. Besides his loss as an interpreter, they were likewise bereft of a guide, and made many unnecessary wanderings and errors in their route. They spent 10 days in travelling from Autiamque to a province called Ayays; and came again to a town situated near to the Washita (or the river of Cayas and Autiamque). Here he passed the river by means of a boat which they built on purpose, but for four days after they could not travel for snow. When the snow had now ceased, they went through a wilderness, and a country so enswamped and full of lakes, that they travelled one time a whole day in water from the knee to the stirrup, and sometimes they were obliged to swim. At length, they arrived at a town called Tutelpinco, which was abandoned, and destitute of maize; near to it there passed a lake communicating with the river, by an outlet which now ran with a considerable current.

De Soto spent a whole day in seeking a passage across this lake, and all without success. Returning at night to the town, he met with two Indians, who showed him the passage, which they effected the following day by means of hurdles or rafts of cane. After travelling three days, they came to a town of the territory of Nilco, called Tianto. Here they took 30 natives, and among them two chiefs. De Soto, according to his custom of levying contribution on the natives, dispatched a party beforehand to Nilco, to prevent the Indians from gaining time to carry away their provision. The party passed through three or four large towns, and in the town where the chief resided, which was four miles from where the governor had remained, they found many Indians armed with their bows and arrows, standing apparently on the defensive. But as soon as the Spaniards began to approach, without more ado, they set fire to the house of the chief, and fled over a contiguous lake, which was not fordable for the horses.

The next day they arrived at Nilco, and lodged in the cazique's town, which stood in a prairie, and was inhabited for the space of half a mile. Within three miles were other large towns, well stored with the usual kind of provision. The Spaniards considered this as the best inhabited country which they had seen in Florida, except Coça and Apalache. A deputation came to Soto in the name of the chief, with a present of a garment of fur, and a string of pearls, to which the commander made a suitable return. This Indian promised to return in two days, but never fulfilled his promise, and in the night, the Indians were perceived carrying away their maize, and erecting cabins on the opposite side of the river.

This river, which ran by Nilco, was again recognized as the same which passed by Cayas and Autiamque, and from its contiguity to the Mississippi, appears to have been the Red river. Near to its confluence, was situated what La Vega calls the province of Guachoya. Three days after his arrival at Nilco, the commander came to Guachoya, where he hoped to hear of the sea, and recruit his men while the brigantines should be building, which he intended to dispatch to the Spanish settlements. He took up his residence in the town of the chief, which was fortified with pickets, and situated about a cross-bow shot from the Mississippi.

The chief of Guachoya came to the commander, accompanied by many of his people, who brought presents of fish, dogs, deer skins, and woven garments. He was asked concerning the distance from hence to the sea, to which he could receive no answer, and was, moreover, informed that no more towns or settlements were to be met with on that side of the river in descending. Soto suspecting the truth of this disagreeable information, sent one of his officers with eight horsemen down the river to acquire more certain intelligence, and to learn, if possible, the distance and practicability of proceeding to the sea. This messenger travelled eight days through sunken lands, and was not able to proceed in all that time more than about 30 miles, in consequence of the obstruction of bayous, cane brakes, and almost impenetrable forests, which were entirely destitute of habitations.

At this news, as well as at the desperate situation of his affairs, the commander fell sick with despondence. But previous to taking to his bed, he sent an Indian messenger to the chief of Quigalta, to declare to him, that he was of the offspring of the sun (a pretention which was supported by the princes of the Natchez), and that, as such, he had been every where obeyed and served; that he requested him to accept of his friendship, and visit him, as he would be gratified by his presence; and that, as a mark of his esteem and obedience, he hoped he would bring something with him, of that which was most esteemed in his country; to which, however, the chief returned the following independent answer:

"That as to his relation with the sun, he would believe it if he would dry up the river. He paid no visits, but, on the contrary, received obedience and tribute, either willingly or by force, from all the people with which he was acquainted. Therefore, if he desired an interview, it would be most proper for him to pay the visit. If his intentions were peaceable, he would be received with hospitality, but if he wished for war, he could attend him in the town where he now resided, but that, for him, or any other mortal, he would not step back a foot."

When the messenger returned with this unexpected answer, the governor was confined to his bed, and sick of a fever, but expressed a mortification that he was not immediately prepared to cross the river (Mississippi), which was here very rapid, and chastise the pride of this chief of Quigalta. [16] The river is here described as being a mile in width, and 16 fathoms deep, having both banks thickly inhabited by the natives.

The enterprising Soto, sensible of the approach of death, called around him the officers of his ruined army, and, in their presence, appointed Louis de Mososco de Alvarado their succeeding captain general and governor. The following day, the 21st of May, 1542, Ferdinand de Soto died, near to the confluence of Red river with the Mississippi. Mososco, now reduced to stratagem, determined to conceal his death from the natives, because that Soto had made them believe that the Christians were immortal, and because they were impressed with a high opinion of his vigilance and valour, and, seeing him now removed by death, they might be instigated to take up arms against the miserable handful of troops that

[16]From the geographical situation, this aboriginal province must have been that of the Natchez. —NUTTALL. [In what follows, read Moscoso for Mososco.]

remained. Knowing the inconstancy of their friendship, and their credulity, de Soto made them believe he possessed the art of prying into their inmost secrets, without their knowledge; and, that the figure which appeared in a mirror, which he showed them, disclosed to him all their intentions, by which means they were often deterred from practising treachery against him.

Mososco, after concealing the body of Soto for three days, had him at length removed and buried in the secrecy of the night, near one of the gates of the town within the wall. The Indians, however, having seen him sick, suspected what in truth had happened; and, passing by the place of his interment, where the earth was fresh, the circumstance became a matter of conversation among them, in consequence of which, Mososco had the body disinterred in the night, and wrapt up with a ballast of sand, and committed to the deep of the river. At length, the chief of Guachoya inquired for Soto, and was informed by Mososco, that he was gone for a while to heaven, as he had often done before, and because his stay was now to be protracted for a considerable time, he had appointed him to fill his place in the interim. The chief, still, however, believed that he was dead, and ordered two handsome Indians to be brought and sacrificed, according to their custom on the death of a chief, in order that they might wait upon him hereafter. Mososco still insisted, that de Soto was not dead, but gone to heaven, and that of his own soldiers, he had taken such as were necessary to serve him, and desiring the Indians to be loosed, advised the chief hereafter to desist from such an inhuman practice. Upon this, the intended victims being set at liberty, one of them refused to return with his chief because of his inhumanity, and attached himself to Mososco.

After some deliberation concerning their intended route, they came, at length, to the conclusion of attempting a passage to New Spain over land, as more practicable than the way by sea. After passing through several Indian towns whose names are now unintelligible, we find him, at length, among the Naguatex (or Natchitoches).

After proceeding in a western direction, about 300 miles from the Mississippi, they came to a river called Daycao, which Purchas conjectures to be the Rio del Oro of Cabeza de Vaca. From hence, after encountering the inclemencies and hardships of the commencing winter, they found it necessary to return to the confluence of Red river and the Missis-

sippi, as it was impossible for them to subsist among the wandering natives of the sterile wilderness they were approaching, and over which, the
natives themselves merely migrated and hunted, being destitute of any
supply of maize, and spending a wandering life, like that of the Arabs,
subsisting upon the Tunas (prickly pears), and roots of the plains.

Having returned to Minoya, considerably reduced by a sickness, which
bordered on the typhus fever, they commenced building boats for the
purpose of descending the Mississippi to the sea. In the month of March,
though there had not been rain previous for a month, the river took such a
rise, that in its overflow it reached to Nilco, 18 miles distant, and from
the natives, Mososco understood that the flood was equally extensive on
the opposite side. In the town occupied by the Spaniards, which was
somewhat elevated, the water reached to the stirrups on horseback; and
for two months they never stirred out of their houses, except on horseback or in canoes.

From an Indian, who was tortured for the purpose, Mososco learnt,
that the caziques of Nilco, Guachoya, Taguanate, and others, to the
number of about 20 chiefs, commanding many people, had determined to
fall upon him by treachery. The signal for the destruction of the Spaniards
on which they had agreed, was the time of making a present to the commander. The Indian, who gave this information, was detained in close
confinement, and the day arriving for the delivery of the first presents, 30
Indians appearing with fish, Mososco ordered their right hands to be cut
off, and sent them back in this condition to their chief. He also sent word
to the cazique of Guachoya, that he and the rest of the conspirators might
come when they pleased, as he was prepared for them, and could readily
divine all their intentions as soon as thought of. This circumstance threw
them into consternation, and the chiefs respectively came forward to excuse themselves.

Their boats being finished in the month of June, the summer flood
again visited the town, and without any farther trouble, the boats were
now launched and conveyed into the Mississippi. They shipped 22 of the
best horses which they had in the camp, and of the rest they made provision. They left Minoya on the second of July, 1543, being now reduced
to 320 men, who occupied seven brigantines. They were 17 days in
descending to the sea, which they considered to be a distance of about 500

miles from the place of their departure; and, indeed, pretty well corresponding with the present estimated distance. In the course of their descent, they were repeatedly attacked by the natives.

On the 18th of July, they arrived in the gulf with a fair wind, and continued with a moderate breeze for two days, to their great astonishment still in fresh water, and were greatly tormented by musquetoes. After coasting two and fifty days, they at length arrived in the river of Panuco the 10th of September, 1543, and were in all 311 men.

Such is a brief sketch of this memorable expedition, which opened the northern hemisphere of the New World to the enterprize and industry of the Europeans, and whence civilized society has derived far more lasting and important advantages, than could ever have accrued from the mere discovery of the precious metals.

SECTION II

————————

THE HISTORY OF THE NATCHEZ

WE SEE NOTHING, says Charlevoix, in their outward appearance that distinguishes them from the other savages of Canada and Louisiana. They seldom made war, living in quiet possession of their country, and having no ambition to distinguish themselves by conquering their neighbours. Their despotic form of government, accompanied by some taste for parade and courtly magnificence, and the great servility of their subjects, appeared to be the shadow of a departing power, and concomitant population, such as had been unparalleled in the history of the northern natives.

Their great chief pretended to derive his origin from the Sun, which was likewise the principal object of their adoration.[1] He was always chosen from the family of the nearest female relative of his predecessor, and his mother was also invested with considerable power,[2] and considered as an auxiliary chief. She, no less than the Great Sun, dispensed with the lives and liberties of their subjects. The lesser chiefs and the people never

[1]The Hurons also, according to the same author, pretended that their hereditary chiefs were descended from the sun, and continued the descent by the females in the same manner. —NUTTALL.

[2]In a speech made to governor Clinton, in 1788, by Domine Peter, a native orator, on the part of the Senecas and Cayugas, the authority of the female chieftains is acknowledged, by the speaker, and thus apoligized [sic]. "Our ancestors considered it a great offence to reject the counsels of their women, particularly (that) of the female governesses (or chieftains). They were esteemed the mistresses of the soil (as they solely attended to the labours of agriculture). Who, said they, bring us into being? Who cultivate our lands, kindle our fires (or administer food to the calls of hunger), but our women? &c." *Governor Clinton's Discourse, December,* 1811, *App. p.* 80.

As the mothers of the slain in battle, the women had the controul of prisoners, either to adopt or destroy them at will, and their interposition to procure peace, and stay hostilities, was universally acknowledged. We have a remarkable example of this in the history of the Delawares, who, at the instigation of the Iroquois, became a nation of mediators, and were thus said to have assumed one of the distinguishing functions of the female sex, and were, consequently, debarred from active war and masculine distinction. *See Heckewelder's History of the Delawares, in the report of the Historical Committee of the American Philosophical Society.* —NUTTALL.

approached them without uttering three salutations, in a loud and mournful tone, which it was necessary to repeat on retiring, and also to walk out from their presence backwards. Even when they happened to meet them, they were obliged to arrange themselves on either side of the path, and repeat the customary salutation as they passed. Their subjects likewise brought them the best of their harvests, of their hunting, and their fishing. And no person, not even their nearest relatives, or those of noble families, when invited to eat with them, had a right to put their hand to the same dish, or to drink out of the same vessel.

Every morning, as the sun appeared, the great chief came to the door of his cabin, and turning himself towards the East, bowed to the earth, and howled three successive times. A pipe dedicated to this purpose was then brought to him, out of which he smoked tobacco, blowing the fume towards the sun, and the other three quarters of the world.[3]

[3]This, which Sir William Jones considered as the ritual of the Tartars, is also employed by the Sioux or Naudowessies, as I have repeatedly witnessed.

According to the observations of Mr. Wm. Bartram, the Creeks likewise practised the same ceremony.

An invocation not very dissimilar to this sacred ceremony, is that of Agamemnon in the Iliad; thus translated by Pope:

> Then loudly thus before th' attentive bands
> He calls the gods, and spreads his lifted hands:
>   O first and greatest power! whom all obey,
> Who high on Ida's holy mountain sway,
> Eternal Jove! and yon *bright orb* that rolls
> From east to west, and views from pole to pole!
> Thou mother *Earth!* and all ye living *Floods;*
> Infernal Furies! and Tartarian Gods;
> ————————Hear and be witness.
>
> *Pope's Iliad,* Book III. lines 344–354.

According to Humboldt, in his Monumens de l'Amerique, vol. ii. pp. 54 and 55, the Mexican cycle of 52 years was divided into four indictions of 13 years, in reference to the *four seasons* of the year, the *four elements,* and the *cardinal points.* The most ancient division of the zodiac, according to Albategnius,* is that into four parts. "These four signs," he adds, "of the equinoxes and the solstices, chosen from a series of 20 signe" (the number of days in the Mexican month), "recal to mind the four *royal stars,* Aldebaran, Regulus, Antares, and Fomahault, celebrated in all Asia, and presiding over the seasons.† In the new continent, the indictions of the cycle of 52 years, formed, as we would say, the four seasons of the *grand year,* and the Mexican astrologers were pleased to see presiding over each period of 13 years one of the four equinoctial or solstitial signs." —NUTTALL.

*De Scientia Stellarum, cap. 2 (ed. Bonon. 1645) p. 3. —NUTTALL.
†Firmicus, lib. vi. c. 1. —NUTTALL.

The actions of the Great Chief were allowed to be without impeachment; and his life, according to an ancient and solemn compact, could never become forfeited by his crimes. Indeed the death of the Great Sun was considered the greatest national calamity which could happen, and superstition had brought it to be considered as an omen of the theocracy, and of the destruction of the world. Their sons were termed nobles, an honour which was likewise attainable by the meritorious of inferior rank. The common people laboured under a degrading appellation, not indeed very different from the French epithet of *canaille,* or our own term the mob, or the vulgar. They carried this distinction even into their language, as there were different modes of addressing the vulgar and nobles.[4]

When either the male or female sun died, all their *allouez,* or intimate attendants, devoted themselves to death, under a persuasion that their presence would be necessary to maintain the dignity of their chief in the future world. The wives and husbands of these chiefs were likewise immolated for the same purpose, and considered it the most honourable and desirable of deaths. More than a hundred victims were sometimes sacrificed to the names of the Great Chief.[5] The same horrible ceremonies, in a more limited degree, were also exercised at the death of the lesser chiefs.

[4]The following example of the noble and common language of the Natchez, is given by Du Pratz.* In calling one of the common people he would say, *aquenan,* that is, "hark ye;" if to a sun or one of the nobles, the address would be *magani,* which also signifies the same. To one of the common people, calling at his house, he would say, *tachte-cabanacte,* "are you there," or "I am glad to see you." To a sun the same thing is expressed by the word *apapegouaiché.* Again, according to their custom, I say to one of the common people, *pechti,* "sit you down;" but to a sun, *caham.* In other respects the language is the same; as the difference of expression seems only to take place in matters relating to the persons of the suns and nobles, to distinguish them from the people. —NUTTALL.

*Hist. Louisian. p. 328. —NUTTALL.

[5]Among the Mexicans, prisoners, rather than domestics and attendants, were devoted to death at the obsequies of the great, as victims to that spirit of revenge so deeply cherished by savage or barbarous nations. So even Achilles, lamenting over the body of Patroclus, says,

> Ere thy dear relics in the grave are laid,
> Shall Hector's head be offer'd to thy shade;
> That, with his arms, shall hang before thy shrine;
> And twelve the noblest of the Trojan line,
> Sacred to vengeance, by this hand expire:
> Their lives effus'd around thy flaming pyre.
>
> *Pope's Iliad,* Book XVIII. lines 391–396.
> —NUTTALL.

At the death of one of their female chiefs, Charlevoix relates, that her husband not being noble was, according to their custom, strangled by the hands of his own son. Soon after, the two deceased being laid out in state, were surrounded by dead bodies of 12 infants, strangled by the order of the eldest daughter of the late female chief, and who had now succeeded to her dignity. Fourteen other individuals were also prepared to die and accompany the deceased. On the day of interment, as the procession advanced, the fathers and mothers who had sacrificed their children, preceding the bier, threw the bodies upon the ground at different distances, in order that they might be trampled upon by the bearers of the dead. The corpse arriving in the temple where it was to be interred, the 14 victims now prepared themselves for death by swallowing pills of tobacco and water, and were then strangled by the relations of the deceased, and their bodies cast into the common grave, and covered with earth.

The Natchez, together with the remains of the Grigras and Thioux, who had become incorporated with them, did not, in 1720, amount to more than 1200 warriors.[6] Only six or seven years prior to this period, their warriors were estimated at 4000. This rapid decrease they attributed to the prevalence of contagious diseases, by which they had been wasted, for it does not appear that they were ever addicted to war, having long lived in peace with the neighbouring nations, who venerated their sacred institutions, and acknowledged their political ascendancy and power. Their dominion once extended from the borders of bayou Manchac to the banks of the Ohio, and they numbered not less than 500 suns or caziques. Descended from, and confederated with them, were the Taensas of the Mobile, and the Chetimashas of bayou Placquemine, remnants of whom still exist, not far from the sites where they were first found by the French colonists, and against whom they waged an unsuccessful war.

The Natchez had a distinct tradition of migrating to the Mississippi, from the coast of the Gulf of Mexico, at two distinct periods of time. A part of the nation (probably about the period of the first establishment of the Mexican monarchy) fled from the threatening oppression of their natural enemies, and living in undisturbed tranquillity for several generations in their newly acquired territory, they became very populous, and were only joined by the Great Sun after the arrival and invasion of the

[6]Du Pratz Hist. Louisian. p. 313 (*Ed. Lond.*). —NUTTALL.

Spaniards, with whom at first they had entered into an alliance. As to their ultimate oriental origin, it appears to be merely connected with their presumption of a descent from the sun, which first illuminates the eastern hemisphere. It was this superstition which proved so fatal to the Mexicans, who venerated as a celestial race the Spanish conquerors, because they had arrived from the region of the rising sun. Traces of the natural worship of the two great luminaries of day and night, were every where visible throughout the regions of the New World, and continue to be practised by those who are still unbiassed by the influence of the European nations.[7] The Hurons, no less than the Muyscas of the plain of Bogata, in

---

[7]The great Deity of the savages of the river Bourbon, and the river St. Therese, Hudson's Bay, is the sun. When they deliberate on any important affair, they make him, as it were, smoke. They assemble at day-break in a cabin of one of their chiefs, who, after having lighted his pipe, presents it three times to the rising sun; then he guides it with both hands from the east to the west, praying the sun to favour the nation. This being done, all the assembly smoke in the same pipe. *Charlevoix, Hist. Journ. p.* 108 (Ed. Lond.). The Sioux also practise the same rites.

Gookin, in 1674, says, "Some, for their God, adore the sun; others the moon; some the earth, others the fire, and like vanities. Yet, generally, they acknowledge one great supreme doer of good; and him they call Woonand or Mannitt; another, that is, the great doer of evil or mischief; and him they call Mattand, which is the Devil, &c." Compare this relation with the invocation of Agamemnon, already quoted, from which it scarcely differs in any particular.

Traces of the adoration of the sun are discoverable also in Colden's History of the Five Nations, not only among the Iroquois, but also with the neighbouring nations: thus among the attestations to a treaty of peace made with the Iroquois, by a band of the Utawas, we find the following. "Let the sun, as long as he shall endure, always shine upon us in friendship." With which apostrophe was delivered a figure of the sun, sculptured of red marble.* A similar figure was again presented to the Five Nations by the Utawas and a branch of the Hurons (called Dionondadies) jointly, in another treaty concluded between them.†

At a treaty in which general Harrison assisted, towards the commencement of the last war, the council-house being crowded, a chief arriving late was suffered to stand some time unheeded, until the general sent him a chair, as from his father. He refused the offer, saying, probably in allusion to their ancient belief, "The sun is my father, the earth my mother, and my seat is the ground."

The sacred, or eternal, fire is also described in the following incidental remark, made by a chief speaker of the Five Nations: "Before the Christians arrived amongst us, the general council of the Five Nations was held at Onondago, where there has, from the beginning (or from the remotest time) been kept a fire continually burning, made of two great logs whose flame was never extinguished."‡ —NUTTALL.

---

*Colden's Hist. Five Nations, third edition, i. p. 115. —NUTTALL.

†Ibid. i. p. 185. —NUTTALL.

‡Ibid. vol. i. p. 176. —NUTTALL.

the equatorial regions, personified the moon in their female deity, Atahentsic, who was the mother of the fratricide Jouskeka, or the sun,[8] betwixt whom were divided the powers of good and evil. The moon possessing the attributes of Hecate, and the sun those of Phoebus, Apollo, or Osiris the brother of Isis, or the moon.[9]

The great ritual of this religion, which obtained throughout America, is the pipe which was filled with the inebriating tobacco, and smoked in offering to this great luminary, and to the four quarters, or the surrounding horizon of the visible world, which it illuminates. Associated with this adoration, as simple as natural, was that of preserving an eternal fire in some sacred place appropriated to this purpose, as well as for the celebra-

[8]Charlevoix, Hist. Journ. 1. 249. (*Ed. Lond.*). —NUTTALL.

[9]In ancient times, before the moon accompanied the earth (says the mythology of the Muyscas or Mozcas Indians), the inhabitants of the plain of Bogota lived like barbarians, naked, without agriculture, without laws, and without worship. Suddenly there appeared among them an aged man, who came from the plains east of the Cordillera of Chingasa: he seemed to be of a different race from that of the indigenes, for he had a long and tufted beard. He was known by three different names; under that of *Bochica*, *Nemquetheba*, and *Zuhe*. This aged person, after the manner of Manco-Capac, taught men to clothe themselves, to construct dwellings, to cultivate the earth, and to unite in society. He brought with him a woman, to whom tradition gave also the three names of *Chia*, *Yubecayguaya*, and *Haythaca*. This female was of an uncommon beauty, but exceedingly wicked, counteracting her husband in every thing which he undertook for the good of men. By her magic art she swelled the river Funzha to such a degree, that the water inundated the whole valley of Bogota. This deluge destroyed the greatest part of the inhabitants, a few only escaping upon the summits of the neighbouring mountains. The old man, irritated, drove the beautiful Haythaca from the earth; she then became the moon, which, from that period, commenced to enlighten our planet during the night. Afterwards Bochica, son of the sun, taking pity on the men who were dispersed upon the mountains, broke, with his powerful hand, the rocks which close the valley on the side of Canaos and Tequendama. By this opening he carried off the water of the lake of Funzha, reunited again the people of the valley of Bogota, constructed towns, introduced the *worship of the sun*, nominated two chiefs, between whom he divided the ecclesiastic and secular power, and then retired, under the name of *Idacanzas*, into the sacred valley of Iraca, near to Tanja, where he devoted himself to exercises of the most austere penance, for the space of two thousand years. *Humboldt's Vues des Cordillères, et Monumens des Peuples indigènes de l'Amérique*. Vol. I. pp. 87,88. (Ed. Octavo.).

The Jouskeka, who destroyed his brother, and the Atahentsic of the Hurons, also, in some measure, resemble the Cihuacohuatl or woman of the serpent, adored by the Mexicans, and figured in their hieroglyphic paintings. This goddess was regarded as the mother of the human race, and in the painting alluded to, published by Humboldt, she is accompanied familiarly by a serpent, and in the same symbolical sketch there are two smaller figures engaged in combat, as if to designate the Cain and Abel of the Hebrews, and which were considered in Mexico as the children of the female deess. *Humboldt*, vol. I. pp. 235, 236. —NUTTALL.

tion of their festivals and deliberative councils. The pipe was brought forward on every solemn occasion, and to ratify every serious pledge of peace, integrity, and friendship. The rites of hospitality, sanctioned by this ceremony, were irrefragable, as well as every commercial and political contract. The Hurons say, that the Indian nations derived the sacred pipe from the great luminary to whom it is dedicated, and, that it was first presented to the western nation of the Pawnees,[10] a tradition which I have found corroborated by the nation of the Mandans and the Minitarees. Those people, as well as the Naudowessies, influenced by an idolatrous regard for the sun, make offerings of the most valuable effects,[11] and, occasionally, even of the lives of their prisoners. The Mexicans immolated hosts of human victims to their cruel and imaginary deities.

If the Natchez refrained from cruel offerings to their gods, they failed not to sacrifice many human victims at the death of their caziques, who pretended to derive their origin from the sun.

In their other superstitions, manners, and customs, they differ too little from the rest of the aborigines to tolerate the repetition. Their peculiar usages are in some degree still kept up by those confederated tribes which we call the Creeks or Muskogolgees, to whom they appear to have been more intimately related, than any other of the remaining aborigines. Among these people fire is still venerated, and the appearance of the new moon announced with festivity and gladness. According to the relation of my venerable friend, Wm. Bartram, there existed also among them a language of distinction and of honour, and an aristocratic acknowledgment of superior and inferior order in their society.

The occasion of that signal depopulation which the Natchez had experienced, when first discovered by the French, must ever remain in unaccountable uncertainty. The prevalence of fatal and contagious diseases at one period more than another, is scarcely admissible in a country which had ever exhibited the same aspect, and amongst a people who had never inhabited crowded towns or cities. From the migratory and unsettled character of the more northern natives, and their acknowledged

[10]Charlevoix, p. 133. —NUTTALL.

[11]They present robes of the bison painted with the rays of the sun, exposing them upon poles, set up in the prairies. —NUTTALL.

superiority in arms, particularly the Iroquois, with whom they warred,[12] may be with more probability deduced the real cause of this destruction. The valley of the Ohio, and the interior of Kentucky and Tennessee, still exhibit unequivocal and numerous remains of a vast population, who had begun to make some imperfect advances towards power and civilization. Works were constructed for public benefit, which required the united energy, skill, and labour of a devoted multitude. We, in vain, look for similar subordination among the existing natives; by their own tradition they destroyed this race, as foreigners, and gained possession of their country and their fortresses, abandoning them as the barbarians of the north did the cities of Europe, and thus prostrating every advance which had been made beyond the actual limits of savage life.

These devoted people, the Mexicans of the north, were not, however, relieved by their acquaintance with the civilized world. They had peaceably suffered the French to settle around them, and assisted them when in the utmost want and necessity. They thus saved the lives of those, who were about to prove their mortal enemies and oppressors.

The first quarrel which took place betwixt the French and Natchez, in the year 1722, was occasioned by the insolence and injustice of a common soldier of the fort, who, demanding in an unreasonable manner a debt from an aged warrior of the White Apple village, proceeded by unjust pretences to instigate the guard to shoot him, which proved mortal, and for which rashness he received from the commander nothing more than a reprimand.

The village, determined on revenge, fell upon two Frenchmen in their neighbourhood, and last upon the settlement of St. Catharine. The great chief, however, called the Stung Serpent, at the entreaty of the commandant of Fort Rosalie, succeeded in producing a cessation of hostilities, and soon afterwards a peace.

Notwithstanding this favourable posture of affairs, M. De Biainville, the governor, violating every principle of honour and of justice, a few months afterwards, in the midst of peace, surprised the unfortunate Natchez of the offending village, and falling upon them in cold-blooded

[12]When La Salle was among the Natchez, in 1683, he saw a party of that people, who had been on an expedition against the Iroquois. Tonti's account of La Salle's Expedition (Ed. Lond.), p. 112. —NUTTALL.

treachery, obliged them to give up their aged chief, whose head he had demanded of his people.

Some years after this affair, the tyranny and injustice of the Sieur de Chopart, who commanded the post of Natchez, had nearly proved fatal to the whole of the French settlement in Louisiana. Soon after arriving at the post, he projected forming an eminent settlement, in order to gratify his ambition, and amongst all the situations which he examined, none could satisfy him but the village of the White Apple, which was not less than a square league in extent. The commandant, without further ceremony, ordered the chief to remove his huts and his people, as soon as possible, to some other quarter. To which the Sun of the Apple deliberately replied, that his ancestors had lived in that village for almost as many years as there were hairs in his head, and that therefore they had a just right to continue there unmolested.

The Sun, without making any impression on the mind of the inexorable Chopart, withdrew, and assembled the council of his village, who represented to the commandant that, at present, their corn was only shooting, and if now neglected, would be lost both to themselves and the French, who were not numerous enough to tend it. But this excuse, though just and reasonable, was menacingly rejected.

At length, the old men proposed to the commandant, to be allowed to remain in their village until harvest, and to have time to dry their corn, on condition, that each hut of the village should pay, at a time appointed, a basket of corn and a fowl, a measure which would also afford them time to deliberate on some method of delivering themselves from the tyranny of the French.

This proposal succeeded with the avaricious Chopart, who pretended to grant them this respite as a favour. The Sun and council of the village, now consulted together on the means of ridding themselves and their nation of the French. They entered into a secret conspiracy to destroy the whole settlement at a blow, on that odious day appointed for the delivery of the stipulated tribute. They were also to endeavor to gain over the other neighbouring nations into the plot, in order to complete their success, and accelerate the fatal project.

To obtain uniformity in the execution, bundles of rods, equal in number, were to be delivered to their several allies, and also retained by themselves in the recess of their temple; one of which was to be withdrawn and broken each day, until the accomplishment of the stated period.[13]

The secret councils which were held among the nobles and elders, gave some alarm to the people, and aroused the curiosity of the Stung Arm, mother to the Grand Sun, who, at length, wrung from this chief the fatal secret. Influenced either by caprice or compassion, she destroyed the concert of the execution, which was to have been seconded by the Choctaws, by withdrawing a number of the rods, and so hastening the approaching time of the massacre. All the warnings which she gave to the commander and other individuals, were treated with disdain, as the effects of fear and cowardice.

On the eve of St. Andrew, 1729, the Natchez left their towns preparatory to the execution of their plot, and to show their contempt for the commandant, they had left his execution in the hands of one of the vulgar, who was armed with a wooden hatchet, no warrior deigning to kill him. At the time appointed, the massacre became general and instantaneous, and of about 700 persons, but few escaped to bear the fatal intelligence to New Orleans, the capital.

The Choctaws were greatly displeased at the acceleration of the period appointed for the accomplishment of the plot by the Natchez, and were, in consequence, easily induced, soon afterwards, to join the French against them. Arriving early in the following spring, the troops appointed by M. Perier, then governor of Louisiana, joined by the Choctaws, made their attack on the fort of the Natchez. After the lapse of several days employed in firing without any great effect, the besieged, fearing the worst, began to sue for peace, and offered as a condition to deliver up all their prisoners. The Natchez gaining time by these offers of pacification, took advantage of the following night, and evacuated their fort with all their families, baggage and plunder.

After the Natchez had abandoned the fort, it was demolished to the ground.

[13]This method of recording the lapse of time was also practised by the Chicasas and Muskogolgees, according to the relation of Adair. —NUTTALL.

A short time after their flight, determined on revenge against the To-nicas, who were allies of the French, they destroyed them by stratagem, under pretence of offering them terms of peace.

The Natchez had now abandoned the east side of the Mississippi, and fortified themselves near to Silver creek connected with the Washita.

M. Perier and his brother, with a considerable armament penetrated to the retreat of the unfortunate Natchez, who, struck with terror at the sight of their relentless and formidable enemies, shut themselves up in their fort, and abandoned themselves to despair and desperation. Soon after the battery had commenced, a bomb happening to fall in the midst of their fort amongst the women and children, they were so struck with terror and grief at the cries of the helpless, that they instantly made the signal of capitulation. They, however, started difficulties again to obtain time. The night was granted them, and they attempted a second flight, but were, for the greatest part, checked and obliged to retire into the fort. Those who did escape, joined a party who were out a hunting, and they altogether retired to the Chicasaws. [14] The rest surrendered themselves prisoners, among whom were the Grand Sun, and the female chiefs; they were carried to New Orleans in slavery, and there consigned to prison, but were shortly after sold in the king's plantations. Bent upon their annihila-tion, the French afterwards transported them to St. Domingo, and in this way terminated the fate of the Natchez as a nation, whose only fault was that of patriotism, and an inviolable love of rational liberty.

It appears that the small party who had sought refuge among the Chicasaws, still insecure from the bitter hostilities of the French, had at last retired into the country of the Creeks; and, at this time occupy a small village called Natchez, on the banks of the Tallipoosee, whose chief, Coweta, fought under the banners of general Jackson. Their language (said to be destitute of the letter r), and their positive affinities to any existing nation of the aborigines, has never yet been ascertained, and remains open to the inquiries of the curious, who will not probably long enjoy the advantage of contemplating the character of this feeble fragment of a once numerous, powerful, and rational people.

[14]Mr. Brackenridge adds, that, after the defeat by Perire, about 200 of the Natchez fortified themselves some distance up Red river, but were attacked and destroyed by St. Dennis. *Hist. Louisiana.* p. 44. —NUTTALL.

SECTION III

OBSERVATIONS ON THE CHICASAWS AND CHOCTAWS

The Chicasaws and Choctaws, who speak a language considerably related, entertain a tradition in common with the Iroquois, the Delawares, the Illinois, and most of the nations of North America, of having once migrated from the west, and crossed the Mississippi to their present residence. They are said to derive their name from two distinguished leaders, Choctawby and Chicasawby, who instigated their warlike and political movements. These personal appellations were frequently employed by the aborigines in the time of Soto, who speaks, for example, of the Kaskaskias and others by those who then held the rule, as the cazique or chief of Casqui, of Nilco, of Cayas, &c., all which, as far as still recognizable, have passed very improperly into so many epithets apparently national, but which were, in fact, as we discover both by language and confederation, merely so many bands of the same people receding from the residence of the original stock, either through ambitious caprice, enterprize, or necessity. This connection among the Delawares or Lleni-lenapés, affording an easy clue of origin, was always readily acknowledged under the epithets of grandfather, the original stock, and brothers or collateral descendants, by which were designated the receding tribes, and by a mere reference to which, never for a moment disputed, the paternal and ruling authority of the ancient household was universally acknowledged and venerated. From a neglect of this genealogical analysis has arisen that confusion of origin, and those fallacious ideas of Indian nations and languages which many suppose to exist; as if the human family in America, had ever consisted of as many paltry and radically dismembered fragments, as there were names employed to designate them.

It is not a little singular, that to all inquiries of ultimate residence which have ever been among the American natives, they should so uniformly refer back apparently almost to the same period and the same country. The occasion of this simultaneous migration, however urgent and important, is now perpetually locked in mystery. It was, undoubtedly, instigated by some important human revolution, which appears to have set in motion a vast hive of the human race in search of some more commodious state of subsistence. They were too barbarous to have adventured in quest of pecuniary wealth, and could have had naturally no other object for separation greater than that which slowly dispersed the first patriarchs of the world. Their migrations, as described by the Mexicans, probably took up a period of ages, and the vicissitudes of fortune which attended their progress, unrecorded by the circumstantial pen of history, and limited by chronology, may, probably, contribute to that extraordinary appearance of simultaneous and uninterrupted movement, which was rather carried on through an extended cycle of time, than in the short space requisite to the completion of an expedition. There is one thing, however, certain in regard to the Chicasaws and their collateral bands, that they have for at least the three last centuries occupied the countries in which we still find them. For it was here that they were discovered by De Soto, and where they had not then apparently by any means recently established themselves. On what footing they had resided as near neighbours to the Natchez, I am unable to ascertain; they appear from the first to have been a jealous and hostile nation, and became the bold, cunning, and successful enemies of the whites from their first interview with the Spaniards, who certainly, as wanton invaders, did not act in a way to conciliate the esteem of the natives. The Natchez asserted that they could once number no less than 500 Suns (or chiefs who pretended to derive their origin from that luminary which they adored), and that their possessions extended in a continual line from Natchez to the mouth of the Ohio. Whether they had been dispossessed and reduced to the feeble state in which they were discovered by the French, through the enmity of the Chicasaws, Iroquois, or the Illinois, we cannot now determine, though, from the contiguity of the latter, and their former strength, we should rather conclude them, or the northern confederates, to have been the destroyers of the Natchez, than the Chicasaws, as we find them and the Choctaws to have been the abettors of the Natchez, in their unfortunate contest with the French, yet of a character extremely versatile and revengeful, insomuch that the Choctaws, who had at one time proffered their assistance, withdrew it in favour of their enemies, in consequence of the unforeseen circumstance which to the Natchez prematurely hastened the secret attack they had concerted against their enemies, and which was to have been regulated by the consummation of a period of time, designated by a bundle of rods deposited in the temple, each of which counted for a day. The completion of this fatal period was, however, secretly hastened, to destroy the concert with the Choctaws, by the revengeful sister of the Great Sun, who, resenting the secrecy her brother had observed towards her, withdrew a number of the tallies, and though by this means the main object was not defeated, yet it excited the fatal jealousy and enmity of the Choctaws, who were consequently disconcerted in completing the intended measure of vengeance.

From the high tone in which the chief of Quigalta answered the requisitions of Soto, (and who, occupying the identical spot where Natchez now stands, could, by the concurrence of their traditions, scarcely have been any other than the same people), we perceive their power and independence, although concentrated within narrower limits, still highly respectable.

In the time of Charlevoix, an active war was carried on betwixt the ever restless and rapacious Chicasaws and the Illinois, who, by them and the Iroquois, in the end appear to have been exterminated as a nation.

From the situation which the Chicasaws and their branches occupied on this continent, from the earliest period of history, we may, I think, consider them as among the most ancient of the existing aborigines. To give a more correct idea of their former extent and influence, considered in the most general point of view, I shall bring together their scattered branches, so as to afford a retrospect of the whole. Although we have chosen to speak of the Chicasaw as the principal band, which it now is, in consequence of the reduction or extinction of most of the rest; yet, in point of numbers, the Mobilians, now, I believe, extinct, must have far exceeded the Chicasaws. They were discovered by De Soto, dwelling in the vicinity of the present bay and river of Mobile. Their name, by De Soto, is Mouvill. Unwilling to acknowledge the arbitrary usurpation of their Spanish discoverers, a battle ensued, which, in consequence probably of the inequality of arms and skill, proved very destructive to the

Mouvillians, who lost 2500 men. From so considerable a loss at the first outset, and that without a surprise, it is evident that their numbers must have been considerable. They were nearly extinct in the time of Charlevoix, who, concerning their religious rite of preserving an eternal fire in a temple, remarks, that it appeared probable, the Mobilians had, over all the people of Florida, a kind of primacy of religion, for it was at their sacred fire that the others were obliged to kindle *that*, which, by accident or neglect, had been suffered to go out.[1] In the vicinity of the Mobilians lived also the Chatots, in the time of Du Pratz, occupying a village of about 40 huts. A little north of Fort Louis, on the Mobile, according to the same author, lived the Thomez, who were not more numerous than the Chatots.

To the north of the Apalaches, who gave name to the mountains so called, lived the Alibamas, and to the north of the Alibamas, were the Abeikas and Conchacs, apparently the same people. Their language was scarcely at all different from that of the Chicasaws, and their name of *conchac* is the Chicasaw word for the knives which they formerly made of sharpened splits of cane.

The Aquelou Pissas, formerly living within three or four miles of the site of New Orleans, had removed, in the time of Du Pratz, to the borders of lake Ponchartrain.

Upon the Yazoo river, lived the Chacchi-oumas (or Red Cray-fish), consisting of about 50 huts. Not far from them, also dwelt the Oufe-Ogoulas (or the Nation of the Dog), occupying about 60 huts. The Tapoussas likewise lived upon the banks of this river, and had not more than 25 cabins. These, as well as the Oumas of the Mississippi, who still lived on the present site of the great plantation of General Wade Hampton, in the time of the author already mentioned, did not use the letter *r* in their language, and, as well as all the above named natives, appeared to be branches of the Chicasaws, as they spoke either that language or its dialects.

Most part of these small nations, after joining the Natchez in their unsuccessful plot against the French, retired among the Chicasaws, and were finally incorporated with them.

The language of the Chicasaws, it appears, was not unknown on the

[1]Charlevoix's Hist. Journ. p. 323. —NUTTALL.

western side of the Mississippi: the Caddoes or Cadoda-quioux, divided into several extensive branches, as well as the Natchitoches, although possessed of a peculiar language, as well as all the Indians of Louisiana generally, were more or less acquainted with the Chicasaw or Mobilian.[2] And it was, no doubt, from this circumstance that John Ortiz, who had escaped the fate of the adventurers of Pamphilo de Narvaez, and who was discovered by De Soto living among the Indians of East Florida, rendered himself so easily understood throughout the whole of the extensive route which was pursued by Soto.

From the earliest settlement of the French on the borders of the Mississippi, the Chicasaws evinced a hostile disposition, which, indeed, they had probably cherished from their ancestors, who had severely punished the little army of De Soto. Their hostility is attributed by Charlevoix to the friendship which subsisted between the French and the Illinois, their enemies. They appear, however, afterwards to have remained neutral, and would have continued so, had not the tyrannical Biainville commenced hostilities against them, for the customary hospitality which they had shewn to the unfortunate remains of the Natchez, whom they had received and adopted. To the requisitions of Biainville to give up the Natchez, whom he was bent on exterminating, the Chicasaws answered, that the Natchez having sought their protection, had been received and adopted by them, so that they now constituted but one people. If Biainville, said they, had received our enemies, should we demand them? or, if we did, would they be given up?

Without listening to reason, Biainville commenced warlike preparations against the Chicasaws. Supplies of ammunition were sent up the Mississippi to the post of Illinois, desiring the commandant to equip as many of the Indians, inhabitants, and troops, as possible, to join him at the Chicasaws, by the 10th of the following May. The Indians attempted in vain to surprise the convoy, which, proceeding in safety to the fort at the mouth of the Arkansa, left the gunpowder there without any manifest reason, which Artaguette, the commandant at Illinois, understanding, from those who had neglected to convey it, immediately sent down a boat for the purpose of obtaining it, which was taken by a party of the Chicasaws, after killing all the crew except two individuals, whom they made slaves.

[2]Du Pratz's Hist. Louisiana, p. 318. —NUTTALL.

In the mean time, Biainville proceeding to fort Mobile, engaged the Choctaws to join him as mercenaries.

On the 10th of March, 1736, the troops being assembled, began their march the 2d of April, and arrived at Tombecbee on the 20th, where they fortified their camp, and remained till the 4th of May, detained by a conspiracy among themselves to destroy the commandant and garrison. The Choctaws, who joined them, were about 1200 in number, and commanded by their principal chief.

On the 26th of May, they marched to the fort of the Chicasaws, crossing an adjoining rivulet of considerable depth; the fort defended the village, which was situated upon an agreeable plain. This defensive position was thrown up on an eminence with an easy ascent, around it stood several huts, and others at a greater distance, which appeared to have been put in a state of defence; and close to the fort ran a little brook, which watered a part of the plain.

On approaching the fort they observed four Englishmen enter it, and that the British flag was flying. The attack was made, and obstinately maintained for a considerable time on both sides, but greatly to the disadvantage of the French. The Indians, protected by a strong stockade, were under cover from every attack, and could have defended themselves by their loop-holes. In addition to which, they formed a gallery of flat pallisadoes quite round, covered with earth, which screened it from the effects of grenadoes. Thus the troops, after lavishing their ammunition against the wooden posts of the Indian fort, were obliged to retreat, with the loss of 32 men killed, and almost 70 wounded; and, abandoning the country, retired to fort Mobile, from whence the militia and Indians were disbanded.

Mr. Artaguette, with his Illinois troops and Indian allies, arriving in the Chicasaw country on the 9th of May, waited the arrival of the French until the 21st, when, hearing nothing of them, and fearful of the impatience of the Indians, made the attack with success, at first, having forced the Chicasaws to quit their village and fort. They also attacked another village with the same success, but hurried away in the pursuit, M. d'Artaguette received two wounds, which caused him and a small body of his men, 46 soldiers and two sergeants, to be abandoned by the Indians, and, after defending their commander all that day, they were at last obliged to surrender. The troops under Biainville having retired, and the Indians consequently finding no opportunity of gaining a ransom for their prisoners, put them all to death by slow fire, except a sergeant, who, meeting with an indulgent master, found means to make his escape.

Biainville, desirous to take vengeance upon the Chicasaws, wrote both to France and Canada, requesting succours.

The reinforcements having arrived from France, proceeded up the Mississippi to the Cliffs of Prud'homme, now called the Chicasaw Bluffs, where they landed, and fortified their encampment, which was situated on a fine plain, and called fort Assumption, in commemoration of the day on which they landed.

They made wagons and sledges, and cleared out roads for the conveyance of cannon, ammunition, and every thing necessary for forming a regular siege. They were also immediately reinforced by the forces which they had requested from Canada, consisting of a mixed multitude of French, Iroquois, Hurons, Epsingles, Algonquins, and other nations, led by the commandant of the Illinois, with the garrison inhabitants and neighbouring Indians, as many as could be brought together, and furnished with a considerable number of horses.

This formidable army, the greatest that had ever been seen in the interior of America, remained in camp without undertaking any thing, from the month of August, 1739, to the succeeding month of March. Provisions, which were at first in plenty, became at last so scarce, that they were obliged to eat up the horses, which were intended to draw the artillery, ammunition, and provisions. They were also seriously attacked by sickness, which at length inclined M. Biainville to have recourse to mild methods. He therefore attached a small body of troops and Canadian Indians against the Chicasaws, with orders to make offers of peace to them in his name, if they were inclined to sue for it.

What the general had foreseen did indeed happen. For no sooner had the Chicasaws seen the French, followed by the Indians of Canada, then they apprehended the approach of the rest of the numerous army, and making signals of peace, came out of their fort in the most humble manner, hazarding all the consequences of such an exposure, in the hope of obtaining peace. They solemnly protested an inviolable friendship to the French, and avowed that they had been instigated by the English to take up arms against them, and seeing their error they had already separated from them, and had, at that very time, two of that nation whom they had made slaves, and of the truth of which assertion, they might, if they pleased, now satisfy themselves.

Lieutenant de St. Laurent, accompanied by a young slave, therefore, went in order to ascertain the truth of their professions; as he passed through the village, the women were heard to demand him as a sacrifice to their hatred, but were prevented by the men from offering him any injury. Peace was now instantly concluded, and a few days after, they accompanied the commander of the detachment in a considerable body, to carry the pipe of peace to the French governor, and to deliver up the two Englishmen. They behaved before M. Biainville with the utmost submission, and offered, if necessary, to attest their friendship by making war upon the English. Thus concluded the war of the French with the Chicasaws, about the beginning of April, 1740.

In the revolutionary war with Great Britain, they appear to have sided with the republicans; and displayed considerable fidelity and courage in the late war against the Creeks, under the command of general Jackson.

After the Iroquois, we are not acquainted with any nation of the aborigines of North America, who have been so restless and enterprising as the Chicsaws, and who have better maintained their ground against every species of hostility. They have not only, says Du Pratz, cut off a great many nations who were adjoining them, but have even carried their love of war and vengeance as far as New Mexico, near 600 miles from the place of their residence, to exterminate a nation that had removed to that distance from them. In this enterprise they were, however, deceived and cut off.

The Choctaws, still equally numerous, reckoned, in the time of Du Pratz, 25,000 warriors. We know but little of them more than a few detached customs, and the tradition, that they had made a sudden arrival in the country which they now occupy. There is a small village of them in the vicinity of the town of Arkansas, but made up principally of those, who had rendered themselves obnoxious to the rest of the nation, who, probably, as well as the Cherokees and Creeks, have found the necessity of introducing corporeal and general punishments, for the benefit and security of society.

As we cannot discover any mention of them by the historian of De Soto, they were perhaps, at that period, included amongst the Chicasaws. And, from the extinction of the Mobilians and other nations, met with by that adventurer, we are inclined to believe them the modern usurpers of the country which they now possess. Many of them live on the borders of the Yazoo, and other parts of the Mississippi and Louisiana territories. It is certain, as we have had already occasion to notice, that they made war against the Chicasaws, in aid of the French, and that, though they professed to aid the cause of the Natchez, yet that afterwards, through mere jealousy, they had joined with the French against them.

The Choctaws, till very late years, had a practice, not indeed peculiar, of exposing their dead upon scaffolds till such time as the flesh decayed, which was then separated from the bones by a set of old men, who devoted themselves to this custom, and were called "bone-pickers," after which, the bones were interred in some place set apart for the purpose.

This custom unquestionably arose out of a veneration for the deceased, and an attachment to their remains, which, among a wandering and unsettled people, were thus conveniently removed. A circumstance of this kind is related by Charlevoix,[3] where the Indians on removing their village, carried with them also the bones of their dead.

[3]Historical Journal, p. 334. (*Ed. Lond.*). —NUTTALL.

—◆—

THERMOMETRICAL OBSERVATIONS IN THE ARKANSA TERRITORY, DURING THE YEAR 1819

		A.M.	deg.	P.M.	deg.
January	20	12	67		
	21	12	67		
March	9	12	50		
	10	12	50		
	12	8	66	3	76
	13		48	3	60
	14		48	3	56
	15		56	3	73
	16	8	28	5	34
	17	8	34	3	48
	18	8	42	3	50
	19	8	38	2	50
	20	8	48	3	58
	21	6	22	5	48
	22	8	48	3	66
	23	7	60	3	72
	24	6	60	2	70
	25	7	54	4	78
	26	7	42	5	64
	27	8	46	1	66
	28	7	52	3	54
	29	6	60	2	54
	30	7	40	3	44
March	31	6½	32	12	58
April	1	7	48	2	68
	2	6½	58	3	60
	3	7	52	2	64
	4	7½	44	2	60

		A.M.	deg.	P.M.	deg.
	5	7	40	2	70
	6	7	50	1	70
	7	6½	60	2	76
				at 7	76
	8	7	64	2	74
	9	7	56	2	66
	10	7	60	1	64
	11	7	52	3	76
	12	7	54	2	74
	13	7	62	3	76
	14	7	64	2	74
	15	7	64	3	78
	16	7	64	3	66
	17	. 7	54	3	70
	18	10	56	4	65
	19	8	54	2	70
	20	6	60	1	74
	21	6	62	3	76
	22		66	6	70
	23	6	56	1	76
	24	6	62	3	72
	25	6	56	2	78
April	26	7	63	3	70
	27	6	56	3	77
	28	6	66	9	75
	29	7	69	1	80
				5	80
	30	6	66	12	75
May	1	8	68		
	2	7	60	4	80
	3	7	68	12	82
				7	82
	4	7	68	3	78
	5	7	68	3	76
	6	7	68	3	68
	7	7	68	3	78
	8	7	60	3	66

		A.M.	deg.	P.M.	deg.
	9	8	68	3	70
	10	8	70	3	86
	11	6	77	4	86
	12	8	76	2	86
	13	7	78	4	68
	14	7	62	4	66
	15	7	54		
June	23			4	80
	24	6	68	3	82
	25	7	74	3	80
	26	6	72	3	76
	27	7	74	3	76
June	28	7	68	3	80
	29	7	70	4	84
	30	7	73	3	88
July	1	7	76	3–5	86
	2	7	72	3–5	84
	3	7	73	3	88
	4	8	72	3	74
	5	7	68	3	74
	6	7	68	3	78
	7	7	69	3	90
	8	7	74	3	88
	9	7	78	3	90
	10	7	80	3	90
	11	7	73	3	86
	12	7	72	3	92
	13	6	78	3	90
	14	7	78	3	90
	15	7	80	3	91
	16	7	76	3	86
	17	6	70	3	84
	18	6	60	3	88
	19	6	64	3	86
	21	7	70	3	76
	22	7	72	3	82

		A.M.	deg.	P.M.	deg.
	23	7	72	3	88
	24	7	78	3	86
	25	7	72	3	85
July	26	7	72	3	90
	27	7	70	3	88
	28	7	73	3	90
	29	7	76	3	90
	30	7	76	3	90
	31	7	76	3	90
August	1	8	76	3	90
	2	8	72	3	90
	3	8	72	3	82
	4	8	72	3	76
	5	8	72	3	84
	6	8	76	3	84
	7	7	76	3	84
	8	7	76	3	84
	9	7	76	3	84
	10	7	78	3	86
	11	8	76	3	86
	12		76	3	86
	13	7	76	3	86
	14	7	76	3	86
	15	7	76	3	86
	16		76	3	86
	17		76	3	86
	18		76	3	86
	19		76	3	86
	20		76	3	86
	21		76	3	86
August	22		74	3	82
	23		70	3	78
	24		70	3	78
	25		70	3	78
	26		70	3	78
	27		70	3	78
	28		70	3	78

		A.M.	deg.	P.M.	deg.
	29		70	3	78
	30		70	3	78
	31		70	3	78
Sept.	1		72	3	82
	2		72	3	82
	3		74	3	86
	4		74	3	86
	5		76	3	86
	6		76	3	86
	7		76	3	86
	8		76	3	86
	9		76	3	86
	10		76	3	86
	11		74		
	12		76	3	86
	13		70	3	86
	14		52		
	17		62	3	88
	18		64	3	86
	19		72	3	86
Sept.	20		74	3	89
	21		68	3	84
	22		62	3	82
	23		60	3	80
	24		58	3	88
	25		49	3	70
	26		51	3	80
	27		54	3	84
	28		64	3	88

Sources Cited by the Author
or Cited and Consulted by the Editor

ADAIR   Adair, James. *The History of the American Indians. . . .* London, Edward and Charles Dilly, 1775.

AM. ST. PAPERS   *American State Papers, Documents, Legislative and Executive, of the Congress of the United States.* Class II, *Indian Affairs.* 2 vols. 1st Cong.–19th Cong., May 25, 1789–March 1, 1827. Class V, *Military Affairs,* 7 vols., 1st Cong.–27th Cong., August 10, 1789–March 1, 1838. Class VII, *Public Lands,* 8 vols., 1st Cong.–24th Cong., July 1, 1790–February 28, 1837.

ANS [1]   Academy of Natural Sciences of Philadelphia *Journal* (First Series), "Description of *Collinsia,* a New Genus of Plants," by Thomas Nuttall, I (1817), 189–92.

ANS [2]   Academy of Natural Sciences of Philadelphia *Journal* (First Series). "Observations on the Geological Structure of the Valley of the Mississippi," by Thomas Nuttall, II (1821), 14–52.

AOU   American Ornithologists' Union. *Checklist of North American Birds.* 6th ed. Lancaster, Pa., 1957.

APS   American Philosophical Society. *Documents Relating to the Purchase and Exploration of Louisiana: William Dunbar, Exploration of the Red, the Black and the Washita Rivers.* Philadelphia, 1904.

ARK. GAZETTE   *Arkansas Gazette,* Arkansas Post and Little Rock, 1819–. Microfilm, Western History Collections, University of Oklahoma, Norman.

AUDUBON   Audubon, John James. *Journal of John James Audubon Made During His Trip to New Orleans in 1820–1821.* Ed. by Howard Corning. Cambridge, Mass., Club of Odd Volumes, 1929.

BANCROFT   Bancroft, George. *History of the United States.* Boston, Little Brown & Co., 1823 onwards almost to the time of the author's death in 1891, in editions of one to ten volumes.

BARTON   Barton, Benjamin Smith. *New Views of the Origin of the Tribes and Nations of America.* Philadelphia, Printed for the Author by John Bioren, 1797; 2d ed., 1798.

BARTRAM   Bartram, William. *Travels Through North & South Carolina, Georgia, East & West Florida, the Cherokee Country, the Extensive Territories of the Muscogulages, or Creek Confederacy, and the Coun-*

try of the Choctaws. . . . Philadelphia, Printed by James & Johnson, 1791.

BATES   Bates, Frederick. *The Life and Papers of Frederick Bates.* Ed.
by Thomas Maitland Marshall. 2 vols. Saint Louis, Mis-
souri Historical Society, 1926.

BEARSS [1]   Bearss, Edwin C. "In Quest of Peace on the Indian Border: The
Establishment of Fort Smith," *Arkansas Historical Quarterly*,
Vol. XXIII, No. 2 (Summer, 1964), 123–53.

BEARSS [2]   ———, and Arrell M. Gibson. *Fort Smith: Little Gibraltar on the
Arkansas.* Norman, University of Oklahoma Press, 1969.

BIEDMA   Biedma, Luys Hernando de, in Buckingham Smith, comp. *Collección de Varios Documentos para la Historia de la Florida y Tierras
Adyacentes.* Vol. I. London, Trübner & Co., 1857. Translated
by the same in *Narratives of the Career of Hernando de Soto in the
Conquest of Florida.* New York, Bradford Club, 1866. Reprinted
in Edward Gaylord Bourne, comp. *Narratives of the Career of
Hernando de Soto,* 2 vols. New York, A. S. Barnes & Co., 1904;
also New York, Allerton Book Co., 1922.

BILLON   Billon, Frederic L. *St. Louis in Its Early Days Under the French
[1]   and Spanish Dominations.* Saint Louis, Printed for the Author,
1886.

BILLON   ———. *Annals of St. Louis in Its Territorial Days from 1804 to
[2]   1821; Being a Continuation of the Author's Previous Work, the Annals of the French and Spanish Periods.* Saint Louis, Printed for the
Author, 1888.

BIRKBECK   Birkbeck, Morris. *Notes on a Journey in America, from the Coast of
[1]   Virginia to the Territory of Illinois.* . . . Philadelphia, Caleb
Richardson, 1817; also London, James Ridgway, 1818.

BIRKBECK   ———. *Letters from Illinois* . . . . London, Taylor and Hussey,
[2]   1818.

BOLTON   Bolton, Herbert, Eugene, ed. *Athanase de Mézierès and the
Louisiana-Texas Frontier, 1768–1780.* 2 vols. Cleveland, Arthur
H. Clark Company, 1914.

BOSSU [1]   Bossu, Jean-Bernard. *Nouveaux voyages dans l'Amérique Septentrionale, contenant une collection de lettres écrites sur les lieux, par
l'auteur; à son Ami, M. Douin.* . . . Amsterdam, Changuion,
1777.

BOSSU [2]   ———. *Nouveaux voyages aux Indes Occidentales* . . . . 2 vols.
Paris, LeJay, 1789.

BOSSU [3]   _____. *Bossu's Travels in the Interior of North America, 1751–1762*. Trans. and ed. by Seymour Feiler. Norman, University of Oklahoma Press, 1962.

BOUQUET   Bouquet, Henry. *The Papers of Henry Bouquet*. Ed. by S. K. Stevens, Donald M. Kent, and Autumn L. Leonard. 2 vols. Harrisburg, Pennsylvania Historical Museum Commission, 1951.

BOURNE [1]   Bourne, Edward Gaylord. *Narratives of the Career of Hernando de Soto*. 2 vols. New York, A. S. Barnes & Co., 1904.

BOURNE [2]   _____. *Narratives of the Career of Hernando de Soto*. 2 vols. New York, Allerton Book Company, 1922.

BRACKEN-RIDGE [1]   Brackenridge, Henry Marie. *Views of Louisiana; together with a Journal of a voyage up the Missouri River in 1811*. Pittsburgh, Cramer, Spear, and Eichbaum, 1814.

BRACKEN-RIDGE [2]   _____. *Journal of a Voyage up the River Missouri Performed in Eighteen Hundred and Eleven*. 2d ed. Baltimore, Coale and Maxwell, 1816; also in THWAITES [1], Vol. VI.

BRACKEN-RIDGE [3]   _____. *Views of Louisiana; containing geographical, statistical and historical notices of that vast and important portion of America*. Baltimore, Shaeffer and Maund, 1817.

BRADBURY   Bradbury, John. *Travels in the Interior of America, in the Years 1809, 1810, and 1811; Including a Description of Upper Louisiana, Together with the States of Ohio, Kentucky, Indiana, and Tennessee, with the Illinois and Western Territories. . . .* Liverpool, Printed for the Author, 1817. Also in THWAITES [1], Vol. V.

BURNET   Burnet, Jacob. *Notes on the Early Settlement of the North-Western Territory*. New York, D. Appleton & Co., 1847.

BUSHNELL [1]   Bushnell, David I. *Villages of the Algonquian, Siouan, and Caddoan Tribes West of the Mississippi*. Bureau of American Ethnology *Bulletin 77*. Washington, D.C., 1922.

BUSHNELL [2]   _____. *The Choctaw of Bayou Lacomb, St. Tammany Parish, Louisiana*. Bureau of American Ethnology *Bulletin 48*. Washington, D.C., 1909.

BUTEL-DUMONT   Butel-Dumont, Georges M. *Mémoires historiques sur la Louisiane, contenant ce qui est arrivé de plus memorable depuis l'année 1687 jusqu'à présent*. Vols. I–II. Paris, 1753. See also DUMONT DE MONTIGNY.

CATLIN   Catlin, George. *Letters and Notes on the Manners, Customs, and Condition of the North American Indians . . . Written during Eight Years' Travel Amongst the Wildest Tribes of Indians in North*

America . . . . 2 vols. London, Published by the Author; Printed by Tosswill and Myers, 1841.

CHAPMAN   Chapman, Carl H. "A Preliminary Survey of Missouri Archaeology, Part II: Middle Mississippi and Hopewellian Cultures," *Missouri Archaeologist*, X (April, 1947).

CHARLE-   Charlevoix, Pierre F. X. de, S. J. *Histoire et description générale de*
VOIX [1]   *la Nouvelle France.* 3 vols. Paris, Myon fils, 1744.

CHARLE-   ————. *Journal of a Voyage to North America. Undertaken by*
VOIX [2]   *Order of the French King.* . . . 2 vols. London, R. & J. Dodsley, 1761.

COBBETT   Cobbett, William. *A Year's Residence in the United States of America.* Boston, Small, Maynard & Company, Inc., 1818; London, Sherwood, Neely and Jones, 1819.

COLDEN   Colden, Cadwallader. *The History of the Five Indian Nations Depending on the Province of New-York in America.* New York, W. Bradford, 1727. Frequently reprinted, notably London, T. Osborne, 1747.

CORKRAN   Corkran, David H. *The Creek Frontier, 1540–1783.* Norman, University of Oklahoma Press, 1967.

CORNING   Corning, Howard, ed. *Journal of John James Audubon Made during His Trip to New Orleans in 1820–1821.* 2 vols. Cambridge, Mass., Club of Odd Volumes, 1929.

CORTAM-   Cortambert, Louis Richard. *Voyage au pays des Osages. Un tour*
BERT   *en Sicile.* Paris, A. Bertrand, 1837.

COTTERILL   Cotterill, Robert Spencer. *The Southern Indians: The Story of the Five Civilized Tribes Before Removal.* Norman, University of Oklahoma Press, 1954.

COX   Cox, Isaac J., ed. *The Journeys of René Robert Cavelier, Sieur de La Salle, as Related by His Faithful Lieutenant, Henri de Tonty; His Missionary Colleagues, Fathers Zenobius Membré, Louis Hennepin, and Anastasius Douay; His Early Biographer Father Christian Le Clerq; His Trusted Subordinate, Henry Joutel; and His Brother, Jean Cavelier; together with Memoirs, Commissions, etc.* 2 vols. New York, Allerton Book Co., 1922.

CUMING   Cuming, Fortescue. *Sketches of a Tour to the Western Country* [1810], in THWAITES [1], Vol. IV.

CUSHMAN   Cushman, Horatio Bardwell. *History of the Choctaw, Chickasaw and Natchez Indians.* Greenville, Texas, Headlight Printing House, 1899.

CUTLER   Cutler, William Parker. *Life, Journals and Correspondence of Rev. Manasseh Cutler.* . . . 2 vols. Cincinnati, R. Clarke & Co., 1888.

CUTRIGHT   Cutright, Paul Russell. *Lewis and Clark: Pioneering Naturalists.* Urbana, University of Illinois Press, 1969.

DAB   *Dictionary of American Biography, Under the Auspices of the American Council of Learned Societies.* . . . Ed. by Allen Johnson, Dumas Malone, and Harris E. Starr. 12 vols. New York, Charles Scribner's Sons, 1964–73.

DANA   Dana, Richard Henry, Jr. *Two Years Before the Mast,* New York, Harper & Bros., 1840.

DARBY [1]   Darby, William. *A Geographical Description of the State of Louisiana* . . . *Being an Accompaniment to the Map of Louisiana.* Philadelphia, Printed for the Author and published by John Melish. J. Bioren, Printer, 1816; also 2d ed., enl. and improved, New York, Published by James Olmstead, sold also by B. Levy & Co., booksellers, New Orleans, J. Seymour, printer, 1817.

DARBY [2]   ————. *The Emigrant's Guide to the Western and Southwestern States and Territories, Comprising a Geographical and Statistical Description of the States.* . . . New York, Kirk & Mercein, 1818.

DEBO [1]   Debo, Angie. *The Rise and Fall of the Choctaw Republic.* Norman, University of Oklahoma Press, 1934.

DEBO [2]   ————. *The Road to Disappearance: A History of the Creek Indians.* Norman, University of Oklahoma Press, 1941.

DENYS DE   Denys de Montfort, Pierre. *Histoire naturelle, générale et particul-*
MONTFORT   *ière des Mollusques.* . . . Paris, Impremerie de F. Dufart, 1802–1805.

DE ROSIER   De Rosier, Arthur H. *The Removal of the Choctaw Indians.* Knoxville, University of Tennessee Press, 1970.

DORSEY   Dorsey, J. Owen. "Omaha Sociology," Bureau of American
[1]   Ethnology *3d Annual Report* (1881–2). Washington, D.C., 1884.

DORSEY   ————. "Osage Traditions," Bureau of American Ethnology *6th*
[2]   *Annual Report* (1884–85). Washington, D.C., 1888.

DORSEY   ————. "A Study of Siouan Cults," Bureau of American
[3]   Ethnology *11th Annual Report* (1889–90). Washington, D.C. 1894.

DOUGLAS   Douglas, Walter B. "Documents, Captain Nathaniel Pryor," *American Historical Review,* Vol. XXIV, No. 2 (January, 1919), 253–65.

DRAKE [1]   Drake, Daniel, M.D. *An Inaugural Discourse on Medical Educa-*
tion Delivered at the Opening of the Medical College of Ohio in Cin-
cinnati, 11 November, 1820. Cincinnati, 1820.

DRAKE [2]   _____. *Physician to the West: Selected Writings of Daniel Drake on*
Science and Society. Ed. by Henry R. Shapiro and Zane L. Miller.
Lexington, University of Kentucky Press, 1970.

DUMONT   Dumont de Montigny, Lt. *Mémoires historiques sur la*
DE   *Louisiane . . . Composés sur les mémoires de M. Dumont, par*
MONTIGNY   *N.L.L.M.* . . . . 2 vols. Paris, C. J. B. Bauche, 1753. Trans.
in B. F. French, comp. and ed. *Historical Collections of*
Louisiana . . . . 5 vols. Philadelphia, Daniels and Smith, 1850,
Vol. V, 1–125.

DU PON-   Du Ponceau, Peter Stephen. *Report of the Corresponding Secretary*
CEAU [1]   *to the Committee of the Progress in the Investigation Committed to*
Him of the General Character and Forms of the Languages of the
American Indians. Philadelphia, American Philosophical Society
Transactions, I (1819), pp. xvii–xlvi.

DU PON-   _____. *Mémoire sur le système grammatical des langues de quelque*
CEAU [2]   *nations indiennes de l'Amérique du Nord.* Paris, A. Pihan de la
Foret, 1833.

EDGERTON   Edgerton, Franklin. "Notes on Early American Work in Linguis-
tics," *The Early History of Science and Learning in America: With*
Especial Reference to the Work of the American Philosophical Society
During the Eighteenth and Nineteenth Centuries, American
Philosophical Society *Proceedings*, Vol. 87 (1942). Philadelphia,
1943.

ELVAS   Elvas, Hun Fidalgo de. *Relaçam verdadeira dos trabalhos que ho*
governador Don Fernando de Souto y certos fidalgos portugueses
passarom no descobrimento da provincia da Frolida. Evora, Andre
de Burgos, 1557. See also HAKLUYT, PURCHAS, SMITH, and
BOURNE.

ESAREY   Esarey, Logan, ed. *Governors Messages and Letters: Messages and*
Letters of William Henry Harrison. 2 vols. Indianapolis, Indiana
Historical Commission, 1922.

FERNALD   Fernald, Merritt Lyndon. *Manual of Botany.* . . . New York,
American Book Company, 1950.

FLETCHER   Fletcher, Alice C., and Francis La Flesche. *The Omaha Tribe,*
AND LA   Bureau of American Ethnology *27th Annual Report* (1905–
FLESCHE   1906). Washington, D.C., 1911.

FLINT [1]   Flint, James. *Letters from America* . . . [1818–20]. Edinburgh, C. and C. Tait, 1822; also in THWAITES [1], Vol. IX.

FLINT [2]   Flint, Timothy. *Recollections of the Last Ten Years.* . . . Boston, Cummings, Hilliard, and Company, 1826.

FLOWER [1]   Flower, Richard. *Letters from Lexington and the Illinois.* . . . London, J. Ridgway, 1819; also in THWAITES [1], Vol. X, 85–109.

FLOWER [2]   ————. *Letters from the Illinois, 1820, 1821.* . . . London, Printed for J. Ridgway, 1822; also in THWAITES [1], Vol. X, 111–69.

FORD   Ford, Alice. *John James Audubon.* Norman, University of Oklahoma Press, 1964.

FOREMAN [1]   Foreman, Grant. *Indians and Pioneers.* Norman, University of Oklahoma Press, 1936.

FOREMAN [2]   ————. *Adventure on Red River: A Report on the Exploration of the Headwaters of the Red River,* by Captain Randolph B. Marcy and Captain G. B. McClellan. Ed. by Grant Foreman. Norman, University of Oklahoma Press, 1937.

FOREMAN [3]   ————. "Red River and the Spanish Boundary in the United States Supreme Court," *Chronicles of Oklahoma,* Vol. II, No. 3 (September, 1924), 298–310.

FOREMAN [4]   ————. "Nathaniel Pryor," *Chronicles of Oklahoma,* Vol. VII, No. 2 (June, 1927), 152–63.

FOREMAN [5]   ————. "The Three Forks," *Chronicles of Oklahoma,* Vol. II, No. 1 (March, 1924), 35–47.

FOREMAN [6]   ————. *Marcy and the Gold Seekers: The Journal of Captain R. B. Marcy, with an Account of the Gold Rush over the Southern Route.* Norman, University of Oklahoma Press, 1939.

FOREMAN [7]   ————. *Pioneer Days in the Early Southwest.* Cleveland, Arthur H. Clark Company, 1926.

FOWLER   Fowler, Jacob. *The Journal of Jacob Fowler, Narrating an Adventure from Arkansas Through the Indian Territory, Oklahoma, Kansas, Colorado, and New Mexico to the Source of Rio Grande del Norte, 1821–22.* Ed. by Elliott Coues. New York, Francis P. Harper, 1898.

FREEMAN   Freeman, John F., comp. *A Guide to Manuscripts Relating to the American Indian in the Library of the American Philosophical Society.* Philadelphia, American Philosophical Society, 1966.

FRENCH   French. B. F., comp. and ed. *Historical Collections of Louisi-ana* . . . . 5 vols. Philadelphia, Daniels and Smith, 1850.

GALLATIN   Gallatin, Albert. *A Synopsis of the Indian Tribes Within the United States East of the Rocky Mountains, and in the British and Russian Possessions in North America*, American Antiquarian Society *Transactions and Collections*, II, 1–422 [Cambridge, Mass., 1836].

GARCILASO   Garcilaso de la Vega [El Inca]. *La Florida del Inca, Historia*
[1]   *del Adelantado H. de Soto, gouernador e capitan general del Reyno de la Florida, y de otros caualleros Espanoles e Indios*. Lisbon, P. Crasbeek, 1605.

GARCILASO   ———. *The Florida of the Inca* . . . . Trans. and ed. by John
[2]   Grier Varner and Jeannette Johnson Varner. Austin, University of Texas Press, 1951.

GATSCHET   Gatschet, Albert Samuel. *Die Sprache der Tonkawas*. Berlin, 1877
[1]   ["Extract from *Zeitschrift für Ethnologie*, 1877"].

GATSCHET   ———. "The Timucua Language," American Philosophical So-
[2]   ciety *Proceedings*, Vol. 16, 625–42; Vol. 17, 490–504; Vol. 18, 465–502.

GATSCHET   ———. *Migration Legend of the Creek Indians, with a Linguistic,*
[3]   *Historic and Ethnographic Introduction*. Vol. I: Philadelphia, D. G. Brinton, 1884; Vol. II: Saint Louis, R. P. Studley & Co., 1888 (also in Academy of Science of Saint Louis *Transactions*, Vol. 5 [1886–91], 33–239).

GATSCHET   ———. *The Karankawa Indians, the Coast People of Texas*. Cam-
[4]   bridge, Mass., Peabody Museum of American Archaeology and Ethnology *Papers*, Vol. V, Nos. 1, 2 (1881).

GATSCHET   ———. *A Dictionary of the Atakapa Language*. Bureau of
[5]   American Ethnology *Bulletin* 108. Washington, D.C., 1932.

GEISER   Geiser, Samuel Wood. "Thomas Nuttall's Botanical Collecting Trip to the Red River, 1819," *Field and Laboratory*, Vol. XXIV, No. 2 (April, 1956), 43–60.

GIBSON   Gibson, Arrell M. *The Chickasaws*. Norman, University of Ok-
[1]   lahoma Press, 1971.

GIBSON   ———. *Wilderness Bonanza: The Tri-State District of Missouri,*
[2]   *Kansas, and Oklahoma*. Norman, University of Oklahoma Press, 1972.

GIBSON   ———, and Edwin C. Bearss. *Fort Smith: Little Gibraltar on the*
[3]   *Arkansas*. Norman, University of Oklahoma Press, 1969.

GIST
Gist, Christopher. "Christopher Gist's First and Second Journals, September 11, 1750–March 29, 1752," in Lois Mulkearn, ed., *George Mercer Papers Relating to the Ohio Company of Virginia.* Pittsburgh, University of Pittsburgh Press, 1954, 7–40.

GITTINGER
Gittinger, Roy. *The Formation of the State of Oklahoma, 1803–1906.* Norman, University of Oklahoma Press, 1939.

GOODMAN
Goodman, George J. "The Story of *Parthenium alpinum*," *Madroño,* Vol. VII, No. 4 (October, 1943), 115–18.

GOOKIN
Gookin, Daniel. *Historical Collections of the Indians in New England....* Boston, Apollo Press, 1792.

GORDON
Gordon, Capt. Harry. "Journal of Captain Harry Gordon," Public Record Office, London: C.O. 5: 85, 123–40. Printed in Newton D. Mereness, ed. *Travels in the American Colonies.* New York, Antiquarian Press, Ltd., 1961, 464–89.

GRAUSTEIN
Graustein, Jeannette E. *Thomas Nuttall, Natrualist: Explorations in America, 1808–1841.* Cambridge, Mass., Harvard University Press, 1967.

GREENE
Greene, Edward L. "Reprint of Fraser's Catalogue," *Pittonia,* II (1890), 114–19.

GREGG [1]
Gregg, Josiah. *Commerce of the Prairies* [1844]. Ed. by Max L. Moorhead. Norman, University of Oklahoma Press, 1954.

GREGG [2]
————. *Diary and Letters of Josiah Gregg.* Ed. by Maurice Garland Fulton, Introduction by Paul Horgan. 2 vols. Norman, University of Oklahoma Press, 1941, 1944.

GRIFFIN-ORR
Griffin, James B., ed. *Archaeology of Eastern United States:* Orr, Kenneth G., "Survey of Caddoan Archaeology," 239–55. Chicago, University of Chicago Press, 1952.

HADLEY AND DEVINE
Hadley, Jarvis B., and James F. Devine. "Seismotectonic Map of the Eastern United States," accompanying *Map Folio 620.* Washington, D.C., Department of the Interior, U.S. Geological Survey, 1974.

HAFEN
Hafen, LeRoy R. "New Light on LaLande, First American in Colorado," *Colorado Magazine,* 24 (1947), 194–97.

HAKLUYT
Hakluyt, Richard. *Virginia rightly valued by the description of the maine land of Florida her next neighbour; out of foure yeares continuall travell and discoverie for above one thousand miles east and west, of Don Fernando de Soto, and six hundred able men in his companie .... Written by a Portugall gentleman of Elvas .... Translated out of Portuguese by Richard Hakluyt.* London, F. Kyng-

ston for M. Lownes, 1609. Another edition, differently titled, by Hakluyt, appeared London, 1611.)

HALL AND KELSON   Hall, E. Raymond, and Keith R. Kelson. *The Mammals of North America.* 2 vols. New York, Ronald Press, 1959.

HANSEN   Hansen, Harry, ed. *Louisiana: A Guide to the State.* New York, Hastings House, 1971.

HARRING-TON   Harrington, M. R. *Certain Caddo Sites in Arkansas.* New York Museum of the American Indian, Heye Foundation, 1920.

HECKE-WELDER [1]   Heckewelder, John Gottlieb Ernestus. *An Account of the History Manners, and Customs of the Indian Nations Who Once Inhabited Pennsylvania and the Neighboring States.* . . . Philadelphia, A. Small, 1818.

HECKE-WELDER [2]   ———. *Comparative Vocabulary of Algonquin Dialects.* Cambridge, Mass., Printed for Wellesley College, 1889.

HECKE-WELDER [3]   ———. ". . . A Correspondence between the Rev. John Heckewelder . . . and Peter S. Duponceau . . . Respecting the Languages of the American Indians," American Philosophical Society *Transactions,* I (1819), 351–448.

HECKE-WELDER [4]   ———. "Words, Phrases and Short Dialogues in the Language of the Lenni Lenape, or Delaware Indians," American Philosophical Society *Transactions,* I (1819), 451–64.

HECKE-WELDER [5]   ———. *Names Given by the Lenni Lenape or Delaware Indians to Rivers, Streams, Places, etc., in the Now States of Pennsylvania, New Jersey, Maryland, and Virginia.* . . . Philadelphia, J. Kay, jun. and Co., 1833.

HEITMAN   Heitman, Francis B., comp. *Historical Register and Dictionary of the United States Army.* 2 vols. Washington, D.C., U.S. Government Printing Office, 1903.

HEMPSTEAD   Hempstead, Fay. *A Pictorial History of Arkansas.* Saint Louis and New York, Thompson Publishing Company, 1890.

HERRERA   Herrera y Tordesillas, Antonio de. *Historia general de los hechos de los Castellanos en las islas i tierra firme del mar oceano.* 5 vols. Madrid, Emprenta Real, 1601–15. See also PURCHAS [1], Part 3.

HODGE   Hodge, Frederick Webb. ed. *Handbook of American Indians North of Mexico,* Bureau of American Ethnology *Bulletin 30.* 2 vols. Washington, D.C., 1907.

HOLMES   Holmes, William H. "Illustrated Catalogue of a Portion of the

Collections Made by the Bureau of American Ethnology During the Field Season of 1881," Bureau of American Ethnology *3d Annual Report*. Washington, D.C., 1885.

HOUCK [1]   Houck, Louis. *The Spanish Régime in Missouri* .... 2 vols. Chicago, R. R. Donnelley & Sons Company, 1909.

HOUCK [2]   ————. *History of Missouri* .... 3 vols. Chicago, R. R. Donnelley & Sons Company, 1908.

HOUSE   *House Executive Document*, 50 Cong., 1 sess., No. 6, Part
EXEC.   II: "Report on the Internal Commerce of the United States,"
DOCUMENT   1887.

HULBERT   Hulbert, Archer Butler. *Historic Highways of America*. 16 vols. Cleveland, Arthur H. Clark Company, 1902–1905. Vol. 5, *The Old Glade (Forbes's) Road*, 1903.

HULME   Hulme, Thomas. "Journal of a Tour in the Western Countries of America—September 30, 1818–August 8, 1819 .... " Part 3 in COBBETT, London edition, 1819; also in THWAITES [1], Vol. X, 19–87.

HUMBOLDT   Humboldt, Alexander von (Friedrich Wilhelm Heinrich Alexander, Freiherr von), and Aimé Bonpland. *Vues des cordillières, et monumens des peuples indigènes de l'Amérique*. 2 vols. Paris, 1816.

HUNTER   Hunter, William A. *Forts on the Pennsylvania Frontier, 1753– 1758*. Harrisburg, Pennsylvania Historical and Museum Commission, 1960.

HYDE   Hyde, George E. *The Pawnee Indians*. Norman, University of Oklahoma Press, 1974.

IRVING [1]   Irving, Washington. *The Western Journals of Washington Irving*. Ed. by John Francis McDermott. Norman, University of Oklahoma Press, 1944.

IRVING [2]   ————. *A Tour on the Prairies* [1835]. Ed. by John Francis McDermott. Norman, University of Oklahoma Press, 1956.

IRVING [3]   ————. *Astoria; or Anecdotes of an Enterprise Beyond the Rocky Mountains* [1836]. Ed. by Edgeley W. Todd. Norman, University of Oklahoma Press, 1964.

IRVING [4]   ————. *The Adventures of Captain Bonneville, U.S.A., in the Rocky Mountains and the Far West* [1837]. Ed. by Edgeley W. Todd. Norman, University of Oklahoma Press, 1961.

IRVING [5]   Irving, Theodore. *The Conquest of Florida Under Hernando de Soto*. 2 vols. Philadelphia, Carey, Lea & Blanchard, 1835.

JACKSON   Jackson, Andrew. *Correspondence of Andrew Jackson*. Ed. by John
[1]   Spencer Bassett. 7 vols. Washington, D.C., Carnegie Institution
               of Washington, 1926–35.

JACKSON   Jackson, Donald, ed. *Letters of the Lewis and Clark Expedition,*
[2]   *with Related Documents, 1783–1854*. Urbana, University of Il-
               linois Press, 1962.

JAMES, E.   James, Edwin, comp. *Account of an Expedition from Pittsburgh to*
[1]   *the Rocky Mountains, Performed in the Years 1819 and '20, Under*
               the Command of Major Stephen H. Long, in THWAITES [1], Vols.
               XIV–XVII.

JAMES, E.   ———. "Catalogue of Plants Collected during a Journey to and
[2]   from the Rocky Mountains during the Summer of 1820," Ameri-
               can Philosophical Society *Transactions,* II (1825), 172–90.

JAMES, T.   James, Thomas. *Three Years Among the Mexicans and Indians*. Ed.
[3]   by Walter B. Douglas. Saint Louis, Missouri Historical Society,
               1916.

JEFFERSON   Jefferson, Thomas. *Notes on the State of Virginia*. Paris,
[1]   MDCCLXXXII [MDCCLXXXIV].

JEFFERSON   ———. Unpublished Algonquian language recordings by Jef-
[2]   ferson, copied by P. S. DuPonceau and preserved in the MSS of
               the American Philosophical Society, Philadelphia, with Jeffer-
               son's surviving Indian vocabularies and grammars.

JEFFERYS   Jefferys, Thomas. *The Natural and Civil History of the French*
               Dominions in North America and South America . . . . Parts I, II.
               London, 1760.

JOHNSON   Johnson, Boyd W. "Frederick Notrebe," *Arkansas Historical*
               Quarterly, Vol. XXI, No. 3 (Autumn, 1962), 269–83.

JONES   Jones, Sir William. *Dissertations and Miscellaneous Pieces Relating*
               to the History and Antiquities, the Arts, Sciences and Literature, of
               Asia. Dublin, P. Byrne, 1793.

KAPPLER   Kappler, Charles J., comp. and ed. *Indian Affairs: Laws and*
               Treaties. 3 vols. Washington, D.C., 1904.

KER   Ker, Henry. *Travels Through the Western Interior of the United*
               States, from the Year 1808 up to the Year 1816'. . . . Elizabeth-
               town, N.J., Printed for the Author, 1816.

LA   La Flesche, Francis. *The Osage Tribe: The Rite of Chiefs, Sayings of*
FLESCHE   *Ancient Men*. Bureau of American Ethnology *36th Annual Report*
[1]   (1914–15). Washington, D.C., 1921.

LA
FLESCHE
[2]

————. *The Osage Tribe: The Rite of Vigil.* Bureau of American Ethnology *39th Annual Report* (1917–18). Washington, D.C., 1925.

LA
FLESCHE
[3]

————. *The Osage Tribe: Two Versions of the Child-Naming Rite.* Bureau of American Ethnology *43d Annual Report* (1925–26). Washington, D.C., 1928.

LA HARPE

La Harpe, Bénard de. *Journal historique de l'établissement des Français à la Louisiane.* New Orleans, A. L. Baimare, 1831.

LAHONTAN

Lahontan, Armand L. de D. *Nouveaux voyages de Mr le baron Lahontan, dans l'Amérique Septentrionale.* La Haye, 1703.

LEE AND
FROST

Lee, D., and J. H. Frost, *Ten Years in Oregon.* New York, Published for the Authors, J. Collord, Printer, 1844.

LE PAGE
[1]

Le Page du Pratz, Antoine Simor. *Historie de la Louisiane . . . .* 3 vols. Paris, De Bure, l'aîné, 1758.

LE PAGE
[2]

————. *History of Louisiana.* London, T. Becket and P. A. De Hondt, 1763 (reprinted, London, T. Becket, 1774).

LEWIS
AND
CLARK

Lewis, Meriwether, and William Clark. *Original Journals of the Lewis and Clark Expedition.* Ed. by Reuben Gold Thwaites. 8 vols. New York, Dodd, Mead & Co., 1904–1905.

LITTLE
[1]

Little, Elbert L., Jr. *Check List of Native and Natrualized Trees of the United States (Including Alaska) Prepared Under the Direction of the Forest Service Tree and Range Plant Name Committee.* Washington, D.C., U.S. Forest Service, 1953.

LITTLE
[2]

————. "American Smoketree (*Cotinus obovatus* Raf.), One of Oklahoma's Rarest Tree Species," Oklahoma Academy of Science *Proceedings,* III (1943), 21–23.

MCKELVEY

McKelvey, Susan Delano. *Botanical Exploration of the trans-Mississippi West, 1790–1850.* Jamaica Plain, Mass., Arnold Arboretum of Harvard University, 1956.

MCREY-
NOLDS

McReynolds, Edwin C. *Oklahoma: A History of the Sooner State.* Norman, University of Oklahoma Press, 1954.

MCVAUGH

McVaugh, Rogers. "A Revision of the North American Black Cherries," *Brittonia,* 7 (1951), 279–315.

MALEY

Maley, John. Journal, in the Silliman Papers, Yale University Library; Microfilm in Bizzell Memorial Library, University of Oklahoma.

MARGRY

Margry, Pierre, ed. *Découvertes et établissements des Français dans l'ouest et dans le sud de l'Amérique Septentrionale (1614–1754).*

Mémoires et documents originaux. 6 vols. Paris, D. Jouaust, 1875–86.

MARQUETTE   Marquette, Père Jacques *Le premier voyage qu'a fait Le P. Marquette vers le nouveau Mexique & comment s'en est formé le dessein* (1674), in THWAITES [2], Vol. 59, 86–163.

MARTIN   Martin, P. S., George I. Quimby, and Donald Collier. *Indians Before Columbus. Twenty Thousand Years of North American History Revealed by Archaeology.* Chicago, University of Chicago Press, 1947.

MATTISON   Mattison, Ray H. "Arkansas Post—Its Human Aspects," *Arkansas Historical Quarterly*, Vol. XVI, No. 2 (Spring, 1957), 117–38.

MAXIMILIAN   Wied-Neuwied, Maximilian Alexander Philipp, prinz von. *Reise in das innere Nord-Amerika in den Jahren 1832 bis 1834.* 2 vols. and Atlas. Coblenz, J. Hoelscher, 1839–41; also in THWAITES [1], Vols. XXII–XXV.

MICHAUX, A.   Michaux, André. "Journal" [1793–96], in THWAITES [1], Vol. III.

MICHAUX, F. A.   Michaux, François André. *Travels to the Westward of the Alleghany Mountains, in the States of Ohio, Kentucky, and Tennessee.* . . . London, J. Mawman, 1805.

MITCHELL   Mitchell, Harry A. "The Development of New Orleans as a Wholesale Trading Center," *Louisiana Historical Quarterly*, Vol. XXVII, No. 4 (October, 1944), 933–63.

MOONEY [1]   Mooney, James. *Myths of the Cherokees.* Bureau of American Ethnology *19th Annual Report*, Part 1. Washington, D.C., 1900.

MOONEY [2]   ———. *The Siouan Tribes of the East.* Bureau of American Ethnology *Bulletin 22.* Washington, D.C., 1895.

MOORE   Moore, Clarence Bloomfield. *Certain Mounds of Arkansas and Mississippi: Part I, Mounds and Cemeteries of the Lower Arkansas River.* Philadelphia, P. C. Stockhausen, Printer, 1908.

MORISON   Morison, Samuel Eliot. *Three Centuries of Harvard.* Cambridge, Mass., Harvard University Press, 1936.

MORRIS   Morris, Wayne. "Traders and Factories on the Arkansas Frontier, 1805–1822," *Arkansas Historical Quarterly*, XXVIII (Spring, 1969), 28–48.

MORRIS AND MC REYNOLDS   Morris, John W., and Edwin C. McReynolds. *Historical Atlas of Oklahoma*. Norman, University of Oklahoma Press, 1965.

MORSE   Morse, Jedediah. *A Report to the Secretary of War on Indian Affairs, Comprising a Narrative of a Tour in the Summer of 1820*. New Haven, 1822.

MULKEARN   Mulkearn, Lois, comp. and ed. *George Mercer Papers Relating to the Ohio Company of Virginia*. Pittsburgh, University of Pittsburgh Press, 1954.

NAEF   Naef, Adolf. *Die Fossilen Tintenfische. . . .* Jena, Verlag von Gustav Fischer, 1922.

NASATIR   Nasatir, Abraham P., ed. *Before Lewis and Clark: Documents Illustrating the History of the Missouri, 1785–1804*. 2 vols. Saint Louis, Historical Documents Foundation, 1952.

NATIONAL ATLAS   U.S. Geological Survey. *National Atlas of the United States of America*. Washington, D.C., 1970.

NAVIGATOR   Cramer, Zadok. *The Navigator. . . .* Pittsburgh, Zadok Cramer, 1801 (and in three later editions, and in seven others, published variously by Cramer and Spear and by Cramer, Spear, and Eichbaum, to 1824).

NEWBERRY   Newberry, Farrar. "Jacob Barkman," *Arkansas Historical Quarterly*, Vol. XIX, No. 4 (Winter, 1960), 314–24.

NILES' REGISTER   *Niles' Weekly Register*. Baltimore, 1811–20.

NUTTALL [1]   Nuttall, Thomas. *A Journal of Travels into the Arkansas Territory during the Year 1819, with occasional Observations on the Manners of the Aborigines*. Philadelphia, T. H. Palmer, 1821. Also in THWAITES [1], Vol. XIII.

NUTTALL [2]   ————. *Genera of North American Plants with a Catalogue of the Species through 1817*. 2 vols. Philadelphia, Printed for the Author by D. Heartt, 1818.

NUTTALL [3]   ————. "Collections Towards a Flora of the Territory of Arkansas," American Philosophical Society *Transactions*, New Series, V (1837), 139–203.

NUTTALL [4]   ————. "Nuttall's Travels into the Old Northwest: An Unpublished 1810 Diary." Ed. by Jeannette E. Graustein. *Chronica Botanica*, Vol. 14, Nos. 1, 2 (Autumn, 1951).

NUTTALL   ————. "Observations on the Geological Structure of the Valley
[5]   of the Mississippi," Academy of Natural Sciences of Philadelphia
                 Journal, First Series, II (1821), 14–52.

NUTTALL   ————. *A Manual of the Ornithology of the United States and*
[6]   *Canada*. 2 vols. Vol. I, *Land Birds*. Cambridge, Mass., Hilliard
                 & Brown, 1832. Vol. II, *Water Birds*. Boston, Hilliard, Gray &
                 Company, 1834.

NUTTALL   ————. "A Catalogue of a Collection of Plants Made Chiefly in
[7]   the Valleys of the Rocky Mountains or Northern Andes, Toward
                 Sources of the Columbia River, by Nathaniel B. [J.] Wyeth,"
                 Academy of Natural Sciences *Journal*, VII (1834), 5–60 and 8
                 plates.

NUTTALL   ————. *An Introduction to Physiological and Systematic Botany*.
[8]   Cambridge, Mass., Hilliard and Brown, 1827.

NUTTALL   ————. *North American Sylva*. Published in parts: Philadelphia,
[9]   Dobson, 1842, 1843; Philadelphia, Ward, 1846; Philadelphia,
                 Smith & Wistar, 1849 (see Editor's Introduction, note 33).

OVIEDO   Fernández de Oviedo y Valdés, Capt. Gonzalo. *Historia general y*
                 natural de las Indias, islas y tierra-firme del mar oceano. Seville,
                 Iuam Cromberger, 1535: Part I, 19½ books; Salamanca, Juan de
                 Junta, 1547: 20th book; Madrid, Real Academia, 1851–55: 3
                 parts, 50 books (Part IV not written at the time of Oviedo's death,
                 1555); in 4 vols., where Ranjel appears and was first translated in
                 any language by Edward Gaylord Bourne: *Narratives of the Career*
                 of Hernando de Soto. 2 vols. New York, A. S. Barnes, 1904;
                 reprinted, New York, Allerton Book Co., 1922.

P.A.   Hazard, Samuel, ed. *Pennsylvania Archives*. First Series. 12 vols.
                 Philadelphia, 1852–56. Second Series, ed. by William H. Egle,
                 John B. Linn, and George E. Reed. 19 vols. Harrisburg, Pa.,
                 1879–90.

P.C.P.   Hazard, Samuel, et al. *Minutes of the Provincial Council [of*
                 Pennsylvania], 10 vols. Harrisburg and Philadelphia, 1838–53;
                 by extension, *Minutes of the Supreme Executive Council [of*
                 Pennsylvania], 1776–1790. 6 vols. Philadelphia, 1838–53.

P.C.R.   Hazard, Samuel, ed. [*Pennsylvania*] *Colonial Records*. 16 vols.
                 Harrisburg and Philadelphia, 1838–53.

PALMER   Palmer, W. P., et al., eds. *Calendar of Virginia State Papers and*
                 Other Manuscripts . . . Preserved . . . at Richmond. 11 vols.
                 Richmond, Va., 1875–93.

PARKER   Parker, David W., comp. *Calendar of Papers in Washington Archives Relating to the Territories of the United States*. Washington, D.C., Carnegie Institution of Washington, 1911.

PEAKE   Peake, Ora B. *A History of the United States Factory System, 1795–1822*. Denver, Colo., Sage Books, 1954.

PENNELL   Pennell, Francis. "Travels and Scientific Collections of Thomas
[1]   Nuttall," *Bartonia* 18 (1936), 1–51.

PENNELL   ————. "Historic Botanical Collections of the American
[2]   Philosophical Society and the Academy of Natural Sciences of Philadelphia," American Philosophical Society *Proceedings*, Vol. 94 (1950), 137–51.

PICKERING   Pickering, John. *An Essay on a Uniform Orthography for the*
[1]   *Indian Languages of North America, as Published in the Memoirs of the American Academy of Arts and Sciences*. Cambridge, Mass., Hilliard and Metcalf, 1820.

PICKERING   ————. *Remarks on the Indian Languages of North America*,
[2]   reprinted Philadelphia, 1836, from *Encyclopedia Americana*, Vol. 6 (1831).

PIKE   Pike, Zebulon Montgomery. *The Journals of Zebulon Montgomery Pike, with Letters and Related Documents*. Ed. by Donald Jackson. 2 vols. Norman, University of Oklahoma Press, 1966.

PITTMAN   Pittman, Philip. *The Present State of the European Settlements on the Mississippi, With a Geographical Description of That River* . . . . Cleveland, Arthur H. Clark Company, 1906.

POST   Post, Christian Frederick. "The Journal of Christian Frederick Post, on a Message from the Governor of Pennsylvania to the Delaware, Shawnese, and Mingo Indians, Settled There" [1758] and "The Journal of Christian Frederick Post, on a Message from the Governor of Pennsylvania, to the Indians on the Ohio, in the Latter Part of the Same Year," in THWAITES [1], Vol. I, 185–233, 234–91.

POURTALÈS   Pourtalès, Count Albert-Alexandre de. *On the Western Tour with Washington Irving: The Journal and Letters of Count de Pourtalès*. Ed. by George F. Spaulding; trans. by Seymour Feiler. Norman, University of Oklahoma Press, 1968.

POWELL   Powell, William H., comp. *List of Officers of the Army of the United States from 1779 to 1900*. New York, L. R. Hamersly & Co., 1900.

PREGALDIN   Pregaldin, Anton J. Letter to Savoie Lottinville, March 24,
            1976, concerning Joseph Bogy *père* and his descendants.

PRUCHA   Prucha, Francis Paul. *The Sword of the Republic: The United States
            Army on the Frontier, 1783–1846.* New York, Macmillan Com-
            pany, 1968.

PURCHAS   Purchas, Samuel. *Purchas his Pilgrimes.* 4 vols. London, W.
[1]   Stansby for H. Fetherstone, 1625 (the résumé of Richard Hak-
            luyt's translation of the Elvas narrative of the De Soto Expedition
            appears in Vol. 4).

PURCHAS   ―――. *Hakluytus Posthumus, or Purchas his Pilgrimes.* 20 vols.
[2]   Glasgow, MacLehose & Sons, 1906.

PURSH   Pursh, Frederick. *Flora Americae Septentrionalis.* 2 vols. London,
            White, Cochrane & Co., 1814.

RAFINESQUE Rafinesque, Constantine Samuel. *New Flora and Botany of
[1]   North America. . . .* 4 parts. Philadelphia, Printed for the Author
            and Publisher, 1836 [1838].

RAFINESQUE ―――. *The American Nations.* Philadelphia, C. S. Rafines-
[2]   que, 1836.

RAND   Rand, Jerry. "Samuel Morton Rutherford," *Chronicles of Ok-
            lahoma,* Vol. XXX, No. 2 (Summer, 1952), 149–59.

RANDALL   Randall, J. W. "Crustacea . . . from the West Coast of North
            America . . . ," Academy of Natural Sciences *Journal,* VIII
            (1839–42), 106–42.

RANJEL   Ranjel, Rodrigo, in Capt. Gonzalo Fernández de Oviedo y Valdés,
            *Historia general y natural de las Indias, islas y tierra-firme del mar
            oceano.* Seville, Iuam Cromberger, 1535– (see OVIEDO).

RICKETT   Rickett, H. W. "John Bradbury's Explorations in Missouri Terri-
            tory," Letter 13, American Philosophical Society *Proceedings,*
            Vol. XCIV, No. 1 (1950).

ROHR-   Rohrbough, Malcolm J. *The Land Office Business: The Settlement
BOUGH   and Administration of American Public Lands, 1789–1837.* New
            York, Oxford University Press, 1968.

ROWLAND   Rowland, Mrs. Dunbar. *Life, Letters and Papers of William Dun-
[1]   bar of Elgin, Morayshire, Scotland, and Natchez, Mississippi,
            Pioneer Scientist of the Southern United States.* Jackson, Press of the
            Mississippi Historical Society, 1930.

ROWLAND   Rowland, Dunbar, and A. G. Sanders. *Mississippi Provincial Rec-
[2]   ords: French Dominion.* 3 vols. Greenville, Mississippi Depart-
            ment of Archives and History, 1927–32.

ROYCE — Royce, Charles C. *Land Cessions in the United States.* Bureau of American Ethnology *18th Annual Report.* Washington, D.C., 1899.

SCHARF — Scharf, John Thomas. *History of St. Louis City and County from the Earliest Periods to the Present Day....* 2 vols. Philadelphia, L. H. Everts & Co., 1883.

SCHOOL-CRAFT [1] — Schoolcraft, Henry Rowe. *Journal of a Tour into the Interior of Missouri and Arkansas, from Potosi, or Mine à Burton, in Missouri Territory, in a South-West Direction Toward the Rocky Mountains; Performed in the Years 1818 and 1819.* London, Printed for Sir R. Phillips and Co., 1821.

SCHOOL-CRAFT [2] — ———. *A View of the Lead Mines of Missouri ....* New York, Charles Wiley & Co., 1819.

SHETRONE — Shetrone, Henry Clyde. *The Mound-Builders: A Reconstruction of the Life of a Prehistoric American Race....* New York, D. Appleton & Co., 1930; rev. ed., 1938.

SHIMER — Shimer, Harvey Woodburn, *Index Fossils of North America ....* New York, J. Wiley & Sons, Inc.; London, Chapman and Hall, Ltd., 1944.

SMITH [1] — Smith, [Thomas] Buckingham, *Collección de Varios Documentos para la Historia de la Florida y Tierras Adyacentes,* Vol. I. London, Trübner & Co., 1857.

SMITH [2] — ———. *Narratives of the Career of Hernando de Soto in the Conquest of Florida.* New York, Bradford Club, 1866.

SMITHER — Smither, Nelle. "A History of the English Theatre in New Orleans, 1806–1842," *Louisiana Historical Quarterly,* Vol. XXVIII, No. 1 (January, 1945), 85–276.

STATUTES — Peters, Richard, ed. *The Public Statutes at Large of the United States of America.* Boston, 1845–.

STEARNS AND WIL-SON — Stearns, Richard G., and Charles W. Wilson, Jr. "Geology and Seismic Hazard in, and East of, the New Madrid Earthquake Zone," in Geological Society of America, *Abstracts with Programs,* Vol. 5, No. 5 (February, 1973), 437.

STEVENS — Stevens, Harry R. "Samuel Watts Davies and the Industrial Revolution in Cincinnati," *Ohio Historical Quarterly,* Vol. 70, No. 2 (April, 1961), 95–127.

STODDARD — Stoddard, Amos. *Sketches, Historical and Descriptive of Louisiana.* Philadelphia, Published by Mathew Carey; A. Small, Printer..., 1812.

SWANTON   Swanton, John R. *Indian Tribes of the Lower Mississippi Valley and*
[1]   *Adjacent Coast of the Gulf of Mexico.* Bureau of American Ethnol-
    ogy *Bulletin 43.* Washington, D.C., 1911.

SWANTON   ———. *Source Material for the Social and Ceremonial Life of the*
[2]   *Choctaw Indians.* Bureau of American Ethnology *Bulletin 103.*
    Washington, D.C., 1931.

SWANTON   ———. "Aboriginal Culture of the Southeast." Bureau of
[3]   American Ethnology *42d Annual Report.* Washington, D.C.,
    1928.

SWANTON   ———. *Early History of the Creek Indians.* Bureau of American
[4]   Ethnology *Bulletin 73.* Washington, D.C., 1922.

SWANTON   ———. *The Indian Tribes of North America.* Bureau of American
[5]   Ethnology *Bulletin 145.* Washington, D.C., 1952.

SWANTON   ———. *The Indians of the Southeastern United States,* Bureau of
[6]   American Ethnology *Bulletin 137.* Washington, D.C., 1946.

SWANTON   ———. *Myths and Tales of the Southeastern Indians.* Bureau of
[7]   American Ethnology *Bulletin 88.* Washington, D.C., 1929.

SWANTON   ———. "Social and Religious Beliefs of the Chickasaw Indians."
[8]   Bureau of American Ethnology *44th Annual Deport.*
    Washington, D.C., 1926–27.

TAYLOR   Taylor, E. G. R. "Samuel Purchase," *Geographical Journal,*
    LXXV (1930), 536–39.

TERR. PA-   National Archives and Record Service. *The Territorial Papers of the*
PERS   *United States.* Comp. and ed. by Clarence E. Carter and John
    Porter Bloom. 28 vols. Washington, D.C., 1934–75.

THOMAS   Thomas, Cyrus. *Report on the Mound Explorations of the Bureau of*
    American Ethnology. Bureau of American Ethnology *12th Annual*
    Report (1890–91). Washington, D.C., 1894.

THWAITES   Thwaites, Reuben Gold, ed. *Early Western Travels, 1748–1846.*
[1]   32 vols. Cleveland, Arthur H. Clark Company, 1904–1907.

THWAITES   ———, ed. *The Jesuit Relations and Allied Documents: Travels and*
[2]   *Explorations of the Jesuit Missionaries in New France, 1610–1791.*
    73 vols. Cleveland, Burrows Brothers Company, 1896–1901.

TIXIER   Tixier, Victor. *Tixier's Travels on the Osage Prairies.* Ed. by John
    Francis McDermott, trans. by Albert J. Salvan. Norman, Univer-
    sity of Oklahoma Press, 1940.

TONTY   Tonty, Henri de. *An Account of M. de la Salle's last expedition and*
    discoveries in North America . . . Made English from the Paris orig-

inal. *Also the adventures of the Sieur de Montauban, Captain of the French Buccaneers on the coast of Guinea, in the year 1695.* London, 1698. 8°.

TORREY AND GRAY   Torrey, John, and Asa Gray. *A Flora of North America.* . . . New York, London, Wiley & Putnam, 1838–43. Reprinted, New York, Hafner Publishing Company, 1969, with introduction by Joseph Ewan.

TOWNSEND   Townsend, John Kirk. *Narrative of a Journey Across the Rocky Mountains.* Philadelphia, Henry Perkins, 1839; also in THWAITES [1], Vol. XXI.

UNITED STATES DE SOTO EXPEDITION COMMISSION   United States De Soto Expedition Commission, John R. Swanton, Chairman. *Final Report of the United States De Soto Expedition Commission,* 76 Cong., 1 sess., House Document No. 71 (10328), 1939.

VARNER   Varner, John Grier, and Jeannette Johnson Varner, trans and eds. Carcilaso de la Vega, *The Florida of the Inca: A History of the Adelantado Hernando de Soto, Governor and Captain General of the Kingdom of Florida, and of Other Heroic Spanish and Indian Cavaliers, Written by the Inca, Garcilaso de la Vega.* . . . Austin, University of Texas Press, 1951.

WEISER   Weiser, Conrad. "The Journal of Conrad Weiser," in P.C.R., Vol. V, 348–58.

WILLEY   Willey, Gordon R. *An Introduction to American Archaeology.* 2 vols. Englewood Cliffs, N.J., Prentice-Hall, 1966, 1971.

WISSLER   Wissler, Clark. "The American Indian and the American Philosophical Society," American Philosophical Society *Proceedings,* Vol. 86, No. 1, 189–204. Philadelphia, 1943.

WOODS   Woods, John. *Two Years Residence in the Settlement on the English Prairie, in the Illinois Country.* . . . London, Longman, Hurst, Rees, Orme, and Brown, 1822; also in THWAITES [1], Vol. X, 179–357.

WRIGHT   Wright, Muriel H. *A Guide to the Indian Tribes of Oklahoma.* Norman, University of Oklahoma Press, 1951.

WÜRTTEMBERG   Paul Wilhelm, Duke of. *Travels in North America, 1822–1824.* Trans. by W. Robert Nitske, ed. by Savoie Lottinville. Norman, University of Oklahoma Press, 1974.

WYETH   Wyeth, Nathaniel Jarvis. "The Correspondence and Journals of Captain Nathaniel J. Wyeth, 1831–6, A Record of Two Expeditions for the Occupation of the Oregon Country," *Sources of the History of Oregon*, ed. by Frederick George Young. Vol. I, Parts 3–6. Eugene, Oreg., University Press, 1899.

Index

Abeika Indians: 306

Aborigines: *see* Indians, American

Academy of Natural Sciences: xvi; membership of, ix, x; Nuttall's election to, xvii

Acarus sanguisugas: see *Amblyomma americanum*

Acer barbatum: 127n.
   dasycarpa: see *Acer saccharinum*
   negundo: 87, 189
   saccharinum: 34&n., 110n., 127&n., 189
   saccharum: 34n., 127n.

Achillea lanulosa: 177n.

Achyranthes: 231&n.

Acolapissa Indians: 306

Adair, James: 148&n.

Adams-Onis Treaty: 105n.

Agkistrodon piscivorus: 173n.

Agrostis arachnoides: 177&n.

Ague: 130&n.; symptoms of, 237; *see also* fever, malaria, sickness

Akron, Ill.: 48n.

Alcyonite: 22&n.

Algonquian Indians: 94n., 137n., 309

Alibamu Indians: 306

Allegheny Mountains: 22–23

Alligators along Arkansas River: 85

Allium: 87&n.

Allmand (Allemand) Creek: 153&n.

Alma Plantation: 261n., 265&n.

Alyssum bidentatum: 82&n.

Amblyomma americanum: 143n., 170

Ambrosia: 227&n., 233

American Philosophical Society: xvi, 240n., 255.; membership of, ix; president of, x; Nuttall's election to, xvii, 272; language collections at, 137n.; interest of, in Indians, 272; Historical and Library Committee of, 273

American primrose: *see Dodecatheon Meadia*

American smoke tree: *see Cotinus obovatus*

Amorpha canescens: 192&n.

Amsonia salicifolia: 202&n.

Andrachne phyllanthoides: 167&n.

Anemone: 134&n.

Anoixi, De Soto to: 285

Anomia trigonalis: 22&n.

Apache Indians, opposed by Osages: 197n.

Apalache Indians: 306

Aplectrum hiyemale: 67&n.

Aquixo: 278–79

Arbuckle, Col. Matthew: 191n.

Arctomys monax: 60&n.

Arikara Indians: 92n.

Aristida: 177&n.

Arkansas (Arkansa, Akansas) Indians: 92–93, 280n.; name of 94; character of, 95; *see also* O-guah-pa Indians, Ozark Indians, Quapaw Indians

Arkansas Post: 72n., 100n., 101n., 102n., 244n.; history of, 81–82n.; Joseph Bogy at, 83n.; mail route from, 133n.; factory at, 151n.; trading at, 249&n.

Arkansas Prairie, trees on: 87

Arkansas River: xviiiff., 66, 72–73; entrance on, 76; ascent of, 77–86, 100–54; settlements on, 87, 100–25, 154; vegetation along, 89–90, 111, 118, 125–27, 141; climate of, 90–91, 101–107, 132; Indians on, 93, 109&n.; islands of, 113, 154, 249; geological formations along, 115, 117, 119, 131, 135, 140, 142, 152, 185–87, 245–46; mountains along, 122&n., 134, 140; survey of, 128–29; wildlife along, 131, 153, 184, 189; earthquakes along, 142; prairies along, 155, 221; high water of, 161–62; current of, 186; tributaries of,